THE POLITICAL ECONOMY OF VIRTUE

Jean-Baptiste Perronneau (1715–83), *Portrait of a Man* (1766). Oil on Canvas, 72.5 × 58.5 cm. Photo © The National Gallery of Ireland. Photographer: Roy Hewson. Reproduced by permission of the National Gallery of Ireland.

The
Political Economy
of Virtue

Luxury, Patriotism, and the Origins of the French Revolution

John Shovlin

CORNELL UNIVERSITY PRESS

ITHACA AND LONDON

First published 2006 by Cornell University Press
First printing, Cornell Paperbacks, 2007

Printed in the United States of America

Library of Congress Cataloging-in-Publication Data

Shovlin, John.
  The political economy of virtue : luxury, patriotism, and the origins of the French Revolution / John Shovlin.
      p. cm.
  Includes bibliographical references and index.
  ISBN-13: 978-0-8014-4479-1 (cloth : alk. paper)
  ISBN-13: 978-0-8014-7418-7 (pbk. : alk. paper)
  1. Economics—France—History—18th century. 2. Luxury—Moral and ethical aspects—France—History—18th century. 3. Patriotism—France—History—18th century. 4. France—History—Revolution, 1789–1799—Moral and ethical aspects. 5. France—History—Revolution, 1789–1799—Economic aspects. 6. France—Intellectual life—18th century. 7. France—Economic conditions—18th century. I. Title.
  HB105.A2S56   2006
  944.04—dc22   2006019342

Cornell University Press strives to use environmentally responsible suppliers and materials to the fullest extent possible in the publishing of its books. Such materials include vegetable-based, low-VOC inks and acid-free papers that are recycled, totally chlorine-free, or partly composed of nonwood fibers. For further information, visit our website at www.cornellpress.cornell.edu.

Cloth printing   10 9 8 7 6 5 4 3 2 1
Paperback printing 10 9 8 7 6 5 4 3 2 1

For Kristel

Contents

Illustrations

Acknowledgments

In many ways this book is the fruit of a collective effort; in writing it I benefited from the generous assistance and encouragement of teachers, colleagues, friends, and family. I thank William H. Sewell Jr. of the University of Chicago for the guidance and encouragement he gave me at every stage. Jan Goldstein, also at the University of Chicago, inspired my initial interest in the French Revolution, and Colin Lucas profoundly shaped my view of the eighteenth century. James Livesey read the entire manuscript at draft stage and offered incisive and invaluable suggestions. For their comments on individual chapters, I thank Herrick Chapman, Frederick Cooper, Nicole Eustace, Rebecca Spang, Richard Wittman, and Amy Wyngaard. I also acknowledge the following individuals whose conversation, suggestions, questions, and encouragement all improved the book: Rafe Blaufarb, Greg Brown, Loïc Charles, Denise Davidson, Pierre Force, Stéphane Gerson, Colin Jones, Steven Kaplan, Michael Kwass, Sarah Maza, and Jay Smith. I extend special thanks to Émilie d'Orgeix for her assistance in locating one of the illustrations. To my friends in the history department at Hobart and William Smith Colleges I owe an enormous debt of gratitude. I also acknowledge the patient assistance of the staff of the Warren Hunting Smith Library at Hobart and William Smith Colleges—and especially the indefatigable labors of Daniel Mulvey at interlibrary loan. I thank my colleagues in the history department at New York University who provided the stimulating atmosphere in which I finished the book. My initial research was assisted by grants from the Social Science Research Council, the American Council of Learned Societies, and the Mellon Foundation. In the later stages of the project, I was the beneficiary of grants from Hobart and William Smith Colleges and the National Endowment for the Humanities. My greatest debts are to my family, and especially to Kristel Smentek. This book is dedicated to her.

J.S.

THE POLITICAL ECONOMY OF VIRTUE

Introduction: Political Economy and Public Life in Eighteenth-Century France

> I have studied many works which are comparatively unknown, and deservedly so, but which, as their composition betrays but little art, afford perhaps a still truer index to the instincts of the age.
>
> —Tocqueville, *L'ancien régime*

The image reproduced on the frontispiece, painted in 1766 by Jean-Baptiste Perronneau, is titled, simply, *Portrait of a Gentleman*. An anonymous subject gazes from the canvas with an expression of startling forcefulness. The sitter's dress is rich but sober; he wears a velvet frock coat; his wig is fastened at the nape of the neck with a black silk ribbon. He is unadorned, except for some indications of wealth and ease: the gold buttons of a waist coat, an elaborate cravat, and a pair of prominent lace cuffs. Clasped in his left hand is a memorandum, handwritten in French, its title clearly legible: "agriculture, arts, et commerce." The subject of the painting looks outward, as if he is thinking intently on something he has just read; the expression is proud, inflexible, and shrewd. He is a man of substance, possibly a landowner, but whether noble or just notable is uncertain. He may be a member of one of the agricultural societies established by the royal administration in the 1760s, or simply part of that general educated reading public that engaged with public affairs in the eighteenth century through the medium of their own writings, or those of their peers. His anonymity mirrors that of the public itself, and his engagement with agriculture, the arts, and commerce emblematizes the broad public interest those subjects aroused in the decades between 1750 and the outbreak of the French Revolution.

Between the 1750s and the 1780s the propertied elite of the old regime turned its attention to economic matters as never before. French authors produced an enormous volume of books, treatises, pamphlets, and brochures dealing with the organization of agriculture, trade, finance, and manufacturing and the impact of these activities on the public welfare. By the 1760s, the term "political economy" was coming into fashion to describe such works.[1] According to Jean-Claude Perrot, French publishers issued a total of 2869 new titles in this vein between the middle of the seventeenth century and the Revolution, with about 80 percent of them appearing between 1750 and 1789.[2] Christine Théré enumerates even larger totals, counting 391 new titles in the 1750s, 613 in the 1760s, 668 in the 1770s, 756 between 1780 and 1788, and a colossal 804 in 1789 alone.[3] By the 1760s, authors writing in French were producing new works of political economy at a faster pace than new novels.[4] Some of these works, moreover, sold remarkably well. The *Affiches de province,* a provincial advertising sheet, remarked in 1754 that the abbé Le Blanc's translation of Hume's political economic essays was being "snapped up as fast as the most agreeably frivolous book."[5] The marquis de Mirabeau's *L'ami des hommes* may have gone through as many as forty editions between its initial publication in 1756 and the end of the century. The book appeared in nearly a quarter of the eighteenth-century private libraries inventoried by Daniel Mornet.[6] In the 1780s, Jacques Necker's massive *De l'administration des finances de la France* (1784) broke all previous records for such a work, selling tens of thousands of copies.[7]

In addition to books and brochures, a specialized press published hundreds of articles on agriculture, commerce, and manufactures. Between 1750 and 1815, publishers founded two dozen new periodicals dealing wholly or substantially with economic affairs, and mainstream journals also devoted in-

[1] On the emergence of the term *économie politique,* see Jean-Claude Perrot, *Une histoire intellectuelle de l'économie politique, XVIIe–XVIIIe siècle* (Paris, 1992).

[2] Perrot, *Histoire intellectuelle,* 75.

[3] Christine Théré, "Economic Publishing and Authors, 1566–1789," in *Studies in the History of French Political Economy: From Bodin to Walras,* ed. Gilbert Faccarello (London, 1998). Théré's inventory is based on different criteria than Perrot's. Perrot counts all texts that include in their titles terms such as *richesses, commerce, finances, impôts, crédit,* and *population*—the standard vocabulary of early modern French economic thought. Théré models her conception of political economy on the classification elaborated by the abbé André Morellet in his *Prospectus d'un nouveau dictionnaire de commerce* (Paris, 1769), and bases her enumeration on a bibliography compiled by Jacqueline Hecht and Claude Lévy at the Institut National d'Études Démographiques: *Économie et population: Les doctrines françaises avant 1800,* ed. Alfred Sauvy (Paris, 1956). This bibliography is based on a reading of content rather than titles, and Théré supplements its findings with reference to major British and American catalogues of economic literature.

[4] Based on a comparison with the figures in Angus Martin, Vivienne G. Mylne, and Richard Frautschi, *Bibliographie du genre romanesque français 1751–1800* (London, 1977).

[5] Claude Labrosse, "Réception et communication dans les périodiques littéraires (1750–1760)," in *La diffusion et la lecture des journaux de la langue française sous l'ancien régime: Actes du colloque international, Nimègue, 3–5 juin 1987* (Amsterdam, 1988). All translations are by the author unless otherwise stated.

[6] Victor Riqueti, marquis de Mirabeau, *L'ami des hommes, ou Traité de la population* (Avignon, 1756); Kenneth E. Carpenter, *The Economic Bestsellers before 1850: A Catalogue of an Exhibition Prepared for the History of Economics Society Meeting, May 21–24, 1975, at Baker Library* (Cambridge, MA, 1975); Daniel Mornet, "Les enseignements des bibliothèques privées 1750–1780," *Revue d'histoire littéraire de la France* 17 (1910): 449–96.

[7] Carpenter, *Economic Bestsellers.*

creasing attention to economic issues.[8] Gentlemanly amateurs of rural economy gathered in agricultural societies to read the *Journal oeconomique*, to discuss new crops and farming techniques, or to debate the unpublished memoranda of their peers. The essay competitions run by provincial academies reflected a new interest in practical economic improvement. Artificial meadows, interest rates, woodland management, silk manufacture, internal navigation, the history of trade—these were all topics of academic essay competitions.[9] The enormous growth in the prominence of economic affairs in the intellectual life of the kingdom can be gauged by the dramatic change in the status accorded to economic matters between the *Encyclopédie* of Diderot and d'Alembert in the 1750s and Panckoucke's *Encyclopédie méthodique* of the 1780s. While the earlier work included only a few dozen entries on economic subjects, the sections of the *Encyclopédie méthodique* devoted to finance, commerce, and *économie politique* ran to several stout volumes.[10]

The breadth, vigor, and sheer scale of economic debate in the old regime has attracted surprisingly little notice. Most historians, when they attend to political economy in eighteenth-century France, think only of the Physiocrats, a small coterie of writers notorious for claiming that commerce and manufactures produce no real wealth. As Catherine Larrère observes, Physiocracy is often conflated with eighteenth-century French political economy *tout court*.[11] This school of political economy was the focal point of most research on eighteenth-century French economic thought until recent decades, and it still attracts a great deal of scholarly attention. Physiocracy enjoys a privileged status in modern scholarship because, in their own day, the self-styled *économistes* were such indefatigable self-promoters (no eighteenth-century doctrine enjoyed such single-minded advocacy) and also because, in the teleological history-of-economic-theory approach, influential in much twentieth-century scholarship, Physiocracy figured as the most advanced eighteenth-century French political economy and therefore as the one deserving of most consideration.[12] But the Physiocrats were only one voice in the din of public debate on economic questions in eighteenth-century France.

---

[8] Jean Sgard, ed. *Dictionnaire des journaux, 1660–1789* (Paris, 1991).

[9] Antoine-François Delandine, *Couronnes académiques, ou Recueil des prix proposés par les sociétés savantes* (Paris, 1787).

[10] Perrot, *Histoire intellectuelle*, 127.

[11] Catherine Larrère, *L'invention de l'économie au XVIIIe siècle: Du droit naturel à la physiocratie* (Paris, 1992), 5. Among the major studies of Physiocracy, in addition to Larrère's work, are Elizabeth Fox-Genovese, *The Origins of Physiocracy: Economic Revolution and Social Order in Eighteenth-Century France* (Ithaca, 1976); I.N.E.D., *François Quesnay et la physiocratie* (Paris, 1958); Ronald L. Meek, *The Economics of Physiocracy: Essays and Translations* (Fairfield, NJ, 1993); Philippe Steiner, *La "science nouvelle" de l'économie politique* (Paris, 1998); Gianni Vaggi, *The Economics of François Quesnay* (Basingstoke, 1987); Georges Weulersse, *Le mouvement physiocratique en France (de 1756 à 1770)*, 2 vols. (Paris, 1910); idem, *La physiocratie sous les ministères de Turgot et de Necker (1774–1781)* (Paris, 1950); idem, *La physiocratie à la fin du règne de Louis XV (1770–1774)* (Paris, 1959); idem, *La physiocratie à l'aube de la Révolution, 1781–1792*, ed. Corinne Beutler (Paris, 1985).

[12] Keith Tribe, "The 'Histories' of Economic Discourse," *Genealogies of Capitalism* (Atlantic Highlands, 1981).

Since the 1980s, important contributions to our understanding of political economy have been made by researchers investigating the economic thought of the circle around J.-C.-M. Vincent de Gournay, a senior royal official in the 1750s, and by others exploring the work of Pierre de Boisguilbert, Richard Cantillon, Jacques Turgot, the marquis de Condorcet, and Jean-Baptiste Say.[13] Invaluable as such work is, most of it remains within a tradition of intellectual history that focuses on a small number of writers distinguished by their virtuosity. The argument in favor of concentrating on such thinkers is that their more sophisticated works offer insight into categories and logics that lesser authors do not, or perhaps cannot, make explicit, but which they nevertheless use. This assumption is true in part. However, it does not follow that less self-conscious writers are doing *no more* than deploying a version of an intellectual paradigm expressed more articulately by others. In fact, they often fuse this framework with much else besides, and their cultural and political significance may lie precisely in that syncretism. To put the same point a different way, we tend to contrast popular political economic ideas—sometimes designated as a "moral economy"—with an elite political economy which tends to be identified with the productions of Enlightenment intellectuals or administrative experts. Such an assumption can be misleading. Just as there is an attenuated relationship today between academic economics and the economic assumptions of middle-class people, so there was often a disjuncture between the political economy of "ordinary" elites and that of the most sophisticated economic writers in eighteenth-century France. If the original minds of eighteenth-century French political economy are now better known than they were formerly, the many unremarkable members of the propertied elite who wrote commonplace works remain obscure.

This book will suggest that the center of gravity of French political economy lay in a public composed of middling elites anxious about the effects of economic transformation on their own social position and on the nation's capacity to compete in the international system. The explosion of political economic literature in the latter half of the eighteenth century was one phase in the rise of an educated reading public claiming for itself the right to pass judgment on public affairs. Writers offered critiques of the monarchy's economic policies, and appeals for new economic initiatives, governed by a rudimentary set of as-

[13] Loïc Charles, "L'économie politique française et le politique dans la deuxième moitié du XVIIIe siècle," in *Histoire du libéralisme en Europe,* ed. Philippe Nemo and Jean Petitot (Paris, 2002); Gilbert Faccarello, *Aux origines de l'économie politique libérale: Pierre de Boisguilbert* (Paris, 1986); Simone Meyssonnier, *La balance et l'horloge: La genèse de la pensée libérale en France au XVIIIe siècle* (Montreuil, 1989); Antoin E. Murphy, "Le développement des idées économiques en France (1750–1756)," *Revue d'histoire moderne et contemporaine* 33 (1986): 521–41; idem, *Richard Cantillon: Entrepreneur and Economist* (Oxford, 1986); Claude Morilhat, *La prise de conscience du capitalisme: Économie et philosophie chez Turgot* (Paris, 1988); Emma Rothschild, *Economic Sentiments: Adam Smith, Condorcet, and the Enlightenment* (Cambridge, MA, 2001); Richard Whatmore, *Republicanism and the French Revolution: An Intellectual History of Jean-Baptiste Say's Political Economy* (Oxford, 2000).

sumptions about how economic activity affects the public welfare. My principal objective has been to explore those assumptions that were most prevalent, to analyze the most pervasive critiques, and to understand the significance of this wide public engagement with political economic issues in the eighteenth century.

One of the primary conclusions of my analysis is that much of the political economy elaborated and embraced by ordinary elites was animated and shaped by a patriotic impulse. Patriotism has emerged in recent years as a crucial category in the study of the eighteenth century. Patriots sought to create a political community in which citizens subordinated their private interests to the welfare of the public, a polity stirred by the same spirit of civic virtue that had characterized the republics of the ancient world. Patriots expected the renewal of such virtue to solve a range of problems. Most believed it would restore French greatness in the international sphere—a pressing concern after the humiliating reverses France suffered in the Seven Years' War (1756–63). Others believed patriotism would counter what they perceived as the increasing despotism of the monarchy. Monarchists, meanwhile, hoped to harness patriotism to increase the popularity of the Crown. Many commentators believed that society had been corrupted by an excessive interest in wealth and that patriotism would reverse this troubling development. With such stakes attached to it, by the 1760s patriotism had become a powerful legitimating category of French politics.[14]

The shadow that patriot preoccupations cast on political economy in this period can be seen in the way many writers combined calls for an expansion of national wealth with attacks on the deleterious effects of money on social, political, and cultural life. The development of economic resources would permit France to regain the position of European supremacy lost to Britain in the Seven Years' War. But most patriots also believed that moral qualities were crucial to the regeneration of France, and that wealth, in the hands of the wrong people, produced in the wrong way, or used perversely, might destroy those qualities. The kind of venal or mercantile ethos that could come with expanding wealth was the very reverse of the disinterested spirit patriots idealized.

At the heart of the broad public engagement with political economy in France lay a modernized and economized version of the ancient problem of luxury. *Luxury* evoked the venality and corruption that were supposed to have destroyed the Roman Republic after the Romans conquered the East and were seduced by its riches and refinement. In the first half of the eighteenth century, Enlightenment moralists attempted to redefine luxury, to represent it as a harmless byproduct of commercial prosperity and a stimulus to economic develop-

[14] David A. Bell, *The Cult of the Nation in France: Inventing Nationalism, 1680–1800* (Cambridge, MA, 2001); Linda Colley, *Britons: Forging the Nation, 1707–1837* (London, 1992); Edmond Dziembowski, *Un nouveau patriotisme français, 1750–1770: La France face à la puissance anglaise à l'époque de la guerre de Sept Ans* (Oxford, 1998); Bailey Stone, *The Genesis of the French Revolution: A Global-Historical Perspective* (Cambridge, 1994), 57–62.

ment. While they succeeded in destabilizing the meaning of the word itself, many of the anxieties traditionally reflected by references to luxury were actually strengthening in the decades after 1750, and were expressed in the burgeoning literature of political economy. Recalling the classical concern with the way luxury hastened the decay of virtue, many eighteenth-century French political economists worried that the material conditions of French life had sapped the French capacity for patriotism. Some held that the pursuit of what they construed as ungrounded, or "unreal" wealth, be it in international commerce, in the luxury trades, or in finance and speculation, had undermined the production of "true" wealth in agriculture or domestic commerce. Though they conceded that such unreal wealth could render a state powerful in the short run, in time it would mine the foundations of a polity's prosperity and power and render it vulnerable to decline. The shadow of the old luxury critique was manifest also in the concern shown by many political economic writers that economic changes were disturbing the proper distribution of honor and status in society. Discussions of how the distribution of honor could best serve the public welfare were ubiquitous in French political economy.

For many French elites who engaged with political economy in this period, the central problem was one of balancing wealth and virtue. France had to create the wealth necessary to meet the British challenge, but she had to do so without jeopardizing the moral qualities crucial to patriotic regeneration. Historians of Anglo-American political thought have long regarded the problem of maintaining an equilibrium between wealth and virtue as central to debates on political economy in the Atlantic World.[15] According to J. G. A. Pocock, Whig defenders of the Hanoverian regime sought to reconcile commerce with virtue by arguing that commercial modernity fostered moral dispositions—manners and civility—that could function as surrogates for an irrecoverable civic virtue. Many French authors, notably Montesquieu, deployed similar arguments, as Albert Hirschman's celebrated discussion of *le doux commerce* suggests.[16] But in the long run this mode of argument proved less persuasive in France than in Britain. It was not principally to trade, but to agriculture that French writers

[15] Istvan Hont and Michael Ignatieff, ed., *Wealth and Virtue: The Shaping of Political Economy in the Scottish Enlightenment* (Cambridge, 1983); Drew R. McCoy, *The Elusive Republic: Political Economy in Jeffersonian America* (Chapel Hill, 1980); David McNally, *Political Economy and the Rise of Capitalism: A Reinterpretation* (Berkeley, 1988); J. G. A. Pocock, *The Machiavellian Moment: Florentine Political Thought and the Atlantic Republican Tradition* (Princeton, 1975); idem, *Virtue, Commerce, and History: Essays on Political Thought & History, Chiefly in the Eighteenth Century* (Cambridge, 1985); Donald Winch, *Adam Smith's Politics: An Essay in Historiographic Revision* (Cambridge, 1978). In recent years, this approach has begun to influence studies of French political economy. See, Steiner, *Science nouvelle;* Whatmore, *Republicanism and the French Revolution.*

[16] Albert O. Hirschman, *The Passions and the Interests: Political Arguments for Capitalism before Its Triumph* (Princeton, 1977). The term "doux" can be translated as "gentle," "sweet," or "soft," and is used in this context to denote the refining and civilizing effects that some eighteenth-century writers attributed to trade.

looked for the foundations of a society that would foster both wealth and virtue (one sees a similar impulse in the Jeffersonian political economy of early national America).[17] Most French political economists believed that a reinvigorated agriculture would constitute a stable foundation for the prosperity of the state while fortifying the moral fiber of the nation.

But it was not enough to revive agriculture; luxury-producing forms of economic activity also had to be curtailed. Principal among such sources of corruption was the system of public finance, and its beneficiaries, known generically as financiers. Financiers were contractors who ran a system of what has been called "private enterprise in public finance."[18] They collected taxes, lent money to the state, made most payments on behalf of the treasury, and advanced money to supply the army, the navy, and other public services. Public finance was big business, and the most successful financiers were among the richest individuals in the country. The growing concern about luxury in the middle of the eighteenth century reflected, in part, the conviction that financiers had risen to a position of new authority and status. By mid century a dense network of marriage alliances linked the highest tiers of finance with the court aristocracy, as did investments in tax farms, government loans, and privileged "court capitalist" ventures in international trade, mining, and manufacturing.

There was vigorous debate in the 1750s and 1760s about whether commerce and manufactures also produced luxury. Unsophisticated writers often viewed trade with a mistrustful eye, seeing the wealth it generated, and the new consumption patterns it made possible, as sources of corruption. Such attitudes changed over time, at least in the mainstream of French political economy. Even among the devotees of agriculture, most came to see that commerce was vital to agricultural prosperity. Defenders of commerce, many associated with the world of trade, elaborated representations validating trade and reconstituting entrepreneurship as a patriotic endeavor. Although some partisans of commerce sought to represent the profit motive itself in positive terms, more commonly champions of trade elided the egotistic dimension of economic behavior and represented merchants, farmers, and entrepreneurs as driven by the desire for honor. No longer actuated exclusively by interest, these might now be seen as potential patriots.

Along with such shifts in the representation of trade, critical changes occurred in the late 1760s and 1770s with respect to thinking about sources of luxury. Critics of luxury argued that the causes of luxury lay in political institutions, not in wealth per se. They elaborated distinctions between a healthy commerce that fostered agriculture, distributed prosperity widely, and supported national power, and harmful speculation, tax farming, and privileged companies that fostered corruption and sapped patriotism. In the 1770s and

---

[17] McCoy, *Elusive Republic*, passim.
[18] J. F. Bosher, *French Finances, 1770–1795: From Business to Bureaucracy* (Cambridge, 1970), 6–12, 74–92.

1780s, the attack on luxury took on an increasingly anti-aristocratic edge. Aristocratic engagement with court capitalism, and connections with financiers, both personal and pecuniary, made the court nobility vulnerable to the charge that it too had become part of a corrupt plutocracy.

A political economy preoccupied by problems of luxury and plutocracy articulated the resentments and the ambitions of middling elites: provincial nobles of modest means, many with a tradition of military service, along with that part of the non-noble elite drawing its income mainly from land, the professions, and office holding. Substantial segments of the propertied class felt threatened in the eighteenth century by the increasing influence money seemed to enjoy as a basis for social status. Many resented the social ascension of families who profited from expanding trade, and especially finance, to achieve ennoblement and the rewards of office and honor. They criticized the protection the state gave to manufactures and commerce and its relative neglect of agriculture. They deplored a tax system that systematically favored financiers, grandees, and "capitalists" at their expense. Patriot political economy expressed these prosaic concerns in an idealized fashion, identifying the interests of middling elites with the interests of the nation. This is not to imply that political economy simply reflected the experiences and interests of such groups. The language they used shaped their perceptions and helped to create common interests by simplifying a complex reality and offering a framework to make sense of it.

The discontent of broad, middling sections of the elite with the existing political economic order had profound political implications: it allowed privileged groups, paradoxically, to feel like victims of a social order from which they richly benefited, and it strained the implicit contract that tied them to the monarchy. Since the seventeenth century, as historians of absolutism have shown, the relationship of elites to the Crown was predicated on an exchange of loyalty for benefits. The elite abstained from rebellion against the authority of the monarchy, while the king guaranteed the integrity of an hierarchical social order in which elites enjoyed a privileged status. The Crown also delivered a wide array of material benefits to the elite in the form of exemptions from taxation, salaries paid to venal office holders, careers in the military and the administration, interest payments on *rentes* (annuities), pensions, and gifts.[19] As Michael Kwass has recently pointed out, this bargain showed signs of breaking down in the eighteenth century as the monarchy introduced universal taxation and pressed elites to pay their share.[20] Of equal importance, I suggest, was the wide-

---

[19] William Beik, *Absolutism and Society in Seventeenth-Century France: State Power and Provincial Aristocracy in Languedoc* (Cambridge, 1985); James B. Collins, *Fiscal Limits of Absolutism: Direct Taxation in Early Seventeenth-Century France* (Berkeley, 1988); idem, *The State in Early Modern France* (Cambridge, 1995); Daniel Dessert, *Argent, pouvoir et société au Grand Siècle* (Paris, 1984); Philip T. Hoffman, "Early Modern France, 1450–1700," in *Fiscal Crises, Liberty, and Representative Government, 1450–1789*, ed. Philip T. Hoffman and Kathryn Norberg (Stanford, 1994).

[20] Michael Kwass, "A Kingdom of Taxpayers: State Formation, Privilege, and Political Culture in Eighteenth-Century France," *Journal of Modern History* 70, no. 2 (1998): 295–339.

spread feeling that the monarchy bilked middling sections of the elite to benefit an aristocratic and plutocratic few. The political economic policies sponsored
by the monarchy, including universal taxation, the Colbertist encouragement
of manufactures and commerce, and the regulation of the grain trade, seemed
to benefit one section of the elite at the expense of another. In the perception of
many middling nobles, and notables, the political economic order sponsored by
the monarchy delivered disproportionate advantages, at their expense, to a
small super-elite defined by its wealth: the court nobility, great merchants and
manufacturers, and financiers. Viewed through the prism of a political economy oriented to problems of luxury, such injustices could also be perceived as
the root cause of the nation's degeneration.

Recognizing that political economic problems were a central feature of what
many elites thought was wrong with the old regime enriches our understanding of the origins of the French Revolution in several important respects. First,
as I have already pointed out, it tells us much about why sections of the French
elite—ostensibly the beneficiaries of absolutism—were alienated from the
absolute monarchy, and why demands for change took the form of a patriot
discourse calling for the regeneration of the nation. Second, an attention to political economy sheds light on why the financial crisis of the 1780s was so symbolically important. It is a truism that the French Revolution was touched off
by the near bankruptcy of the state, a predicament exacerbated by a sharp economic slump. This crisis is often viewed instrumentally, as a trigger, or opening, to be exploited by the monarchy's critics, rather than as a powerful impetus
to revolutionary transformation in its own right. What is not appreciated is the
heavy symbolic charge the financial and economic crises carried, the powerful
way such breakdowns bore out claims critics had been making for decades: that
the monarchy was sponsoring a political economic order that was ungrounded,
destructive of the "real" economy, vulnerable to collapse, and inimical to the
regeneration of national power. The administration sought to regain credibility in the only way it could, by sponsoring a program of deep political economic
reform to regenerate the nation. This move lent further authority to the critics
without restoring confidence in the Crown.

To understand the negative public response, one must see the royal reform
project in the context of earlier failed initiatives. In the 1760s the monarchy
made a concerted effort to identify itself with the forces of political economic
revitalization, sponsoring agricultural improvement, deregulating the grain
trade, and revoking the privilege of the Indies Company. The abandonment of
most of these efforts in the early 1770s by a deeply unpopular ministry shook
the faith that the monarchy would transform the political economic order. A
second round of reform and retreat followed under Turgot, controller general
from 1774 to 1776. When the monarchy once again proclaimed its commitment to regeneration in 1787, the public was rightly skeptical.

Mistrust was heightened by the fact that the royal administration in the
1780s appeared to be presiding over an extraordinary expansion of unreal and
corrupting wealth. Fueled by royal borrowing, and the establishment of new

joint-stock companies, the Paris stock exchange of the 1780s played host to wild speculation. Speculation became the fixation of many political economic writers, the most recent and disturbing avatar of the luxury they had railed against since the 1750s. Through its reform plan, the monarchy had placed sweeping transformation on the political agenda but it failed to persuade elites that it should be the agency of that transformation.

Attention to political economic debates also helps explain why hostility to absolutism morphed so readily into antagonism to aristocracy in 1789. In their attack on aristocracy, critics borrowed heavily from old regime critics of luxury, who had long castigated the monarchy for patronizing a plutocratic order that benefited only financiers and court nobles. Critics charged that the nobility was a corrupt plutocracy wallowing in luxury, whose existence was inimical to agriculture and commerce, a group that pursued its own pecuniary interests at the expense of the public. There is certainly an irony here, if not a paradox, because the provincial nobility had pioneered this language to criticize financiers and the court, and now it was turned against them by their erstwhile allies, nonnoble provincial elites. In fact, I will suggest, this critique of plutocracy was modular—it could readily be invoked by any group to challenge a rival distinguished from it by relative wealth.

To view the Revolution from the standpoint of the patriot political economy that had flourished in the old regime is also to see the economic transformations it wrought in a clearer light. Scholars have tended to measure the economic significance of the Revolution in terms of its contribution to the development of capitalism, or economic growth, and many have judged it a failure on both counts. But these are not the only metrics of structural change. A large literature on the French economy in the old regime has shown us what was self-evident to most eighteenth-century political economists: that the economy was structured, through and through, by the exercise of political authority.[21] Fundamental transformations of the locus and character of political authority necessarily had structural implications for the formatting of the economy by the state. Once the power of the aristocracy had been broken and absolutism replaced with new constitutional arrangements, patriots dismantled the institutional order they regarded as a source of luxury and took steps to regenerate France economically. They lifted regulations on the grain trade, abrogated the exclusive privileges and monopolies enjoyed by court capitalist enterprises, dis-

---

[21] See, for example, Judith A. Miller, *Mastering the Market: The State and the Grain Trade in Northern France, 1700–1860* (Cambridge, 1999); Philippe Minard, *La fortune du colbertisme: État et industrie dans la France des lumières* (Paris, 1998); Jean-Laurent Rosenthal, *The Fruits of Revolution: Property Rights, Litigation, and French Agriculture, 1700–1860* (Cambridge, 1992); Michael Sonenscher, *Work and Wages: Natural Law, Politics, and the Eighteenth-Century French Trades* (Cambridge, 1989). For theoretical accounts of the structuring role of the state in the economy, see Fred Block, "The Roles of the State in the Economy," *The Handbook of Economic Sociology,* ed. Neil J. Smelser and Richard Swedberg (Princeton, 1994); Michel Callon, ed., *The Laws of the Markets* (Oxford, 1998); Karl Polanyi, *The Great Transformation* (Boston, 1944).

mantled the system of private enterprise in public finance, and created a new paper currency, nominally based on the value of land, to bring order to the public finances. These reforms were intended to remove the political economic obstacles to the emergence of a polity combining prosperity with patriotism. In the short term, they mostly failed. In aggregate, and in the longer run, however, the Revolution altered basic political economic structures in ways commensurate with the critiques elaborated before 1789, creating a France more attuned than the old regime to the interests and values of the former middling elites.

Behind the palpable and dramatic transformations of the revolutionary decade and the tempests of eighteenth-century French politics another quieter revolution was taking place: a shift in the relationship of elite culture as a whole to the economic, mediated by political economic debate. It has long been recognized that the late eighteenth century was a significant moment in the reorientation of elite attitudes toward the economy, but the precise character of that adaptation is disputed. Some scholars have traced in the final decades of the eighteenth century the rise of "market culture," a set of cultural schemas and categories that classified and ordered aspects of social reality according to how they fit into the logic and modalities of a market system.[22] Others have argued that in the course of the eighteenth century representations of pecuniary interest were transformed, and profit-directed activities came to be validated as innocuous, if not socially beneficial.[23] Historians who explore nineteenth-century attitudes, by contrast, argue that suspicion of interest, economic individualism, and the market remained central features of French culture long after the French Revolution.[24] An attention to the massive literature of political economy produced in the eighteenth century, much of it authored by ordinary French elites, allows us to clarify the exact nature of the cultural transformation underway in this period.

Through the political economic debates that played out in the public sphere, economic activity was remade as a quasi-patriotic pursuit, and economic agents—farmers, merchants, and manufacturers—came to be seen as potentially capable of civic engagement in a way they had not been before. The primary impetus behind this change was the need to engage with the problem of national success in a competitive international order where wealth was a basic determinant of power. Ordinary elites were more willing to view the work of farmers, entrepreneurs, and merchants as patriotic when they came to see it as

[22] William M. Reddy, *The Rise of Market Culture: The Textile Trade and French Society, 1750–1900* (Cambridge, 1984). See also, Jean-Pierre Hirsch, "Revolutionary France, Cradle of Free Enterprise," *American Historical Review* 94 (1989): 1281–89; Pierre Rosanvallon, *Le libéralisme économique: Histoire de l'idée de marché* (Paris, 1989).

[23] Hirschman, *Passions and the Interests.*

[24] Sarah Maza, *The Myth of the French Bourgeoisie: An Essay on the Social Imaginary 1750–1850* (Cambridge, MA, 2003); Victoria E. Thompson, *The Virtuous Marketplace: Women and Men, Money and Politics in Paris, 1830–1870* (Baltimore, 2000); Lisa Tiersten, *Marianne in the Market: Envisioning Consumer Society in Fin-de-Siècle France* (Berkeley, 2001).

vital to the national well-being. These changes were effected not through a successful repackaging of the profit motive as benign, or by embracing the idea that
market exchange was a peculiarly beneficent mode of social intercourse. Instead, economic activity was recast as patriotic through the virtual elision of the
profit motive. Economic agents were represented as acting out of a civic regard
for their fellow citizens or, more often, out of a desire to win legitimate honor
and esteem.

To be sure, there was an alternate tradition that rose to prominence at several critical moments during the eighteenth century. Writers in this tradition
tended to represent the economy as an auto-regulatory mechanism governed by
the laws of the market. They embraced interest and economic individualism as
the basic and legitimate motors of all economic life. Such views enjoyed some
traction in the old regime where they could be used to solve particular political
problems, such as defending the government's liberalization of the grain trade
in the 1760s. Ultimately, however, the economic imaginary that underpinned
such approaches did not fit well with the way most French elites thought about
the sources of order in material life. The state, or the political community, was
always viewed as the ordering matrix of the economic world. The only moment
at which this dominant imaginary was seriously challenged was during the
1790s. As the Revolution veered in more radical directions, and began to seem
a threat to property, some elite revolutionaries claimed that further economic
transformations might precipitate a collapse of national wealth. Their premise
was that the economy is not infinitely malleable to exertions of sovereign will.
They posited a natural economic order which was refractory to political tin-
kering, a mechanism that might break down completely in the face of a *coup
d'autorité,* precipitating the nation into a new barbarism. This rhetorical move
constituted a virtual "invention" of the economy for political purposes.

The debates of the revolutionary period gave an impetus to such recogniz-
ably "liberal" modes of representing the economy, and a liberal political economic tradition enjoyed a position of prestige in French higher education during
the nineteenth century. Liberals also exerted some influence on public debate,
but never in a way authoritative enough to decisively challenge the major tradition emerging from eighteenth-century political economy. The primary legacy
of the long public engagement with economic matters in the old regime was a
continuing suspicion of consumption, a preference for agriculture over industry, and a proclivity to validate economic activity not for its own sake but for
its patriotic contribution to the nation. It would be easy to view this sensibility
as a rejection of economic modernity and a hankering for an earlier simpler society. But this would be a mistake. From the provincial notables of the old
regime to the economic planners of the twentieth century, such an orientation
mediated a sometimes reluctant embrace, rather than a backward-looking rejection, of economic development.

CHAPTER 1

Commerce, Finance, and the Luxury Debate

I know that our philosophy, always fertile in singular maxims, claims against the experience of all ages, that luxury is what underpins the splendor of a state; but ... will it deny that good manners are essential to the duration of empires, and that luxury is diametrically opposed to good manners? Let luxury be regarded as a sure sign of riches; let it serve, if you will, to multiply them: what is to be concluded from this paradox so worthy of having arisen in our time; and what will become of virtue if wealth must be acquired at any cost?

—J.-J. Rousseau, *Discours sur les sciences et les arts* (1750)

In a chapter of *De l'esprit* (1758) illustrating the kinds of fruitless debates that occur when disputants do not first agree upon the meaning of words, Claude-Adrien Helvétius contrasted two competing views of luxury. According to its defenders, he noted, luxury augments the power of states by putting financial resources at their disposal to buy stores, fill magazines, and subsidize foreign armies. In the domestic sphere, luxury improves moral habits, moderates brutal dispositions, and generates happiness by disseminating ease, comfort, and diversion. It provides employment for artisans, accelerates the circulation of goods and money, and stimulates industry. The critics of luxury took the opposite view. "The happiness and apparent power that luxury for a time imparts to nations," they insisted, "may be compared to those violent fevers from which, during the paroxysms, the patient derives an astonishing strength, and which seem to augment his powers only to deprive him at once, when the fit is over, both of this strength and his life." The true source of a nation's might, they claimed, resided in the number and vigor of its inhabitants and their patriotism. Luxurious nations were sooner or later struck by despotism because neither the elite, mired in pleasure-seeking, nor the poor, in pinching want, would fight to preserve liberty. Wealth, moreover, produced happiness in a state only if it was evenly distributed, while luxury gave rise to grotesque inequalities that generated only misery.[1]

---

[1] Claude-Adrien Helvétius, *De l'esprit* (Paris, 1758), 16–30.

One of the principal claims of this book is that anxieties about luxury permeated much of the French political economy produced in the second half of the eighteenth century. The principal function of this chapter is to explore what was at issue in thinking about luxury, to show that anxieties about luxury were resurgent at mid-century, and to consider the social and cultural grounding of anti-luxury sentiment. Forewarned by Helvétius, however, I do not propose to write a concept history of luxury. My principal concern is not to trace what men and women meant when they used the word—few used it carefully or with any consistency. Like Helvétius, Denis Diderot singled out luxury as emblematic of those words whose uncertain meaning led to interminable and pointless intellectual wrangling.[2] Even within a single work, writers often used the term in a variety of ways. In his *Spirit of the Laws,* Montesquieu employed luxury in at least four different senses: as the imitation of consumption patterns characteristic of one's social superiors; to refer, more broadly, to the extravagant consumption of the rich; as a desire for material goods beyond real needs that nurtured egotism and corrupted civic spirit; or, simply, as the traffic in expensive consumer goods.[3] The imprecision with which contemporaries used the term did not mean that it lacked meaning. On the contrary, luxury was a word whose significance and power inhered in the capacity to evoke a range of ideas or feelings not contained in any formal definition.[4]

I am less interested in pinning down some reified meaning, or meanings, of the word than in discovering what was at issue when it was invoked. Under the sign of luxury, eighteenth-century men and women argued about whether, and how, activities in the material realm could damage the proper functioning of the polity. Given the structure of early modern economies, "material realm" implies not only the circuits of production, exchange, and consumption, but the interactions of the state with society. According to the critics of luxury, activities in the material realm, in this broad sense, might destabilize the social order, impair the morality or civic spirit of citizens, facilitate despotism, or weaken the power of the state in international competition. Apologists rejected such charges and often claimed for luxury an array of moral, social and political benefits. One did not have to invoke the *word* luxury to have these kinds of debates; indeed, one could do so while insisting that luxury was something altogether more specific and narrow (a particular form of consumption, for example). Buffeted by the winds of debate, the meaning of the word itself was unstable. However, even those eighteenth-century commentators who maintained

---

[2] Denis Diderot, "Encyclopédie," *Encyclopédie, ou Dictionnaire raisonné des sciences, des arts et des métiers par une société de gens de lettres,* vol. 5 (Paris, 1751). See also Pierre Rétat, "Luxe," *Dix-huitième siècle* 26 (1994): 79–88.

[3] Charles de Secondat, baron de Montesquieu, *The Spirit of the Laws,* trans. Anne M. Cohler, Basia Carolyn Miller, and Harold Samuel Stone (Cambridge, 1989), bk. 7, chaps. 1–4; bk. 20, chap. 10.

[4] Quentin Skinner, "Language and Social Change," in *Meaning and Context: Quentin Skinner and His Critics,* ed. James Tully (Oxford, 1988).

a narrow and specific definition of luxury would have recognized that many of their contemporaries used the term to evoke a far wider range of issues. Thus, I will occasionally claim in this book that commentators are engaging in debate about luxury, even when they expressly used the word in a narrower way, and inveighed against its looser usage.

Many scholars treat the expansion of trade and the development of new consumption practices in the eighteenth century as the fundamental source of debate about luxury, and there is obvious justification for doing so.[5] The middle decades of the eighteenth century were a time of relative economic growth and prosperity, and the new consumption that accompanied this wealth stimulated the speculations of both critics and defenders of *luxe*. Modest economic expansion occurred in the countryside, as markets developed and regional specialization intensified.[6] Manufacturing increased its share of the French gross domestic product from a mere 5 percent of the total in 1700 to about 13 percent by the 1780s, a testament to growth in the textile industry, in particular. French international trade, and especially colonial commerce, was dynamic. Between 1730 and the late 1770s, foreign trade expanded between five- and six-fold, despite the interruptions and losses associated with the period's many wars, while colonial commerce increased tenfold. By the 1780s, a million metropolitan jobs may have depended on colonial investment.[7] Economic growth was reflected in the steady development of French cities. The number of French towns with a population over 10,000 increased from 60 in 1700 to 88 in 1780 and the total population of these urban centers rose from 1.85 to 2.8 million. Port cities, benefiting from the profits of colonial trade, grew particularly quickly. Bordeaux, for example, more than doubled its population between 1700 and 1790.[8]

---

[5] Maxine Berg and Helen Clifford, *Consumers and Luxury: Consumer Culture in Europe, 1650–1850* (Manchester, 1999); Cissie Fairchilds, "Fashion and Freedom in the French Revolution," *Continuity and Change* 15, no. 3 (2000): 1–15; Michael Kwass, "Ordering the World Of Goods: Consumer Revolution and the Classification of Objects in Eighteenth-Century France," *Representations* 82 (2003): 87–116; Sarah Maza, *Myth of the French Bourgeoisie*, 41–68.

[6] Philip T. Hoffman, *Growth in a Traditional Society: The French Countryside, 1450–1815* (Princeton, 1996); David R. Weir, "Les crises économiques et les origines de la Révolution française," *Annales ESC* 4 (1991): 917–47.

[7] Jan Marczewski, "The Take-Off Hypothesis and French Experience," in *The Economics of Take-Off into Sustained Growth*, W. W. Rostow, ed. (London, 1963), 119–38; T. J. Markovitch, *Les industries lainières de Colbert à la Révolution* (Geneva, 1976); *Des dernier temps de l'âge seigneurial aux préludes de l'âge industriel (1660–1789)*, vol. 2 of *Histoire économique et sociale de la France*, ed. Fernand Braudel and Ernest Labrousse (Paris, 1970–82), 503; Laurent Dubois, *Avengers of the New World: The Story of the Haitian Revolution* (Cambridge, MA, 2004), 21.

[8] On urbanization, see Bernard Lepetit, "Urbanization in Eighteenth-Century France: A Comment," *Journal of Interdisciplinary History* 23, no. 1 (1992): 73–85. For a less sanguine view of the figures, see Philip Benedict, "Was the Eighteenth Century an Era of Urbanization in France?" *Journal of Interdisciplinary History* 21, no. 2 (1990): 179–215; idem, "Urbanization in Eighteenth-Century France: A Reply," *Journal of Interdisciplinary History* 23, no. 1 (1992): 87–95; François Crouzet, "Bordeaux: An Eighteenth-Century Wirtschaftswunder?" in *Britain, France, and International Commerce: From Louis XIV to Victoria*, ed. François Crouzet (Aldershot, Hampshire, 1996).

Especially sweeping were changes in consumption. In the course of the eighteenth century, the ordinary people of Paris, for the first time, became active and conscious pursuers of fashion. The value of plebeian wardrobes, especially those of Parisian women, increased sharply both in absolute terms and as a percentage of an individual's total assets.[9] Similar if less spectacular changes in consumption occurred in provincial cities. A citizen of Montpellier fretted in 1768 that "In this town, from one season to the next, all of this [fashion] changes, and it is truly an occupation, for those who wish to be fashionable, to study and to practice the changes that occur daily."[10] The consumer revolution extended beyond the sartorial realm. Cheap imitations of luxury items, such as pocket watches, fans, ornate buttons, and fancy buckles flooded the market.[11] It became far more common for people of modest means to own consumer goods that in previous generations had been the province of the well-to-do. "Showy pieces of furniture such as writing-tables, card-tables and coat stands [became] more common; wallpaper, wall-hangings, mirrors, snuff-boxes, teapots, razors, chamber pots, and clocks [were] found in greater abundance."[12] Provincial noble families with the means to do so changed their consumption practices radically. The seventeenth-century norm of provisioning the household from the estate shifted to a pattern of buying almost all household needs.[13] Such broad changes could hardly fail to generate debate, and the language of luxury was used to assess the meaning of these transformations.

Middling elites, both noble and nonnoble, often reacted with considerable ambivalence, if not downright hostility to the economic changes going on around them. Some were disturbed by the consumer revolution, which allowed plebeians to insinuate themselves into polite society by purchasing the traditional markers of elite status. It was easy to blame such disquieting changes on the policies of a monarchy which, since the seventeenth century, had encouraged the development of luxury manufactures and international trade. But attacks on luxury reflected more than antipathy to new patterns of consumption; middling elites were concerned that money was becoming the sole avenue to

[9] Daniel Roche, *The People of Paris: An Essay in Popular Culture in the Eighteenth Century* (Berkeley, 1987), 169–94; idem, *The Culture of Clothing: Dress and Fashion in the 'Ancien Régime,'* trans. Jean Birrell (Cambridge, 1994), 108–11.

[10] Joseph Berthelé, ed., *Montpellier en 1768, d'après le manuscrit anonyme, intitulé: État et description de la ville de Montpellier, fait en 1768* (Montpellier, 1909), 99.

[11] Cissie Fairchilds, "The Production and Marketing of Populuxe Goods in Eighteenth-Century Paris," in *Consumption and the World of Goods,* ed. John Brewer and Roy Porter (London, 1993).

[12] Colin Jones, "Bourgeois Revolution Revivified: 1789 and Social Change," in *Rewriting the French Revolution,* ed. Colin Lucas (Oxford, 1991), 89. See also Annik Pardailhé-Galabrun, *La naissance de l'intime: 3000 foyers parisiens, XVIIe–XVIIIe siècles* (Paris, 1988), and Daniel Roche, *A History of Everyday Things: The Birth of Consumption in France, 1600–1800* (Cambridge, 2000).

[13] Jonathan Dewald, *Pont-St-Pierre 1398–1789: Lordship, Community, and Capitalism in Early Modern France* (Berkeley, 1987), 193–99. See also François-Joseph Ruggiu, *Les élites et les villes moyennes en France et en Angleterre (XVIIe–XVIIIe siècles)* (Paris, 1997), 199–210.

political authority and social status, and the foundation of this fear was as much the ascendancy of financiers as the expansion of commercial wealth. Financiers were contractors who undertook much of the everyday business of government. Indirect taxes were collected by syndicates of businessmen—the Farmers General, most notably—who advanced sums of money to the Crown in return for the right to collect a particular tax over a specified period. The collection of direct taxes—the *taille,* the *vingtième,* and the *capitation*—was entrusted to Receivers General, who also worked for their own profit in serving the state. The Crown also depended upon contractors to advance money and make payments on the government's behalf for all manner of goods and services; these advances were, in effect, short-term loans on which the monarchy paid interest.[14]

Financiers had been the chief target of the anti-luxury critique in seventeenth-century France, and the resurgence of concern about luxury in the middle of the eighteenth century reflected, in part, the conviction that they had risen to a position of new eminence. By the 1740s, a dense network of marriage alliances linked financiers with the court aristocracy, giving their children access to the highest offices in the land.[15] The worlds of finance and the court were also united by investments in the realm of public finance, tax farms, international trade, and large-scale manufacturing.[16] Integration between the worlds of court and finance was nothing new, but the perception that financiers were ascendant grew in the 1740s, catalyzed by the elevation of a daughter of finance, Madame de Pompadour, to the powerful position of royal mistress. The considerable influence of the new royal favorite emblematized the power that the financial class had acquired in the world of the court.

I do not mean to deny that commercial expansion and the consumer revolution played a key role in prompting public debate over the relationship between material life and the public welfare. But I suggest that these factors have too often been viewed outside the full political economic framework within which they took on meaning. Why, one must ask, was there so much more resistance in France than in Britain to the proposition that trade diffused numerous benefits—political, social, and moral—to the societies it invigorated? Why did the cult of commerce, which was such a marked feature of English public life in the eighteenth century, have such a relatively harder time taking hold in France? An important part of the answer, it seems to me, is that the social and cultural effects of commerce and expanding consumption were difficult to separate, in the French context, from the effects of wealth generated in

[14] Bosher, *French Finances,* 6–12, 74–92.

[15] Guy Chaussinand-Nogaret, *The French Nobility in the Eighteenth Century: From Feudalism to Enlightenment,* trans. William Doyle (Cambridge, 1985), 124.

[16] George V. Taylor, "Types of Capitalism in Eighteenth-Century France," *English Historical Review* 79 (1964): 487–92; Guy Chaussinand-Nogaret, *Gens de finance au XVIIIe siècle* (Paris, 1972), 68–77; Guy Richard, *Noblesse d'affaires au XVIIIe siècle* (Paris, 1974), 229–54; Herbert Lüthy, *La banque protestante en France de la révocation de l'Édit de Nantes à la Révolution,* 2 vols. (Paris, 1959–61), 2:42–43.

public finance. The very distinction between trade and finance was somewhat artificial: financiers were business men, and were among the most important investors in commerce and manufactures, both directly as entrepreneurs in their own right and indirectly as partners of other business people. Moreover, they were prominent consumers, visibly using the wealth generated by their public charges to insert themselves into the upper reaches of the social hierarchy. The language of luxury as it was used in eighteenth-century France tended to further confound the effects of trade with those of finance. A significant theme to be explored at the end of this chapter is the emergence, during the 1750s, of a serious effort to separate the two conceptually. Only in the 1770s, however, was this distinction fully assimilated into public debate, and even then it remained fragile. The intervening sections of the chapter will sketch the development of French thinking on luxury in the first half of the eighteenth century, and explore the ways in which luxury became newly problematic in the late 1740s and 1750s.

The Luxury Debate in Early Modern France

In seventeenth-century France the critique of luxury was part of a political tradition calling for a renewal of "virtue" in public life, and it was in association with this idiom that antipathy to luxury revived in the eighteenth century. Luxury was meaningful within a view of human affairs, derived from classical antiquity, holding that a separation ought to exist between the political sphere and a subordinate realm of production, labor, and exchange. In antiquity, this hierarchy of politics over economics corresponded to a division between a minority of male, property-owning citizens deemed to possess the rationality and orientation to public affairs—the virtue—to exercise authority, and the women, slaves, laborers, and traders who did not. In the broadest sense, luxury was a breach of the boundary between the economic and political spheres that threatened to corrupt the functioning of the political, thereby jeopardizing the health of the community as a whole. Such a breach could occur when the base appetites of the lower sphere found a place in the higher, enlarging the place of interest and appetite in the personality of the citizen, and drawing him away from public affairs. If left unchecked, luxury would lead men to subordinate public affairs to private interests. In a polity corrupted by luxury, persons lacking virtue—slaves, money-lenders, even women—might rise out of their proper sphere and usurp authority. The example of the ancient Roman Republic which, according to Roman moralists, had been corrupted and destroyed by luxury, loomed large in the thinking of those who worried that wealth could be a harbinger of decline. According to such luminaries as Livy, Sallust, and Plutarch, luxury enervated and feminized men, sapping their capacity for military virtue; it was a tool of despots who used it to weaken the commitment of their subjects to liberty; it made both rulers and their subjects self-serving, vitiating their capacity to place the public welfare before private interest.[17]

Though it evolved in the classical republics, critics could draw on this tradition in Bourbon France to deplore the usurpation of noble prerogatives by the merely moneyed, especially financiers. Moralists selectively mapped aspects of classical political thought onto the aristocratic institutions and culture of seventeenth-century France. The nobility regarded itself as the political class, the group with the virtue necessary to wield public authority. The usurpations of nonnobles constituted an attempt on the part of people lacking such virtue to elbow their way into the governing elite. The adoption of magnificence by people of low origins, critics argued, led to the "confounding of ranks," the dissolution of the boundaries that distinguished the estates.[18] The proper hierarchy was threatened not only by usurping consumption, but by venality—the sale of public offices. The monarchy sold offices on a massive scale to raise revenues in the seventeenth and eighteenth centuries.[19] Building on the classical precept that a state of luxury exists when men driven by appetite occupy positions of authority, critics argued that venality was filling the ranks of the governing class with such men. Merchants, tax farmers, and financiers were incapable of virtue. Their occupations taught them habitually to value personal gain above higher goods, and they could not be expected to unlearn this habit on taking up public business.[20]

During the seventeenth century, several ideological challenges arose to this anti-luxury tradition, most significantly, perhaps, "commercial humanism." This body of thinking had its roots in late-fifteenth-century Italy, where writers favorable to the claims of the cities sought to present trade as the source of certain social virtues and as an antidote to the idleness of the lordly class. In Henry Clark's useful summation, "'Commercial humanism' may be defined as the tradition of attempts to render comprehensible the ways in which a commercial society, with its emphasis on liberal property rights, on social exchange, and on material prosperity, may be reconciled with the classical concern for virtue as both a moral and a political imperative."[21] Commercial humanists in seven-

[17] Christopher J. Berry, *The Idea of Luxury: A Conceptual and Historical Investigation* (Cambridge, 1994), 45–86; John Sekora, *Luxury: The Concept in Western Thought, Eden to Smollett* (Baltimore, 1977), 30–40.

[18] Renato Galliani, *Rousseau, le luxe et l'idéologie nobiliaire: Étude socio-historique*, in *Studies on Voltaire and the Eighteenth Century*, no. 268 (Oxford, 1989), 11, 63–68, 118.

[19] Roland Mousnier, *La vénalité des offices sous Henri IV et Louis XIII*, 2nd ed. (Paris, 1971); William Doyle, *Venality: The Sale of Offices in Eighteenth-Century France* (Oxford, 1996).

[20] The contrast between the disinterestedness of men of birth and the avarice of recently ennobled financiers was highlighted, for example, in the mid-century attacks on Cardinal Mazarin. Jay M. Smith, *Culture of Merit: Nobility, Royal Service, and the Making of Absolute Monarchy in France, 1600–1789* (Ann Arbor, 1996), 116.

[21] Henry C. Clark, "Commerce, the Virtues, and the Public Sphere in Early Seventeenth-Century France," *French Historical Studies* 21, no. 3 (1998): 415–40.

teenth-century France challenged the classical discourse on luxury by claiming for merchants some of the capacity for public virtue associated with nobles, and by claiming for commerce some of the public utility associated with the profession of arms.

A quite different challenge to the classical discourse on luxury was articulated by representatives of the self-styled *mondain* position, many of them female salon hosts, who advocated the admission into polite society of all people of merit—merit defined to include self-enrichment in commerce or finance, buying venal offices, or successfully intriguing at court. According to Carolyn Lougee, the women who dominated salon life, defended the rapid accumulation of fortunes by tax farmers and financiers, and criticized noble prejudices against commerce. They accepted "misalliances"—marriages between nobles and wealthy commoners—appealing to theories of romantic love to justify them. They even argued occasionally that money alone ought to be the basis of social status.[22]

A third challenge to the anti-luxury perspective emerged from the *bureaux* of the monarchy. Jean-Baptiste Colbert and his administrative successors held that the power of states was a function of national wealth, and that the rise and fall of empires could be explained in economic terms: "commerce is the source of finance, and finance is the sinews of war."[23] With the explosion in the size of armies and the costs of warfare that occurred in early modern Europe, the ability of a state to tax and borrow became the basic determinant of its power.[24] The Colbertist perspective left little room for the kind of political moralizing characteristic of the language of luxury; virtue was largely irrelevant to the well-being of the political community. Political economists in the Colbertist tradition worried about luxury only to the extent that habits of consumption diminished the money supply or adversely affected the balance of trade.[25] Indeed, toward the end of the seventeenth century some began to argue that luxury increases the power of states by stimulating trade and creating employment for the poor.[26]

Colbertism, along with the *mondain* position, were chief targets of the last great seventeenth-century critic of luxury: Archbishop Fénelon. As preceptor to Louis XIV's grandson, the duc de Bourgogne, Fénelon led an aristocratic "conspiracy of reform" at the turn of the eighteenth century.[27] He and his circle op-

[22] Carolyn C. Lougee, *Le Paradis des Femmes: Women, Salons, and Social Stratification in Seventeenth-Century France* (Princeton, 1976), 42–52.

[23] Martin Wolfe, "French Views on Wealth and Taxes from the Middle Ages to the Old Régime," in *Revisions in Mercantilism*, ed. D. C. Coleman (London, 1969), 201.

[24] Geoffrey Parker, *The Military Revolution: Military Innovation and the Rise of the West, 1500–1800* (Cambridge, 1988); Richard Bonney, ed., *Rise of the Fiscal State in Europe* (Oxford, 1999).

[25] Charles Woolsey Cole, *French Mercantilist Doctrines before Colbert* (New York, 1931), 12–13.

[26] Lionel Rothkrug, *The Opposition to Louis XIV: The Political and Social Origins of the French Enlightenment* (Princeton, 1965), 104–5.

[27] Ibid., 256.

posed many of the policies of Louis XIV and hoped that, one day, Bourgogne would be a vehicle for the transformation of the French monarchy. This drive for reform came to nothing when the young prince died in 1712, but Fénelon's thinking formed a vital political legacy for the following century. The archbishop sought systematically to bolster the social status and political power of the nobility. In the *Tables de Chaulnes,* a program of reform he drew up during the autumn of 1711 when the accession of Bourgogne to the throne seemed imminent, he proposed to reverse the centralization of administrative authority, to abolish the corps of intendants—the chief bureaucratic representatives of the monarchy in the provinces—and to turn over responsibility for taxation, trade, and agriculture to provincial estates. He sought to curtail misalliances, to reserve court and military offices for nobles, and to abolish venality in the army. A hallmark of his politics was his hostility to financiers and to fiscalism.[28] He sought to dismantle the fiscal apparatus of absolutism, to abolish the *gabelle* (the royal salt monopoly), the tax farms, and the *capitation,* which was a new poll tax falling on all subjects, including the privileged.[29]

Fénelon denounced Colbertism. He argued that the state's encouragement of manufactures and international trade, combined with a tax structure that overburdened the peasantry, had led to the disastrous neglect of agriculture and to rural poverty and depopulation. Characterizing this as a state of luxury, he represented it as a threat to the long-term well-being of the state. The archbishop held that agriculture is the true basis of the prosperity and power of states and that rulers ought to do everything in their power to foster it. A state was suffering from luxury, in his view, when agriculture was sacrificed to the pursuit of less solid prosperity in commerce and manufactures, and when the countryside was neglected for the benefit of the towns. This, he believed, was the systematic tendency of states governed under the principles of Colbertism, where, to keep manufacturing costs down, low agricultural commodity prices were favored, undercutting both land values and rural standards of living. Such policies created an economic order that was dazzling but ungrounded, masking the real poverty of the country behind a façade of grand enterprises.

Fénelon was by no means an enemy of commerce; indeed, he drew upon a strain in the tradition of commercial humanism arguing that God had established an international division of labor in order to create a universal interdependence between peoples that would be the foundation for peace among them.[30] He held that nobles should be allowed to go into commerce without fear of derogation in order to revitalize their fortunes.[31] The archbishop argued that it was not the power of commercial states to tax and borrow that made

[28] By "fiscalism" I mean administrative practices created to facilitate the extraction of taxes (rather than, for example, to foster prosperity or public order).

[29] Gilbert Gidel, *La politique de Fénelon* (Geneva, 1971), 70–76.

[30] Rothkrug, *Opposition to Louis XIV,* 275. On this tradition, see Geoffrey Butler, *Studies in Statecraft* (London, 1970).

[31] James Herbert Davis, Jr., *Fénelon* (Boston, 1979), 128.

commercial peoples formidable, but the deeply ingrained practice of justice and good manners. Manners had a sense in the eighteenth century that is largely lost in modern English, but that persists in the French *moeurs,* a term that refers to both mores and to moral habits. According to the moralist Charles Pinot Duclos, when one refers to the *moeurs* of an individual, this "signifies nothing other than the practice of moral virtues." As applied to a nation, however, *moeurs* connoted customs and usages, "those that influence the manner of thinking, of feeling, and of acting."[32] In his masterwork, the *Adventures of Telemachus,* written for the instruction of the duc de Bourgogne, Fénelon described the manners of an idealized trading people, the Tyrians, as economical, industrious, clean, sober, patient, faithful, and sincere.[33]

Moeurs, or *manners,* was a key word in the moral and political discourse of eighteenth-century Europe because many moralists saw in such moral dispositions a substitute for a civic virtue that was difficult to sustain in the conditions of commercial modernity. Some commentators claimed, notoriously, that virtue was irrelevant to the welfare of modern commercial societies. In his *Fable of the Bees* (1714), Bernard Mandeville argued that vices rather than virtues make a state wealthy and formidable. Mandeville explored the positive unintended consequences of selfish and even criminal behavior, arguing that prosperity, and thus power, depends on the economic stimulus supplied by citizens' pursuit of their irrational and selfish desires. Not only was virtue superfluous, it might be positively harmful. If the people of a great state were suddenly to abandon their egoistic drives, Mandeville argued, the economy would disintegrate, population would collapse, and the state would be rendered vulnerable to invasion.[34] This view was not widely accepted, however. Instead, British, Dutch, and French moralists argued that modern dispositions such as manners might form a new basis for the kind of behavior that made people good citizens. Such arguments were the stock in trade of "Court Whigs," the chief apologists for the Hanoverian regime in Britain, while in the Netherlands, according to Wyger Velema, publicists elaborated a republican conception of politeness that would allow the citizen "to put the common good before his own direct interest and thus to serve the community as a whole."[35]

In the decades following his death in 1715, a critical component of Fénelon's position was contested by a new generation of moralists. For Fénelon, while

[32] Charles Pinot-Duclos, *Considérations sur les moeurs de ce siècle,* ed. F. C. Green (Cambridge, 1939), 8–9.

[33] François de Salignac de La Mothe-Fénelon, *Aventures de Télémaque,* ed. Jacques Le Brun (Paris, 1995) [1699], 168.

[34] Bernard Mandeville, *The Fable of the Bees; or, Private Vices, Publick Benefits,* ed. F. B. Kaye (Indianapolis, 1988).

[35] Pocock, *Virtue, Commerce, and History,* 37–50; Shelley Burtt, *Virtue Transformed: Political Argument in England, 1688–1740* (Cambridge, 1992); Wyger R. E. Velema, "Ancient and Modern Virtue Compared: De Beaufort and Van Effen on Republican Citizenship," *Eighteenth-Century Studies* 30, no. 4 (1997): 437–48.

commerce and virtue were compatible, luxury and virtue were not: luxury destroyed *moeurs*. This view was disputed by Enlightenment moralists who extolled the social and cultural benefits of luxury. Along with arguments deriving from the Colbertist and *mondain* positions, the Enlightenment apology for luxury articulated in France in the 1730s and 1740s deployed a moral discourse claiming that commerce fosters modern virtue. For many Enlightenment moralists, commerce fostered sociability and humanity; it stimulated the arts and letters, generated employment for the poor, redistributed wealth, and thus created a more egalitarian social order; it suffused a spirit of liberty by reducing personal dependency; it animated industry, enriched the state, and thus made societies more secure. Moreover, the quiet and orderly pursuit of profit was a happy alternative to the religious zealotry of an earlier age.[36]

The most influential French contribution to the debate, J.-F. Melon's *Essai politique sur le commerce* (1734), depended mainly on political economic arguments. Melon argues that luxury renders a state stronger, not weaker. It is a spur to effort and industry, "a destroyer, of sorts, of laziness and idleness," and thus a stimulus to national prosperity and power. But Melon also drew on the position that luxury fostered certain social virtues. It destroys crude vices, such as drunkenness, he argued, and among soldiers the highly developed modern sense of honor compensated for a diminished hardiness.[37] In the two years following its initial publication in 1734, Melon's *Essai* appeared in eight French editions and was reviewed extensively in the press.[38] It may have inspired Voltaire to launch his own apology for luxury in two polemical poems, "Le mondain" (1736) and "Défense du mondain, ou L'apologie du luxe" (1737), which, as their titles suggest, were extensions of the seventeenth-century *mondain* tradition.[39] Voltaire specifically mocked Fénelon's *Telemachus*, with its "sadly virtuous" antique citizens. Following Melon, he argued that luxury reduces inequality by inducing the rich to spend and the poor to work, while enriching the state and rendering it more powerful. The high-water mark of the apology for luxury came with the publication in 1754 of the abbé Le Blanc's translation of Hume's *Political Discourses* (1752).[40] The second essay in the

[36] Hirschman, *Passions and the Interests;* Jerry Z. Muller, *The Mind and the Market: Capitalism in Modern European Thought* (New York, 2002), 23–36; Anthony Pagden, "The 'Defence of Civilisation' in Eighteenth-Century Social Theory," *History of the Human Sciences* 1, no. 1 (1988): 33–45.

[37] Jean-François Melon, *Essai politique sur le commerce* (n.p., 1734), chap. 9.

[38] Carpenter, *Economic Bestsellers;* J. Q. C. Mackrell, *The Attack on "Feudalism" in Eighteenth-Century France* (Toronto, 1973), 81.

[39] Voltaire, "Le mondain," and "Défense du mondain, ou L'apologie du luxe," *Oeuvres complètes de Voltaire,* vol. 10 (Paris, 1877) [1736–37]. See also André Morize, *L'apologie du luxe au XVIIIe siècle et «Le mondain» de Voltaire: Étude critique sur «Le mondain» et ses sources* (Geneva, 1970) [1909].

[40] *Discours politiques de Monsieur Hume traduits de l'anglois* (Amsterdam, 1754), 48–93. On the publishing history, see Loïc Charles, "French Cultural Politics and the Dissemination of Hume's Political Discourses on the Continent (1750–1770)," in *Essays on David Hume's Political Economy,* ed. Margaret Schabas and Carl Wennerlind (New York, 2006).

volume, "Of Luxury," articulated a powerful justification of luxury as the foundation of productivity, power, and civil virtues. The core of Hume's defense of luxury was that ages of luxury are also the most virtuous because a highly developed commercial economy provides conditions for the diffusion of knowledge, the enlivening of sociability, and the refinement of manners. "Thus industry, knowledge, and humanity, are linked together by an indissoluble chain," he argued, "and are found, from experience as well as reason, to be peculiar to the more polished, and what are commonly denominated, the more luxurious ages."[41]

By the time Hume's essay appeared in France, however, disquiet about luxury was reemerging. The publication of Rousseau's first two discourses in 1750 and 1755 are particularly significant benchmarks of a changing perspective among intellectuals. Rousseau doubted that those private moral dispositions seized upon in the first half of the eighteenth century as substitutes for civic virtue would in fact flourish under modern conditions. He argued that the physiological and psychological underpinning of modern virtue—sensibility, or sympathy—is damaged in conditions of modern sociability. Rousseau denied that politeness, worldly sociability, and enlightenment enlivened virtue, claiming that natural sympathy for others was systematically corrupted and muted in the conditions of modern society.[42]

This claim was not peculiar to Rousseau. Albrecht von Haller, professor of anatomy at the University of Göttingen, suggested that it was only among peasants who lived simple, ascetic lives that true innocence, health, and happiness were to be found. P.-J. Boudier de Villemaire insisted that luxury "has succeeded in stifling all our senses . . . . The excess to which we have brought feeling will soon reduce us to the point of feeling nothing."[43]

If the central thrust of Rousseau's critique was to deny that civilization and refinement produced moral improvement, he also attacked the idea that luxury fortifies the state in international competition. Rousseau reiterated the classical critique of luxury, charging that it led to the corruption of manners, that it sapped martial virtues, was a tool of despotism, and a cause of political degeneration. One of the central arguments of his *Discourse on the Sciences and the Arts* is that luxury undermines the security and stability of states by destroying citizenly virtue. The "essential question" in the discussion of luxury, according to Rousseau, is the following: "Is it better for an empire to be brilliant and short-lived, or virtuous and lasting?" Rousseau rejected the Colbertist view that it was commerce and money that underpinned the power and secu-

[41] Hume, *Essays,* 271. Hume changed the title of the essay to "Of Refinement in the Arts" in the British edition that appeared in 1760. The new title was retained in subsequent editions.
[42] Jean-Jacques Rousseau, *Discours sur l'origine et les fondements de l'inégalité parmi les hommes* (Amsterdam, 1755).
[43] R. F. Brissenden, *Virtue in Distress: Studies in the Novel of Sentiment from Richardson to Sade* (London, 1974), 39–40; Pierre-Joseph Boudier de Villemaire, *L'andrométrie, ou Examen philosophique de l'homme* (Paris, 1753), 89–90.

Fig. 1. *Inside the Port of Marseilles* by Joseph Vernet, 1754.
The foreground of Joseph Vernet's painting of the port of Marseilles teems with merchants from Africa, the Ottoman Empire, and Europe who converse freely and peacefully together. This image is the visual counterpart to the commercial humanism that sought to represent trade as a bond tying diverse peoples harmoniously together. Indeed, the peaceful commerce of all nations as represented here mirrors Voltaire's famous description of the London Stock Exchange in the *Letters on England* (1734) "where the representatives of all nations meet for the benefit of mankind." Réunion des Musées Nationaux/Art Resource, NY.

rity of states. He granted that luxury might make a state rich, but questioned whether wealth was really a solid basis for power. He implied that the progress of luxury had paralleled the development of absolute government in France and that luxury rendered men servile.[44]

The rejection of the Enlightenment apology for luxury that emerged in the late 1740s and 1750s articulated the perspective of provincial elites who felt themselves shut out from the cultural prestige and economic privilege of *le monde*. Country gentlemen, provincial *officiers*, and down-at-heel abbés could have felt little attraction to a philosophy that celebrated a world from which they were excluded for want of polish, connections, and money. The provincial notables of the Dijon Academy who awarded Rousseau a prize for his first discourse felt deep ambivalence about the Voltairean apology for luxury. In an essay written in 1749, the president of the prize jury, Lantin de Damerey, expressed anxiety concerning the progress of luxury, despite the strength it was

[44] Jean-Jacques Rousseau, *Discours sur les sciences et les arts,* ed. François Bouchardy (Paris, 1964), 43.

supposed to lend to a state. Another member of the jury, J.-B. Fromageot, submitted an essay to the Academy of Montauban in 1753 on the topic: "The corruption of taste always follows that of manners," remarking that "the corruption of manners is always a public calamity for a nation." "What virtues, what success," Fromageot asked, "awaits a people that tramples under foot the laws of modesty and decency, among which the love of the *patrie* [fatherland] and the public good is no more?"[45]

Rousseau's criticisms also hit their mark in Paris. After the 1750s, as we shall see, the philosophes were more reticent in their praise of luxury and more willing to recognize its potential pitfalls. The power of Rousseau's critique, Mark Hulliung suggests, was that it articulated an anxiety about the effects of civilized modernity—an autocritique of Enlightenment—that many of the philosophes, at some level, shared.[46] The change in tone is perceptible even in the approved Voltairean refutation of the *Discourse on the Sciences and the Arts,* Charles Borde's *Discours sur les avantages des sciences et des arts* (1751). What is striking about Borde's work is how much it concedes to Rousseau: Borde admits that luxury is harmful. Rather than defending it, he seeks to disentangle the sciences and the arts from their damaging association with *le luxe.*[47] The French Enlightenment apology for luxury continued into the latter half of the century (the *summa* of the tradition was Georges-Marie Butel-Dumont's *Théorie du luxe,* published in 1771).[48] But by the 1770s, many philosophes took a more circumspect view. Not until the late 1790s did apologists for luxury recover some of the momentum they enjoyed in the first half of the century. Much of the remainder of this chapter will be preoccupied with exploring the moment at which luxury reemerged as a pressing cultural problem, and in considering what the timing of that reemergence can tell us about its significance.

Pompadour, Financiers, and the Resurgence of Luxury

The final years of the 1740s constituted a crucial turning point for the luxury debate in France, with a marked resurgence of disquiet about luxury in elite culture. Renewed hostility to luxury was associated with the reemergence of a political discourse in the mold of Fénelon bemoaning the corruption of the court, attacking the influence of financiers and women in public life, and calling for the renewal of virtue. The ultimate source of this recrudescence of hos-

[45] Marcel Bouchard, *L'académie de Dijon et le premier discours de Rousseau* (Paris, 1950), 72–75.

[46] Mark Hulliung, *The Autocritique of Enlightenment: Rousseau and the Philosophes* (Cambridge, MA, 1994).

[47] Charles Borde, *Discours sur les avantages des sciences et des arts, prononcé dans l'assemblée publique de l'Académie des sciences & belles-lettres de Lyon, le 22 juin 1751* (Geneva, 1752).

[48] Georges-Marie Butel-Dumont, *Théorie du luxe, ou Traité dans lequel on entreprend d'établir que le luxe est un ressort non seulement utile, mais même indispensablement nécessaire à la prospérité des états* (n.p., 1771).

tility to luxury was the status financiers had acquired over the course of the century in the life of both court and society. But the immediate catalyst was the rise of Jeanne-Antoinette Lenormand d'Étiolles, soon to be marquise de Pompadour, to the position of royal mistress in 1745. In an age of personal government, the emergence of a royal favorite could have a profound impact on the competition for power that structured court life. Madame de Pompadour exerted enormous political influence. In 1747 she had her protégé, Puisieulx, appointed Minister for Foreign Affairs to replace the marquis d'Argenson. In 1749 she engineered the disgrace and exile of the comte de Maurepas, Minister of the Navy, hitherto a close friend and confidant of the king.[49] According to Julian Swann, "ministers discussed their affairs with her before presenting them to the council."[50] She even played a role in brokering the Treaty of Versailles which created an alliance between France and the Austrian Empire in 1756. The Austrian ambassador, Starhemberg, informed Vienna that "It is certain, that we owe all to Madame de Pompadour, and ought to expect all in the future [from her]."[51]

For Pompadour's enemies, the political tradition associated with Fénelon proved a powerful weapon in court politics. Beginning in 1747, an effort was made to revive that tradition by publishing the archbishop's *Directions pour la conscience d'un roi*. Originally titled *Examen de conscience sur les devoirs de la royauté*, the *Directions* had been composed at the turn of the century by Fénelon for the guidance of the duc de Bourgogne. Taking the form of an examination of conscience in preparation for confession, the *Directions pour la conscience d'un roi* was a harsh indictment of the reign of the Sun King. Fénelon criticized Louis's dynastic wars, the luxury of his court, and the role of favorites in royal government. So inflammatory did the French government consider its contents that Cardinal Fleury intervened in 1734 to have the first edition suppressed before the book could come to market. Thus the 1747 editions, appearing in London and The Hague, were the first to reach the public.[52] The *Correspondance littéraire* predicted that the new work would cause a sensation, and indeed, in 1747 and 1748 alone, seven editions of the *Directions pour la conscience d'un roi* appeared.[53] The work could have been custom-made to

[49] Henri Carré, *La marquise de Pompadour: La règne d'une favorite* (Paris, 1937), 105, 116.

[50] Julian Swann, *Politics and the Parlement of Paris under Louis XV, 1754–1774* (Cambridge, 1995), 54–55.

[51] Carré, *Marquise de Pompadour*, 191–92.

[52] François de Salignac de La Mothe-Fénelon, *Directions pour la conscience d'un roi, composées pour l'instruction de Louis de France, duc de Bourgogne* (The Hague, 1747). This was the title of the more successful Dutch edition, and it was under this title that the work acquired notoriety. The modern edition used here is François de Salignac de La Mothe-Fénelon, "Examen de conscience," in *Fénelon: Oeuvres*, ed. Jacques le Brun (Paris, 1997). On the publishing history of the essay, see Albert Cherel, *Fénelon au XVIIIe siècle en France (1715–1820)* (Geneva, 1970) [1917], 334–35.

[53] Friedrich Melchior Grimm et al., *Correspondance littéraire (1747–1777)*, ed. M. Tourneux (Paris, 1877–82), 1:91. On the editions of Fénelon's works, see Cherel, *Fénelon au XVIIIe siècle*, appendix.

rebuke Louis XV for succumbing to the charms of Pompadour. Fénelon admonishes kings to guard themselves against the blandishment of favorites, particularly women. Indeed, he advocates the exclusion of young women from the court, and their containment within the domestic sphere of home and family (a theme he discussed at greater length in his *De l'éducation des filles*).[54] The very form of the *Directions pour la conscience*—a guide to a royal confession—was significant in the context of the sexual politics of the court. The last time the king had confessed and received absolution was at Metz in 1744 when he believed he was dying. The bishop of Soissons, who attended him, forced Louis to abjure his mistress—at that time, the duchesse de Châteauroux—before he would grant him the sacraments. Once he recovered, the king went back to his dissolute ways but, for the remainder of his reign, royal mistresses dreaded the prospect of the king's confession because it must be a preliminary to their own disgrace.

The publication of Fénelon's *Directions* in 1747 marks the revival of a political vision underlining the centrality of virtue to a healthy polity. The *Directions* allowed critics of the king's behavior to use royal debauchery as a symbol of deeper problems of national degeneration. Fénelon rejected the view that private royal vices have no public significance. "Ordinarily it is said to Kings that they have less to fear from their vices as individuals than from the faults to which they are prone in royal functions," Fénelon observes, but "for myself, I boldly affirm the contrary, and I hold that all their faults in the most private areas of life are of infinite consequence for royalty."[55] The private morality of kings was critical, according to Fénelon, because the king established the moral tone for the rest of society—royal subjects calibrated their own morals to those of the monarch. Rejecting the fashionable Machiavellism of the seventeenth century, the archbishop argued that morality was crucial to the health of a polity.[56] As he emphasized at great length in *Telemachus*, it was the chief business of government to cultivate the capacity of its subjects for virtue.[57]

It is unlikely that the renewal of a Fénelonian politics was serendipitous at a moment when its message was so germane to current political circumstances. The group that stood to benefit most from its publication was the *parti dévot*, a court faction composed of the dauphin, his sisters, the queen, the duc de La Vauguyon (governor of the royal children), and a number of other sympathetic courtiers and ministers.[58] The *parti dévot* continued a political tradition of what

---

[54] Fénelon, "Examen de conscience," Paragraph XI. On Fénelon as a proponent for domesticity, see Lougee, *Le Paradis des Femmes*, 173–87.

[55] Fénelon, "Examen de conscience," Paragraph X.

[56] Rothkrug, *Opposition to Louis XIV*, 249–86.

[57] Fénelon, *Aventures de Télémaque*, 226, 253, 398.

[58] Swann, *Politics and the Parlement of Paris*, 214–15. It is difficult, however, to link the appearance of the *Directions* directly to anti-Pompadour forces. The Dutch edition emanated from the publishing house of Prosper Marchand, a Huguenot with republican leanings and links to the radical enlightenment. See Christiane Berkvens-Stevelinck, *Prosper Marchand, la vie et l'œuvre (1678–1756)* (Leiden, 1987).

Dale Van Kley calls "devout humanism," which stretched back through Fénelon into the seventeenth century.[59] Leading *dévots* had been involved in the effort to force the king to renounce his mistress when he lay ill at Metz in the summer of 1744, and they suffered for it when he regained his health. The chief object of their hatred by 1747 was Madame de Pompadour.[60] The *dévots* were behind attacks on Louis XV and his mistress that were prompted by the Treaty of Aix-la-Chapelle in 1748. The treaty was widely viewed as unfavorable, and there was particular anger at the clause that required the French king to expel the son of the Stuart Pretender, an action regarded as humiliating for France. According to Thomas Kaiser, the expulsion of Prince Charles Edward drove the *parti dévot*, who were ardent Jacobite sympathizers, to launch a propaganda offensive against the king.[61] To whatever extent the *dévots* were behind it, by 1749, Arlette Farge argues, a political climate had emerged whose "leitmotif was essentially ethical: public life ought to be moral. Since the king gave the lead, the king ought to offer worthy images of himself and his entourage." Disdain for a "tyrannical and immoral king" was the central theme of an explosion of *mauvais discours*—popular mutterings—directed against the Crown.[62]

The renewal of the political tradition with which Fénelon had been associated, and the political circumstances under which that renewal occurred, both drove a resurgence of criticisms against luxury. The corruption of virtue and the problem of luxury were fused in the person of Madame de Pompadour. The career of the marquise exemplified the blurring of social boundaries and the usurpation of noble prerogatives by those of low birth. The king's previous mistresses had an aristocratic lineage as old as the monarchy itself.[63] Pompadour had a title only by virtue of the marquisate bestowed upon her by the king. Playing on her family name—Poisson, or "fish"—one versifier implied that she had literally come up from the marketplace to usurp a position of power and eminence: "If the court is degraded/Why is one surprised?/Is it not from the market/That fish comes?"[64] Popular grumbling recorded by the police accused Pompadour of trafficking in honors and influence.[65] Her extravagance was no-

[59] Dale Van Kley, *The Religious Origins of the French Revolution: From Calvin to the Civil Constitution, 1560–1791* (New Haven, 1996), 39–43, 47–49, 51–58, 140.

[60] Thomas E. Kaiser, "Madame de Pompadour and the Theaters of Power," *French Historical Studies* 19, no. 4 (1996): 1025–44.

[61] Thomas E. Kaiser, "The Drama of Charles Edward Stuart: Jacobite Propaganda and French Political Protest, 1745–1750," *Eighteenth-Century Studies* 30, no. 4 (1997): 365–81. The Stuart prince's mother was a friend of the queen, a fellow Polish aristocrat. His uncle by marriage was the duc de Bouillon, a *dévot* leader who had been disgraced following his role in the Metz affair. The *dévot* Bishop of Soissons, who had played the pivotal role at Metz, was another leading Jacobite—a grandson of James II by an illegitimate line.

[62] Arlette Farge, *Subversive Words: Public Opinion in Eighteenth-Century France* (University Park, PA, 1995), 153–61.

[63] Yves Durand, *Les fermiers généraux au XVIIIe siècle* (Paris, 1971), 67.

[64] Kaiser, "Madame de Pompadour," 1030.

[65] Durand, *Fermiers généraux*, 74n.

a generation.[77] Sons and brothers of financiers routinely served as intendants in the second half of the eighteenth century.[78] Many of the officials who served as controllers general in the 1750s were from the financial milieu. François-Marie Peyrenc de Moras, who inherited the *contrôle général* in 1756 from his father-in-law, Jean Moreau de Séchelles, was the son of one of the most successful of the Mississippi speculators. Peyrenc de Moras's successor, Jean-Nicolas de Boullongne was the son of a tax farmer, and his successor, Étienne de Silhouette, was the son of a tax receiver and the brother-in-law of a tax farmer.[79]

The court nobility and great financiers increasingly shared the same lifestyle of spectacular consumption. Court nobles built magnificent Paris town houses, they gambled and lost immense sums, and spent extravagantly on clothing. For them, luxury consumption was not discretionary; they consumed to preserve their power, rank, and influence.[80] Among the bases of both political power and social order in the old regime was the use of commodities to create a dazzling display of wealth and social distinction—a theater of power.[81] The men and women who occupied the heights of the French social hierarchy dressed in clothing distinguished by its sumptuousness and visibility. Court noble families normally spent in excess of 10,000 livres a year on clothing—more than the average income of a well-off provincial noble or barrister.[82] They spent lavishly on horses and carriages, averaging in many cases over 30,000 livres a year.[83]

The richest of the financiers enjoyed a style of living akin to the greatest aristocrats. Antoine Crozat had the Hôtel d'Évreux (now the Élysée palace) built for his daughter and son-in-law, the duc d'Évreux. It was bought by Madame de Pompadour in 1752 for half a million livres and sold after her death for twice

---

[77] François Bluche, *Les magistrats du Parlement de Paris au XVIIIe siècle (1715–1771)* (Paris, 1960).

[78] Vivian R. Gruder, *The Royal Provincial Intendants: A Governing Elite in Eighteenth-Century France* (Ithaca, 1968), 170–71; Matthews, *Royal General Farms*, 241n.

[79] Chaussinand-Nogaret, *Gens de finance*, 44–45, 59.

[80] Natacha Coquery, *L'hôtel aristocratique: Le marché du luxe à Paris au XVIIIe siècle* (Paris, 1998), 119–20; Mathieu Marraud, *La noblesse de Paris au XVIIIe siècle* (Paris, 2000), 305.

[81] Peter Burke, *The Fabrication of Louis XIV* (New Haven, 1992), 5. See also Jean-Marie Apostolidès, *Le roi-machine: Spectacle et politique au temps de Louis XIV* (Paris, 1981); José Antonio Maravall, *Culture of the Baroque: Analysis of a Historical Structure* (Minneapolis, 1986).

[82] Coquery, *L'hôtel aristocratique*, 129–30.

[83] Ibid., 135–36. Jennifer Jones notes that the eighteenth century marked a shift in the centre of gravity of fashion culture away from the royal court toward the city, inaugurating a more inclusive fashion regime in which ordinary people could play a more significant role. While no doubt this is true, the needs of the court nobility exerted a real influence on the world of fashion and even, indirectly, on the popular consumer revolution. The competitive drive for distinction among courtiers, Natacha Coquery has emphasized, stimulated the fashion trades to produce unending novelties, and court nobles helped fuel popular consumption by selling used luxury clothing back to merchants in partial payment for new fashion wares. Jennifer M. Jones, *Sexing La Mode: Gender, Fashion, and Commercial Culture in Old Regime France* (Oxford, 2004), 73–74; Natacha Coquery, "The Language of Success: Marketing and Distributing Semi-Luxury Goods in Eighteenth-Century Paris," *Journal of Design History* 17, no. 1 (2004): 71–89.

that sum to Nicolas Beaujon, banker to the court. A Scottish nobleman, passing through Paris in 1763 observed: "The houses of the financiers are the best in Paris. Their tables are sumptuously appointed. One meets in their homes the whole French aristocracy. Most of these *gentlemen* have 100,000 pounds of revenue, while a noble who has 4,000 passes for wealthy." Radix de Sainte-Foy, a *trésorier général de la Marine* from 1764 to 1771, owned houses in Paris and Neuilly that the salon gossip Bachaumont appraised at two million livres; he was said to keep forty horses for his equipages. Claude Baudard de Sainte-James owned an hôtel on the Place Vendôme, several other Paris town houses, and a magnificent country house at Neuilly known as the "folie Sainte-James," which he had constructed to rival the lavish Château Bagatelle built by his neighbor, the brother of the king.[84]

Such conspicuous displays of wealth by the very rich had long been regarded as scandalous, and they helped catalyze a resurgence in criticisms of luxury around mid-century. A critique of the baneful effects of luxury which doubled as an attack on the political influence of financiers, Étienne de La Font de Saint-Yenne's *Réflexions sur quelques causes de l'état présent de la peinture en France* excited considerable public interest when it was published in 1747. La Font suggested that the arts had degenerated comprehensively in France since the seventeenth century. He particularly attributed this decline to the use of mirrors and varnished paneling in interior decoration, claiming that these fashions had banished paintings from positions of prominence in modern apartments. This new predilection for expensive and gaudy adornments La Font attributed to the "excess and the eccentricity of our luxury."[85] The only paintings spared in the general rout, he claimed, were portraits, but the trend toward portraiture was itself a cause of debasement because the subjects of these works were individuals of no exemplary merit. The *Réflexions* was an attack on the direction of French painting since the Regency, a period when art increasingly served private pleasures rather than public grandeur. Against the background of Enlightenment claims that the arts and sciences progress in proportion as luxury advances, La Font's insistence on decline assumed pointed critical significance.

Thomas Crow argues that the *Réflexions* expressed La Font's antagonism toward the administration of the arts that Madame de Pompadour helped to install in 1746. The royal mistress had her father-in-law and former protector, Lenormand de Tournehem, appointed *Directeur général des bâtiments du roi*, a position that gave him control over royal art patronage. On Tournehem's death the position was to pass to Pompadour's brother, the marquis de Marigny.[86] Both Marigny and Lenormand de Tournehem were major patrons of

[84] Durand, *Fermiers généraux*, 68; Chaussinand-Nogaret, *Gens de finance*, 123; Legohérel, *Trésorier généraux*, 331–32.

[85] Étienne de La Font de Saint-Yenne, *Réflexions sur quelques causes de l'état présent de la peinture en France* (The Hague, 1747), 18.

[86] Thomas E. Crow, *Painters and Public Life in Eighteenth-Century Paris* (New Haven, 1985), 112.

such Rococo masters as François Boucher, Carle Van Loo, and Charles Natoire, as was the marquise herself. (Marigny owned at least nineteen paintings by Boucher.)[87] This was the kind of artistic work that La Font deplored; he expressly condemned some of the works Boucher and Van Loo had executed for Pompadour.[88] Painting, as La Font made clear both in his *Réflexions* and in his later *Sentimens sur quelques ouvrages de peinture, sculpture et gravure* (1754), ought to be "a school of manners."[89] He advocated the revival of history painting, which could communicate the great actions and virtues of celebrated men in a more vibrant fashion than any other medium. In the *Sentimens,* he recommended as subjects for painters exemplars of severe republican virtue, among them the Roman magistrate, Brutus, who condemned his sons to death for conspiring against the republic, and the general Fabricius, celebrated for his asceticism.[90] La Font was no isolated crank. His intervention in 1747 sparked a chorus of complaints that the fine arts had degenerated and that a general reform of the arts was needed to make them, once again, an instrument for improving manners and inspiring men with patriotic zeal.[91] Indeed, art historians regard his essay as a foundational work in a tradition of criticism that stimulated the development of neoclassicism. With its celebration of Roman virtue, and a stylistic austerity that rejected the extravagance and play of the Rococo, neoclassicism was the visual counterpart to the eighteenth-century anti-luxury campaign.

If La Font's critique constituted an attack on Pompadour and her financier friends, it also articulated a disquiet about the effects of commercialization on French culture. La Font's obsession with mirrors has to be read both figuratively and literally. As Katie Scott suggests, the prevalence of mirrors was a metaphor for the ills of a social world increasingly ravaged by the passions and illusions unleashed by commerce. "The mirror," she argues, "functioned in La Font's text as immediate and material evidence of industrial growth and the corruption of taste that accompanies it, and as a metaphor for the specular values (of desire, gain, duplicity, emptiness, of something in nothing) that were essential to the projection of a commercial society, and yet the cause of its numerous maledictions."[92] As she also notes, mirrors were increasingly being used as interior decoration in the homes of the very rich—testament to the success of one of the luxury industries established by Colbert. Most of the mirrors sold in France emanated from the Royal Plate Glass Company of Saint-Gobain

[87] James A. Leith, *The Idea of Art as Propaganda in France 1750–1799: A Study in the History of Ideas* (Toronto, 1965), 74.

[88] Katie Scott, *The Rococo Interior: Decoration and Social Spaces in Early Eighteenth-Century Paris* (New Haven, 1995), 255.

[89] Étienne de La Font de Saint-Yenne, *Sentimens sur quelques ouvrages de peinture, sculpture et gravure, écrits à un particulier en province* (n.p., 1754), 76.

[90] La Font de Saint-Yenne, *Sentimens,* 92.

[91] Leith, *Idea of Art as Propaganda,* 8–9.

[92] Scott, *Rococo Interior,* 254.

founded in 1665 to supplant imports of plate glass and mirrors from Venice. By the late eighteenth century, the Saint-Gobain works had grown to be one of the largest manufacturing operations in Europe. It employed 4,000 people in 1790 and held assets of 23 million livres. As major shareholders in the plate glass works, financiers were principal beneficiaries of the increasing use of mirrors. In the 1750s, the company was making a net profit of over one million livres a year, and occasional extraordinary dividends paid to shareholders ran to hundreds of thousands of livres. Through a perverse feedback mechanism, Colbertist court capitalism stimulated luxury consumption which, in turn, lined the pockets of that characteristically luxurious class, the financiers.[93]

Criticisms of the effects of commercialization on French society and culture were closely associated with attacks on the influence of financiers because the latter were among the most important direct beneficiaries of an expanding commerce. They were key players in the long commercial expansion that marked much of the eighteenth century. An illustrative example is Gabriel Prévost, a Treasurer General of the royal agency superintending bridges and highways, who, according to John Bosher, had a portfolio typical of many financiers. In the 1770s, Prévost had investments in a Spanish gunpowder company and in a Lisbon-based shipping concern, 60,000 livres in a Paris insurance company, 50,000 in mining concerns, 50,000 in a military hospital contractor, 30,000 livres in a cloth factory, 30,000 in forges, 12,000 in a spinning shop, and 4,000 in the manufacture of acid.[94] Financiers had been major investors in trade and manufacturing since the seventeenth century, according to Daniel Dessert; because of their ability to mobilize large sums of capital, they became "the almost mandatory partners" of merchant manufacturers.[95] In industries that supplied the state, such as armaments, gunpowder manufacture and naval supply, they played a more direct role. Typical in this respect was Babaud de la Chaussade, who in the late 1740s established an enterprise to supply anchors and chains to the navy and the Indies Company. Through the good offices of his father, a former financier to Leopold of Lorraine, and a senior clerk in the *contrôle général,* Babaud secured a government subvention, a loan from the Indies Company, additional investment capital from a syndicate of tax farmers, and an exclusive privilege to furnish anchors and chains to the navy for a period of seven years. Here we see all the crucial ingredients of court capitalism: a large-scale manufacturing operation, underwritten by financier capital, sufficient political influence to secure government contracts, and a monopoly guaranteed by privilege.[96]

From the seventeenth century onward, financiers invested in foreign trade,

[93] Claude Pris, *Une grande entreprise française sous l'ancien régime: La manufacture royale des glaces de Saint-Gobain (1665–1830)* (New York, 1981), 1:143–44; Warren C. Scoville, *Capitalism and French Glassmaking, 1640–1789* (Berkeley, 1950), 27, 144–45.

[94] Bosher, *French Finances,* 102.

[95] Dessert, *Argent, pouvoir et société,* 384–86.

[96] Chaussinand-Nogaret, *Gens de finance,* 70.

Fig. 2. *Portrait of Samuel Bernard* by Hyacinthe Rigaud, 1726.

Framed by an imposing architecture, enfolded by sumptuous drapery, with the cordon of the Order of Saint-Michel draped over his right shoulder, Samuel Bernard (1651–1739) emblematizes the wealth and status achieved by the greatest of the financiers. The globe at Bernard's left hand and the fleet at anchor to his right allude to one of the sources of his fabulous wealth, international trade. The greatest of Louis XIV's financiers, Bernard is reputed to have left a fortune of 33 million livres at his death. He acquired nobility and established his children in brilliant social positions. Bernard paid 7,200 livres for his portrait, a sum equivalent to a year's income for a prosperous provincial noble. Réunion des Musées Nationaux/Art Resource, NY.

and especially in the privileged companies founded in the age of Colbert.[97] Taking advantage of the peace that followed the Treaty of Aix-la-Chapelle in 1748, financiers established two major slaving ventures, the Angola Company with a capital of 2 million livres, and the Guinea Company with a capital of 2.4 million.[98] Not all major financiers invested in trade. Most of the Farmers General avoided commerce; only 14 out of the 224 men who held the position in the eighteenth century had commercial investments, and these were concentrated in the Indies Company and the slave trade.[99] But many of the greatest eighteenth-century financiers were also merchant princes. Nicolas Beaujon, receiver general and banker to Madame de Pompadour, was also a shipping magnate and major grain trader. Philippe Tavernier de Boullongne, a tax farmer whose son served as Controller General from August 1757 to March 1759, participated in colonial commerce through investments in Bordeaux and Saint-Malo merchant houses. Jean-Joseph de Laborde, a banker to the court through much of the 1760s, had major investments in the Spanish trade through Bayonne. Magon de la Balue, briefly a court banker in the late 1760s, emanated from a Saint-Malo shipping dynasty and was a director of the Indies Company. The Treasurer General of the Navy and Colonies, Claude Baudard de Sainte-James, had major investments in a canvas sail manufacture, an arms factory, the Paris Water Company, mines, metallurgy, and shipping.[100]

Commercial society, in the French context, was a social world where plutocratic financiers-cum-merchants appeared increasingly ascendant. Against such a background, the Enlightenment celebration of commercial society could sound like an endorsement of a corrupt order characterized by the naked power of money, a danger all the more acute given the close links between financiers and many of the philosophic party. Robert Darnton has suggested that by the 1770s the High Enlightenment had formed a cozy relationship with the powerful.[101] But elements of this intimacy developed much earlier. Voltaire was part of the circle of Madame de Pompadour, frequenting her house before she became involved with the king. He was patronized by the Pâris brothers, and invested in their business as a sleeping partner.[102] Jean-François Melon had been

---

[97] Dessert, *Argent, pouvoir et société,* 390; Catherine Manning, *Fortunes à Faire: The French in Asian Trade, 1718–48* (Aldershot, 1996), 21.

[98] Lüthy, *La banque protestante,* 2:42; Chaussinand-Nogaret, *Gens de finance,* 68, 73–75; Richard, *Noblesse d'affaires,* 238.

[99] Marraud, *Noblesse de Paris,* 324.

[100] Chaussinand-Nogaret, *Gens de finance,* 53, 71–72; Henri Sée, "The Ship-Owners of Saint Malo in the Eighteenth Century," *Bulletin of the Business Historical Society* 2, no. 4 (1928): 3–9; Bosher, *French Finances,* 331; Denise Ozanam, *Claude Baudard de Sainte-James: Trésorier général de la marine et brasseur d'affaires (1738–1787)* (Geneva, 1969).

[101] Robert Darnton, *The Literary Underground of the Old Regime* (Cambridge, MA, 1982), 1–40.

[102] Carré, *Marquise de Pompadour,* 13; Daniel Roche describes Voltaire as the "protégé" of the Pâris. *France in the Enlightenment,* trans. Arthur Goldhammer (Cambridge, MA, 2000), 141. See also H. N. Brailsford, *Voltaire* (London, 1963), 35.

John Law's secretary, and had tried to become a director of the Indies Company. Helvétius was a retired tax farmer. Madame de Houdetot, an Enlightenment *salonnière*, was the daughter of the tax farmer La Live de Bellegarde.[103] Madame Geoffrin, whose salon was a pillar of the French Enlightenment, was the widow of a director of the Saint-Gobain manufactory.[104] At the heart of intellectual and cultural life, and in the corridors of power at Versailles, money exerted an influence that, to contemporaries, seemed greater, more visible, and more blatant, than ever before. The renewal of the French anti-luxury tradition that began at mid-century was a reaction to this perceived state of affairs. I have already suggested that this tradition appealed to the kinds of men and women who were never likely to receive an invitation to the salon of a Madame Geoffrin, or a Madame de Houdetôt, much less to the court at Versailles. It is to these ordinary, provincial elites we now turn.

Nobles, Notables, and the Critique of Luxury

At mid-century, hostility to luxury resonated with the ethos and interests of important sections of the middling elite, especially elements of the provincial nobility, and some of the *rentiers*, professionals, and office-holders who enjoyed a position of respectability in provincial cities.[105] Such middling elites—nobles and notables—made up the numerical preponderance of the general reading public, the men and women with the means, the education, and the orientation to public affairs to buy and read newspapers, periodicals, and pamphlets. The attacks on luxury launched at mid-century resonated with their values and social practices. Middling elites were doing quite well economically in the conditions of commercial expansion that marked the middle decades of the eighteenth century. As landowners, they profited from rising prices for cereals, wine, and wood, and the steady augmentation of their rents.[106] But if their absolute economic position was improving, their wealth relative to competing social groups was not. The consequence was a threat to the social status of many middling elites. Those who sought social promotion faced increasingly stiff com-

---

[103] Chaussinand-Nogaret, *Gens de finance*, 124.

[104] Dena Goodman, *The Republic of Letters: A Cultural History of the French Enlightenment* (Ithaca, 1994), 307.

[105] I am reluctant to use the label "bourgeois," in any blanket sense, to describe these latter groups. In the register of Marxist historiography, this label refers expressly to merchants and manufacturers—groups with a different perspective to that of the nonnoble elites I focus on here. Moreover, in many provincial cities, the category *bourgeois* was reserved for a particular class of elite nonnobles, families living off revenues from real estate and *rentes*, and no longer engaging in any profession or trade. See Michel Vovelle and Daniel Roche, "Bourgeois, *Rentiers*, and Property Owners: Elements for Defining a Social Category at the End of the Eighteenth Century," in *New Perspectives on the French Revolution: Readings in Historical Sociology*, ed. Jeffry Kaplow (New York, 1965).

[106] Braudel and Labrousse, *Histoire économique et sociale*, 2:386–87, 396, 399, 455–56.

petition from the world of trade and finance, while those who merely wished to preserve their status could feel their rank subject to subtle but inexorable erosion in a world where money increasingly mattered.

The provincial nobility lived according to an ethic of economic discipline and antipathy to frivolous expenditure, and comparable values prevailed among nonnoble elites. Most nobles resident in the provinces—about 90 percent of the order—engaged in consumption necessary to mark their status but eschewed the prodigal expenditure on clothing and equipages in which the court nobility and financiers indulged. "Family and friends usually intervened as a corrective to the dangerous spending habits of a wayward squire," Robert Forster notes; "sobriety, not profligacy, was the dominant note in the provincial noble family."[107] Provincial nobles could hardly have done otherwise. Among them only families in very happy circumstances had revenues of more than 10,000 livres a year, and 5,000 marked a solid prosperity.[108] Such incomes placed nobles in a different universe to the court nobility, and their plutocratic cousins, the financiers, who often enjoyed revenues twenty times greater. Not dissimilar to middling nobles in their attitudes to luxury were professionals, especially lawyers. The culture of the bar had traditionally frowned upon courtly luxury.[109] Provincial lawyers did not have the means to indulge in ostentatious spending, but most did not have the aspiration to do so either. The family of Daniel Lamothe, a Bordeaux barrister who died in 1763, bought fine clothes as befitted their station, but never spent to excess; they kept account of every expense to the last penny.[110] The barristers of eighteenth-century Toulouse were no different, manifesting "little desire to compete for prestige among their peers through high levels of consumption."[111]

There is some debate about whether elite nonnobles actively and avidly pursued social mobility, or whether they were primarily concerned to conserve a social status already acquired. "For the Lamothe family," according to Christine Adams, "conservation of resources, status, and family were primary goals, rather than risky and psychologically threatening efforts towards social mobility."[112] Those engaged in social ascent sometimes felt deeply ambivalent about it. Paul-François Depont, an ennobled merchant and *officier* from La Rochelle, was "racked by status anxieties, incapable of reconciling provincial with Pari-

[107] Robert Forster, "The Provincial Noble: A Reappraisal," *American Historical Review* 68, no. 3 (1963): 689.

[108] Forster, "Provincial Noble"; Chaussinand-Nogaret, *French Nobility*, 52–61; Robert Forster, *The Nobility of Toulouse in the Eighteenth Century* (New York, 1971), 175; Ruggiu, *Les élites et les villes moyennes*, 179-80.

[109] David Bell, "The 'Public Sphere,' the State, and the World of Law in Eighteenth-Century France," *French Historical Studies* 17, no. 4 (1992): 912–34.

[110] Christine Adams, "Defining État in Eighteenth-Century France: The Lamothe Family of Bordeaux," *Journal of Family History* 17, no. 1 (1992): 25–45.

[111] Lenard R. Berlanstein, *The Barristers of Toulouse in the Eighteenth Century (1740–1793)* (Baltimore, 1975), 57.

[112] Adams, "Defining État," 25.

sian standards of behavior, economy with *éclat,* and Christian principles with social ambition." Paul-François was particularly disturbed at his son's move to Paris to pursue a career in the royal administration because, for the elder Depont, "sin, glitter, flux, and insecurity were inextricably linked in that Babylon on the Seine." He advised his son to get in touch with the *dévot* duc de La Vauguyon, a correspondent of Paul-François, and a man who shared his principles.[113] Other nonnobles undoubtedly welcomed the opportunity to compete with the nobility that money afforded to commoners. "Since finance and commerce have procured rapid fortunes for those who have practiced these professions," observed a citizen of Montpellier in the late 1760s, "the second order [nonnoble elites] has acquired by the expenses of its luxury a consideration which the first [nobles] uselessly envies them. It was by a sort of necessity that they should be confounded." Elite commoners such as barristers, doctors, notaries, merchants, and even financiers deserved to enjoy such status, because "this class is always the most useful, the most considerable, and the richest, in every kind of country."[114]

The same writer, however, could also display a marked hostility to luxury. He deplored continuous changes of fashion, and questioned the value of manufactures because they produced superfluities, which he regarded as unhealthy, and which introduced luxury. He accused clerics who employed substitutes to perform their jobs of "displaying a luxury which revolts poverty," and he complained about the promotion of inexperienced, but presumably well-connected, young men above individuals of superior merit in the church and the magistracy. His sympathetic attitude toward social mobility categorically did not extend to those below him on the social scale. He fiercely criticized the display by artisans and servants of the markers of polite status. If servants must be allowed to appear in public at all, he argued, "one should be able to pick them out with a badge indicating their station and making it impossible to confuse them with everyone else."[115] Concerned as they were with the conservation of status, many nonnoble elites felt threatened by the usurping consumption of the lower orders. The Paris bookseller Antoine-Prosper Lottin complained that "everyone wants to lose the marks of their estate and tries to disguise themselves with the mask of a higher station."[116] Joseph Charon grumbled that luxury had established "a confusion of ranks and estates" in all the great cities. He protested that professions were accorded respect not according to how useful they were but in proportion to their monetary rewards.[117]

There has long been debate among historians about whether social mobility

[113] Robert Forster, *Merchants, Landlords, Magistrates: The Depont Family in Eighteenth-Century France* (Baltimore, 1980), 26, 48.

[114] Berthelé, ed., *Montpellier en 1768,* 67–68.

[115] Ibid., 28, 34, 68–69, 98–99.

[116] Quoted in Jones, *Sexing La Mode,* 148.

[117] Joseph Charon, *Lettre ou mémoire historique sur les troubles populaires de Paris en août & septembre 1788* (London, 1788), 41–42.

slowed for the French bourgeoisie in the second half of the eighteenth century. For some nonnobles, clearly, it was easier than ever to pass into the nobility in the eighteenth century. William Doyle argues that in the eighteenth century the French nobility was the most open in Europe with at least 10,000 ennoblements (that is, probably 50,000 new nobles) over the course of the century.[118] From the 1730s, the office of *secrétaire du roi* (king's secretary), which ennobled after just twenty years service, created nobles at a rate of nearly one family a week.[119] By the 1770s, over a third of all ennoblements annually were accounted for by this most rapid and expensive route into the nobility.[120] But the existence of unprecedented opportunities for nobility did not mean that everyone could take advantage of them. Rapid ennoblement was increasingly difficult for anyone outside finance or large-scale commerce. By 1789 a position of *secrétaire du roi* cost an average of 120,000 livres in Paris and 80,000 in the provinces: as much as twenty times the income of a reasonably prosperous provincial notable. Successful manufacturers, merchants, and financiers, who sometimes enjoyed much larger incomes, and had greater access to credit, were better placed to take advantage of opportunities for mobility.[121] In the provincial city of Abbeville in 1784, among sixteen families that had recently entered the nobility, eight had a revenue above 10,000 livres, and three of the five richest men in the town were recent *anoblis* (ennobled persons).[122] As the price of most ennobling offices spiraled, those middling elites outside the world of business faced extraordinarily stiff competition, and many presumably had either to abandon their quest for nobility or content themselves with offices that required several generations to ennoble.[123]

Even those families concerned only to preserve their social status found it increasingly difficult to do so in a social world where people at a lower rung in the social hierarchy could so easily use money to surpass their former superiors. This situation was all the more galling because nobility was supposed to represent the antithesis of the grasping, self-interested spirit of trade and fi-

---

[118] Doyle, *Venality,* 319. When a venal officeholder acquired nobility, it brought all his direct descendants into the Second Estate. For an older man, this might include a clan of children, grandchildren, and even great grandchildren.

[119] David Bien, "Manufacturing Nobles: The Chancelleries in France to 1789," *Journal of Modern History* 61, no. 3 (1989): 445–86.

[120] Michael P. Fitzsimmons, "New Light on the Aristocratic Reaction in France," *French History* 10, no. 4 (1996): 418-31.

[121] Georges Lefebvre mentions a manufacturer of printed calicoes in Orléans whose income was estimated at 300,000 livres in 1779. "Urban Society in the Orléanais in the Late Eighteenth Century," *Past and Present* 19 (1961): 50. The Treasurer General of the Navy, Baudard de Sainte-James, made nearly half a million livres per year from his office in peacetime, and three times that in wartime. The annual income of the Farmers General certainly ran into the hundreds of thousands of livres. See Ozanam, *Claude Baudard de Sainte-James,* 12; Matthews, *Royal General Farms,* 263–68.

[122] Ruggiu, *Les élites et les villes moyennes,* 183.

[123] Colin Lucas, "Nobles, Bourgeois and the Origins of the French Revolution," *Past and Present* 60 (1973): 84–126.

nance. If public service in a small town magistracy formed an excellent train-
ing for eventual inclusion in the nobility, self-enrichment in the tax farms or
colonial commerce did not. A veritable hostility to business and to those enriched by it marked many nonnoble elites from professional or *rentier* back-
grounds. The future Madame Roland said of business that "[I] could never lend
myself to anything of this kind, nor could I respect anyone who is thus occupied from morning till night."[124]

This use of wealth by financiers and entrepreneurs to acquire prestige and
access to honors also represented a threat to the social status and identity of
middling nobles. It seemed to many that such "luxury" was the principal obstacle preventing them from serving the king in the army. The rich sons of the
ennobled could more readily shoulder the heavy financial burden of an officer's
commission, and enjoyed preferential access to promotion in the service.[125] The
royal administration set out systematically to lower the financial obstacles to
service in the military for middling nobles during the second half of the century,
but competition with wealthy *anoblis* remained a source of resentment for military nobles until the end of the old regime.[126]

If middling elites, noble and nonnoble, shared a sense that the social world
was being corrupted by money, their different social locations and cultural commitments nevertheless inclined them to divergent perspectives both on the precise nature of the problem and on its solution. Ultimately, for nobles, luxury
was a threat to the corporate identity and superior status of the Second Estate.
For many, the answer was to limit further encroachments by commoners, and
to institute measures to give preferential access to careers to members of old noble families. In the general *cahiers* of 1789—lists of grievances composed by all
three estates—50 percent of the noble *cahiers* called for a total end to ennoblement through venal office; only half as many of the Third Estate *cahiers* did
so.[127] Though they tended to agree that money alone should not ennoble, any
blanket exclusion of commoners from office or honors was, obviously, both offensive and threatening to the nonnoble part of the elite. The kind of friction
such different perspectives could cause between nobles and nonnobles is evident in the storm caused by the famous Ségur Ordinance of 1781, which closed
the officer corps to most men who lacked four generations of nobility in their
families. Aimed not against commoners so much as against wealthy *anoblis*, the
measure nevertheless enraged many nonnoble elites.

In claiming that the ethos and interests of middling elites inclined them to-

---

[124] Quoted in Elinor Barber, *The Bourgeoisie in Eighteenth-Century France* (Princeton, 1955),
63. Such attitudes were still widespread in the 1790s. See, Marcel Reinhard, "Sur l'histoire de la
Révolution française: Travaux récents et perspectives," *Annales* 14 (1959): 560.

[125] David Bien, "The Army in the French Enlightenment: Reform, Reaction and Revolution,"
Past and Present 85 (1979): 68–98.

[126] Rafe Blaufarb, *The French Army, 1750–1820: Careers, Talent, Merit* (New York, 2002), 16–
32.

[127] Doyle, *Venality*, 269.

ward hostility to luxury, I do not mean to imply that the critique simply articulated or expressed interests that had an entirely separate, pre-existing reality.
Rather, the language of antipathy to luxury, operating within the social context
just described, played some role in creating those interests and organizing them
in a coherent fashion. It is only through systems of meaning that one can experience a grievance, a sense that one is not receiving one's due. The language
that "expresses" an interest thus plays some role in bringing that interest into
being. If economic interests, in some unmediated sense, are alone considered,
the middling provincial elite might be regarded as a single, unified class. But the
effect of the language they used to articulate those interests was precisely to mil-
itate against class consciousness. Much as they disliked the court nobility (and
there is plenty of evidence of real aversion), and much as they had in common
with other provincial landowners, nobles could not form a stable coalition with
elite nonnobles. For them, the language of luxury was a language of corporate
distinctiveness. The anti-luxury idiom could drive a wedge between nonnobles
and nobles also because of its modular quality; it could be used by any group
against any other stratum enjoying a greater share of wealth and its advantages.
Both nobles and notables occasionally gave vent to the view that the court nobility had become part of a selfish and corrupt plutocracy. But nonnobles could
turn the same weapon against middling nobles. Despite all his pretensions—his
country residence, his adoption of the noble-sounding *particule*—the provincial notable was often much less wealthy than the local marquis or baron with
his 10,000 a year.[128] The language of luxury was an inherently fissiparous idiom; it was far easier to use as a rhetorical flail than as a basis for solidarity.

One other caution is required before leaving behind an analysis of the social
foundations of the luxury critique. If this language derived much of its force
from the way it resonated with the concerns of middling elites, its elaborators
were by no means necessarily drawn from such groups; some indeed were part
of strata that were often the butt of the luxury critique. A case in point is La
Font de Saint-Yenne who was the scion of an ennobled house of Lyon silk merchants. He held the court office of gentleman of the queen from 1729 to 1737,
having acquired it with money made in the luxury trades.[129] There is nothing
especially surprising in this, any more than it should surprise us to find recent
anoblis drafting a *cahier* in 1789 "of such exclusiveness as to suggest that every
one of its signatories descended from a crusader."[130] For some commentators,
criticism of luxury may have been a way to distance themselves from a past they
would as soon forget. For others it may have been a means to close a door
through which they had already passed. Once the critique had acquired some

---

[128] The lifestyle of the typical Chartres notable, for example, "was usually much less resplendent;
his house was generally quite small and shabby in comparison with the mansions of the Chartres
nobility, and he had far fewer servants." Vovelle and Roche, "Bourgeois, *Rentiers,* and Property
Owners," 37.

[129] Étienne Jollet, ed., *La Font de Saint-Yenne: Oeuvre critique* (Paris, 2001), 9.

[130] Lefebvre, "Urban Society in the Orléanais," 47.

momentum, moreover, it could function as a weapon in the factional struggles that were the stuff of French politics in the old regime. Thus, in the 1770s and 1780s, financiers and speculators deployed criticisms of luxury to focus public anger on competing cartels. Nor were middling elites the sole consumers of writings attacking luxury; these might appeal to members of any social group alarmed by the perception that France was weakening, or degenerating, vis-à-vis its European rivals—a view increasingly widespread in the 1750s. The same perception of decline, however, also gave rise to a quite different intellectual impulse in the 1750s. Those who believed that the chief means to envigorate the kingdom lay in the animation of trade elaborated this view in a new literature of political economy during the 1750s. The resurgence of luxury as a central cultural problem created an ideological problem with which the new political economists would have to wrestle.

The Political Economy of the Gournay Circle

In the 1750s, a key figure in the royal administration of trade, J.-C.-M. Vincent de Gournay, patronized a circle of writers, encouraging them to translate works from English and to produce political economic writings of their own. Gournay and his acolytes saw commerce as the basis of power in the international system, and they generally endorsed the arguments of Enlightenment moralists that commerce improves manners and redistributes wealth. As the son of a Saint-Malo merchant, and the manager of his family's trading concerns in Cadiz, Gournay understood and valued the world of trade. He was well-versed in the works of English economic writers, and he had visited the ports of northern Europe on spying missions for the French government.[131] Several of Gournay's associates were also close to the world of trade: François Véron de Forbonnais came from a family that made a fortune in manufacturing; Simon Clicquot de Blervache was a substantial merchant in Reims; and Jean-Gabriel Montaudouin de la Touche was the scion of a Nantes slaving dynasty.[132]

In encouraging such men to produce works of political economy, Gournay was motivated principally by a fear that France's position was slipping in relation to her competitors in the international order.[133] France had emerged as the premier continental power by the middle of the seventeenth century. The French could, and did, continue to think of themselves as the dominant European state until the middle of the eighteenth. Though the disastrous wars of Louis XIV's final years shook that confidence, they nevertheless demonstrated that the concerted opposition of all Europe was necessary to check French power. Critical reflection was occasioned, however, by the War of Austrian Succession (1741–

---

[131] Meyssonnier, *Balance et l'horloge*; Gustave Schelle, *Vincent de Gournay* (Geneva, 1984) [1897].

[132] Meyssonnier, *Balance et l'horloge*, 180; Robert Louis Stein, *The French Slave Trade in the Eighteenth Century: An Old Regime Business* (Madison, 1979), 154.

[133] Charles, "French Cultural Politics."

48), the first conflict to engage all the great powers since 1713. The war had by no means proved disastrous for France, but the expenditure of much blood and treasure had not placed the nation on a better footing. The Parisian diarist, Edmond-Jean-François Barbier complained that "of all the belligerent powers we shall have gained least by this war which has cost us immense sums and the loss of three or four hundred thousand men."[134] Moreover, far from marking the dawn of a new era of harmony, the Peace of Aix-la-Chapelle (1748) seemed merely the harbinger of future conflict. Indeed, a new age of international discord and uncertainty was opening and, by the early 1750s, war with a dynamic Britain again seemed imminent.[135] Gournay believed that only a greater attention to developing her economic resources would serve to recover France's position, which is why he led a campaign to promote political economy as a key discourse of public affairs.

That campaign was a resounding success. Louis-Joseph Plumard de Dangeul's *Remarques sur les avantages et les désavantages de la France et de la Grande Bretagne* aroused extraordinary public interest in 1754. Assuming the identity of an English gentleman, Dangeul drew up a balance sheet of relative British and French strengths and weaknesses. The *Remarques* quickly became the talk of Paris, went into a second edition within a fortnight, and two more before the end of the year. Mainstream periodicals excerpted the book, and even the king claimed to be reading it.[136] Forbonnais' *Élémens du commerce*, published in the same year, also captured the attention of readers and several editions appeared. J.-C. Herbert's *Essai sur la police générale des grains* (1753) ran to five editions and stimulated public discussion on the grain trade.[137] In March 1755, the *Correspondance littéraire* remarked that "over the last eighteen months nothing has been more common that works on trade."[138] Among Gournay's other associates who would become celebrated in political economic debate were the abbé Coyer, the abbé André Morellet, later to distinguish himself in the fight over the grain trade and the East Indies Company, and Jacques Turgot, who served as controller general in the 1770s. With the connivance of figures inside the royal administration, notably Daniel Trudaine, the head of the Bureau of Commerce, and Chrétien-Guillaume Lamoignon de Malesherbes, the director of the Book Trade, there was an upsurge in the number of books published on economic subjects in the 1750s.

To make their case for economic development as the foundation of national greatness, Gournay and his acolytes had to grapple with the critique of luxury resurgent in the late 1740s and 1750s. Instead of rejecting outright the claims

---

[134] Edmond-Jean-François Barbier, *Chronique de la Régence et du règne de Louis XV (1718–1763), ou Journal de Barbier*, 4 vols. (Paris, 1885), 4:309.

[135] M. S. Anderson, *The War of the Austrian Succession, 1740–1748* (London, 1995), 219.

[136] David T. Pottinger, *The French Book Trade in the Ancien Régime 1500–1791* (Cambridge, MA, 1958), 204.

[137] Details on the number of editions can be found in Carpenter, *Economic Bestsellers*.

[138] Quoted in Antoin E. Murphy, *Richard Cantillon: Entrepreneur and Economist* (Oxford, 1986), 308–10.

of those who saw in the rising power of money a threat to their own social position and a source of national degeneration, the writers around Gournay distinguished between two kinds of luxury, the one beneficent and the other malign. Gournay and his acolytes enthusiastically embraced the popular consumer revolution, and other vivifying effects of trade, but condemned the parasitic self-enrichment of financiers and aristocrats. They argued that well-distributed, general prosperity and high consumption are the conditions of a flourishing economy and hence of a powerful state. Forbonnais observed that a state "is not rich through the great fortunes of a few subjects, but when everyone . . . is able to spend above real needs. It is in this sense that luxury is really useful in an Empire." Such luxury, he suggested, generates a useful competition among men to be esteemed by others, a competition that drives them to work harder, making the state stronger and more prosperous. Forbonnais saw in Hume's arguments a convenient corrective to the moralized vision of the opponents of luxury. Citing the *Political Discourses* for support, he claimed that luxury "humanizes mankind, polishes their manners, softens their humors, spurs their imagination, perfects their understandings."[139]

Unlike some of the earlier apologists for luxury, however, the men around Gournay did not dismiss criticism of luxury as over-rigorous moralism or mere prejudice. Alongside their celebration of the benefits of consumption, some of Gournay's disciples acknowledged the existence of a pernicious luxury which they associated with aristocrats and financiers. According to Forbonnais, if the source of luxury was not commerce, if it was confined to a small number of cities, or to just one, if useless occupations multiplied while the most productive sectors of society languished, luxury had certainly become destructive. The defenders of luxury were defending a paradox, he argued, if they did not think such excesses were capable of undermining a polity. "If luxury is not general," he insisted, "if it is not the fruit of national affluence, one will see disorders capable of destroying the political body arise along with it."[140] Dangeul equated destructive luxury with excessive inequality in the distribution of wealth, particularly when great fortunes were acquired by means other than commerce or agriculture. Twenty households with an income of 1000 livres stimulate production far more than one household disposing of 20,000, he argued. The baneful effects of such luxury are exacerbated, he argued, if wealth is concentrated in one place—as it was in Versailles and Paris—and if labor is attracted out of essential sectors, particularly farming, into unproductive occupations such as domestic service. "Well ordered luxury consumes," Dangeul concluded, while "excessive luxury abuses and destroys."[141]

---

[139] François Véron de Forbonnais, *Considérations sur les finances d'Espagne* (Dresden, 1753), 171–2; idem, *Élémens du commerce* (Leiden, 1754), 2:291, 299–300.

[140] Forbonnais, *Élémens du commerce*, 2:302–4.

[141] Louis-Joseph Plumard de Dangeul, *Remarques sur les avantages et les désavantages de la France et de la Grande Bretagne, par rapport au commerce, & aux autres sources de la puissance des états. Traduction de l'anglois du Chevalier John Nickolls*, 2nd ed. (Leiden, 1754), 65.

This effort to define an unhealthy luxury and to link it with financiers fit into a larger critique of fiscalism. According to Gournay and his disciples, the system of public finance imposed a crushing burden on productive activity. Dangeul argued that farmers were impoverished and overburdened by taxes; land lay uncultivated but peasants hesitated to bring a new field under the plow for fear of increasing their tax burden. Fiscalism fettered manufacturing, he argued, because guild regulation had become almost purely a fiscal device. Another poisoned fruit of the French state's fiscal operations, according to Dangeul, were high interest rates generated by excessive government borrowing. Funds that could be employed with such profit in "usury," he argued, would not be used to improve land.[142] The importance of low interest rates for national prosperity was also underlined by another member of Gournay's circle, Simon Clicquot de Blervache, who attributed the superior commercial position of England to the lower rates of interest that prevailed there. High interest rates, he argued, constituted the single cause most likely to injure commerce and agriculture. Where the interest rate was too high, he observed, work was not honored because idleness paid greater dividends, and merchants were drawn out of trade because they could make more money as *rentiers*. Clicquot criticized those who lived off *rentes* as idlers who lived off the sweat of the cultivator and the merchant. Every interest payment, he claimed, was a tax levied by laziness on industry.[143]

It is probable that Vincent de Gournay was part of the motley coalition of forces that opposed Pompadour and her financier allies. He was a protégé of the comte de Maurepas, the Minister of the Navy disgraced in 1749 after falling afoul of the marquise. Maurepas had been part of an anti-Pompadour faction at court, and he continued to direct efforts to discredit her from his provincial exile.[144] Members of Gournay's circle were involved in an effort to rein in the depredations of finance during the brief ministry of Étienne de Silhouette in 1759. Silhouette wanted to raise taxes and temper the policy of borrowing to meet expenses pursued by the three preceding controllers general. With Forbonnais as his advisor, Silhouette imposed what was in effect a 50 percent super-tax on the profits of the Farmers General.[145] He also adopted a host of new duties to curb what he called the "prodigality and luxury" of the cities.[146] The financiers forced his ouster after just a few months in office.

The Gournay circle placed political economy at the heart of public debate in

---

[142] Dangeul, *Remarques*, 22, 27, 70.

[143] Simon Clicquot de Blervache, *Dissertation sur les effets que produit le taux de l'intérêt de l'argent sur le commerce et l'agriculture* (Amiens, 1755), 5, 14, 22.

[144] Carré, *Marquise de Pompadour*, 113; Kaiser, "Drama of Charles Edward Stuart."

[145] Marcel Marion, *Histoire financière de la France depuis 1715* (Paris, 1921), 1:191–92; Gabriel Fleury, *François Véron de Fortbonnais: Sa famille, sa vie, ses actes, ses oeuvres 1722–1800* (Mamers, 1915), 48–49.

[146] James C. Riley, *The Seven Years War and the Old Regime in France: The Economic and Financial Toll* (Princeton, 1986), 152.

the 1750s. There, it shared center stage uneasily with the competing perspective that traced the polity's woes to luxury rather than to an underdeveloped economy. The two frameworks were not antithetical—they could find common ground in a hostility to finance—but they were incongruous bedfellows. One might have expected a battle royal eventually to have been conducted between the proponents of the two approaches, and there was certainly some sniping. But as chapter 2 will show, in the late 1750s and 1760s a middle position emerged as the dominant attitude within public discourse.

Writers seized upon the viewpoint made fashionable by Vincent de Gournay and his associates to recast the problem of luxury in powerful new terms. In the 1750s and 1760s, they elaborated a political economy with an economized version of the problem of luxury at its core—a political economy of virtue. The writers who developed this viewpoint accepted the premise that wealth is the foundation of the power of states, but they were equally committed to the view that no state could long remain stable and powerful without civic commitment and the manners that sustained it. They argued that France had undermined both prosperity and patriotism by neglecting agriculture in favor of more brilliant but less grounded forms of wealth. They held that the containment of luxury combined with the regeneration of agriculture would revivify national wealth and also remove a central obstacle to the cultivation of patriotism. In so doing, they also produced a political ideology that identified the interests of provincial landholders with the well-being of the *patrie* and that offered them a new place in national life.

CHAPTER 2

Constructing a Patriot Political Economy

> The best moving force of a government is love of country and this love is cultivated with the fields.
>
> —Rousseau, *Constitution for Corsica* (c. 1765)

> Perhaps too wide a commerce is as great an ill for a kingdom as a domination extended over provinces too vast.
>
> —Mably, *Des principes des négociations* (1757)

On November 5, 1757, the forces of Frederick the Great inflicted a decisive defeat on the French army at Rosbach. As the Seven Years' War unfolded, that early reverse proved an omen of future calamity. On land, French forces failed to achieve victory over Prussia, a state that France dwarfed in population and wealth. In the colonial sphere, Britain was triumphant everywhere, defeating the French in India, North America, and the Caribbean. As early as 1759, it was clear that only a humiliating peace would extricate France from the conflict. The war stirred the loyalties and national sentiments of French elites. Patriotic feeling, which had ebbed and flowed in cultural importance over the previous half century, flowered during the hostilities so that by the end of the war patriotism had become a leading feature of public life. The monarchy deliberately stimulated patriotism in an effort to mobilize the population behind the war effort, but the enthusiastic response it elicited suggests that official propaganda tapped an authentic ground swell of sentiment. Thus the failure of French arms left in its wake not just a chastened military, and a ballooning royal debt, but a public inspired by patriotic feeling, anxious to understand the sources of national debility and eager to regenerate the *patrie*.[1]

It was easy to read the failure of French arms as a validation of the claim

---

[1] Bell, *Cult of the Nation in France*, 63–68; Edmond Dziembowski, *Un nouveau patriotisme français*, passim; Liah Greenfeld, *Nationalism: Five Roads to Modernity* (Cambridge, MA, 1992), 160; Stone, *Genesis of the French Revolution*, 57–62.

that France was crippled by luxury. In fact, patriotism drew heavily on the Fénelonian politics of virtue, and antipathy to luxury was one of its central features.[2] Patriots insisted that civic virtue was crucial to the fortunes of the state and that luxury was inimical to the preservation of such virtue. They imagined an economic order free of luxury as the basis for a regenerated polity. In his *Dissertation sur le vieux mot de patrie* (1755), the abbé Coyer argued that patriotism could not be expected to thrive in a social system characterized by great inequality and an excessive pursuit of private interest. In a description of ancient Rome that served as a metaphor for modern France, he asked why anyone should experience love of country when all wealth was concentrated in the hands of a few, when excessive luxury taunted extreme poverty, and when citizens were forced to neglect the public welfare to attend to their own. Coyer's vision of a true *patrie* was one marked by "wealth and mediocrity, but no paupers; men great and small, but nobody oppressed." When the Roman emperor Trajan sought to reestablish patriotism after the reigns of the tyrants who preceded him, Coyer argued, he attacked luxury at its source by reducing taxes, selling palaces, succoring the poor, blocking excessive enrichment, restoring abundance, and returning authority to the Senate.[3]

But if the language of luxury offered an intuitively compelling account of French weakness, it did not blind patriots to the lessons of the political economy made fashionable by Gournay and his circle in the 1750s. Anyone committed to recovering French supremacy in the international order had to take seriously the call to increase national wealth. Patriotic feeling spurred a generation of French elites to engage with political economic ideas. A case in point is the young Pierre-Samuel Dupont who spent the war years in a patriotic fervor, dreaming up plans to storm the British fortress at Gibraltar, and who was soon to make his name as a political economist.[4] However, the political economy of the Gournay circle was not well adapted to the celebration of virtue that was the stock in trade of patriotism. In embracing political economy, patriots remade it in their own image: not just wealth, but virtue, must be regenerated. The period from 1756 to 1763 saw the emergence of a new political economy in France, suffused with patriotic motifs, and deploring luxury as a source of national decline.

Though it was far from a unified and coherent discourse, some common themes can be discerned in the political economy elaborated in this period. Writers in the late 1750s and early 1760s repudiated major aspects of the existing political economic order as destructive of both virtue and national pros-

---

[2] Sarah Maza, "Luxury, Morality, and Social Change: Why There was no Middle-Class Consciousness in Prerevolutionary France," *Journal of Modern History* 69, no. 2 (1997): 199–229.

[3] Gabriel-François Coyer, "Dissertation sur le vieux mot de patrie," *Gabriel-François Coyer, Jacob-Nicolas Moreau: Écrits sur le patriotisme l'esprit publique et la propagande au milieu du XVIIIe siècle,* ed. Edmond Dziembowski (La Rochelle, 1997) [1755], 45–47.

[4] Pierre-Samuel Dupont de Nemours, *L'enfance et la jeunesse de Du Pont de Nemours racontées par lui-même,* ed. H. A. Du Pont de Nemours (Paris, 1906), 182–83.

perity. Many complained that the fiscal system, regulation of the grain trade, and scorn for cultivators had destroyed the prosperity of French agriculture. Some held that the international commerce and luxury manufactures encouraged by Colbert and his administrative successors had fostered the growth of an ephemeral wealth while neglecting the genuine riches of the land. Power founded on mobile wealth was subject to "revolutions," they held; it could strengthen a state in the short term, but such vigor was evanescent; an excessive dependence on commerce and manufactures could render a polity vulnerable to decline. The most significant unifying theme in this entire corpus of texts was the tendency to privilege agriculture as the principal source of national wealth. There was much attention to the supposedly thriving state of British farming, and the study of agronomy became something of a national fad in the late 1750s and early 1760s. Agriculture was the symbolic ground on which it proved possible to reconcile wealth and virtue. Increasingly, political economists represented agriculture as the most real source of wealth, as the true basis of national prosperity, and also as the font of the moral dispositions that would make it possible to sustain civic spirit. It was widely held that agriculture was in wretched straits and that the primary route to national regeneration lay through the creation of rural prosperity.

Aspects of the new political economy appealed strongly to the middling nobility, and they played a crucial role in elaborating it. The paradigmatic expression of this new perspective was the literary blockbuster of 1757, the marquis de Mirabeau's *L'ami des hommes, ou Traité de la population,* a work motivated by a desire to renew the nobility, to create prosperity, and to regenerate patriotic virtue. The book represented a counter-offensive against some of the writers associated with Gournay, who claimed that nobles made little contribution to the prosperity and power of the state, and that noble honor, in particular, was an impediment to economic development. The abbé Coyer popularized a version of this argument in 1756 with the publication of his pamphlet, *La noblesse commerçante,* which advocated that nobles abandon traditional pursuits and values and make themselves useful to the *patrie* by becoming traders. Mirabeau's attack on luxury and his claim that agriculture was the foundation of long-term prosperity and power resonated with the values of the provincial nobility, and equated their economic interests as landowners with the national interest. But Mirabeau's success must also be seen as part of a broader trend: a growing elite fascination with agriculture.

The Agromania of the 1750s

A craze for agricultural improvement swept France in the 1750s as interest in the new English agriculture of Jethro Tull, Thomas Hale, and Lord Townshend crossed the channel. The introduction of Tull's ideas into France in the guise of Henri-Louis Duhamel du Monceau's *Traité de la culture des terres*

(1750) marked the beginning of the new fashion.[5] Duhamel dwelt on the disadvantages of leaving land fallow, proposing that fodder crops such as turnips be cultivated as an alternative. In the course of the 1750s, André Bourde writes, "a whole world of amateurs, of experimenters, of improving landlords," emerged.[6] A sense of this upsurge of interest can be gleaned from a bibliography of writings on rural economy published in 1810 by the agronomist Victor-Donatien de Musset (father of the poet Alfred de Musset).[7] It shows that a greater number of works on agriculture were published in the 1750s than during the previous half century. The proliferation of writings was so marked by the early 1760s that the term *agromania* was coined to describe it.[8] The journalist Fréron picked up the expression remarking that "this agromania, if one can call it that, can only produce considerable benefits."[9] In addition to books on agricultural improvement, the promotion of agriculture was undertaken between 1750 and 1789 by a half dozen specialized periodicals, beginning with the *Journal oeconomique* in 1751.[10] The promotional efforts of agronomists and agricultural improvers contributed significantly to disseminating the idea that the foundation of national regeneration lay in the land.

The new interest in agriculture emerged from the same intellectual and political conjuncture as the political economic literature of the 1750s. It was, in

[5] Henri-Louis Duhamel du Monceau, *Traité de la culture des terres, suivant les principes de M. Tull, anglois* (Paris, 1750–61); André J. Bourde, *The Influence of England on the French Agronomes, 1750–1789* (Cambridge, 1953), 40–42.

[6] André J. Bourde, *Agronomie et agronomes en France au XVIIIe siècle* (Paris, 1967), 365.

[7] Victor-Donatien de Musset, *Bibliographie agronomique, ou Dictionnaire raisonné des ouvrages sur l'économie rurale et domestique et sur l'art vétérinaire* (Paris, 1991) [1810].

[8] Laurent-Benoit Desplaces, *Préservatif contre l'agromanie, ou L'agriculture réduite à ses vrais principes* (Paris, 1762). Desplaces criticized what he perceived as the contemporary mania for agronomy. What irritated him was not the interest in agriculture—his *Préservatif* was itself an agronomic how-to manual. He was simply annoyed by the trifling quality of much of the contemporary discussion of the subject.

[9] Quoted in Bourde, *Influence of England*, 63n.

[10] In 1754, seeing the potential for a second journal dealing with rural economy, the publishers of *La nouvelle bigarrure* transformed their publication into the *Nouvelliste oeconomique et littéraire*. Over the next seven years, the journal published a mix of literary criticism and rural economy. On broader issues of the political economy of agriculture, the Physiocratic *Éphémérides du citoyen*, and the *Journal de l'agriculture* were the two dominant journals. The *Gazette du commerce*, established in 1763, and renamed the *Gazette du commerce, de l'agriculture et des finances* in 1765, was devoted primarily to commercial information of a practical sort but it also reported on agricultural improvement. Later in the century, the *Journal de physique* (1771–93), the *Journal d'agriculture, commerce, arts et finances* (1779–83) and the *Bibliothèque physico-économique, instructive et amusante* (1782–97) took over as the key agronomic organs. The general press showed a great deal of interest in agriculture also, especially during the late 1750s and 1760s. Of all the non-specialized journals, Fréron's *Année littéraire* (1749–76) offered perhaps the most enthusiastic coverage. In the early 1760s, the *Journal de Trévoux* also carried extensive coverage of agricultural and agronomic literature. The *Journal des sçavans* carried occasional extracts from agronomic works, as did the *Mercure de France*. The provincial *Affiches,* or advertising press, also contained notices and information on agronomic activities.

large measure, the fruit of comparisons between France and England in the period after the War of Austrian Succession. In the prosperity of the English countryside, French writers discerned an arena in which England enjoyed a marked superiority. The abbé Le Blanc celebrated the prosperity of rural England in his best-selling *Lettres d'un Français sur les Anglais* (1745). In an image which, as Bourde points out, must have seemed incredible to his French readers, Le Blanc described farm laborers taking tea—still an expensive commodity in the 1740s—before going out to the fields.[11] There was growing attention in the 1750s and 1760s to the relationship between Britain's power and her "improved" agriculture. Among the writers impressed by English agriculture were the abbé Coyer, who discoursed at length about its productivity in *La noblesse commerçante*, Ange Goudar, who affirmed that British power ought to be attributed to her "new system of agriculture," and Edmé-Jacques Genet who claimed that in British farming lay "the principle of the true wealth of England."[12]

To many French elites, the chief lesson of the War of Austrian Succession was that commerce was not the foundation of lasting international supremacy. The war had revealed a radical decline in the power of the Netherlands, a paradigmatically commercial state. As early as November 1741, the marquis de Stainville wrote, "As for Holland, I regard her as a dead power who will be the victim of her drowsiness," and it was imminent Dutch collapse that forced her ally, Great Britain, to the bargaining table in 1748.[13] The authority of Colbertist assumptions owed much to the example of the Dutch Republic. With a population one-tenth the size of France, the Netherlands had been capable of mobilizing disproportionate military force in the seventeenth century. Colbertism was, in part, an attempt to imitate the Dutch model on a grander scale. The Dutch collapse of the 1740s undermined this whole policy perspective. A lesson that some drew from the Dutch experience was that commerce lent only a temporary strength to states. "The Dutch amass for a conqueror as a miser saves for his inheritors," wrote the chevalier d'Arcq.[14] Goudar, too, was struck by the decline of the Netherlands, noting in 1756 that "Holland has just lost two-thirds of her power." He concluded that power built on commerce was like a house built on sand; landed wealth was more "real."[15]

Different, but in some respects complementary, conclusions could be drawn from the other major developments of the war: the breakthrough of Prussia as

---

[11] Bourde, *Influence of England*, 19–20.

[12] Gabriel-François Coyer, *La noblesse commerçante* (London, 1756), 56–60; Ange Goudar, *Année politique* (Paris, 1758), 36; Edmé-Jacques Genet, *Essais historiques sur l'Angleterre* (n.p., 1761), iii.

[13] Anderson, *War of the Austrian Succession*, 111.

[14] Philippe-Auguste de Sainte-Foix, chevalier d'Arcq, *Mes loisirs* (Paris, 1755), 187.

[15] Ange Goudar, *Les intérêts de la France mal entendus, dans les branches de l'agriculture, de la population, des finances, du commerce, de la marine et de l'industrie, par un citoyen* (Amsterdam, 1756), 1:6.

a great power and the continuing rise of Russia. Prussia emerged as a military dynamo during the 1740s and, despite its diminutive size, joined the league of major powers. The country governed no colonies and possessed no navy, but had a reputation as a modern Sparta.[16] Russia too, with its vast peasantry and relative commercial underdevelopment, saw its strength wax. These facts did not escape the notice of contemporaries. Barbier followed the progress of Russian forces during the War of Austrian Succession with fascination, while the marquis de Mirabeau observed in 1756 that the power of the Prussian king and the tsar had grown prodigiously.[17]

Though principally promoters of commerce, Gournay and his closest collaborators also underlined the importance of agricultural prosperity to the wealth and power of states. In a co-authored work of 1758, Gournay and Clicquot de Blervache argued that the principal problem facing the French economy was the neglect of agriculture. Despite France's natural economic advantages over England, they noted, the French had been bested by their rivals. They concluded that there must be a "hidden vice" in the French administrative or legal order, namely, "the too great preference given in France to manufactures over agriculture." Arguing that farmers were the "drive wheel" that animated commerce, they called for a greater development of agricultural resources. Manufactures had undermined agriculture in France by attracting labor off the land into less necessary sectors of the economy. "Because [commerce] is not based on our productions," the two men wrote, "it is only precarious, dependent and transient." It was pointless to consider the reform of the arts and trades—the primary concern of the work—unless agriculture was placed on a sound footing.[18]

Close links tied several members of the Gournay circle to the agricultural improvers who sought to revivify French agriculture. Gournay performed agronomic experiments on his lands and was a correspondent of Duhamel du Monceau (Duhamel recommended the writings of Gournay, Clicquot, and Forbonnais to his readers).[19] Forbonnais set up a model farm and was the author of the article "Culture des terres" in the *Encyclopédie*. His father, François-Louis Véron du Verger, became the permanent secretary of the Agricultural Society of Le Mans when it was founded in 1761, and Forbonnais himself joined in 1764.[20] Turgot's brother was one of the leading lights of the Paris Agricul-

---

[16] Voltaire, for one, was fond of this comparison. Peter Gay, *Voltaire's Politics: The Poet as Realist* (New York, 1965), 150–51n, 171n.

[17] Suzanne Cornand, "La fin de la guerre de succession d'Autriche: Le témoignage de Barbier," in *1748, l'année de l'Esprit des lois*, ed. Catherine Larrère (Paris, 1999), 34; Mirabeau, *Ami des hommes*, 3:209.

[18] Simon Clicquot de Blervache and Jacques-Claude-Marie Vincent de Gournay, *Considérations sur le commerce, et en particulier sur les compagnies, sociétés et maîtrises* (Amsterdam, 1758), 4–12.

[19] Bourde, *Agronomie et agronomes*, 333; Henri-Louis Duhamel du Monceau, *École d'agriculture* (Paris, 1759), 12, 17n.

[20] Frank A. Kafker and Serena L. Kafker, *The Encyclopedists as Individuals: A Biographical Dic-*

tural Society. One of Gournay's administrative patrons, Daniel Trudaine, was an associate member of the Agricultural Society of Orléans, and both he and his son, Trudaine de Montigny, became associate members of the Paris society. The other sponsor of the Gournay Circle, Malesherbes, was an enthusiastic *agronome* and protector of the *Journal oeconomique.*[21]

If the celebration of agriculture was one of the factors that mediated the development of a political economy oriented to patriot objectives, the other was the penetration into political economic thought of preoccupations with degeneration. The erroneous notion that the country's population had fallen precipitously was widely shared at mid-century.[22] Gournay argued that depopulation had occurred on a grand scale in France.[23] The abbé Coyer concurred, claiming that while France had a population of twenty million under Charles IX, a century later Vauban counted only nineteen, and the present population was only eighteen million.[24] Dangeul complained that both the farming and artisanal classes were daily being depleted, and he regarded this depopulation as a major source of French weakness.[25] Those who worried about depopulation in the 1750s may have been influenced by the marked increase in mortality across Northern Europe that occurred in the 1740s, brought on by unusually severe weather conditions.[26] But many writers believed that luxury was responsible. Jacques-Claude Herbert blamed depopulation on an excessive luxury unfavorable to agriculture.[27] Dangeul also saw luxury as a significant factor in causing depopulation. It had become more respectable to own half a dozen horses, he complained, than to live in mediocrity and "give children to the state."[28]

François Quesnay claimed that the population of France had declined by a third since the days of Henri IV, in the early seventeenth century, and he attributed this fall to luxury and the degeneration of French agriculture. France formerly produced annually at least seventy million *septiers* of grain, in comparison to a mere forty-five million by the 1750s, Quesnay argued. The past

---

tionary of the Authors of the Encyclopédie (Oxford, 1988); Fleury, *François Véron de Fortbonnais,* 22, 88.

[21] Allison, *Lamoignon de Malesherbes,* 72; Weulersse, *Le mouvement physiocratique en France,* 1:27.

[22] Carol Blum, *Strength in Numbers: Population, Reproduction, and Power in Eighteenth-Century France* (Baltimore, 2002), passim; James C. Riley, *Population Thought in the Age of the Demographic Revolution* (Durham, NC, 1985), 52–53; Joseph J. Spengler, *French Predecessors of Malthus: A Study in Eighteenth-Century Wage and Population Theory* (Durham, NC, 1942), 57–74. Modern estimates suggest that French population actually grew slowly from about 21.5 million at the beginning of the eighteenth century to about 24.5 million by 1750.

[23] Meyssonnier, *Balance et l'horloge,* 185.

[24] Coyer, *Noblesse commerçante,* 67–70.

[25] Dangeul, *Remarques,* 25.

[26] John D. Post, "Climatic Variability and the European Mortality Wave of the Early 1740s," *Journal of Interdisciplinary History* 15, no. 1 (1984): 1–30.

[27] J.-C. Herbert, *Essai sur la police générale des grains* (Berlin, 1755), 344–47.

[28] Dangeul, *Remarques,* 17–18.

abundance was "a happy consequence of the economic government of M. de Sully," Henri IV's finance minister.[29] Quesnay expressed his admiration for Sully, claiming that this "great minister grasped the true principles of the economic government of the kingdom," that the "supposed advantages of manufactures of every kind did not seduce him," and that he had established "the riches of the king, the power of the state, and the happiness of the people on the revenues of the land."[30] A veritable eighteenth-century cult of Sully dates from the publication in 1745 of the abbé de L'Écluse's *Mémoires de Maximilien de Béthune, duc de Sully*, a rewrite of Sully's own unreadable memoirs.[31] At least five editions of L'Écluse's work appeared between 1745 and 1752. Sully's name was a byword for hostility to luxury and to financiers (which was ironic since he invested in tax farms himself).[32] As Fénelon would do later, Sully argued that because agriculture was the foundation of virtue, agricultural prosperity was the key to the health of the body politic.[33]

But if Quesnay connected his arguments to the long tradition of antipathy to luxury, he did so almost entirely within a political economic idiom. He argued that Colbertist policies to foster industrial development by keeping consumer prices (and thus manufacturing wages) low had artificially depressed the price of cereals. The manufacturer's gain came at the expense of the cultivator, and the wealth that manufacturers claimed to be creating was really a transfer of profit from the cultivator without any absolute national benefit. To obtain a few millions by making and selling cloth, France had sacrificed billions in agricultural wealth: "The nation bedecked in gold and silver cloth, believed itself to enjoy a flourishing commerce," he remarked, but "these manufactures have plunged us into a disordered luxury." Quesnay argued that a nation that depended on manufacturing wealth was in a "precarious and uncertain state."[34] Though sympathetic to the agenda of the agricultural improvers—the agronomists Henry Patullo and Georges Leroy were friends and collaborators of Quesnay, and his son was a prominent agricultural experimenter—Quesnay saw free trade as the real solution to problems of agriculture.[35] He demanded freedom of export to raise French cereal prices to the level of European markets in the expectation that export opportunities would permanently raise

[29] François Quesnay, "Grains," *François Quesnay et la physiocratie* (Paris, 1958), 2:471–72.

[30] In December 1758, Quesnay printed a copy of his "Tableau économique" with a set of maxims for the government of an agricultural kingdom under the title "Extrait des économies royales de M. de Sully." Henry Higgs, *The Physiocrats: Six Lectures on the French Économistes of the 18th Century* (London, 1897), 41.

[31] Maximilien de Béthune, duc de Sully, *Mémoires de Maximilien de Béthune, duc de Sully, . . . mis en ordre; avec des remarques par M. L. D. L. D. L.,* ed. Pierre-Mathurin de L'Écluse des Loges (London, 1745).

[32] Rothkrug, *Opposition to Louis XIV*, 74; Dessert, *Argent, pouvoir et société,* 352.

[33] Charles Rupin, *Les idées économiques de Sully et leurs applications à l'agriculture aux finances et à l'industrie* (New York, 1970) [1907], 41–42, 52.

[34] Quesnay, "Grains," 459–60, 499.

[35] Jacqueline Hecht, "La vie de François Quesnay," in *François Quesnay et la physiocratie,* 1:253–54.

French domestic prices. If the price of grain rose to its true level, he argued, total agricultural production would more than triple in cash value, and the enormous increase in national wealth would regenerate the fortunes of the state.[36]

Though a resident of the court at Versailles, and personal physician to Madame de Pompadour, Quesnay manifested a deep hostility to courtiers and financiers. In correspondence with the marquis de Mirabeau, he condemned courtiers as petty and frivolous and described the wealth of financiers as "base," complaining that it blurred social distinctions and eclipsed the nobility.[37] He turned down a position as a tax farmer for his son Blaise-Guillaume, lending him forty thousand livres instead so that he could enrich himself "in a manner useful to the *patrie*."[38] An important contributory factor to the devastation of agriculture, Quesnay argued, were the evils of fiscalism. France's most important land tax, the *taille*, fell not only on the profits of agriculture but on the advances that the cultivator needed to reinvest in order to achieve comparable production the following year. If taxation cut into the *avances*, the result must necessarily be a fall in production and a decline in tax revenues for the following year. "If the cultivator is ruined by the financier, the revenues of the kingdom are annihilated." Quesnay argued that taxation should be strictly proportional to the rent of farms. This would allow the farmer to figure the cost of taxation into the lease price and would ensure that his advances would be untouched by the fisc. The reform of the tax system, Quesnay argued, would attract a large number of proprietors out of the towns, would "reanimate the cultivation of the land" and "reestablish the strength of the kingdom."[39]

By 1756, a political economic version of the problem of luxury was emerging, but there were tensions between this new political economy and the Fénelonian critique of luxury. Political economists assumed, by and large, that the appropriate agent of economic reform was the administrative monarchy; they manifested little concern that absolutism was sapping the foundations of patriotic virtue. Indeed, Forbonnais mounted a spirited defense of absolutism in his first published work, a critique of Montesquieu's *De l'esprit des lois*.[40] Most of Gournay's circle were, or eventually became, agents of the Crown. Clicquot de Blervache became an Inspector General of Manufactures; Morellet served as a consultant to controller general Maynon d'Invau; Forbonnais was appointed Inspector General of the Mint; Turgot would go on to become the Intendant at Limoges and, later, controller general.[41] Gournay's associates were

---

[36] Quesnay, "Grains," 478.

[37] Georges Weulersse, ed., *Les manuscrits économiques de François Quesnay et du marquis de Mirabeau aux Archives nationales (M. 778 à M. 785)* (Paris, 1910), 28.

[38] Hecht, "Vie de François Quesnay," 1:245.

[39] Quesnay, "Grains," 492.

[40] François Véron de Forbonnais, "Du gouvernement d'Angleterre, comparé par l'auteur de l'Esprit des loix au gouvernement de France," in *Opuscules de M. F**** (Amsterdam, 1753), 3:173–213.

[41] Minard, *La fortune du colbertisme,* 335; Léonce de Lavergne, *Les économistes français du dix-huitième siècle* (Geneva, 1970) [1870], 347; Fleury, *François Véron de Fortbonnais,* 48; Swann, *Politics and the Parlement of Paris,* 237–38.

not interested in regenerating the power and prestige of traditional elites. One of the central thrusts of Dangeul's *Remarques* was that France was burdened by an excessively feudal social structure and by outdated aristocratic attitudes inimical to the growth of commerce.[42] Most importantly, at this stage, few political economic writers took seriously the idea that virtue needed to be regenerated. In this respect, Goudar was quite typical. His objections to luxury were not that it sapped civic virtue. The Romans arrived at grandeur through poverty and virtue, he conceded, but it was quite otherwise with modern states, which required wealth.[43] The writers of Gournay's circle maintained that men are driven by passions and self-interest. Jacques-Claude Herbert, for example, observed that "it will be in vain to find means to fertilize the land if the cultivator is not animated there by his personal interest," while Morellet remarked pointedly that "one ought not expect from men more virtue than they've got."[44] Many of the tensions that patriots had to work through as they married political economy with a politics of reviving civic virtue were played out in the course of the greatest political economic controversy of the 1750s, the debate aroused by Coyer's *La noblesse commerçante*. For that reason, the controversy would prove foundational for the development of a patriot political economy.

The *Noblesse commerçante* Debate

In *La noblesse commerçante,* Coyer argued that nobles ought to be allowed, and indeed encouraged, to become merchants. In reply, the chevalier d'Arcq published his *La noblesse militaire, ou le patriote françois* (1756) in which he asserted that a trading nobility would disastrously undermine French military prowess.[45] Coyer published a reply to his critics, and journalists gave the dispute extensive attention in the press.[46] Numerous other commentators weighed in on the question in the years following, and the controversy even attracted attention abroad.[47] The debate between Coyer and d'Arcq, as Jay Smith points out, was a clash within a common idiom of patriotism.[48] As is obvious from the subtitle of d'Arcq's work—*Le patriote françois*—the author saw himself as

---

[42] Dangeul, *Remarques,* 15–19.

[43] Goudar, *Intérêts de la France,* 1:4–8, 26–29, 3:247.

[44] Herbert, *Essai sur la police,* 52; Abbé André Morellet, *Réflexions sur les avantages de la fabrication et de l'usage des toiles peintes en France* (Geneva, 1758), 46.

[45] For a good general account of the controversy, see J. Q. C. Mackrell, *The Attack on "Feudalism" in Eighteenth-Century France* (London, 1973), 77–103.

[46] Gabriel-François Coyer, *Développement, et défense du système de la noblesse commerçante* (London, 1768) [1757].

[47] Henry Higgs, *Bibliography of Economics, 1751–1775* (Cambridge, 1935); Ulrich Adam, "Nobility and Modern Monarchy—J. H. G. Justi and the French Debate on Commercial Nobility at the Beginning of the Seven Years War," *History of European Ideas* 29, no. 2 (2003): 141–57.

[48] Jay M. Smith, "Social Categories, the Language of Patriotism, and the Origins of the French Revolution: The Debate over *Noblesse Commerçante,*" *Journal of Modern History* 72 (2000): 339–74.

a patriot. Having published the *Dissertation sur le vieux mot de patrie* in 1755, Coyer was already a leading patriot voice; his argument in *La noblesse commerçante* is framed by a patriotic concern that France successfully meet the challenge of her British rival.

The work demanded, first, that patriots take the lessons of political economy into account in any scheme to regenerate the nation—to square their projects with political economic realities or be undercut by them. Second, it made the question of the role of the nobility, and of noble values, in French society central to thinking about patriotic national renewal. Finally, Coyer's work forced all who followed him to grapple with questions of the proper social distribution of honor.[49]

Coyer argued that Britain had made herself powerful through a more thorough exploitation of her commercial resources than France, a feat she had achieved because, while the French scorned commerce and the merchants who pursued it, the British honored them. He argued that commerce in France was retarded by the dishonor under which it labored, a claim he borrowed from Dangeul, who regarded this lack of honor as a key obstacle to French economic development.[50] The worthiness of trade was an especially pressing question in France, Coyer argued, because, while other nations might be contented with enriching themselves, "the Frenchman wants glory."[51] In engaging nobles to trade, Coyer hoped to use their social prestige to make commerce honorable. In this he was following in the French tradition of commercial humanism, which sought to confer legitimacy on commerce by endowing it with noble qualities. In the words of Henry Clark, it was rather by "conceptualizing merchant activities in noble terms" than by revaluing specifically merchant qualities that commercial humanists tried to legitimate commerce.[52]

The chevalier d'Arcq, by contrast, argued that Coyer's scheme for a trading nobility would destroy the sense of honor that was the animating spirit of successful military officers. He contended that the nobility ought to stay out of trade lest they become infected with a spirit of calculation—the antithesis of the self-sacrificing spirit of honor.[53] D'Arcq argued that only nobles were sen-

---

[49] Coyer may have written *La noblesse commerçante* at the behest of the administration, and possibly at the suggestion of Vincent de Gournay. The practice of preparing the public for administrative initiatives by commissioning pamphlets became increasingly common in the second half of the eighteenth century and, at the moment when the pamphlet appeared, the *Conseil de commerce* had decided to reiterate the principle that nobles could engage in wholesale commerce without derogation—formal loss of noble status. (Richard, *Noblesse d'affaires*, 62.) The controller general may have felt the need for some propaganda favorable to the project because a trading nobility had been criticized by Montesquieu in 1748 and more recently in an article by the marquis de Lassay published in the *Mercure de France* in December 1754. Montesquieu, *Spirit of the Laws*, bk. 20, chap. 21; "Réflexions de M. le marquis de Lassé, mort en 1738," *Mercure de France* (December, 1754).

[50] Coyer, *Noblesse commerçante*, 3; Dangeul, *Remarques*, 31–35.

[51] Coyer, *Noblesse commerçante*, 192. See also Coyer, *Développement*, 2:79.

[52] Clark, "Commerce, the Virtues, and the Public Sphere," 438.

[53] D'Arcq, *Noblesse militaire*, 49, 56–57, 67.

Que sert ce vain amas d'une inutile gloire?

Fig. 3. Frontispiece to abbé Coyer, *La noblesse commerçante*, 1756.

The frontispiece to Coyer's *La noblesse commerçante* exemplifies the thesis of his polemic: that nobles should be permitted to engage in commerce both for their own benefit and for the good of the country. Coyer's explication of the image states that "This gentleman one sees here, tired of living in poverty and uselessness, displays his marks of nobility, an escutcheon, a crest, or armorial helmet, and a parchment which contains his titles, gifts of birth from which he has drawn no fruit. He is leaving them behind and is going to embark to serve the *Patrie* by enriching himself in trade." Courtesy of Kroch Library (Rare and Manuscript Collections), Cornell University, Ithaca.

sitive enough to honor to be valorous in battle and thus to be effective military officers. Once the animating passion of commerce, pecuniary interest, had taken root in a noble's soul, it would accustom him to an egoistic calculus of the costs and benefits of any action, destroying his capacity for selfless valor. D'Arcq's argument was seconded by many other participants in the war of words that followed the publication of *La noblesse commerçante*. One contributor to the debate, a Madame Belot, alerted her readers to the dangers of introducing the "spirit of calculation" in place of the "military spirit," noting that "a vast kingdom has needs that a great number of citizens prefer the vanity of rank, public consideration . . . to the tranquil *douceurs* of opulence." If the military spirit ceased to be the soul of the nation, Belot feared, the French Empire would fall either to the Scylla of invasion or the Charybdis of despotism.[54] Similarly in his *Lettre à l'auteur de la noblesse commerçante*, the abbé Barthoul noted that it is honor, the desire for glory and distinction, that has made the French soldier invincible. If Coyer's scheme were realized, he argued, interest would take the place of honor, and France would become a nation of calculators.[55]

The *noblesse commerçante* debate exposed a fault line in patriotic thinking about how best to harness the human passion for honor to direct self-interested individuals toward satisfying public needs. In the first half of the century, as moralists began to look to manners as a substitute for antique virtue, many argued that the love of honor—sometimes labeled "emulation"—could direct men to perform socially useful acts. (Emulation was a form of gentlemanly competitiveness—a drive to imitate or surpass others in virtue or merit—but moralists often assumed that such striving was linked with a desire to make a name for oneself.)[56] Hume insisted on a close connection between virtue and the desire for repute: "Vanity is so closely allied to virtue, and to love the fame of laudable actions approaches so near the love of laudable actions for their own sake, that . . . it is almost impossible to have the latter without some degree of

[54] Octavie Guichard, dame Belot, *Observations sur la noblesse et le Tiers-État* (Amsterdam, 1758), 7, 111.

[55] Abbé Barthoul, *Lettre à l'auteur de la noblesse commerçante* (Bordeaux, 1756), 31–38. Numerous other commentators agreed. See, for example, J.-J. Garnier, *Le commerce remis à sa place; réponse d'un pédant de collège aux novateurs politiques* (n.p, 1756), 24–26; Grimm, *Correspondance littéraire*, 3:170–79; De La Hausse *La noblesse telle qu'elle doit être, ou Moyen de l'employer utilement pour elle-même et pour la patrie* (Amsterdam, 1758), 7; E.-L. Billardon de Sauvigny, *L'une ou l'autre, ou La noblesse commerçante et militaire, avec des réflexions sur le commerce et les moyens de l'encourager* (Mahon, 1756), 54.

[56] That emulation was prompted by the lure of honor is illustrated in a piece of advice attributed to the father of the economist François Quesnay. The elder Quesnay told his son that "the temple of virtue is supported by four columns, honor, reward, shame and punishment." His son should choose one of these columns as the basis of his own virtue, "because it is necessary to choose to do good through emulation, through interest, through decency, or through fear." As reward is aligned with interest, and punishment with fear, so honor is linked with emulation. Hecht, "Vie de François Quesnay," 1:213.

the former." He suggested that a sense of honor would restrain excessive egoism in a commercial society.[57] Montesquieu accorded a decisive role to competitive striving for honor as a substitute for civic virtue. He argued that the drive for honor produces benefits in a monarchy in ways parallel to the functioning of public virtue in the ancient republics. In the pursuit of honor, "each individual advances the public good, while he only thinks of promoting his own interest."[58] The dispute between Coyer and d'Arcq turned on whether the maximum social benefit could be derived from the passion for honor by structuring competition for esteem within a traditional society of orders, or by democratizing honor and using the passion for distinction common to all Frenchmen to induce them to behave in socially useful ways.

The different perspectives of Coyer and d'Arcq on this question also reflected a disagreement about whether wealth or virtue was more important to the power and well-being of the polity. Coyer argued that the basis of power was wealth. "[I]n the end," he argued, "the nation which has the most money, that is to say, the most commerce, will obtain victory for itself."[59] D'Arcq, by contrast, suggested that it was not commerce so much as military virtue that was the fundamental basis of power. A concentration on creating wealth to the exclusion of nurturing virtue rendered a country vulnerable to conquest. Moreover, commerce led to luxury, which was the most redoubtable enemy of the state.[60] D'Arcq was not blind to the state's need for wealth. But he was mistrustful of the social and political consequences of an extensive commerce. In a work published in 1755, he suggested that agriculture was a firmer basis than trade for the power of states.[61]

Luxury was associated, in d'Arcq's mind, with despotism. Great financial resources in the hands of the monarch allowed him to hire mercenaries, or to suborn powerful subjects. Drawing on Montesquieu, he argued that noble pride was crucial to preventing the degeneration of the French monarchy. According to Montesquieu, the "principle" of monarchy—honor—acted as a brake preventing monarchy from degenerating. "In monarchical and moderate states," he argued, "power is limited by that which is its spring; I mean honor, which reigns like a monarch over the prince and the people."[62] The same sense of honor that made nobles effective soldiers also made them a bulwark against despotism. D'Arcq argued that encouraging nobles to trade would jeopardize this sense of honor—nobles would become "calculators" who would no longer care enough about their honor to resist a tyrant. He insinuated that Coyer's scheme of effacing the distinctions between the nobility and the trading classes

---

[57] Hume, *Essays*, 86, 276.

[58] Montesquieu, *Spirit of the Laws*, bk. 3, chap. 7.

[59] Coyer, *Noblesse commerçante*, 152.

[60] D'Arcq, *Mes loisirs*, 79.

[61] Ibid., 75, 77, 130.

[62] Montesquieu denounced the idea of a commercial nobility arguing that it was contrary to the "spirit of monarchy." *Spirit of the Laws*, bk. 3, chap. 10; bk. 20, chap. 21.

would precipitate a "revolution" that would threaten the existing form of government and allow France to drift toward tyranny.[63]

At the core of the *noblesse commerçante* controversy was a disagreement about the role the nobility should play in French national life, and within what kind of social order—a commercial society, rid of the last traces of feudalism, or a revivified society of orders. To its champions, like Coyer, the commercialization of society was progressive; the fruit of commercial society would be the enlightenment and humanity celebrated by Voltaire and Hume. Commercial society would also signal a break with an anachronistic, feudal social order. Coyer saw the attitudes he was struggling against—that commerce is dishonorable, for instance—as a vestige of the "Gothic spirit," a cultural remnant as irrational and baneful as trial by ordeal.[64] The true danger of despotism, he implied, came not from the monarchy but from nobles who tyrannized ordinary folk, a domineering spirit he associated with impoverished provincial squires.[65] Coyer also represented a pernicious luxury as a vestige of feudalism. Instead of enriching the country by improving their estates, *grands seigneurs* locked up productive land in parks and banished the plow in favor of carriages. The countrymen they threw out of work flocked to the cities where they "serve and share our luxury, lose the love of work and the *moeurs* of nature."[66]

D'Arcq's perspective on what a commercial society meant was diametrically different. For the chevalier, a commercial society would be a realm governed by money. The mischievous consequences of such an order were already apparent in the army, where wealth rather than merit attracted consideration and ensured promotion. Sumptuous apparel and courtly connections, rather than competence and service, determined the rank accorded to officers.[67] In rejecting a plutocratic social order that gave precedence to wealthy *anoblis* over noble merit, d'Arcq came close to rejecting a conception of nobility based on title in favor of one based on service. In an earlier work, he had written that "real merit alone creates real distinctions. He who occupies himself with the duties of society and the interests of the *patrie* is a true *grand* seigneur."[68] In *La noblesse militaire* he argued that "The gentleman is a citizen before being a noble . . . and the only privilege to which his nobility entitles him is the right to choose among the important services that the state can and must expect from him. The moment he stops thinking in this way, he ceases to be noble."[69]

D'Arcq was here espousing a view common among military nobles. As a number of scholars have shown, nobles of modest means used a rhetoric of merit to deplore the fact that courtiers and the wealthy sons of the ennobled

---

[63] D'Arcq, *Noblesse militaire*, iii., 6, 45.
[64] Coyer, *Noblesse commerçante*, 7–8, 112–13, 168.
[65] Ibid., 14–15.
[66] Ibid., 62–63, 80.
[67] D'Arcq, *Noblesse militaire*, 89.
[68] D'Arcq, *Mes loisirs*, 154.
[69] D'Arcq, *Noblesse militaire*, 188.

were being promoted faster than deserving provincial nobles with family tra-
ditions of military service. The army high command was acutely aware of this
problem and pursued reforms from the early 1750s to restrain the effects of
money on promotion and to create a more Spartan army after the model of
Frederick the Great's Prussia.[70] Royal military schools were established to bring
the sons of poor noble families into the service (Napoleon Bonaparte was a beneficiary), and the sale of commissions was restricted. The reform movement
reached its apogee under the comte de Saint-Germain, appointed War Minister
in 1775. He believed that "all the poor nobility, destined by birth to serve and
form the backbone of the army, is absolutely excluded," replaced by "the sons
of big merchants . . . of *fermiers généraux*."[71] Within the military there was
some consensus that the importance of money, and the spread of a venal spirit,
was weakening the nation, not strengthening it. Military officers called for an
army and, by extension, a country, in which duty replaced pecuniary interest,
and virtue rather than wealth was the source of advancement and authority.
D'Arcq, who led a company of cavalry in the War of Austrian Succession, and
received the Croix de Saint-Louis after Fontenoy, echoed this point of view.[72]

It is tempting to link the very different perspectives on social order embodied in *La noblesse militaire* and *La noblesse commerçante* to the biographies of
the texts' authors. Coyer was born in provincial obscurity, one of thirteen children of a draper. His origins, perhaps, influenced his positive outlook on trade.
But Coyer would also have understood the military perspective. After working
for a time as tutor to the son of the *dévot* duc de Bouillon, he was appointed
chaplain to a cavalry corps, presumably with the patronage of his employer,
and served in the Low Countries during the War of the Austrian Succession.[73]
In contrast to the humble Coyer, d'Arcq had royal blood in his veins; he was
the bastard son of Louis XIV's bastard, the comte de Toulouse. Yet, other than
his military experience, what probably shaped his outlook most was the struggle to make ends meet. D'Arcq was far from poor; his father left him a landed
estate and 12,000 livres a year from *rentes*. But in the courtly circles on whose
fringes he was raised, these were trifling sums. D'Arcq's half brother, the duc de
Penthièvre, enjoyed an annual income in the millions. The chevalier absorbed
from his upbringing the casual attitude toward spending typical of the courtly
class; by 1775 he was in deep financial trouble and had to sign over his *rentes*
to his creditors. If he belonged to the court nobility by birth, and upbringing,
d'Arcq was excluded from it by a lack of money.[74]

Neither Coyer nor d'Arcq prevailed in the *noblesse commerçante* debate.

[70] Bien, "The Army in the French Enlightenment"; Blaufarb, *French Army,* 16–32.

[71] Blaufarb, *French Army,* 17.

[72] E. Forestié Neveu, *Notice biographique: Le comte de Sainte-Foy, chevalier d'Arcq, fils naturel du comte de Toulouse* (n.p., 1878).

[73] Adams, *Coyer and the Enlightenment,* 20–24.

[74] Forestié Neveu, *Notice biographique;* Jean Duma, *Les Bourbon-Penthièvre (1678–1793): Une nébuleuse aristocratique au XVIIIe siècle* (Paris, 1995), 199.

Both of their positions informed the patriot political economy that developed in the latter half of the 1750s. A key part of the debate's significance is that it put the question of the distribution of honor at the center of French political economy, a shift that would permit significant rethinking of representations of commerce in the 1760s and 1770s. D'Arcq's position in the debate influenced later writers in its emphasis on disinterested civic virtue as a crucial ingredient of national power and a critical rampart against despotism. But most subsequent commentators placed far more emphasis than he did on the imperative of boosting national wealth. In this respect, Coyer's arguments were unanswerable. The abbé's claim that an engagement in modern economic life was the key to revitalizing the nobility was also eagerly taken up by others, though his scheme of encouraging nobles to enter trade was not. Other writers—many of them noble—began to think of agriculture as the key to invigorating the fortunes of the nobility. The nobility, after all, was a landowning class and agriculture had irrefutable associations with simplicity, virtue, and good *moeurs*. The animation of agriculture would allow patriot political economists to square the circle: to stimulate prosperity while fostering civic virtue.

The marquis de Mirabeau and Noble Regeneration

The text that, more than any other, made fashionable the idea that the fortunes of the nation might be revived by stimulating agriculture was the marquis de Mirabeau's *L'ami des hommes*. Implicitly, the work also offered a program of renewal for the nobility. In terms of its impact on political economy, this was by far the most important work of the 1750s. For a short time in 1757, *L'ami des hommes* made its author the most celebrated writer in France. Mirabeau was fêted in Paris; it was rumored at Court that the dauphin wanted him appointed preceptor to his son; from Saint-Malo in Brittany, the marquis's brother reported that he was basking in the reflected glory of the "friend of mankind."[75] It was certainly not the literary merits of *L'ami des hommes* that won it such acclaim. The work is long and tedious, written in an eccentric, often tortuous, style. Grimm acknowledged as much when he criticized the book but praised Mirabeau's principles, which he described as "the only ones that a wise government ought to follow."[76] Mirabeau's success was due to his fusion of political economy and patriotism, and to the program for national, and noble, regeneration that he produced in the process. The marquis implicitly accepted the premise that wealth is the foundation of the power of states, but he was equally committed to the view that no state can long remain stable and powerful without civic commitment and the *moeurs* that sustain it. He argued that

[75] Humbert de Montlaur, *Mirabeau: Ami des hommes* (Paris, 1992), 183–4; Louis de Loménie, *Les Mirabeau: Nouvelles études sur la société française au XVIIIe siècle* (Paris, 1889), 2:169–70.
[76] Quoted in Loménie, *Les Mirabeau*, 2:140.

France had undermined both its prosperity and the bonds that tie citizens to the community by sacrificing agriculture to a luxury economy that was both ungrounded and morally corrupting. If France took steps to contain luxury and revivify agriculture, it would give an enormous stimulus to national wealth along with *moeurs* and patriotism.

The political economic text that inspired Mirabeau to produce this hybrid perspective was Richard Cantillon's *Essai sur la nature du commerce en général*. The first draft of *L'ami des hommes* is a paragraph by paragraph commentary on Cantillon's work.[77] Mirabeau read the essay as a vindication of the classical political insight that all states degenerate due to luxury and are eventually surpassed by poorer neighbors. This was not actually Cantillon's own view; he seems generally to have used the word *luxury* in a narrow way to refer to the consumption of expensive commodities, regarding such consumption as disadvantageous only to the extent that luxury purchases were imports. But Mirabeau read Cantillon's argument about the long-term effects of an increase in the money supply as a claim about the way luxury will eventually weaken a state's ability to compete internationally. Cantillon argued that a sustained favorable balance of trade, by bringing money into a country, increases prosperity and enhances the capacity of a state to wage war. In the long run, however, an increasing money supply will cause domestic prices and wages to rise excessively, undercutting the competitiveness of the affected country in the international marketplace. This is hardly an argument about the degenerative effects of luxury on state power. However, Cantillon confused matters by claiming that the Roman Empire was destroyed as a consequence of the mechanism he analyzed: "the Roman Empire fell into decline through the loss of its money before losing any of its estates. Behold what Luxury brought about and what it always will bring about in similar circumstances."[78] It is hardly surprising that Mirabeau drew a civic humanist inference from such statements.

But Mirabeau's is a very different kind of work than Cantillon's. It can be regarded as an effort by a moralist in the mold of Fénelon to appropriate elements of political economy to bolster a thesis about the destructive effects of luxury. In *L'ami des hommes,* and his earlier *Mémoire concernant l'utilité des états provinciaux* (1750), Mirabeau echoed some of Fénelon's central themes. He described as a "vast project of universal tyranny" the desire to establish a mercantile empire at the expense of one's neighbors, arguing that justice, not the "cruel and ruinous sophisms of exclusive interest," ought to be the sole rule of foreign policy. He deeply admired the archbishop, and praised *Telemachus* lavishly, claiming that the book contained more "wise policy" in a few pages than did his own entire treatise. Mirabeau argued that patriotic virtue was necessary to sustain the health of a monarchy; indeed, besides Providence, patriotism was the "sole support" of monarchy. He held that agriculture was the true

[77] Weulersse, ed., *Manuscrits économiques*, 3.
[78] Richard Cantillon, *Essai sur la nature du commerce en général,* trans. Henry Higgs (London, 1964), 199.

foundation of national wealth and that luxury undermined the power of states. "I am going to finally prove," Mirabeau stated, "that luxury is . . . the ruin of a large state even more so than of a small one."[79]

Mirabeau's conception of luxury confounded economic meanings of the term with older political and moral senses. He condemned luxury as a type of consumption that disturbed the proper hierarchical arrangement of society, claiming that "the lowest classes who make pecuniary fortunes," by the "apotheosis of gold" overthrow this order. Like d'Arcq, Mirabeau argued that patriotic virtue could only be fostered in a revivified society of orders with the nobility dominating its upper reaches. He wrote that the "prejudices that constitute honor make up a real part of the treasure of the state," and that it was therefore "important to preserve . . . to the greatest extent possible that portion of the people among whom this money has the greatest currency, that is, the nobility." Mirabeau rejected a social order in which status was determined by wealth. When honor, prestige, and esteem are lavished on riches, rather than on birth or merit, he argued, the passion for honor draws men to pursue profit rather than to serve the public. Mirabeau also used luxury in the classical sense to mean a corrupting venality inimical to patriotism and public virtue, commenting that France would go the same way as ancient Rome if it continued to allow luxury to flourish. Finally, for the marquis, luxury was an economic order in which there was excessive attention to the acquisition of mobile wealth, and not enough attention to agriculture, which he regarded as the true basis of national prosperity. The core of Mirabeau's political economy was that agriculture had been sacrificed to the pursuit of a mercantile wealth that was at once illusory and destructive in its social, economic, and moral effects. *L'ami des hommes* called for the renewal of peasant cultivation and for noble proprietors to return to their estates and become active stewards of their lands.[80]

In engaging political economy, I suggest, it was Mirabeau's intention to forge a new place in national life for the provincial nobility, a social group to which he was tied by upbringing and affinity. At the time he published *L'ami des hommes,* Mirabeau had been preoccupied for at least a decade by problems of the nobility's situation in the French polity. He grappled with the issue in his first written work, a political testament he produced in 1747, where he called for the regeneration of seigneurial power via-à-vis the monarchy.[81] He pursued the theme further in his *Mémoire concernant l'utilité des états provinciaux,* demanding the establishment of provincial estates in provinces without representative assemblies.[82] A political economy, like Mirabeau's, that figured agri-

[79] Mirabeau, *Ami des hommes,* 3:201, 2:94, 2:78, 1:iv.

[80] Ibid., 3:180, 2:84, 1:32; 2:102–6, 132.

[81] Gino Longhitano, "La monarchie française entre société d'ordres et marché: Mirabeau, Quesnay et le *Traité de la monarchie (1757–1759)," Marquis de Mirabeau & François Quesnay, Traité de la monarchie (1757–1759)* (Paris, 1999), x.

[82] Victor de Riqueti, marquis de Mirabeau, *Mémoire concernant l'utilité des états provinciaux* (Rome, 1750). The marquis dedicated the *Mémoire* to the duc de Bourgogne and claimed to have derived its central ideas from Fénelon.

culture as the foundation of the national welfare, and luxury as its antithesis, appealed to both the interests and the sentiments of many provincial nobles. Mirabeau proposed to establish an economic order that was advantageous to middling nobles rather than inimical to their needs. He offered the nobility a modern idiom in which to condemn an old enemy: luxury. He aligned their interests with the national interest and made of their values a patriotic ethic.

The claim that agriculture is the foundation of national prosperity and power interpellated different nobles in different ways, the provincial nobility more than the nobility of Paris and Versailles and, among the former, those in better circumstances rather than the truly poor. I have already noted that the attack on luxury as the wellspring of national decline, so prominent in Mirabeau's thinking, resonated with the values and prejudices of provincial nobles. An economic philosophy that identified the success of agriculture with the well-being of the state tended to align their chief economic interests with the interest of the nation. Most provincial French nobles in the latter half of the eighteenth century derived their principal income from land and managed their estates directly. Many still lived on the land; over half the nobility still lived outside cities at the end of the eighteenth century, and the figure was much higher in some provinces.[83] Others resided in provincial cities adjacent to their estates. In the diocese of Toulouse at mid-century, nobles owned 44 percent of the land, with longer established families holding an average of 424 acres. The representative noble in this district, according to Robert Forster, was a country gentleman who "managed his estate directly and personally."[84] In Upper Normandy, nobles were also closely involved in farming and estate management.[85] In Bordeaux, agriculture, especially viticulture, remained the most important source of wealth for the noble magistrates of the parlement, and their account books show them to have been careful estate managers.[86] Landed gentlemen of this sort could appreciate Mirabeau's *L'ami des hommes,* as did the head of the Cadenet de Charleval family, magistrates in the Parlement of Aix, who recommended it as an excellent work in his family's *livre de raison.*[87]

The rich Paris noble was also a proprietor, but his relationship to land was neither as intimate nor as obligatory as that of the country gentleman. The great noble could visit his estates only occasionally and for short periods. Scattered in distant provinces, it was difficult to exercise a close supervision over them. While the provincial noble knew and prided himself on every acre, the courtier necessarily had a more distant relationship with his property.[88] Magistrates of

---

[83] Mathieu Marraud, *La noblesse de Paris au XVIIIe siècle* (Paris, 2000), 25.

[84] Forster, *Nobility of Toulouse,* 36–38.

[85] Dewald, *Pont-St-Pierre,* 99–101.

[86] William Doyle, *The Parlement of Bordeaux and the End of the Old Regime, 1771–1790* (New York, 1974), 62, 87–97.

[87] François Bluche, *La noblesse française au XVIIIe siècle* (Paris, 1995) [1973], 188.

[88] Marraud, *Noblesse de Paris,* 295–98, 303; Robert Forster, *The House of Saulx-Tavanes: Versailles and Burgundy, 1700–1830* (Baltimore, 1971), 205.

the Paris Parlement tended to own land in the Île-de-France and, when they finished business in September, traveled to their estates to oversee the harvest. But land represented a relatively small proportion of their total assets; their holdings in urban real estate were more significant, and they often held half or more of their total capital in *rentes*.[89] The *grand seigneur*, also, derived a much smaller proportion of his income from agriculture than did the nobility of the provinces. Court nobles were involved in the same kinds of large-scale, commercial and industrial enterprises as financiers. Members of the aristocracy, among them the duc de Montmorency, the vicomte de Ségur, the comte de Jaucourt, and the marquis de la Ferté-Imbault, figured prominently among the shareholders of the Saint-Gobain works. The duc de Choiseul and the duc de Penthièvre invested in the royal steel manufactory at Amboise, one of the largest industrial operations in France. The comtesse de Sabran, the comtesse de Boisgelin, and the duc de Nivernais had investments of 50,000, 96,000, and 200,000 livres, respectively, in a company manufacturing woolen cloth. The ducs de Liancourt, de Béthune-Charost, and de Bouillon set up manufacturing operations on their estates, as did the marquis de Caulaincourt, and the marquis de Sinéty. The chief shareholder in the Anzin mines, the largest in France, was the prince de Croy; from it he derived an income of fifty thousand livres a year. Other notable mining magnates were the duc de Charost, the prince de Conti, and the duc de Castries. Castries' chief rival for control of the Grand Combe mining concession in Languedoc, the nonnoble Pierre-François Tubeuf, was backed by the marquis and marquise de Chaulieu, who invested a quarter of a million livres in his company.[90]

Certain court noble families played an important role in ocean-going commerce. The Maurepas and Bourmont clans invested in the slave trade as sleeping partners of the Montaudouin, the richest of the Nantes slavers.[91] The Magon of Saint-Malo took on silent partners, recruited not just among other merchants but from the financiers and the nobility of Paris.[92] Indeed, at Saint-Malo, most vessels, even the smaller ones, were held by companies of shareholders, many of them nobles. In 1764, there were twenty-seven shareholders in the *Duchesse-de-Choiseul*, a boat of only thirty tons destined for the Newfoundland fisheries, and most of these were resident in Versailles or Paris.[93] The Jacobite nobility, linked by marriage to court grandees, were prominent share-

[89] Swann, *Politics and the Parlement of Paris*, 22; Marraud, *Noblesse de Paris*, 309, 316.

[90] Chaussinand-Nogaret, *French Nobility*, 102–3; Pris, *Grande entreprise française*, 1:146–48; Marraud, *Noblesse de Paris*, 313–5; Gwynne Lewis, *The Advent of Modern Capitalism in France, 1770–1840: The Contribution of Pierre-François Tubeuf* (Oxford, 1993), 51. See also Charles A. Foster, "Honoring Commerce and Industry in 18th-Century France: A Case Study of Changes in Traditional Social Functions," Ph.D. diss., Harvard University, 1950.

[91] Pierre Goubert, *The Ancien Régime: French Society, 1600–1750*, trans. Steve Cox (New York, 1973), 191.

[92] See, "Ship-Owners of Saint Malo."

[93] Richard, *Noblesse d'affaires*, 237.

holders in the Indies Company. The Guyana Company, charged to colonize and provision Cayenne in the early 1760s, found investors in the duc de Duras, the comte de Maillebois, the marquis de Saisseval, de Montgeroult, de Champcenetz, and de Choiseul-Meuse. A number of Paris nobles owned sugar and coffee plantations in Saint-Domingue, among them the Beauharnais, Céreste-Brancas, Choiseul-Meuse, Choiseul-Praslin, Gouy d'Arsy, Pardailhan, and Vaudreuil. Colonial commerce also engaged the interests of some parlementary families in both Paris and Bordeaux, though in general the magistracy steered clear of investments in trade or manufacturing. Commercial covetousness, as Mathieu Marraud observes, was regarded as antithetical to judicial ethics. The ennobled sons of financiers also tended to steer clear of trade, distancing themselves from their families' tawdry past. It was the ancient nobility that could trade with least unease; its honor was unassailable.[94]

Courtiers were further insulated from the performance of the agricultural economy by the proceeds of court office and pensions, which made up a significant proportion of total income for many grandees. Court offices often carried enormous stipends: the Grand Master of France drew almost 140,000 livres; the High Steward, nearly 135,000; the chief lady in waiting to the queen, 78,000. Provincial governorships also supplemented the income of courtiers. The incumbent in Guyenne was paid 100,000 livres, Burgundy, 150,000, and Languedoc, 160,000. Finally, there were pensions which, in the late 1770s, totaled 8.6 million livres a year shared out between 569 dignitaries of the court.[95] Between 1755 and 1775, the duc de Coigny had an average income of 90,000 livres per year. His revenues expanded to an average of 250,000 livres from 1776 to 1787 after he acquired the office of *premier écuyer*. During these years, 60–80 percent of his income came from offices and pensions. Coigny was not unusual in this respect. Offices brought the duc de Choiseul 700,000 livres a year, more than three quarters of his income. The comte d'Artois enjoyed 540,000 livres in income from his enormous estates, but received nearly three million more from his brother, Louis XVI.[96]

One must be careful not to overstate the contrast between Paris and the provinces; the distinction between capital and country noble was muddied by numerous exceptions. Mirabeau himself demonstrates how difficult it can be to separate the rich provincial nobility from the nobility of the court. As a more or less permanent resident of Paris, or its environs, and with estates in Provence, the Limousin, and the Gâtinais, the marquis was hardly a simple provincial gentleman. Moreover, he was something of a court capitalist, operating a mining concession at Glanges in the Limousin between 1763 and 1776 with three dukes, five marquises, and a financier named Isaac Panchaud as sleeping part-

[94] Marraud, *Noblesse de Paris,* 312–13, 321–25; Doyle, *Parlement of Bordeaux,* 102–4.
[95] Chaussinand-Nogaret, *French Nobility,* 52–61.
[96] Coquery, *Hôtel aristocratique,* 152–53.

ners.[97] Court nobles, moreover, could be dedicated agriculturalists. Among the most notable agricultural improvers of the eighteenth century were the maréchal de Noailles, the duc de Béthune-Charost, and the duc de La Rochefoucauld. Nobles of the port cities also blurred the line between Paris and the provinces with their often substantial investments in colonial commerce and international trade. Finally, virtually no noble families derived all their income from land. Most provincial noble families held at least some assets in *rentes*; widows and unmarried daughters were often pensioned off in this fashion.[98] Many provincial nobles drew royal pensions, though the vast majority were for paltry sums and derived from military service. Exceptions notwithstanding, a loose dividing line can be drawn between a provincial nobility heavily dependent on agriculture for its economic well-being, and a Paris nobility with a very much weaker relationship to land.

The appeal of agriculture-centered political economies to the middling nobility was not just a question of interest, however, but of sentiment. Some of those nobles most enthusiastic about agriculture were members of families that had recently lost a direct connection to the land. More apt to idealize country life than their contemporaries who still managed estates, these individuals could manifest a powerful nostalgic and sentimental enthusiasm for country life. Such was Jean-Baptiste Cotton des Houssayes, a cleric from a poor noble family who helped found the Rouen Agricultural Society, and who worked to establish a journal in Normandy devoted to economic matters. Cotton was forced off the land and into a clerical career by the straightened circumstances of his family. He celebrated agriculture and dreamed of returning to the countryside, but his pleasure in contemplating rural life was sentimental; as Jonathan Dewald observes, it was "that of an urban individualist." He embraced the language of patriotic agricultural regeneration; for him, the farming estate was "the last where frivolity and luxury are concerned." He demanded that the administration forbid peasants from leaving the land for the cities, and he embraced the language of patriotism, peppering his writings with references to the *patrie*, citizenship, and duty. Cotton was part of a growing class of nobles who left the land during the two or three generations before the Revolution. In some rural parishes in Upper Normandy there were 60 percent fewer noble families in 1788 than at the beginning of the century.[99]

Mirabeau was not the only writer who saw in political economy a means to bolster the position of the nobility. Quesnay was critical of Coyer's scheme to involve nobles in trade, recommending commercial agriculture for them in-

[97] Taylor, "Types of Capitalism in Eighteenth-Century France," 495; Lüthy, *Banque protestante*, 2:425.

[98] In the provincial city of Abbeville, according to François-Joseph Ruggiu, there was only one noble who held a share in the Indies Company, and he had married into a Paris robe family and was mainly resident in the capital. Ruggiu, *Les élites et les villes moyennes*, 192.

[99] Dewald, *Pont-St-Pierre*, 113–14, 119–24; Marraud, *Noblesse de Paris*, 27.

stead. "This occupation is more appropriate to their condition," Quesnay argued, "than the station of retail trader in the towns."[100] Rather than pushing them into trade, Ange Goudar recommended, the government should encourage nobles to "give themselves over to agriculture."[101] Henri Goyon de la Plombanie, a provincial noble and military officer, also rejected Coyer's proposal, fearing that if nobles entered commerce, the "spirit of interest" would "smother that of bravery," ruining the "austere virtue of our ancient nobility." Instead, Goyon argued, the nation must find a way to increase the value of noble estates, to use commerce to increase the landed revenues of the nobility. Like many of his contemporaries, Goyon believed that the problem lay with low prices for cereals and a shortage of specie which impeded economic activity. He proposed the establishment of a "Company of Agriculture" to regulate and coordinate the grain trade, and to stimulate agricultural investment by issuing a paper money backed by the value of land.[102] The potential of political economy as a program of renewal for the nobility was obvious by the early 1760s, and nobles gravitated in large numbers to the new literary mode. Of the identifiable authors of political economic tracts published between the 1750s and the 1780s, as many as 40 percent were noble; nobles, by contrast, made up only 15 percent of authors in belles-lettres.[103] Nobles also distinguished themselves as authors of works on agricultural improvement, and from the late 1750s this literature increasingly took on the ethos, and echoed the perspectives, of the developing political economy of noble and national regeneration.

Patriotism, Luxury, and the Call for Agricultural Regeneration

In the wake of Mirabeau's *L'ami des hommes,* the literature of agricultural improvement became increasingly imbued by a patriotic sensibility, by calls for the retrenchment of luxury, and by criticisms of the existing political economic order. The shift is perceptible between the editions of Duhamel du Monceau's *Traité de la culture des terres* published in the early 1750s and works by the same author at the end of the decade. The early works contain no references to patriotism, while the later writings are replete with references to the *patrie.* Because of its largely technical character, the literature of rural economy, or agronomy, is not usually regarded as relevant to the study of political economy. However, most of these texts were framed by simple political economic assumptions, usually stated explicitly in the preface or introductory pages. A central assumption of most of the authors who wrote on agricultural improvement

[100] Quesnay, "Grains," 491.

[101] Goudar, *Intérêts de la France,* 1:68.

[102] Henri Goyon de la Plombanie, *La France agricole et marchande* (Avignon, 1762), 53–61. See also Simone Gout, *Henri Goyon de la Plombanie, économiste périgourdin: Ses idées, sa place dans l'histoire des doctrines économiques* (Poitiers, 1933), 23–26.

[103] Perrot, *Histoire intellectuelle,* 78.

in the late 1750s and 1760s was that agriculture is the foundation of both prosperity and civic virtue and that luxury is agriculture's anti-principle. Exemplary
in this respect is Jean-Baptiste Dupuy Demportes, author of perhaps the most
widely read work of the 1760s advocating agricultural improvement, *Le gentilhomme cultivateur* (1761–63).

In language charged with references to patriotism and citizenship, Dupuy
Demportes calls for the regeneration of agriculture in order to bolster the power
of the state and the virtue of its population. "How can it be," he asks, "that the
example of Rome has had so little ascendancy over enlightened minds?" The
military power of Rome was based on the land: "Nobody is unaware that in
[the time of] its rustic but happy simplicity it owed the extent and the solidity
of its power only to agriculture." Roman soldiers were great because they were
farmers. But Rome was corrupted and eventually brought low by luxury, which
led in turn to the abandonment of agriculture. "Hardly had Rome gloried in its
conquests but it was corrupted by the riches of Nations" he remarks. "Soon it
moved away from its first principles, abandoned reality for appearance, was
softened by luxury, and saw its original splendor insensibly eclipsed."[104] In
fact, Dupuy Demportes claimed, Rome had exchanged a form of wealth that
was healthy and solid for a form that was corrupting and illusory. The richer
Rome believed itself to be, the poorer it was in fact. The same misstep, he argued, would corrupt any polity. "Is it not," he asked, "from this harmful error
that dates the fall of all Monarchies and of all the empires that luxury . . . has
overthrown?" Great military exploits could not be expected of a nation in
which farming had been systematically neglected and disdained—a pointed
comment in light of the military disasters of the ongoing war. One could not
hope to produce another Fabricius, another Cato, another Cincinnatus, Dupuy
Demportes argued, when husbandry was held in contempt. He placed the blame
for this state of affairs on Colbert, complaining that Colbert gave too much attention to "luxury arts" at the expense of agriculture, while Sully encouraged
cultivators.[105]

Dupuy Demportes's themes were central to the discourse on agriculture that
proliferated in the late 1750s and 1760s. The founder of the agronomic movement, Duhamel du Monceau, asserted in his *École d'agriculture* (1759) that
agriculture was the basis of the prosperity and strength of states, and he implied that in neglecting the land in favor of luxury manufactures France had
jeopardized its international standing. France would become the most powerful and opulent monarchy in the world, he argued, if it fostered agriculture, but
conversely, "to neglect [agriculture] is to allow a state to weaken."[106] Like

---

[104] Jean-Baptiste Dupuy Demportes, *Le gentilhomme cultivateur, ou Corps complet d'agriculture,
traduit de l'anglois de M. Hale* (Paris, 1761–64), 1:i–iv. Like Duhamel du Monceau's *Traité de la
culture des terres*, the *Gentilhomme cultivateur* was a loose adaptation of the works of an English
agronomist, Thomas Hale. On its dissemination, see Bourde, *Influence of England*, 65–66.

[105] Dupuy Demportes, *Gentilhomme cultivateur*, iii–v.

[106] Duhamel du Monceau, *École d'agriculture*, 41.

Dupuy-Demportes, Duhamel du Monceau blamed the neglect of agriculture on Colbertism, and many other authors followed suit. The editors of the *Journal oeconomique* remarked in 1765 that "M. Colbert, too taken with the brilliance of external commerce, sacrificed the solidity to the decoration of the edifice."[107] In his *Le patriote artésien,* the agronomist and retired cavalry lieutenant, Louis-Joseph Bellepierre de Neuve Église, criticized Colbert for destroying the prosperity of the farmer by favoring manufactures and commerce excessively. Through the policies of Louis XIV's minister, the nation had embraced a "fashionable commerce" that has depopulated the countryside, destroyed circulation, and "brought the Nation to the point of despising the most solid of its Arts."[108]

A leitmotif of the literature on agricultural improvement was that the neglect of cultivation rendered states vulnerable to "revolutions." One of the sources of this idea was Cantillon's crises of competitiveness, as we have seen in the case of Mirabeau. Agricultural improvers were also quick to point to the example of Spain which, they argued, abandoned farming to pursue gold and silver. Once the most powerful country in Europe, Spain had looted the Americas of their treasure but had failed to develop her own resources; the quest after an illusory wealth left the Spaniards bankrupt. This theme had been adumbrated by Mirabeau who claimed that "Gold will ruin us as it devastated Spain."[109] Cantillon traced the decline of Spain, but Mirabeau may also have been influenced by Forbonnais who observed in an article written for the *Encyclopédie* that Spain and Portugal had been convinced that as "the proprietors of the metals which are the measure of everything, they would be the mistresses of the world," but "they have learned since that that which is the measure of subsistence goods belongs necessarily to he who sells these goods."[110] While Forbonnais affirmed the value of commerce and manufacturing, many of the agronomists were more hesitant. Most claimed not that a nation could do without trade, but that agriculture needed to be sustained and developed as much or more than commerce and manufactures. According to J.-G. Hirzel, the author of *Le Socrate rustique* (1762), manufactures attracted into countries not only basic commodities but riches of every sort, causing the power of such lands to grow "to a prodigious degree." "However," he warned such power would "always be precarious and lacking in solidity so long as agriculture is neglected in a country." Even the best "constitutions . . . lose their force," he insisted, and

---

[107] *Journal oeconomique* (February 1765), 63.

[108] Louis-Joseph Bellepierre de Neuve-Église, *Le patriote artésien* (Paris, 1761), x.

[109] On Spain's economic reputation, see Paul Burton Cheney, "The History and Science of Commerce in the Century of Enlightenment: France 1713–1789," Ph.D. diss., Columbia University, 2002, 144–61.

[110] Mirabeau, *Ami des hommes,* 3:183. François Véron de Forbonnais, "Commerce," *Encyclopédie, ou Dictionnaire raisonné des sciences, des arts et des métiers, par une société de gens de lettres* (Paris, 1753), 3:693.

cannot keep a state from ruin when agriculture is neglected.[111] First published in Switzerland and translated from the original German by a lieutenant-colonel in the French army who dedicated the translation to the marquis de Mirabeau, *Le Socrate rustique* enjoyed at least four editions in French, and was still being excerpted in the press during the 1790s.[112]

If the stakes of regenerating agriculture were to avoid the fate of Rome, for most agricultural writers this was a question not simply of creating wealth but of maintaining virtue. Fortunately, they held, both wealth and virtue could be acquired through the cultivation of the soil. Eighteenth-century *agronomes* were thoroughly convinced of the connection between farming and good *moeurs*. The anonymous author of an *Essai sur l'administration des terres* (1759) claimed that the Romans preserved their virtue so long as they remained an agricultural people.[113] Duhamel du Monceau advised priests to try to inspire in their flocks a love of the farming life because "there is no surer means of keeping their parishioners on the path of virtue than to make them love an estate that keeps them quite naturally from vice."[114] In the first issue of the *Journal oeconomique,* the editor remarks that agriculture was dear to the Romans and Greeks while they still preserved their virtue. He observes that there is an air of "modesty," "gentleness," and "tranquility" attached to the cultivation of the soil that draws people away from vices.[115]

Writers attributed to peasants the capacity for feeling associated with the virtues of humanity, benevolence, and sympathy. As the agricultural improver Sarcey de Sutières observed, "the man who makes agriculture his essential occupation is virtuous and beneficent."[116] Contrasting the country environment to the town, the marquis de Mesmon remarked that "in the countryside man left to himself is wholly natural . . . . Far from great interests, he is exempt from great passions; his tranquil heart is opened to natural sentiments."[117] Sentimental drama vulgarized and diffused such representations widely.[118] Artists

---

[111] Jean-Gaspard Hirzel, *Le Socrate rustique, ou Description de la conduite économique et morale d'un paysan philosophe* (Zurich, 1762), 24–25. See also *Journal oeconomique* (November 1769), 482.

[112] Paul H. Johnstone, "The Rural Socrates," *Journal of the History of Ideas* 5, no. 2 (1944): 151–75.

[113] *Essai sur l'administration des terres,* vi–vii. Musset's *Bibliographie agronomique* attributes this work to Quesnay's son, Blaise-Guillaume, who was an enthusiastic and successful agronomic experimenter. The work has, on occasion, been wrongly attributed to François Quesnay himself. Hecht, "Vie de François Quesnay," 1:245.

[114] Bourde, *Agronomie et agronomes,* 995.

[115] *Journal oeconomique* 1 (1751).

[116] Bourde, *Agronomie et agronomes,* 995.

[117] Auguste Oncken, ed., *Oeuvres économiques et philosophiques de F. Quesnay* (Frankfurt, 1888), 75.

[118] See, for instance, Michel-Jean Sedaine, *Le roi et le fermier* (1762); Charles-Simon Favart, *Les moissonneurs* (1768).

such as Jean-Baptiste Greuze made careers for themselves depicting the simple virtues of country people in moving visual language, and reports in the press on events like the Rose Festival of Salency celebrated the simple virtues of country people.[119]

Representations that cast agriculture as the foundation of patriotic virtue also drew heavily on the Georgic literary tradition, which underlined the contrast between a wholesome and virtuous life on the land and the corrupting artificiality of the city. The Georgic was a plastic idiom that had served in seventeenth-century England as a basis for radical claims for the redistribution of wealth, but became in the eighteenth century an ethos principally associated with the improving country gentleman.[120] Enthusiasm for agricultural experimentation was often framed in terms of this paean to rural life. French agricultural improvers were fond of quoting passages from Cato, Cicero, Varro, Virgil, Columella, Palladius, Pliny, and Horace, which emphasized the simplicity and healthiness of life on the land.[121] Translations and imitations of the Georgic form proliferated. In 1760, *The Seasons,* by the English poet James Thompson, was translated with a foreword written by the marquis de Mirabeau.[122] Saint-Lambert's *Saisons* followed in 1768. Perhaps the most successful Georgic of the eighteenth century was the abbé Delille's new translation of Virgil's *Georgics,* which was published in 1770 and won the abbé entry to the Académie française in 1774.[123] Quotations from Delille's *Georgics* were common in agronomic texts of the latter part of the century.

Landowners who lived on their estates also emerged as icons of virtue in patriotic discourse. That a single great landholder could make an enormous difference to the area in which he held his estates was a common assumption of writers on agriculture. In his *Éloge de Sully* (1763), Antoine-Léonard Thomas praised Sully for encouraging proprietors to stay on their lands and damned Richelieu for attracting grandees to court. "A man who is often useless at Versailles could, on his lands, be the benefactor of the Nation," Thomas argued.[124] The gentleman who left his estates to serve his country on the battlefield, returning to a quiet rustic life at the conclusion of hostilities, was a particular favorite of agricultural improvers. The model for such a citizen was Cincinnatus, the Roman patrician who, as dictator, led Rome twice to military victory in the

---

[119] Sarah Maza, *Private Lives and Public Affairs: The Causes Célèbres of Prerevolutionary France* (Berkeley, 1993), 98; Amy S. Wyngaard, *From Savage to Citizen: The Invention of the Peasant in the French Enlightenment* (Newark, DE, 2004).

[120] See Anthony Low, *The Georgic Revolution* (Princeton, 1985), and Andrew McRae, *God Speed the Plough: The Representation of Agrarian England, 1500–1660* (Cambridge, 1996).

[121] Bourde, *Agronomie et agronomes,* 447.

[122] Loménie, *Les Mirabeau,* 2:168.

[123] Jacques Delille, *Les Géorgiques de Virgile, traduction nouvelle en vers françois avec des notes* (Paris, 1770).

[124] Antoine-Léonard Thomas, *Éloge de Maximilien de Béthune, duc de Sully, surintendant des finances, &c. principal ministre sous Henri IV. Discours qui a remporté le prix de l'Académie française en 1763* (Paris, 1763), 79.

Fig. 4. *Caius Furius Cressinus Accused of Sorcery* by Nicolas-Guy Brenet, 1777.
   This painting represents the story of the Roman farmer, Caius Furius Cressinus, whose success as a cultivator led to accusations that he practiced sorcery. The farmer defends himself by pointing to the instruments of his success: his family, his plow, and the oxen that pull it. The image is a visual distillation of the discourse linking agriculture with Roman civic virtue. The painting is a copy of one commissioned by the abbé Terray, controller general from 1769 to 1774. The original was exhibited to the public in 1775, perhaps to persuade viewers that its owner was not, as was widely believed, the enemy of patriotic schemes for agricultural regeneration. Musée des Augustins, Toulouse. Photo: STC Mairie de Toulouse.

fifth century. In a story familiar to every eighteenth-century schoolboy, when his country called upon him to lead it, Cincinnatus was found, covered in grime and sweat, working his own small farm. Figuratively and literally, agriculture was the grounding of his civic virtue. The marquis de Turbilly, one of the most active promoters of agronomy in the 1760s, and a cavalry colonel who served in the War of Austrian Succession, represented himself in such a light.[125] Later, representations of George Washington also owed much to this trope.

The association of virtue, good *moeurs,* and patriotism with agriculture allowed publicists to infer that a shift from the excessive focus on commerce and luxury manufactures back to the cultivation of the land would bring about a regeneration of manners and a renewal of public spirit. Perhaps the most striking example of this argument is the *Réflexions sur les avantages inestimables de l'agriculture,* probably written by Pierre-Philippe Roussel de la Tour, a robe noble with Jansenist leanings serving in the Parlement of Paris. The author advises his fellow citizens to leave their professions and give themselves over to work in the countryside, where they will find "repose of spirit," "innocence of heart," and "vigor of soul." Roussel insists that God did not authorize us to "heap up money, or to shroud ourselves beneath the decorations of a revolting luxury." He recommends that all classes of people corrupted by luxury be sent back to the land where they would "reestablish their degraded manners" and "no longer corrupt those of others." For Roussel de la Tour, such personal moral regeneration would underpin a regeneration of the state.[126]

It is unlikely that most of the partisans of agriculture thought in such literal terms. The point is that an agriculture-based strategy of economic development had emerged as a means to revivify the civic spirit of the nation. Agriculture was the ground on which wealth and virtue might be reconciled. The point was expressed, perhaps, most clearly by Pierre-Samuel Dupont de Nemours in the cahiers of the Third Estate for Nemours which he drafted in 1789. Dupont said of landowners, especially landowners of the Third Estate, that "This class of citizens has not a single concern which opposes those of their fellow citizens. The better they pursue their own affairs, the more food is created, and raw materials, goods and riches for all men, prosperity for the country and power for the state."[127] Through agriculture, Dupont implied, the pursuit of self-interest was reconciled with the good of society and the needs of the public.

By the time Dupont deployed this idea for political purposes in the early stages of the French Revolution, it had acquired enormous authority in French political culture. The patriots, agricultural improvers, and political economists who advanced this view during the Seven Years' War could hardly have achieved

---

[125] Louis-François-Henri de Menon, marquis de Turbilly, *Mémoire sur les défrichemens* (Paris, 1760), flyleaf.

[126] Pierre-Philippe Roussel de la Tour, *Réflexions sur les avantages inestimables de l'agriculture, relatives aux circonstances présentes* (n.p., n.d.), 3–5, 14.

[127] John Markoff, *The Abolition of Feudalism: Peasants, Lords, and Legislators in the French Revolution* (University Park, PA, 1996), 188.

such a status for their perspective unaided. They benefited from the assistance of an unlikely set of allies. In the 1760s, powerful interests at court, including Pompadour and some of her circle, began to adopt some of the projects of the political economic and agronomic publicists as their own. The royal administration also saw in patriot political economy a body of ideas and enthusiasms from which elements useful to the state might be fashioned. Under these propitious circumstances, political economic schemes focused on the animation of agriculture flourished in the 1760s. As we shall see in the following chapter, though, the effects of official patronage were also to disaggregate the multiple strands of patriot political economy into a series of widely divergent, competing programs of reform.

CHAPTER 3

Regenerating the *Patrie:* Agronomists, Tax Reformers, and Physiocrats

Of the able and wise Sully,
Nothing remains to us but the image;
Today this great personage
Will live again in Laverdy.

—Verse on a snuff box presented to controller general L'Averdy by
Mme de Pompadour (1764)

Let us only overthrow the tax farms, and we will have done enough for regeneration!

—marquis de Mirabeau, private correspondence (1760)

From the late 1750s, some of the most powerful figures at the French court began to sponsor initiatives for agricultural reform. Madame de Pompadour became a patron both of Physiocracy and agronomy: the agronomist Patullo was one of her protégés, as was the chief ministerial sponsor of agricultural improvement, and free trade in grain, Henri Bertin.[1] François Quesnay was her personal physician and lived in quarters adjoining hers at Versailles, though he also had ties with the opposing *dévot* faction at court.[2] We ought to see such patronage in the context of other initiatives undertaken by the marquise and her associates. Responding to critics like La Font de Saint Yenne, Pompadour's brother, the marquis de Marigny, as *Directeur général des bâtiments du roi,* made a serious effort to encourage the revival of history painting.[3] Financiers and courtiers took up "patriotic" art collecting, favoring native French artists over foreign old masters.[4] In what was surely an effort to mollify criticism from

---

[1] Steven L. Kaplan, *Bread, Politics, and Political Economy in the Reign of Louis XV* (The Hague, 1976), 131.

[2] Hecht, "Vie de François Quesnay," 256.

[3] Leith, *Idea of Art as Propaganda,* 73–77. Thomas Crow documents the failure of this initiative. See Crow, *Painters and Public Life,* 154ff.

[4] Colin B. Bailey, *Patriotic Taste: Collecting Modern Art in Pre-Revolutionary Paris* (New Haven, 2002).

middling nobles, the war contractor Pâris-Duverney patronized the *École royale militaire,* founded in 1751 to educate the sons of poor nobles for military careers.[5] There is no reason to reject outright the sincerity of such expressions of public spirit; financiers and courtiers were not necessarily the selfish bloodsuckers they were represented to be. But it would also be naïve not to read such initiatives as modes of image management in a cultural climate increasingly hostile to plutocracy.

A key figure behind reform in the 1760s was the duc de Choiseul, a protégé of Pompadour, and at one time or another minister of war, the navy, and foreign affairs. Choiseul was the dominant character in the royal administration during the 1760s. An unlikely reformer, the duke personally epitomized courtly luxury: he married a granddaughter of Antoine Crozat, one of the greatest of Louis XIV's financiers, was a notorious spendthrift, and used his many high offices to enrich himself.[6] While it is difficult to be certain what Choiseul stood for, there is little doubt that he was behind several initiatives to regenerate French power by promoting economic development. According to Louis Cullen, "In the 1760s the economic policies he stood for or backed . . . were remarkably coherent. They embraced (in a mix which did not uniformly please any interest) the restructuring of the East Indian traffic, the freeing of the grain trade, and the breaching of the exclusive regime in the colonies."[7] That Choiseul was publicly identified with economic reform is suggested by the fact that the young Pierre-Samuel Dupont, who approached the minister in 1764 in search of employment and favor, presented him with a memoir proposing to encourage agriculture, establish liberty of commerce, and suppress onerous taxes.[8]

Choiseul was hardly a partisan of the kind of agriculture-centered strategy of economic regeneration favored by many gentleman political economists. "In the present state of Europe it is colonies, trade and in consequence sea power, which must determine the balance of power upon the continent," he wrote, and as navy minister he pursued a vigorous and costly policy to rebuild France's shattered fleet.[9] However, Choiseul recognized luxury as a social and political problem. As war minister, he undertook an extensive reform of the army in the same anti-luxury spirit as the maréchal de Belle-Isle before him, decreasing the influence of wealth on advancement by relieving officers of some of the burdensome administrative costs they had previously had to shoulder.[10] He believed, or affected to believe, that the regeneration of patriotism would play a

---

[5] I am grateful to Richard Wittman for this observation.

[6] Guy Chaussinand-Nogaret, *Choiseul (1719–1785): Naissance de la gauche* (Paris, 1998); Coquery, *Hôtel aristocratique,* 153.

[7] L. M. Cullen, "History, Economic Crises, and Revolution: Understanding Eighteenth-Century France," *Economic History Review* 46, no. 4 (1993): 652.

[8] Gustave Schelle, *Du Pont de Nemours et l'école physiocratique* (Geneva, 1971) [1888], 9.

[9] Paul Kennedy, *The Rise and Fall of the Great Powers: Economic Change and Military Conflict from 1500 to 2000* (New York, 1989), 113.

[10] Blaufarb, *French Army,* 25–27.

role in reviving French national fortunes. In a letter to the king written in 1765, he remarked that "patriotic virtue degenerates every year in France . . . . One of the objects of my system of administration is to reestablish the interest, the love, of the *patrie* in French hearts; better that we should prefer the interest of our village, of our province, of our kingdom, to our own interest."[11] Though he intrigued against Henri Bertin, the administrative patron of the agricultural improvers, he had him replaced by Clément-Charles-François L'Averdy, who was also committed to reform. The administration established thirteen agricultural societies in Paris and the provinces in the early 1760s and provided tax incentives for the reclamation of land. In 1763, Bertin introduced domestic freedom of the grain trade, with an exception for the provisioning of Paris, and in July 1764, L'Averdy granted freedom to export grain. The royal administration did not look with equal favor on all schemes for economic reform. Those that required sweeping transformations were rejected, while more modest solutions were embraced enthusiastically. If agricultural production could be stimulated by such means, then further changes—changes that touched the heart of a system of aristocratic and plutocratic wealth and power—might be avoided.

The availability of such administrative patronage had complex effects on the movement for economic regeneration. It contributed to the crystallization of distinct schools of thought among reformers on the most appropriate means to regenerate agriculture. Because some schemes were more officially welcome than others, the agricultural improvers who most actively courted government patronage had to play down certain themes, especially hostility to financiers and fiscalism, while they were encouraged to emphasize others, notably the dissemination of improved farming techniques and proposals to increase the honorability of agricultural activity. The fruit of this devil's bargain was that these more moderate initiatives, along with the whole foundation of assumptions and beliefs on which they were predicated, received powerful validation and institutional support. While official patronage could contribute to the public standing of this body of ideas, however, it exposed the reformers who espoused such views to criticism from others for their overly cozy relationship with the government.

A second school of thought that was powerfully shaped by its interactions with the administration was Physiocracy. The Physiocrats offered a comprehensive critique of all the political economic arrangements sponsored by the monarchy, but as it became clear that the Crown would back the freeing of the grain trade and not other reforms, the *économistes* concentrated more of their energies on defending this one reform proposal. The theory of politics articulated by the Physiocrats may also have been intended to appeal to the absolute monarchy. This readiness to collaborate with the Crown, along with Physiocratic promotion of large-scale commercial agriculture, attracted sharp criti-

---

[11] Quoted in Chaussinand-Nogaret, *Choiseul*, 129.

cisms from other political economists in the latter half of the 1760s. These other reformers contested the view that peasant agriculture was less productive, and argued that the moral and political advantages of keeping more families on the land outweighed any economic benefits of concentration. Such critics increasingly claimed that Physiocracy was the dogma of *grands seigneurs* and the rich.

The hostility of the administration to any scheme for deep fiscal reform made such policy proposals more difficult and more dangerous to articulate. The two most incendiary critics of financiers and the fiscal system during the 1760s, the marquis de Mirabeau and Edmé-François Darigrand, both spent time in prison for their temerity. Nevertheless, critics of the tax system, who charged that it undermined agricultural production and systematically disadvantaged peasants and landholders, did get a sympathetic hearing from the parlements. The long-standing hostility between the sovereign courts and the financiers, together with the combative stance that some of the parlements took towards the Crown in the 1760s, made the courts a center for criticism of royal fiscal policy. Under the auspices of parlementary resistance to new taxation, a great public debate on the reform of the fiscal system blossomed in 1763. The large number of mainly clandestine pamphlets published in this context went far beyond the traditional criticisms of the parlements, however, and disseminated a barrage of proposals for the radical and fundamental remaking of the fiscal system.

Agronomy and the Royal Agricultural Societies

One of the primary means to regenerate agriculture that patriots championed in the 1760s was agronomy, or agricultural improvement. Agronomy offered a technical vision of how to resolve the problems of agriculture: by adopting crop rotation instead of leaving land fallow, through more intensive manuring, and by improving livestock breeds, farming could be made more productive. Agronomists also called for the enclosure of common land, and the restriction of communal use rights on private property, because, they argued, such traditional institutions limited innovation.[12] These were local, technical solutions that, in aggregate, improvers hoped would regenerate the agriculture of the kingdom as a whole. The one global remedy they championed was the use of prizes and honors to raise the prestige of farming. Claiming that the low status of agriculture was a critical obstacle to regeneration, they called on the government to honor cultivators—indeed, this demand was probably the most important legacy of agronomy to the wider climate of political economic ideas.

Agronomes did not eschew calls by Physiocrats and others for fiscal reform

---

[12] On the agronomic movement in eighteenth-century France, see Bourde, *Agronomie et agronomes;* idem, *Influence of England;* Jean Boulaine, *Histoire de l'agronomie en France* (Paris, 1992); Jean Boulaine and Jean-Paul Legros, *D'Olivier de Serres à René Dumont: Portraits d'agronomes* (Paris, 1998).

or freedom of the grain trade because they thought such political economic reform was unnecessary. The fiscal system was self-evidently a major obstacle to agricultural improvement, and almost everyone agreed in the early 1760s that a greater measure of liberty would stimulate the trade in agricultural commodities. The improvers focused on technical measures, because this seemed the most likely means of winning administrative support. They were right. In the early 1760s, the government established a network of societies devoted to agricultural improvement. Technical works on rural economy received privileges from the royal censors; many were dedicated to courtiers, officers of the crown, and prelates. Mme de Pompadour accepted the dedication of Patullo's *Essai sur l'amélioration des terres* in 1758. The comte d'Artois had an agronomic manual entitled *Le patriote artésien* dedicated to him in 1761. As controller general, Bertin promulgated an edict freeing land newly brought into cultivation from tax obligations for ten years. His successor L'Averdy extended these tax incentives to fifteen years for land reclaimed from marshes, and two years later he expanded the immunity to all types of newly cultivated land. As a consequence, between 1766 and 1769 about 360,000 acres of new land were brought into cultivation.[13] At L'Averdy's instigation, or at least with his support, the *Journal de l'agriculture* was established in 1765. Sponsorship of agronomic improvement was a popular, politically inexpensive means for the royal administration to promote the prosperity of agriculture, or at least to claim to be doing so. Unlike the other major proposals for agricultural regeneration in the 1760s, promoting technical innovations offended nobody, except perhaps peasants.

No figure in the royal administration was more closely associated with the *agronomes* and with the agronomic solution to the regeneration of agriculture than Bertin, controller general from November 1759 to December 1763. A protégé of Madame de Pompadour, Bertin is sometimes linked by association with the Physiocrats because he promulgated a key Physiocratic demand in 1763—the internal deregulation of the grain trade. But a relaxation of the regulations that policed the trade in cereals was the demand of a wider group of economic publicists than the *économistes*, as they were known to contemporaries. Herbert placed it at the center of the reform agenda with his *Essai sur la police générale des grains* (1753), and his call had been echoed by the other political economists around Vincent de Gournay. It was with members of the latter group, primarily, that Bertin surrounded himself when he came to power. Among the associates of Gournay who served him were Louis-Paul Abeille, Plumard de Dangeul, the abbé Morellet, and Turgot. He was also advised by the marquis de Turbilly, the author of a celebrated agronomic work, the *Mémoire sur les défrichemens* (1760), and it was Turbilly who was Bertin's chief collaborator in the foundation of a network of agricultural societies in the 1760s.[14]

[13] Douglas Dakin, *Turgot and the Ancien Régime in France* (New York, 1965) [1939], 81–83.
[14] Joël Félix, *Finances et politiques au siècle des lumières: Le ministère L'Averdy, 1763–1768* (Paris, 1999), 187–90; Kaplan, *Bread, Politics, and Political Economy*, 101–13, 131.

The societies were the primary institutional vehicle through which the administration hoped to encourage agriculture. That a network of such associations be established was a demand frequently mooted by members of Gournay's circle. In his *Remarques sur les avantages et les désavantages de la France et de la Grande Bretagne,* Dangeul pointed to the success of the Royal Dublin Society in promoting the improvement of the arts and agriculture in Ireland, and he called for the establishment of similar societies in France.[15] As Intendant of Commerce, Gournay used his contacts with Abeille, a Rennes lawyer, and Jean-Gabriel Montaudouin de la Touche, scion of a wealthy Nantes merchant house, to encourage the Estates of Brittany to set up a Society of Agriculture, Commerce, and the Arts in January 1757.[16] The new society was to have nine *bureaux* of six members meeting twice weekly in each of the dioceses of the province, along with a *bureau général,* which was to meet once a month in Rennes.[17] The press celebrated the foundation of the society, with the *Journal encyclopédique,* the *Journal des sçavans,* and the *Journal oeconomique* all lavishly praising the Breton Estates.[18] Duhamel du Monceau called for the establishment of such societies in every province, observing that patriotism had far more vitality in *pays* that administered themselves.[19] "Rustic academies" began to form in a few areas during the late 1750s where enthusiasts met to read the *Journal oeconomique* and to discuss agricultural improvement.[20] In 1759, the Intendant at Limoges assembled a group of local gentlemen to meet weekly to discuss agricultural affairs.[21] In Picardy, private gentlemen founded an agricultural club patronized by the duc de Chaulnes.[22]

In August 1760, Bertin ordered the intendants to establish agricultural societies in their jurisdictions. In 1761 societies were founded in Paris, Tours, Lyons, Riom, Orléans, Rouen, and Soissons, and the agricultural committee at Limoges was expanded into a full society. The following year, other societies came into existence at Bourges, Alençon, Auch, La Rochelle, Montauban, and Caen. In 1763, a society was established in the *généralité* of Hainaut and Cambrésis, and in 1765 the last official agricultural society was created in Aix-en-Provence (though it appears to have been moribund from the start).[23] Most agricultural

---

[15] Dangeul, *Remarques,* 170–73, 184ff.

[16] Schelle, *Vincent de Gournay,* 155–56.

[17] On the structure and history of the society, see *Établissement d'une société d'agriculture, de commerce, et des arts dans la province de Bretagne, délibérations des États* (Rennes, 1757); Louis de Villers, *Histoire de la société d'agriculture de commerce & des arts établie par les États de Bretagne (1757)* (Saint-Brieuc, 1898).

[18] *Journal encyclopédique* (15 June 1757); *Journal des sçavans* (August 1757), 519; *Journal oeconomique* (November 1757), 124.

[19] Duhamel du Monceau, *École d'agriculture,* 31–32.

[20] Bourde, *Agronomie et agronomes,* 365–66.

[21] Émile Justin, *Les sociétés royales d'agriculture au XVIIIe siècle (1757–1793)* (Saint-Lô, 1935), 47–48.

[22] Ibid., 74.

[23] Ibid., 75, 81, 92.

societies established *bureaux* in smaller neighboring towns. The Paris society had such branches in Meaux, Beauvais, and Sens, for instance, while the Lyons society set up subsidiaries at Montbrison, Saint-Étienne, Roanne, and Villefranche. Bertin formed an administrative committee in 1761, to meet weekly under his own chairmanship, to coordinate the societies and to gather information from them.[24]

The agricultural societies disseminated patriotic rhetoric about farming of the sort popularized in the late 1750s. At a session of the Paris agricultural society in 1761, Turbilly observed that states whose power is based on agriculture possess greater solidity and durability that polities constituted on other foundations.[25] An associate of the Limoges society, Pierre-Louis-Raimond de Massac, suggested that while the "bel-esprit" may assess power in terms of the "splendor of cities, the magnificence of buildings, the sumptuousness of furnishings," the "true statesman takes no other rule for his observations than the greater or lesser affluence of farmers." Massac noted a number of encumbrances burdening agriculture: the fact that much fertile land remained uncultivated; the flight of labor from the land; and the excessive preference given to manufactures. "If agriculture languishes," he asked, "is this not perhaps because we have been too busy up to now with multiplying the arts and trades, and manufactures of every kind, beyond the product of agriculture?" He also drew attention to the problem of the high interest rates the state paid its creditors. These, he argued, caused individuals to invest their money in *rentes* rather than land.[26]

The societies provided opportunities for an office-holding and landowning elite to dabble in agronomic experimentation and to converse with other amateurs of agricultural improvement. Works on agronomy and political economy circulated within the societies. Jullien, the Intendant at Alençon, made available to the agricultural society a set of works from his own library, including Turbilly's *Mémoire sur les défrichemens,* Patullo's *Essai sur l'amélioration des terres,* and Mirabeau's *L'ami des hommes.*[27] In 1768 the Limoges society read and discussed an abridged edition of Turbilly's *Mémoire.*[28] The members of the agricultural societies also published and distributed memoirs themselves.[29] They maintained a correspondence with other societies and with their associ-

[24] Bourde, *Agronomie et agronomes,* 1105.

[25] Louis-François-Henri de Menon, marquis de Turbilly, *Observations sur l'établissement des sociétés royales d'agriculture dans les différentes généralités du royaume, lues à l'assemblée de la Société royale d'agriculture de la généralité de Paris, au bureau de Paris, le 10 septembre 1761, par M. le marquis de Turbilly, membre de la Société* (Paris, 1761).

[26] Pierre-Louis-Raimond de Massac, "Discours sur l'établissement des sociétés royales d'agriculture, lû à l'assemblée du bureau de Brives le 10 mars 1762," in *Discours et mémoires relatifs à l'agriculture* (Paris, 1763).

[27] Louis Duval, *Un gentilhomme cultivateur au XVIIIe siècle: Samuel de Frotté de La Rimblière, membre de la Société royale d'agriculture d'Alençon, son livre de compte* (Alençon, 1908), 66.

[28] Dakin, *Turgot and the Ancien Régime,* 81.

[29] Justin, *Sociétés royales d'agriculture,* 125.

ates (the Lyons society, for instance, corresponded with sister organizations in Milan, Turin, Bath, and Manchester).[30] A small number of societies took more practical steps to effect agricultural improvements in their localities. The Paris society opened an agricultural school for abandoned children, and the Alençon society opened a similar establishment in Lower Normandy. One active member of the Alençon society, Coulombet, curé of the parish of Saint-Denis-sur-Sarthon, organized local notables into a charitable society to make loans of seed available to local farmers. The society distributed 89 bushels of barley in 1767, and 300 in 1775.[31] The Limoges society established an experimental farm, and Lyons and Riom sought to do the same.[32]

The most characteristic activity of the agricultural societies was the distribution of prizes to encourage agronomic improvement.[33] Turbilly was an enthusiastic advocate of the use of prizes and medals to animate the zeal of cultivators.[34] In 1754, he established two prizes for the peasants on his own estate, which he noted with pride, "have excited a singular emulation among the inhabitants and have done such good that I advise all *seigneurs,* whether ecclesiastical or lay, to offer them also on their lands." Anecdotal evidence suggests that Turbilly's advice did not fall on deaf ears. In 1765, Rigaud de l'Isle of Crest in the Dauphiné instituted an annual "fête champêtre" at which prizes were awarded to encourage local farmers. The following year, Father Coulombet of the Alençon society offered prizes to cultivators in his parish with the support and encouragement of the local seigneur, who was also a member of the agricultural society.[35] Another proprietor mobilized the energies of farmers in the village of Saint-Louis by establishing a festival of "vaillants et francs laboureurs."[36]

Offering prizes to cultivators would serve a double function: to stimulate agricultural improvement at an individual and communal level, and to address a structural obstacle to agricultural regeneration—the dishonor that burdened the farmer. It was axiomatic for the *agronomes* that one of the chief causes of the backwardness of French agriculture was that the *état* of the farmer was held in contempt. As one agronomist noted, "Hunger . . . persuaded mankind to cultivate the earth; honor . . . which often prevails even over hunger in strong and vigorous souls, seems today, by a cruel abuse to drive us away from that inno-

[30] Ibid., 130.

[31] Ibid., 163–64.

[32] Dakin, *Turgot and the Ancien Régime,* 80–81; Justin, *Sociétés royales d'agriculture,* 48–49.

[33] Bourde, *Agronomie et agronomes,* 1060–61; Justin, *Sociétés royales d'agriculture,* 130–33. Limoges offered prizes for memoirs in 1775, 1776, and 1780; Paris in 1764, 1766, 1786, 1787, 1788, 1789 and 1791; Soissons offered two in 1778; Lyons in 1768 and 1770; Orléans in 1769 and in 1774, and Laon in 1786.

[34] Louis-François-Henri de Menon, marquis de Turbilly, *Mémoire sur les défrichemens* (Paris, 1760), 230–36.

[35] Justin, *Sociétés royales d'agriculture,* 132–33; Duval, *Gentilhomme cultivateur,* 66.

[36] Weulersse, *Mouvement physiocratique,* 2:156.

cent occupation."[37] In the early 1760s, the parish priest of Saint-Xantin, and secretary of the Brive bureau of the Limoges society, drew attention to the fact that the countryside was deserted, while a multitude of useless people flocked to the cities.[38] The root of the problem, he suggested, was the scorn unjustly attached to those who worked the land. Children of peasants tried to escape from the dishonorable profession of their parents while artisans' children were happy to remain in the supposed distinction of their *métier*. If agriculture was honored and disdain visited upon craftsmen, he argued, people would return from the cities to the countryside.[39] The idea that honoring and distinguishing cultivators would regenerate agriculture was ubiquitous in agronomic literature. "If the Cross of St-Louis has produced heroes," the agronomist Richard suggested, "a medal would produce a new species of cultivators."[40] Pattullo recommended that prizes for agricultural improvement be used to raise the prestige of cultivation.[41] Nor was this sort of reasoning confined to French thinkers. The Italian jurist and political economist, Beccaria, noting "the extreme abjection" into which farming had fallen, suggested that the most industrious farmers of a village be awarded a distinctive sign that, by attracting admiration, "would excite a praiseworthy emulation."[42]

Some commentators expressed skepticism that cultivators had the sophistication to find honors alluring. An article published in the *Journal de commerce* in 1759 suggested that the farmer was not interested in this kind of reward: "Gentleness, humanity, equity in a superior, good food and good clothing; it is these that constitute the happiness of the cultivator . . . . His ambition does not raise itself to more exalted objects of ambition at all."[43] But other authors testified that even the humblest peasants could be actuated by the desire for distinction. A noble, and founding member of the Breton agricultural society, Pinczon du Sel des Mons, remarked that peasants would exert all their efforts to win a prize at a *fête*, even if it were only a ribbon.[44] Other writers, while not discounting the power of emulation, suggested that the basic needs of farmers would have to be met before they were susceptible to the lure of honor. "Before

---

[37] Vaudrey, *Nouveau mémoire sur l'agriculture, sur les distinctions qu'on peut accorder aux riches laboureurs; avec des moyens d'augmenter l'aisance & la population dans les campagnes* (Paris, 1767).

[38] Sélébran, "Mémoire pour l'établissement d'un prix dans chaque paroisse, en faveur des agriculteurs," in *Discours et mémoire relatifs à l'agriculture* (Paris, 1763).

[39] Ibid., 33–34.

[40] Bourde, *Agronomie et agronomes*, 1061.

[41] Henry Pattullo, *Essai sur l'amélioration des terres* (Paris, 1758), 188, 215, 269.

[42] Cesare Bonesana de Beccaria, *Principes d'économie politique appliqués à l'agriculture* (Paris, 1852), 35–37.

[43] "Réflexions sur le mérite du négociant & sur la considération qui lui est due," *Journal de commerce* 1 (1759): 53–54.

[44] Pinczon du Sel des Mons, *Considérations sur le commerce de Bretagne* (n.p., 1756), 35–36. On his involvement in the establishment of the agricultural society, see Justin, *Sociétés royales d'agriculture*, 37.

a peasant knows what honor is, he must know what comfort is," the encyclopedist Antoine-Léonard Thomas remarked.[45]

Some regarded the very existence of the agricultural societies as a means to honor cultivators. In a letter sent in 1761 to the Intendant of Picardy, the curé of Bayonvilliers cited the need to correct urban prejudices. It was necessary, he wrote, "that the lowest inhabitants of the towns cease regarding cultivators, country curés, and seigneurs with the most detestable disdain." He encouraged the intendant to found an agricultural society "to shelter us henceforth from this sort of contempt."[46] The Intendant of Auch, a member of the local agricultural society, wrote that he doubted such societies offered much practical benefit, but they should be maintained, nonetheless, because "they are at least a token in honor of the first and most useful of the arts."[47] The role envisioned for the societies in raising the prestige of agriculture may help to explain why they privileged social status over practical expertise in recruiting their members. To take a typical example, among the original members of the society of Tours were the Vicar-General of the archbishopric, the canons of the churches of Saint-Pierre, Saint-Martin, and Saint-Côme, the marquis de Beaumont-la-Ronce, the marquis d'Effiat, and M. Aubry, *président* of the *trésoriers de France* of Tours. In choosing their associates, the societies were even more prestige-conscious. The Rouen society, for instance, recruited Bertin and the maréchal duc de Luxembourg as associates, and the cardinal de Rochechouard patronized the Laon society.[48]

It was the king, the chief font of honor, whom agronomists were most eager to draft as a protector of agriculture. They never tired of reminding their readers of the honor lavished on cultivation by the emperor of China. According to the winning entrant to an essay competition organized by the Caen Academy in 1767, the Grand Mandarin of each province in China sent the name of the cleverest farmer of his district to the emperor and the emperor accorded the selected farmer the dignities of a mandarin.[49] The author of the essay could have borrowed this reference either from Montesquieu's *Spirit of the Laws,* where the custom of the Chinese emperor is praised, or from the article "Agriculture" in the *Encyclopédie,* where Diderot lauds the emperor's action.[50] The

---

[45] Antoine-Léonard Thomas, *Éloge de Maximilien de Béthune, duc de Sully, surintendant des finances, &c. principal ministre sous Henri IV. Discours qui a remporté le prix de l'Académie française en 1763* (Paris, 1763), 76–77. One of its correspondents admonished the Paris society that honors could not be mobilized when farmers lacked basic comforts. Girout, "Sur les prix proposés par la Chambre royale d'agriculture de la généralité de Paris," *Journal oeconomique* (February 1765), 60–62.

[46] Quoted in Justin, *Sociétés royales d'agriculture,* 74.

[47] Quoted in Bourde, *Influence of England,* 196.

[48] Justin, *Sociétés royales d'agriculture,* 120.

[49] *Éphémérides du citoyen, ou Bibliothèque raisonnée des sciences morales et politiques* 1 (1767): 166–67.

[50] Montesquieu, *Spirit of the Laws,* bk. 14, chap. 8; Denis Diderot, "Agriculture," in *Encyclopédie, ou Dictionnaire raisonné des sciences, des arts et des métiers* (Paris, 1751), 1:184. The original source seems to have been Jean-Baptiste du Halde's *Description de l'empire de la Chine* (Paris, 1735).

emperor of China became a stock figure of agronomic discourse. It was hardly surprising that the population of China was so prodigious, one writer pointed out, when the emperor "plows a field himself on a certain day of the year."[51] In 1768, the future Louis XVI, presumably in imitation of the Chinese emperor, lent a hand in plowing a field, attended by his Physiocratic governor, the duc de La Vauguyon and his two brothers (see figure 5). The future emperor of Austria, Joseph II, performed a similar ceremony the following year.[52]

In general, the effectiveness of the agricultural societies as lobbies for agricultural improvement was hobbled by their close association with the administration. Their position as official organs of the monarchy bound them to a stultifying prudence and conservatism. Turbilly warned his colleagues in the Paris society of their responsibility not to demand measures that the administration could not deliver.[53] He need hardly have worried. The members and associates of the society were closely linked to the court and the administration. Pompadour's brother, the marquis de Marigny, and her former patron, Pâris-Duverney, were associates of the society. Three groups were disproportionately represented among the other members and associates: there were seven members of the Academy of Sciences, eight officials from the controller general's office, and five financiers.

The limitations of the agricultural societies were evident almost from the beginning. In the early 1760s, Quesnay was enthusiastic about the establishment of such bodies. He thoroughly approved of the Société d'agriculture, du commerce, et des arts de Bretagne, arguing that the estates in every province ought to form similar establishments, and he noted with enthusiasm in 1762 that the Estates of Provence had begun to discuss the creation of an agricultural society at Aix-en-Provence. But Quesnay disdained those government sponsored bodies dominated by intendants which, he argued, were forbidden to discuss the ruinous practices of the administration. These functioned simply to mislead the public into thinking that the administration cared about agriculture.[54] From a Physiocratic perspective, the societies ought to function as pressure groups for political economic reform, or as centers for educating public opinion. As Intendant of Limoges, the Physiocratic sympathizer Turgot attended the agricultural society's meetings regularly, but one of the first things he did was to shut down its experimental farm on the grounds that it was a waste of money. Turgot used the society primarily as a means to disseminate the Physiocratic view that the deregulation of the grain trade was the most important means to effect rural regeneration. Through the Limoges society, he distributed copies of Phys-

[51] Beardé de l'Abbaye, *Dissertation qui a remporté le prix à la Société libre et économique de St. Pétersbourg, en l'année MDCCLXVIII* (Amsterdam, 1768), 16.

[52] Johnstone, "Rural Socrates," 164.

[53] Louis-François-Henri de Menon, marquis de Turbilly, *Réflexions sur les sociétés royales d'agriculture, des différentes généralités du royaume, lues à la première assemblée de la Société royale d'agriculture de la généralité de Paris, au bureau de Paris, le 12 mars 1761* (Paris, 1761).

[54] Weulersse, ed., *Manuscrits économiques*, 86–88.

MONSEIGNEUR LE DAUPHIN
Quel est Donc O Ceres ce nouveau Triptoleme ?
Quelles mains de ton art Essaient les Leçons ?
Dedié à Monseigneur

LABOURANT
D'un Pere bien faisant c'est le plus doux Emblème
L'Image de Louis l'heritier des Bourbons.
Le Dauphin L'an 1769.
Par son très humble et très respectueux Serviteur Isidor le Fevre.

Fig. 5. *My Lord the Dauphin Plowing* by François-Marie-Antoine Boizot, 1769.

This print depicts the future king Louis XVI plowing a field under the direction of his governor, the duc de La Vauguyon, a patron of the Physiocrats. The engraving is a representation of what was, apparently, a real incident reported in the *Mercure de France* in September 1769. The image plays on a favored motif of the literature of agricultural improvement. Improvers never tired of celebrating the actions of the emperor of China who, once a year, took a hand in plowing a field himself in order to honor agriculture. French agronomists were convinced that scorn for agriculture was a major obstacle to national prosperity, and they constantly sought ways to increase its prestige. One way to do so was to link the honor of great nobles, and the monarchy itself, with agricultural activities. Réunion des Musées Nationaux/Art Resource, NY.

iocratic tracts such as Pierre-Samuel Dupont's *De l'exportation et de l'importation des grains* (1764)—a disquisition originally read to the agricultural society of Soissons—and Guillaume-François Le Trosne's *La liberté du commerce des grains*.[55]

The agricultural societies do not seem to have exerted much impact on popular farming practices in France. Yet they cannot be regarded as complete failures. In terms of their influence on elite culture, the agricultural improvers may have been the single most successful reform lobby of the 1760s. A principal goal of the improvers was to raise the status and profile of agriculture—to change the public discourse about farming and to identify the work of the cultivator with the good of the *patrie*. In this they succeeded admirably. With the authority and prestige of the monarchy behind them for nearly a decade, those who saw in agriculture the font of national renewal enjoyed powerful public validation for their ideas. In raising the status of farmers, moreover, they inadvertently contributed to an egalitarian strand of thinking that would issue later in a critique of the nobility's claim to a monopoly on honor and office. The effect of official patronage, however, was also to divide the agronomic reformers from those with more radical, and politically thorny, visions of regeneration, notably those who called for a reform of the fiscal system.

Reforming the Fiscal System—the *Richesse de l'État* Debate

The most crushing legacy of the Seven Years' War was the immense public debt the conflict left in its wake. Of the 1325 million livres the administration spent to finance the war, nearly two-thirds was borrowed. At the end of the War of Austrian Succession, the long-term debt had reached 1,200 million livres, entailing annual debt service charges of 85 million. By 1764 the debt had risen to over 2,300 million livres, involving costs of 196 million a year, or more than 60 percent of the state's revenue.[56] To meet the enormous fiscal burden, Bertin decided, counter to public expectation, to continue some of the tax increases instituted over the course of the war. In 1756, the *vingtième*, a levy of 5 percent on income that fell mainly on land, was doubled, and in the 1760s it was tripled; in addition, the *capitation* had also been doubled. Bertin introduced an edict in April 1763 that, while allowing the third *vingtième* and the second *capitation* to expire at the end of the year, prolonged the first *vingtième* indefinitely and the second until 1770. His edict also called for a national land survey to be used to reapportion the *taille* and the *vingtième*.[57] The April tax edict unleashed an

---

[55] Dakin, *Turgot and the Ancien Régime*, 80–81. The agricultural society of Orléans also became a bastion of Physiocracy. The marquis de Mirabeau was an associate, and Le Trosne, Saint-Péravi, and Dupont de Nemours were members. Justin, *Sociétés royales d'agriculture*, 120.

[56] Riley, *Seven Years War*, 142–43, 182.

[57] Michael Kwass, *Privilege and the Politics of Taxation in Eighteenth-Century France: Liberté, Égalité, Fiscalité* (Cambridge, 2000), 161–93; David Hudson, "The Parlementary Crisis of 1763 in France and Its Consequences," *Canadian Journal of History* 7 (1972): 97–117.

explosion of protest in the parlements. According to Michael Kwass, in this period "the scale, language, and publicity of fiscal dispute reached heights unprecedented since the Fronde," the great aristocratic revolt of the mid seventeenth century.[58]

As Kwass has shown, taxation was a sensitive issue for the French elite in the eighteenth century. One of the foundations of the old regime's tacit partnership between the monarchy and elites was the exemption from direct taxes enjoyed by nobles and many privileged nonnobles. That partnership was threatened by universal taxation—taxes that fell on all wealth and that were specifically designed to tax the income of the privileged. The chief universal taxes were the *capitation,* a poll tax taking 1–1.5 percent of imposed revenues, and the *dixième* and *vingtième,* taxes that took 10 and 5 percent respectively. The *vingtième* was often doubled or even tripled in periods of stringency, with an additional 20 percent surcharge on the first *vingtième,* making it a truly onerous tax by eighteenth-century standards. The monarchy introduced universal taxation during the 1690s, but the *vingtième* did not become a regular part of peace-time taxation until 1749 when controller general Machault replaced the expiring *dixième* with a *vingtième* which was to form the basis for a sinking fund to pay off the war debt. This initiative aroused fierce opposition (indeed, it was the stimulus for Mirabeau's first public foray into the literary world with his *Mémoire concernant l'utilité des états provinciaux.*)[59]

Universal taxation did not affect all the privileged evenly but fell most heavily on middling elites. Provincial nobles, or nonnoble elites with most of their assets in land or venal office, felt the imposition more than either the urban robe nobility or *les grands,* who had the political influence to shelter their wealth from the full brunt of taxation. According to William Doyle, the magistrates of the Bordeaux Parlement probably never paid more than 5 percent of their income, though tax rates ranged between 11 and 16 percent.[60] The situation of *grands seigneurs* was even happier. In 1788, the duc de Trémoille paid only 7000 livres in tax on a total income of 280,000 livres (192,000 of it revenue from land). The duc d'Orléans paid hundreds of thousands of livres less than he should have.[61] A more complicated dynamic operated at local level. François-Joseph Ruggiu notes that the intendant at Alençon tended to give tax breaks to impoverished nobles. Very wealthy nobles also paid a disproportionately small share of their income, but nobles of middling fortune, those with incomes between 3,000 and 10,000 livres, tended to be assessed at the full rate. Presumably, the wealthiest nobles had the influence to lower their assessments, while the poorest could appeal to the charity of the administration: middling nobles

[58] Kwass, *Privilege and the Politics of Taxation,* 161.
[59] Marion, *Histoire financière,* 1:173–75.
[60] Doyle, *Parlement of Bordeaux,* 59–60.
[61] Kathryn Norberg, "The French Fiscal Crisis of 1788 and the Financial Origins of the Revolution of 1789," *Fiscal Crises, Liberty, and Representative Government 1450–1789,* ed. Philip T. Hoffman and Kathryn Norberg (Stanford, 1994).

could do neither.[62] More generally, those elites with the bulk of their assets in land rather than mobile wealth were at a marked disadvantage. It was notoriously difficult to assess the profits of trade, so the *vingtième* was imposed mainly on landed income. Universal taxation also fell with full force on the interest payments (*gages*) the monarchy made on the capital value of venal offices. Again, middling elites could feel that the political economic order systematically disadvantaged them while protecting a powerful and wealthy few.

Their resentment was greatly exacerbated by the knowledge that a significant proportion of the revenues collected in taxation went straight into the pockets of the financiers. The profits of finance were clouded in obscurity, and only the wealthiest financiers made truly substantial fortunes, but here perception was more important than reality.[63] Tax farming may ultimately have been a reasonably efficient mode of revenue collection; it obviated the need for a large public bureaucracy, and may have cost the French state only slightly more than the British system of collection, which did not depend on tax farmers. Moreover, the government depended on the financiers as a source of short-term loans, using the enormous personal credit generated by their reputation for great wealth to borrow indirectly from the public. But if the financial costs of the French system were modest, and its advantages to the state significant, its political cost was crushing. One of the principal reasons there was so much resistance to taxation in France was that the system of tax collection was perceived to be illegitimate, and one of the chief reasons for this lack of legitimacy was the perception that parasitic financiers were getting rich on the backs of their fellow subjects.

Elite resentment at the burdens of taxation gave rise to violent tax disputes during the Seven Years' War. In 1757 the government had to imprison four magistrates belonging to the Parlement of Besançon to force it to register a doubling of the *vingtième*.[64] Matters grew worse in 1760 when the administration added a third *vingtième*, while doubling the *capitation* on the privileged. The Parlement of Rouen refused to register the new taxes and published biting remonstrances attacking the financiers and drawing attention to the disparity between what the people paid in taxes and what the king actually received. They asserted that the people and the nobility were already ruined and exhausted by taxation. In reality, taxes in 1763 were no higher in real terms than they had been a

---

[62] Ruggiu, *Les élites et les villes moyennes*, 178–79.

[63] It is not possible to estimate with complete accuracy the income of tax farmers and other financial officers from their offices, but an order of magnitude can be established. In 1774 every Farmer General had a guaranteed income of 161,200 livres made up of salary (24,000 livres), expenses (4200 livres), 10 percent interest on the first million livres of the capital invested in his office, and 6 percent on the rest. But this was only a portion, and perhaps not the greatest portion, of his revenue. The tax farmer also profited from the difference between the amount raised in taxation and the lease price paid to the administration. Estimates as to the size of this profit vary wildly. One conservative source estimates the profits of the Lease David (1774–1780) at 156,000 livres per Farmer, per year. It seems likely then that each Farmer General earned a minimum of 300,000 livres per year from his office by the 1770s, and the true figure may have been a great deal higher. Matthews, *Royal General Farms*, 263–68.

[64] Hudson, "Parlementary Crisis."

decade earlier. So strong was resistance to taxation that the Crown resorted to borrowing to meet most of the costs of the war and moved to increase taxes only after nearly exhausting its credit.[65]

A milestone in the development of fiscal protest was the publication of the marquis de Mirabeau's *Théorie de l'impôt* in December of 1760. Mirabeau contested the right of the monarchy to raise taxes without consent, and he proposed that the existing tax system, including the tax farms, be abolished, to be replaced by a single land tax collected by provincial estates rather than financiers. The marquis borrowed the idea of a single land tax from François Quesnay with whom he had developed a close relationship since the publication of *L'ami des hommes*. Quesnay believed that agriculture alone actually produces wealth; the net product of land—the amount left over after costs of cultivation, and after a profit for the farmer had been paid—represented the whole economic surplus of society. To collect taxes on revenues other than the net product was merely to increase the costs of collection to the loss of the state and the benefit of financiers. Mirabeau, like Quesnay, assumed that the financial problems of the monarchy would be solved by the economic expansion that a healthy fiscal system would make possible. But as Kwass observes, for Mirabeau the underlying cause of the financial crisis was moral as much as technical; because the Crown governed through bureaucratic agents and left the nation out of the decision making process, tax payers attended to their own interests rather than to the general good.[66]

The *Théorie de l'impôt* was an immense success with the public, but Mirabeau's intemperate attacks on the financiers forced the government to act. The marquis was arrested within a week of the book's appearance and imprisoned at Vincennes. A week later he was released and banished to his estate at Bignon outside the capital for three months. Mirabeau must have had friends in high places, however, because the police lieutenant who came to arrest him is supposed to have told him, "Monsieur, my orders do not extend to rushing you. Tomorrow, if you don't have time today."[67] Mirabeau's arrest certainly helped to make the fortune of the *Théorie de l'impôt*, which ran to eighteen editions and made the marquis, once again, the man of the hour.[68]

The 1763 debate on the reform of the fiscal system was initiated in the parlements, but it moved into the public domain in May with the publication of Pierre-Philippe Roussel de la Tour's *Richesse de l'État*, a pamphlet that called for a radical reorganization of the fiscal system.[69] In an argument reminiscent of Vauban's *Dîme royale*, Roussel suggested that the existing tax system should

[65] Riley, *Seven Years War*, 144.

[66] Kwass, *Privilege and the Politics of Taxation*, 234–36.

[67] Jean-Claude Perrot, "Nouveautés: L'économie politique et ses livres," in *Le livre triomphant*, ed. Henri-Jean Martin and Roger Chartier (Paris, 1984), 241.

[68] Kwass, *Privilege and the Politics of Taxation*, 231.

[69] Pierre-Philippe Roussel de la Tour, *Richesse de l'État* (n.p., 1763). The edition referred to here is the copy reproduced in *Richesse de l'État, à laquelle on a ajouté les pièces qui ont paru pour et contre* (Amsterdam, 1764).

be scrapped in favor of a single progressive income tax falling on the richest two million subjects, divided by wealth into twenty classes of 100,000 individuals. He had a dual objective: to diminish the burden of taxes supposed to be crushing agriculture and to resolve the state's financial embarrassments. He argued that the tax system had to be simplified in order to reduce the costs of collection and to close the enormous gap between what the people paid and what the king received. The poorest peasants, not making up part of the two million richest householders, would pay nothing. Tax payers in the lowest bracket would pay only three livres per year, yet the system would realize 698 million livres annually for the state, more than doubling its current revenues. The *Richesse de l'État* sparked a debate that generated over forty pamphlets in the following two years.

Roussel de la Tour's argument derived much of its critical force from his assertion that the existing tax system was inimical to agriculture. The state had little option but to engage in reform as the tax burden on the land could not be increased; the *vingtièmes* were "the ruin of the countryside, of the nobility and of cultivators." The *conseiller* suggested that the increased revenues made available to the state should be invested in the improvement of agriculture, which he claimed would be "money placed with usury to the profit of the State." He proposed that the government distribute livestock to individuals and communities, observing (with admirable practicality) that the extra manure produced would improve husbandry more effectively than all the "systems and academies of agriculture." The claim that the stakes of tax reform were the well-being of agriculture set the terms for the following debate as both allies and critics of Roussel de la Tour assessed the effects of fiscal reform on cultivation. The author of *La balance égale* argued that it was impossible to raise taxes; the farmer already paid all he could and more than he should have to. The state must not force him to abandon agriculture and to "give himself up to slavery in the cities."[70] *Tous est dit,* an attack on the *Richesse de l'État,* suggested that far from lightening the burdens of the farmer, Roussel de la Tour would double the direct tax on land, crippling cultivators.[71] That the ultimate stakes of fiscal reform were agricultural regeneration was made starkly clear in the most violent pamphlet produced during the whole controversy, Edmé-François Darigrand's *L'anti-financier.* The frontispiece of the work, with its accompanying explication, depicts the monarch granting an edict to the nation creating a single tax and suppressing all existing taxes and *"traitants"* (financial contractors) (see figure 6). "France" accepts the edict on her knees, with "Abundance" holding her hand. Standing on the other side of the king is "Justice" forcing a financier to make restitution of his ill-gotten gains. The financier pours out his gold while a farmer gathers it, signifying, according to the explication, "that the gold

[70] Anon., *La balance égale, ou La juste imposition des droits du roi: Ouvrage digne d'un grand ministre, & d'un contrôleur citoyen* (n.p., n.d.), 5.

[71] Anon., "Tous est dit," in *Richesse de l'État, à laquelle on a ajouté les pièces.*

Fig. 6. Frontispiece to Edmé-François Darigrand, *L'anti-financier*, 1763.

Darigrand's frontispiece vividly summarizes the central claim of this violent attack on the existing tax system: that the renewal of agriculture will be the primary fruit of fiscal reform. As the text accompanying the image explains: "The King accords to France an edict ordaining the creation of a Single Tax, & the suppression of all existing levies along with the Financiers. France on her knees receives this benefit; she holds the hand of Abundance .... Justice on the steps of the pedestal, which bears the Statue of the King, forces the Financiers to make restitution. A Financier reluctantly pours out his gold; a farmer gathers it up, which signifies that the gold which fattened the *Traitans* will turn henceforth to the profit of Agriculture, & will relieve the Countryside." Courtesy of Kroch Library (Rare and Manuscript Collections), Cornell University, Ithaca.

which fattened the *Traitans* will turn henceforth to the profit of agriculture and will relieve the countryside."[72]

The administration, alarmed by the stir Roussel de la Tour's radical scheme was generating, commissioned a response from Jacob-Nicolas Moreau, a close associate of Bertin.[73] Moreau's *Doutes modestes sur la Richesse de l'État* brilliantly exploited fault lines dividing noble from nonnoble elites to attack the proposed fiscal reform. Moreau mobilized anxieties about the confounding of ranks by suggesting that Roussel de la Tour's scheme would undercut the social distinctiveness of the nobility.[74] The *Doutes modestes* is constructed as a dialogue between the author, a chevalier, and an abbé. The chevalier, modeled perhaps on the chevalier d'Arcq, complains that if the system of the *Richesse de l'État* were instituted he, a noble, would be placed in the same tax class as his shoemaker (who is as rich as he), dissolving the symbolic distinctions between social ranks. The chevalier goes on to argue that the destruction of the nobility would entail the removal of the chief rampart against despotism. Moreau understood his audience and adroitly mobilized elite concerns that wealth was replacing honor as the basis for status in order to undercut Roussel de la Tour's call for radical tax reform.

That many critics of the fiscal system were also concerned about the threat luxury posed to the coherence of the social order is indicated by the torrent of invective they produced condemning the luxury of financiers. Darigrand complained that the immense riches of the *traitants* attracted "the respect [due to] nobility," and "astounded the public and made it indignant through their splendor"; financiers had acquired "the most beautiful lands" and established their children in "the first offices of the kingdom."[75] One anonymous author accused financiers of a splendor that, by failing to "observe the order of ranks," had degenerated into luxury.[76] The anonymous author of *La balance égale* observed that the king must be shocked by the "pride" and "luxury" of the financiers; even princes of the blood were "effaced" by them.[77] The abbé Baudeau, complained that "the rapid and considerable fortunes of these money merchants augment luxury and the dissolution of *moeurs*." He described luxury as "the

[72] Edmé-François Darigrand, *L'anti-financier, ou Relevé de quelques-unes des malversations dont se rendent journellement coupable les fermiers-généraux, & les véxations qu'ils commettent dans les provinces: Servant de réfutation d'un écrit intitulé Lettre servant de réponse aux remonstrances du Parlement de Bordeaux* (Amsterdam, 1763).

[73] Jean Egret, *Louis XV et l'opposition parlementaire 1715–1774* (Paris, 1970), 95; Kaplan, *Bread, Politics, and Political Economy*, 131; Edmond Dziembowski, "Les débuts d'un publiciste au service de la monarchie: L'activité littéraire de Jacob-Nicolas Moreau pendant la guerre," *Revue d'histoire diplomatique* 4 (1995): 305–22.

[74] Jacob-Nicolas Moreau, "Doutes modestes sur la Richesse de l'État, ou lettre écrite à l'auteur de ce système, par un de ses confrères," in *Richesse de l'État, à laquelle on a ajouté les pièces*.

[75] Darigrand, *L'anti-financier*, 40.

[76] Anon., "Épître aux critiques des Richesses de l'État," in *Richesse de l'État, à laquelle on a ajouté les pièces*.

[77] Anon., *Balance égale*, 5.

son of a false and pernicious opulence introduced into the State by the unfortunate complications of the finances."[78]

Some authors rejected outright Moreau's claim that Roussel de la Tour's scheme would overturn the social order. Darigrand argued that the distinction of the nobility was not based on the fact that "their name is found on one form rather than another in the file boxes of the *bureau de finance*."[79] An author who identified himself only as B*** was not fooled by Moreau's move to represent himself as a friend of the nobility, suggesting, rather, that he was an ally of the tax farmers.[80] Echoing Voltaire's *Lettres philosophiques*, B*** noted that in England a peer of the realm was, for tax purposes, treated no differently than the most abject person—paying taxes on the same basis as another man did not make him one's equal. The author of *La patrie vengée* sought to circumvent the problem by rearranging the top tax classes.[81] The premier tax class would contain the greatest nobles alone, without requiring all to pay the same sum. The second class, composed of high magistrates, would follow the same pattern. The third class would contain all other magistrates, the remainder of the nobility, and other persons holding offices and dignities, all of whom would be required to pay 1000 livres a year. The author proposed to make an exception however, for nobles who lived in provincial cities or on their estates, whose revenues would not permit them to be taxed in the top classes. These should be placed in subsequent classes according to their capacity to pay. This caveat threw off the entire logic of tax classes based on honor and left the author open to precisely the objection he sought to sidestep.

In fact, Moreau's criticism of the *Richesse de l'État* exposed a crucial tension in the thinking of his adversaries and drove a wedge between provincial nobles and the nonnoble elites with whom they had much in common. The reformers wanted to shift some of the burden of taxation from the poor to the rich, and from agriculture to trade and finance. Their critique was predicated on an unstated vision of society that drew sharp dividing lines between the very rich and the less affluent, on the one hand, and between a moneyed interest and a country interest, on the other. This was, in many ways, a structurally accurate vision of French society, but it also underscored the division that separated provincial nobles from the rich nobility of Paris and Versailles. As such it ran counter to the commitment of many provincial nobles to preserve the unity of the Second Estate and to reinvigorate the distinction between nobles and nonnobles.

Moreau also pursued a divide and conquer policy in his second contribution

[78] Nicolas Baudeau, *Idées d'un citoyen sur l'administration des finances du roi* (Amsterdam, 1763), 11–12.

[79] Darigrand, *Anti-financier*, 76.

[80] Anon., "Mes rêveries sur les Doutes modestes," in *Richesse de l'État, à laquelle on a ajouté les pièces*.

[81] "La patrie vengée, ou La juste balance," in *Richesse de l'État, à laquelle on a ajouté les pièces*.

to the controversy, where he attempted to divert blame for the current financial mess from the fiscal system onto the *rentiers* who profited from the national debt.[82] Moreau accused the government's creditors of luxury and dissipation, charging that they had become the richest people in the state. We have two nations in France, he argued, "The people of *rentiers* is a vampire that sucks dry the landowning people"; one cultivated, the other amused itself. Taxes fell on the land, while those individuals whose wealth was in their portfolios paid hardly anything. Moreau was highlighting the fact that the public debt functioned as a mechanism to transfer wealth out of the pockets of landowners into those of *rentiers*. The heavier the interest payments the administration had to make to its creditors, the more it had to raise taxes, the more proprietors had to pay, and the lower the rents they could expect from their tenants.

Again, Moreau struck a chord. The author of *La balance égale* described *rentiers* as "idle people living in indolence" whose manners are corrupt, and insisted that their wealth be taxed. Pierre-Samuel Dupont disparaged the creditors of the state, claiming that they lived "in indolent idleness, from the sweat and blood of their fellow citizens." For Dupont, the very existence of such wealth was a source of luxury and the corruption of *moeurs*.

> This species of riches has a destructive opulence; and, when they become common among a people, nothing is more proper to hastening its ruin. Independent of the excessive taxes they necessitate, they lead to the loss of *moeurs* and that respectable spirit of antique maxims that is the great impulse of States. . . . Mad luxury is born. The noble himself, indignant at seeing himself eclipsed by a man above him, learns to attach importance to offices only when they offer a salary capable of placing him on a footing of equality: everything is thus perverted.[83]

The first president of the Rouen Parlement, Miromesnil, told Bertin that there was little sympathy for the position of *rentiers* in the provincial parlements where, unlike in Paris, the wealth of the magistrates was still overwhelmingly in land.[84] Many provincial magistrates considered a bankruptcy preferable to high taxes.[85]

The debate sparked by Roussel de la Tour was conducted, to a considerable extent, within the framework of a political economy pervaded by antipathy to luxury, hostility to financiers, and calls for the regeneration of agriculture. To what extent had this language found an institutional home in the parlements? The *Richesse de l'État* was originally a speech its author had given before the

---

[82] Jacob-Nicolas Moreau, "Entendons-nous, ou le radotage du vieux notaire, sur la Richesse de l'État," in *Richesse de l'État, à laquelle on a ajouté les pièces.*

[83] Dupont de Nemours, "Réflexions sur l'écrit intitulé: Richesse de l'État," in *Richesse de l'État, à laquelle on a ajouté les pièces.*

[84] Kwass, *Privilege and the Politics of Taxation.* See also Hudson, "The Parlementary Crisis of 1763."

[85] Quoted in Kwass, *Privilege and the Politics of Taxation,* 182.

Parlement of Paris in 1760.[86] Darigrand was a lawyer attached to the Cour des aides, a partner of the parlement in its resistance to taxation, and he wrote his *L'anti-financier* to defend the Parlement of Bordeaux. Julian Swann suggests that proposals such as Roussel de la Tour's were not typical of the Paris Parlement as a whole.[87] Nevertheless, there is substantial overlap between the rhetoric the parlements used in their remonstrances to the Crown and the idiom that pamphleteers had deployed in the *Richesse de l'État* debate. As Steven Kaplan observes, the Parlement of Paris resorted regularly to the claim that agriculture was ruined and exhausted by taxation.[88] Among the Bordeaux magistrates, according to William Doyle, few doubted that "the seemingly limitless growth in taxation would bring about their ruin, through the destruction of the country's greatest resource—agriculture."[89]

The parlements were especially fond of condemning the luxury of financiers. In 1764, the Parlement of Dijon blamed financial wealth for causing moral corruption, destroying social bonds, and undermining the legitimate pursuit of wealth. The immense fortunes of finance undercut the hierarchical social order appropriate to a monarchy—the judges regretted, in particular, the fusion of *la finance* with the nobility through marriage. The parlement denounced

[T]hat corrupting leaven, that silver rust that gnaws at the heart, debases souls, exhausts sentiments; which has confounded all ranks and destroyed that gradation so essential to a monarchical state; which has staggered all minds when one has seen, through so many sudden fortunes, that it was no longer fashionable to increase one's own slowly through labor, domestic care, and good conduct, since one could in a moment become rich from the goods of the state by direct gains, or through vile secret associations, or through base alliances that corrupt in every way the purest of French blood.[90]

Citing the regenerative effects of a complete reform of the fiscal system, the Parlement of Aix argued that "France will change its aspect when we dry up the well-spring of those immense fortunes that are formed from the spoils of your unfortunate subjects," fortunes that "introduce a corrupting luxury." While no office ought to be "devoid of appropriate emoluments," the magistrates conceded, none ought to be a source of "those immense profits that inflame cupidity and that soon extinguish, in indolence, the taste for virtue and for labor."[91]

The kinds of attitudes toward financiers and the tax system as a whole revealed in the debate of 1763–64 illuminate the roots of resistance to taxation

---

[86] Swann, *Politics and the Parlement of Paris*, 188.

[87] Ibid., 192.

[88] Kaplan, *Bread, Politics, and Political Economy*, 175–76.

[89] Doyle, *Parlement of Bordeaux*, 62, 69.

[90] Egret, *Louis XV et l'opposition parlementaire*, 126.

[91] Ibid., 127.

in the old regime. Such tax resistance was one of the key factors contributing to the structural financial problems of the French monarchy that would come disastrously to a head in the late 1780s. As comparative studies have shown, the French were far less heavily taxed per capita than the English, yet there was considerably less resistance to taxation across the channel than there was in France.[92] Because there was such violent hostility to new fiscal exactions French administrations had enormous difficulty raising taxes. Adjusted for inflation, per capita tax rates in France probably fell between the 1680s and the 1780s, while, during the same period in Britain, real per capita tax rates more than tripled.[93] The fiscal dispute of 1763 was resolved with a compromise which preserved the second *vingtième* until 1768, established an inquiry into other European tax systems, and invited the parlementaires to submit schemes for reform to the Crown.[94] In a further attempt to mollify the magistrates, the king replaced Bertin with L'Averdy, who had been a leader of opposition in the Parlement of Paris. The change did not represent a fundamental shift in royal policy. L'Averdy continued the measures Bertin had taken to encourage agriculture. As the new minister himself noted in a memorandum to the king, agriculture is "the first basis of all wealth and all commerce . . . it is always by this first article that one ought to seek to cure the ills of an exhausted state."[95]

The Physiocratic Vision of Commercial Society

One of the new minister's first initiatives was to permit the export of grain, a policy for which the Physiocrats had been calling since the 1750s. The first stirrings of Physiocracy are to be found in the economic articles François Quesnay published in the *Encyclopédie* in 1756, where he called for the total deregulation of the grain trade and the expansion of English-style commercial farming practices in France.[96] Quesnay's thinking might have developed no further, however, had he not managed to enlist as a collaborator the "friend of

[92] Peter Mathias and Patrick O'Brien, "Taxation in Britain and France, 1715–1810: A Comparison of the Social and Economic Incidence of Taxes Collected for the Central Governments," *Journal of European Economic History* 5 (1976): 601–50. Taxation was more legitimate in England for several reasons: because, unlike in France, English counties or regions did not enjoy formal tax privileges; because such formal privileges were not accorded in England to particular social groups or corporations, as they were in France; because institutions representing elite tax payers consented to tax increases in Britain; and because tax farming had been abandoned in England in the 1680s. John Brewer, *The Sinews of Power: War, Money and the English State, 1688–1783* (Cambridge, MA, 1988).

[93] Norberg, "French Fiscal Crisis," 263; Brewer, *Sinews of Power*, 91.

[94] Kwass, *Privilege and the Politics of Taxation*, 188; Riley, *Seven Years War*, 216.

[95] Félix, *Finances et politiques*, 184–86. Bertin was not disgraced but was made a secretary of state and given charge of a specialized mini-department with responsibility for the agricultural societies, internal navigation, and mines. Bourde, *Agronomie et agronomes*, 1131–32.

[96] Hecht, "Vie de François Quesnay," 1:255.

mankind" himself, the marquis de Mirabeau. When he read *L'ami des hommes* in the summer of 1757, Quesnay was struck by the similarity of Mirabeau's conclusions to some of his own and invited the marquis to visit him at Versailles. Years later, Mirabeau would claim that his meeting with Quesnay resulted in his "conversion" to what he described as a truth "so luminous and abundant that everything changes in principle."[97] After he and Quesnay had worked out the basic principles of the doctrine, Mirabeau became an indefatigable, if not always a very effective, propagandist for Physiocratic ideas, and the two men also recruited a handful of talented and energetic collaborators—Pierre-Samuel Dupont, Guillaume-François Le Trosne, the abbé Baudeau, J.-N.-M. Guérineau de Saint-Péravi, and Paul-Pierre Le Mercier de la Rivière. The intellectual production of these individuals over the decades was prodigious.

Physiocracy constituted the only coherent "school" of eighteenth-century political economists consistently following the same line over several decades: so much so, in fact, that their enemies derided them as a "sect." The Physiocrats demanded a complete deregulation of the grain trade, in particular, the relaxation of laws against export. Only by allowing French prices to rise to the level of European markets could French agriculture be revivified. While *agronomes* highlighted the importance of bringing more land under the plow, the Physiocrats insisted that it was more important to farm existing lands effectively and intensively than to create more acreage for an unproductive and unprofitable peasant agriculture. They called for a shift away from peasant cultivation towards capital-intensive farms managed by commercial farmers and worked by landless agricultural laborers. They called for a single land tax to replace the existing fiscal system, arguing that the current tax system damaged agricultural investment. Quesnay and his acolytes argued that property rights were the basis of the social order and that the use of property should be unfettered. They claimed that inequality was natural, and that it grew with the progress of society. They also argued in favor of absolute liberty to work and trade, a position that set them against the guilds which regulated parts of the French urban economy. The *économistes* were unusual in the 1760s in their enthusiastic approbation of the profit motive. Although they identified the market economy as natural, the Physiocrats did not believe that free markets could be maintained without the exertions of the state. They sought to motivate the monarchy to override the vested interests that were blocking the development of the "natural order" by turning it into a "legal despotism," an authority not subject to any constitutional checks. This innovation was directed against the financiers, the court, and the parlements, which the Physiocrats construed as selfish defenders of corporate interests.

The decision of the royal administration to pursue a policy of liberalizing the grain trade in the 1760s is often attributed to Physiocratic influence. However, the Physiocrats were only one voice among many calling for the liberalization

[97] Loménie, Les Mirabeau, 2:199.

of the grain trade. In fact, they had a much more difficult relationship with the administrations of Bertin and L'Averdy than is often assumed. It was under Bertin's ministry, in 1760, that Mirabeau was imprisoned for the *Théorie de l'impôt*. Moreover, when Mirabeau and Quesnay's *Philosophie rurale* appeared in November 1763, at the height of the conflict between the parlements and the monarchy over fiscal reform, the administration suppressed it. It was only in 1764, after the government had worked out a compromise with the parlements, that it permitted the work to be sold publicly.[98] L'Averdy's connection with the Physiocrats was little closer than his predecessor's. It is true that when the *Journal de l'agriculture, du commerce et des finances* was established in 1765 with his support, the editorial position was given to Dupont de Nemours, who quickly moved to turn the journal into a mouthpiece of Physiocracy.[99] But this exclusivity quickly led to Dupont's ouster in 1766. Henceforth, with L'Averdy still in office, the *Journal de l'agriculture* took an anti-Physiocratic line.

The Physiocrats enjoyed their closest relationship with the royal administration in the latter part of the 1760s. Under the ministry of L'Averdy's successor, Maynon d'Invau (controller general from October 1768 to December 1769), they began to play an important role as propagandists for the official policy on the grain trade. After the adoption of deregulation in 1764, there was a considerable rise in grain prices; poor harvests in the late 1760s led to further steep price increases, and grain riots erupted in numerous towns and cities. The administration was criticized bitterly, most notably by Guillaume-François Joly de Fleury, Advocate General of the Paris Parlement, and by Leprévost de Beaumont who started the rumor that Louis XV was attempting to create an artificial famine in order to speculate in grain.[100] In these circumstances, the Physiocrats emerged as the most important advocates for the government policy. Dupont de Nemours wrote a pamphlet called *Lettre d'un conseiller de Rouen* that was printed clandestinely by Turgot in Limoges and that the Norman parlement condemned to be burned. Mirabeau defended free export in print as did the abbé Roubaud and Guillaume-François Le Trosne. Baudeau also defended the official line from the pages of the *Éphémérides du citoyen*. Physiocracy enjoyed a certain official favor during this period, primarily because the Physiocrats were willing to battle the parlements in defense of the official policy. Some historians have discerned an important conduit of Physiocratic influence on government in Maynon d'Invau's relationship with Dupont de Nemours and Trudaine de Montigny.[101] The controller general was married to the latter's sister, and he hosted a dinner each week to which Dupont was invited, along with two former associates of Gournay, Louis-Paul Abeille and the abbé Morellet. This theory of Physiocratic influence is improbable, however,

---

[98] Hecht, "Vie de François Quesnay," 1:263.
[99] Jean Sgard, ed. *Dictionnaire des journaux, 1660–1789* (Paris, 1991).
[100] Kaplan, *Bread, Politics, and Political Economy*, 389–95.
[101] Schelle, *Du Pont de Nemours*, 133; Léonce de Lavergne, *Économistes français*, 347.

because Maynon d'Invau was a loyal creature of Choiseul, and the latter was hostile to the "sect." The Physiocrats were influential in so far as their ideas coincided with administrative policy; where there was divergence, they were ignored. In fact, the relationship of influence worked inversely. The Physiocrats focused their efforts increasingly on the grain trade, deemphasizing fiscal reform, as the administration showed its willingness to pursue the former policy but not the latter.

It is not my intention here to say more about the Physiocrats' campaign for freedom of trade in grain, a subject amply explored by other historians.[102] Rather, I intend to read Physiocracy in the context of the wider currents of political economic thought explored in this and the preceding chapters. The Physiocratic doctrine spoke directly and powerfully to the problem at the heart of a patriot political economy preoccupied with luxury—how to reconcile the twin imperatives of wealth and virtue in a commercial society. But the Physiocrats transcended the existing terms of the debate completely and forged a mode of thinking far more hospitable to commerce. There is little overt discussion of the corruption of virtue in mature Physiocratic writings, and little bemoaning of the fact that a mercantile spirit has replaced disinterestedness. After their early writings, Quesnay and Mirabeau moved toward a vocabulary of rights and interests that, on its face, seems inimical to their original idiom of virtue and corruption. The shift is especially marked for Mirabeau. But beneath the new terminology, the older concerns never disappeared; it was rather that mature Physiocracy offered its initiates a way to make their peace with commercial society.

The most powerful evidence that Physiocracy responded to the same problems articulated by a patriot political economy is the ease with which Quesnay recruited Mirabeau as a partner. The winning of Mirabeau to Physiocracy is in some respects surprising. He met Quesnay at the height of his literary fame, while Quesnay was as yet unknown. The doctor's views were contrary to Mirabeau's in several important respects. The marquis celebrated small-scale peasant production, while Quesnay condemned such *petite culture*; Mirabeau distrusted *philosophie*, and was hostile to the *Encyclopédie*, while Quesnay was an encyclopedist. Mirabeau's conversion is the more enigmatic in light of his difficult personality. As his troubled relationship with his own family demonstrates, the marquis was a proud and obstinate man, protective of his authority and dogmatic in his opinions.[103] Mirabeau's retrospective acknowledgment of a road to Damascus conversion may have been a distortion of what really happened in July 1757. He may not have recognized immediately all the ways in which his own vision was at odds with that of the doctor. The attrac-

[102] Kaplan, *Bread, Politics, and Political Economy*; Félix, *Finances et politiques*; Miller, *Mastering the Market*.

[103] At one point or another, Mirabeau had his son, his daughter, and his wife imprisoned by *lettres de cachet*. Henry, *Mirabeau père*, 10.

tiveness of collaboration with Quesnay may have been a function of the older man's links with Madame de Pompadour, a potentially important source of patronage.[104] But whatever the nature of the initial meeting of minds, Mirabeau and Quesnay entered into a long and fruitful partnership at the end of which the marquis had come to see Quesnay as his intellectual master.

During the course of this collaboration, Mirabeau subordinated some of his core ideas to those of Quesnay. Money, one of the mainsprings of disorder in *L'ami des hommes*, emerged as a principle of social cohesion in the *Philosophie rurale* (1763).[105] Mirabeau embraced a commercial vision of society and attacked peasant cultivation in the *Philosophie rurale*. The profit motive, vilified in his earlier work, was legitimized, becoming the basis of the most natural human behavior in his mature Physiocratic writings. He remarked in the *Lettres sur la législation* (1775) that, "In general, interest is, and ought to be the true and durable motivation of men."[106] He jettisoned a vision of social order based on rank and estate, stating that "Persons, dignities, superiority, inferiority count for nothing . . . it is the physical essence of things which alone we will consider."[107] Mirabeau asks if the reader would miss any of the traditional three estates should a "*tabula rasa*" be instituted "in order to recognize no constitution but property, unassailable and sacred property?"[108] Instead of using a language of hereditary distinctions, in his later work Mirabeau referred to "classes" of individuals based on their economic function. These classes were the basic units of society; the person who did not fit into any of them was an "extrasocial being."[109]

This was a vision of society that was far more inclusive of nonnoble proprietors than the noble-centered views of Mirabeau's earlier work. Nonnobles might certainly have found aspects of *L'ami des hommes* appealing, but this work, and others like it, were self-consciously oriented toward the nobility. Nobles were far from the only landowners in France. Nonnoble elites owned about a quarter of the land in the country, as much in aggregate as the nobility, though the average nonnoble holding was much smaller.[110] In the provincial city of Chartres, it was common for the upper crust of the Third Estate to have a house in the town and another in the country. The father of the future revolutionary, Jacques-Pierre Brissot, owned about 250 acres scattered in four or five plots in

[104] Shortly after their first meeting, Mirabeau asked Quesnay to help secure the ministry of the navy for his brother, a general of the galleys, and one-time governor of Guadeloupe. Hecht, "Vie de François Quesnay," 1:256.

[105] Victor Riqueti, marquis de Mirabeau, and François Quesnay, *Philosophie rurale, ou Économie générale et politique de l'agriculture* (Amsterdam, 1763), 1:52, 10–11.

[106] Victor Riqueti, marquis de Mirabeau, *Lettres sur la législation, ou L'ordre légal, dépravé, rétabli et perpétué*, 3 vols. (Berne, 1775), 2:667.

[107] Mirabeau and Quesnay, *Philosophie rurale*, 1:193.

[108] Mirabeau, *Lettres sur la législation*, 1:202.

[109] Ibid., 1:xlvii.

[110] *Histoire économique et sociale de la France*, ed., Braudel and Labrousse, 2:476.

the Beauce.[111] The Lamothe family of Bordeaux owned several pieces of rural property, engaged actively in viticulture, and mobilized the whole family for the grape harvest.[112] Elite nonnoble families in the city of Toulouse owned, on average, over forty acres of land in the surrounding countryside.[113] Physiocracy made no distinction between nobles and nonnobles; it was landowning that mattered.

Mirabeau was willing to give up deeply held views because the political economic vision he and Quesnay developed together offered a compelling solution to the tensions between wealth and virtue that preoccupied him in his earlier work. Physiocracy promised to deliver a socio-political order in which the preservation of virtue and the pursuit of wealth would no longer be at odds, in which luxury would be contained. One of the clearest Physiocratic statements to this effect comes in the conclusion to Le Mercier de la Rivière's *L'ordre naturel et essentiel des sociétés politiques* (1767), the most complete single statement of Physiocratic principles. For Le Mercier de la Rivière, a critical advantage of the Physiocratic social and political order was that it would put an end to luxury, which he characterized in the darkest terms. He explained that degeneration occurred in ancient polities because virtue could not fight forever against interest. The "natural order" that the Physiocrats hoped to institute, however, would never degenerate, because, there, interest would be in harmony with virtue, so that it would be "morally and socially impossible for every individual to be other than virtuous."[114] Physiocracy emerges here as the solution to the age-old problem of the decay of political virtue central to classical political theory.

How is the Physiocratic argument in favor of "legal despotism" to be understood in light of such a perspective? It might seem incongruous to claim that thinkers concerned with virtue in the civic sense could use the term "despotism" to refer to their ideal political regime. Indeed this usage marks the rupture with a civic idiom that Physiocracy represents. But Quesnay's legal despotism was not a vision of arbitrary government. A "legal despot" would be a sovereign governing not by caprice but according to fixed laws, derived from the natural order. This authority would be despotic only in the sense that the sovereign would be unhindered by the powerful vested interests that stymied the development of the natural order. If the monarch's authority was supreme, it was nevertheless quite restricted. Quesnay surrounded the sovereign with councils of magistrates expert in the laws of the natural order which would oversee the administration. Acts of authority would also be subject to the oversight of a public opinion enlightened by public instruction and liberty of the press.

---

[111] Vovelle and Roche, "Bourgeois, *Rentiers*, and Property Owners," 36.

[112] Christine Adams, *A Taste for Comfort and Status: A Bourgeois Family in Eighteenth-Century France* (University Park, PA, 2000), 59.

[113] Forster, *Nobility of Toulouse*, 36.

[114] Paul-Pierre Le Mercier de la Rivière, *L'ordre naturel et essentiel des sociétés politiques* (Paris, 2001) [1767], 468, 476.

In his manuscript notes, the doctor criticized absolutism as it had developed
in France in the seventeenth and eighteenth centuries. He condemned Louis XIV
for failing to understand the difference between "a great potentate and a great
King," and suggested that if all the provinces had enjoyed provincial estates,
Louis "would have been better informed than by [his minister] Louvois, who
inspired in him nothing but [the taste for] war." Quesnay described despotism
as a "destructive barbarism," and claimed that ministers were the greatest enthusiasts of despotic power. In his notes on a draft of Mirabeau's *Théorie de
l'impôt,* Quesnay explained that "Sovereignty and kings are not the same thing
. . . . everywhere sovereignty ought to be what it was in the nation before the
nation was deprived of it [*s'en soit démise*]. Thus it is no less the rule of the sovereign than that of the subjects." Quesnay denied that the king had an unlimited right to tax; there would be extraordinary instances of need where the state
should be able to tax beyond the usual rule, but these cases would be as obvious to the subjects as to the king, and proprietors, who would bear the brunt
of such emergency taxes, ought to be the judges with the king on this question.
Without the advice of a permanent council, representing all classes, he argued,
monarchy was little better than "a madman with a sword in his hand."[115]

For Quesnay, legal despotism appears to have had a tactical quality. He had
no faith in the virtue of princes: one must speak to sovereigns, he wrote, "as if
there were neither God nor the Devil, neither justice nor injustice, neither faith
nor right nor law; because they know only that which physically arrests their
wills."[116] Quesnay assumed that the instructed monarch would be restrained
by his own interest, and that if he ignored this rule he would quickly be pun-
ished by a reduction in his revenue and his power. Rather than embracing some
notion of enlightened despotism, in many ways the Physiocratic conception of
the state anticipates the Constituent Assembly of the French Revolution—a system of administrative decentralization combined with an all-powerful legislative sovereignty. Be that as it may, Physiocratic calls for "legal despotism"
repelled many contemporaries who might otherwise have endorsed the Physiocratic project for the regeneration of agriculture. Mably sharply criticized the
theory of legal despotism, as did Turgot.[117]

Mirabeau was not the only economic writer preoccupied by luxury who
found Physiocracy appealing; the abbé Nicolas Baudeau followed a parallel
course. In the early 1760s, Baudeau was a critic of the existing economic order
in the same mold as the "ami des hommes." He founded a journal modeled on
Addison's *Spectator* in 1765, named the *Éphémérides du citoyen,* and used it
as a forum to denounce the corrupting excesses of luxury. Baudeau celebrated
agriculture as the basis of national virtue and contrasted landed wealth with

[115] Weulersse, ed., *Manuscrits économiques,* 27, 32, 53–54.
[116] Ibid., 65–66.
[117] Gerald J. Cavanaugh, "Turgot: The Rejection of Enlightened Despotism," *French Historical
Studies* 6, no. 1 (1969): 31–58.

the "false riches" that made the cities "shine with an illusory splendor." He argued that France had degenerated since the seventeenth century. Agriculture was neglected by Richelieu, and cultivators came to be despised; a "legion of parvenus" acquired wealth and nobility, a development fatal to *moeurs* and to "the antique simplicity of true nobility." Baudeau condemned financiers as a "sect of egoists," and criticized the artists and artisans who catered to their luxury. These were "lost for the truly patriotic arts."[118]

Baudeau, who had initially been critical of the Physiocrats, underwent a change of heart in 1766. In January 1767, he relaunched the *Éphémérides* as the organ of the Physiocratic movement, giving it a new subtitle, *Bibliothèque raisonnée des sciences morales et politiques*. In the writings he produced after 1766, he grafted Physiocracy onto his original concerns rather than abandoning them. The first substantial work he published after his conversion was a pamphlet on luxury.[119] The language Baudeau used to talk about luxury changed markedly: his impassioned rants against financiers and the corruption of *moeurs* were replaced by the pseudo-scientific accents of Dr. Quesnay. Baudeau himself was acutely aware of the shift, contrasting the moralistic conception of luxury to which he had formerly adhered with the new scientific definition he had come to embrace. Prodigality is not necessarily luxury, he noted; private pomp is usually referred to as *luxe* by the vulgar, but it is not always so. He proceeded to define luxury as "the inversion of the natural, essential order of national expenditures, which augments the mass of unproductive expenditures to the prejudice of those that serve production." (His prose, certainly, was not the better for his conversion). What Baudeau meant was that spending was only luxurious when it undermined production, as when a landowner spent money on Chinese silks rather than on a land drainage project. Though he made little reference to *moeurs* in the *Principes sur le luxe*, implicitly they played just as important a role in his thinking. The proprietor had to spend his money wisely; if he spent too much on luxury and not enough on agricultural investment, then the country would be impoverished. Nor did Baudeau retreat from his conviction that luxury had reached ruinous proportions in France; he argued that agriculture groaned under its burden.

Physiocracy was appealing to men like Baudeau and Mirabeau because of the way it imaginatively reconfigured commerce and stripped it of some of its threatening qualities. Physiocracy can appear self-contradictory on the subject of commerce: on the one hand, according to Quesnay, trade was "sterile," producing no real wealth, but, on the other, it was the condition of wealth creation on the land. Market-oriented cultivation, for which the Physiocrats had

---

[118] "De l'esprit agricole," *Éphémérides du citoyen, ou Chronique de l'esprit national* 1, no. 4 (1765); "Des sciences et des arts," ibid., 1, no. 16 (1765); "De Paris," ibid., 4, no. 3 (1766).

[119] Nicolas Baudeau, *Principes de la science morale et politique sur le luxe et les loix somptuaires* (Paris, 1767).

a marked preference, depended on the capacity to exchange an agricultural surplus for other goods, be they necessities, conveniences, or even luxuries. The development of a commercial agriculture required a merchant class to facilitate exchanges and manufacturers to produce goods for which farmers might trade their surplus. If no such goods were available, the farmer would lapse back into subsistence production. The Physiocratic "natural order" was no rustic utopia; it was a commercial society in which agricultural production enjoyed a privileged status. Everyone in such a society would be a trader; even the farmer would be a specialist, producing only what he could grow most efficiently and trading for the rest of his needs. With agriculture and commerce linked in this fashion, some of the solidity and virtue of the farmer inevitably rubbed off on the merchant.

By the 1770s, the claim that agriculture depended on commerce for its prosperity enjoyed wide acceptance beyond Physiocracy. The way such an understanding of commerce could be grafted onto the stock of patriotic agricultural improvement is illustrated by Louis-Étienne Arcère's *De l'état de l'agriculture chez les Romains,* a dissertation written for the *Académie royale des inscriptions* in 1776. Arcère, an Oratorian priest, was the secretary of the agricultural society of La Rochelle.[120] Much of what he wrote echoed the standard assumptions of patriot thinking on agriculture in the 1750s and 1760s. He argued, for instance, that the Roman descent into luxury was linked to the decadence of agriculture. Yet Arcère insisted that agriculture and commerce were mutually dependent. He criticized the Romans for failing to attach enough importance to trade, remarking that "this want of industry must essentially harm the productions of the soil." "Agriculture and commerce are so dependent on one another," Arcère argued, "that they have in a sense a common existence; separate them, they languish; you will never see them flourish."[121]

Physiocracy functioned to legitimate commerce—at least for members of the "sect" itself—in a second important way: by giving commerce a firmer ontological grounding. Part of what disturbed people about commerce in the eighteenth century was its apparently foundationless character. Trade was viewed as "a dimension of life radically unstable, uncertain, and fluid."[122] It was commonplace among the partisans of agriculture in the 1750s and 1760s to refer to "revolutions" in commerce, a metaphor implying a vulnerability to unexpected and disturbing changes in fortune. Economic drives, particularly those supposed to underlie commercial exchange and consumption, were represented as expressions of fancy, imagination, and the passions. The apparent volatility of the commercial world was amplified in the eighteenth century by the speed-

[120] Forster, *Merchants, Landlords, Magistrates,* 77, 80.

[121] Louis-Étienne Arcère, *De l'état de l'agriculture chez les Romains, depuis le commencement de la république jusqu'au siècle de Jules-César, relativement au gouvernement, aux moeurs & au commerce. Dissertation qui a obtenu l'accessit du prix de l'Académie royale des inscriptions & belles-lettres, en 1776* (Paris, 1777), 73, 97.

[122] Clark, "Commerce, the Virtues, and the Public Sphere," 420.

ing up of the cycle of fashion, by the wider use of credit, and the proliferation of paper monies of various kinds. That fickle goddess of commercial society—fashion—ruined merchants and threw artificers out of work when she willed, affirmed one commentator.[123] Because of the unpredictability of trade, another wrote, a man rich in commercial wealth might easily die in the poorhouse.[124] No merchant's fortune was entirely secure, argued another writer, because it is always subject to "the reverses of commerce, and its terrifying vicissitudes."[125] For men like Baudeau and Mirabeau, the world of trade was a realm radically disconnected from reality where unmoored signs usurped the place of real things. Baudeau castigated his own age as "a reign of silver . . . when we allow ourselves to be dazzled by the universal right of representation which [silver] enjoys as money, without penetrating beyond this, that is, to the riches represented." He suggested that the consolidation of real wealth was ever more difficult in a climate characterized by "the illusory principle which reduces all to money, considered as *reality,* instead of being [considered] as *image.*"[126]

In Physiocracy, by contrast, all of economic life, even the unproductive realms of commerce and manufacturing, acquired an aura of necessity and reality. For the Physiocrats, commerce was no less necessary than agriculture because without the stimulus of trade, society would not be able to sustain an agricultural productivity great enough to feed its swollen population. According to Mirabeau, "The entire physical bond of society consists in a single point: the transmutation of superfluity into necessity."[127] Commerce converts the unnecessary, even the frivolous, goods of luxury manufactures and international trade into bread. The Physiocrats pioneered a language of economics that figured all economic activity as material, representing it as an imperative imposed on man by Nature—the production of subsistence. In the words of its founders, the new science would explicate the "constant rules of movement imprinted on matter."[128]

The key to the Physiocratic reimagining of the economic order was their reconceptualization of economic agency. It was not fancy, imagination, and the passions that drove economic activity in their view, but an avoidance of pain and a quest for corporeal satisfactions. Such quasi-biological drives connected human beings to fundamental realities. The Physiocrats borrowed this model of agency from eighteenth-century sensationism, of which Quesnay was a leading exponent in France. Modifying Locke's schema, eighteenth-century episte-

---

[123] Antoine Prosper Lottin, *Discours contre le luxe: Il corrompt les moeurs, & détruit les empires* (Paris, 1783), 32.

[124] Jean-François Butini, *Traité du luxe* (Geneva, 1774), 99–101.

[125] Fresnais de Beaumont, *La noblesse cultivatrice, ou Moyens d'élever en France la culture de toutes les denrées que son sol comporte, au plus haut degré de production* (Paris, 1778), 11.

[126] *Éphémérides du citoyen, ou Bibliothèque raisonnée des sciences morales et politiques* 1 (1767): 104. For very similar language, see *Journal de commerce* (July 1760): 159.

[127] Mirabeau and Quesnay, *Philosophie rurale,* 1:47–48.

[128] Ibid., 1:xxxix.

mologists argued that there are aspects of reality to which human beings must have access without the mediation of the abstract ideas forged by reason. Without such a capacity, primitive man, whose reasoning is poorly developed, would never have survived. A capacity to experience all sensations either as pleasurable or painful, sensationists argued, allowed the mind to distinguish whether an object could satisfy a need or pose a hazard. The basic knowledge which emerged from this mechanism was grounded in the nature of things, unmediated by reason and language.[129] The Physiocrats considered economic activity a direct emanation of this same faculty. For Baudeau,

> Man is born to seek his preservation and his well-being. His heart is avid and even insatiable for the enjoyments which form his felicity; he flees and detests pain and displeasure. The Author of nature has placed in all our souls this universal spring, primary motivation of human actions: it was necessary to the perpetuation, to the multiplication, to the happiness of the species. It is through it that the reasonable and free man may know the principles of the moral and political order, the natural Law and the social Laws, evidently derived from the physical order, instituted by the Supreme Being.[130]

The same faculty implanted in human beings for their survival both motivates human beings to be economic actors and is the cognitive capacity that gives them access to reality. In the article on epistemology he wrote for the *Encyclopédie*, Quesnay argued that will is a simple response to pleasure or pain: "Will can be reduced to finding a sensation agreeable, disagreeable, or indifferent."[131] The economic actor imagined by Physiocracy—even the merchant or manufacturer—was a being whose activities were connected, in a direct sense, to the natural order. Such a conceptualization of economic agency may not have won wide acceptance in eighteenth-century France, but it is surely an important precursor of the economic materialism of the nineteenth century.

Physiocracy offers a window onto some of the central problems with which political economic writers were grappling in France during the 1760s and 1770s, but it should not be viewed as a typical response to those problems. In certain respects, Physiocracy overlapped with other political economies focused on regenerating agriculture, but it also diverged from them sharply. The Physiocratic call for free trade in grain was commonplace. Their insistence on the sole-productivity of agriculture was a fundamentalist version of the widely held view that agriculture was a firmer and more significant source of wealth than any other, while their antipathy to luxury, and insistence on the economic importance of simple manners, was also mainstream. But Physiocracy was ex-

---

[129] For a full development of this argument, see David Hume, *Philosophical Essays concerning Human Understanding*, 2nd ed. (London, 1753), 91.

[130] *Éphémérides du citoyen* 1 (1767): 17–18.

[131] François Quesnay, "Évidence," in *Encyclopédie, ou Dictionnaire raisonné des sciences, des arts et des métiers*, 6:156.

ceptional in the extent to which it endorsed interest, economic individualism, and the profit motive. It alienated many contemporaries in its championing of commercial agriculture and condemnation of peasant farming. It was further marginalized by a tendency to rely on a pseudo-scientific vocabulary, rather than a civic idiom, and went totally beyond the pale in its endorsement of "despotism." Nothing would have surprised the political economic authors of the eighteenth century so much as the tendency of some modern scholars to view Physiocracy as the accepted, or prevailing, economic doctrine of the period.

The Critique of Physiocracy and Aristocratic Property

By the end of the 1760s, the Physiocrats had become the object of a barrage of criticism from other political economic publicists. Though Physiocracy was, arguably, a more socially inclusive perspective than some of the noble-centered political economies of the 1760s, the *économistes* were charged with favoring the interests of speculative grain merchants and plutocratic *grands seigneurs*. Bad harvests in the late 1760s in conjunction with the deregulation of the grain trade produced high prices; substantial landowners enjoyed windfall profits while the less fortunate majority found itself increasingly pinched. The consequence, according to Steven Kaplan, was the development of "a sort of class struggle" between the rich and the poor.[132] The Physiocrats were perceived in this context as defenders of the rich. They were especially vulnerable to such a charge because of the way they embraced economic individualism and distanced themselves from a more civic, or patriotic, rhetoric. The attack on the Physiocrats shows how an antipathy to plutocracy initially mobilized to criticize financiers and courtiers could be redirected to attack landowners, nobles, or the rich *tout court*. Though of little political significance in the context of the late 1760s, such a critique would be taken up and developed in the following decades, and would eventually serve as ideological dynamite in the revolutionary assault on aristocracy.

One of the most unpopular positions taken by the Physiocrats was their opinion that large-scale agriculture—*grande culture*—was superior to peasant farming—*petite culture*.[133] Some critics simply denied that the *économistes* were right about this, holding that *petite culture* was more productive than estate agriculture—a position with which a number of modern scholars agree.[134] Others claimed that the moral benefits of maintaining a certain equality, and keeping families on the land, outweighed economic considerations. Malesherbes noted that "The best legislation possible is that which would multiply as much as pos-

[132] Kaplan, *Bread, Politics, and Political Economy,* 503.
[133] Bourde, *Influence of England,* 99.
[134] Peter McPhee, "The French Revolution, Peasants, and Capitalism," *American Historical Review* 94, no. 5 (1989): 1265–80; Dewald, *Pont-St-Pierre,* 5.

sible the number of small farmers. This is something which our modern econ-omists [the Physiocrats] do not realize."[135] According to the abbé Rozier, "The support of the state is not that there be very great tenant farmers but that there be a great multitude of tenant farmers."[136] A number of substantial landown-ers took this dictum to heart and subdivided their estates. In 1761 and again in 1768, the comte de Maurepas, Pompadour's disgraced foe, and later Louis XVI's mentor, created small tenancies to give farms to as many families as possible. The *Gazette d'agriculture, commerce, arts et finances* remarked that those who benefited would "bless forever this other Sully."[137] The chancelier d'Aguesseau, the maréchal de Mouchy, the duc de Liancourt, and the duc de Penthièvre un-dertook similar well-publicized operations.[138]

Opposition to Physiocratic *grande culture,* combined in some cases with an attack on estate agriculture, can be discerned in many of the essays submitted in the late 1760s to an essay competition organized by the Free Economic So-ciety of St. Petersburg. The Russian society, which received over 150 entries, asked whether it was advantageous to a state for peasants to possess their own lands.[139] In the Russian context, the question concerned serfdom, but many en-trants to the competition, including the winner, a doctor of canon law from Aix-la-Chapelle named Beardé de l'Abbaye, used the question to promote peasant cultivation over estate-based agriculture. The subtext was obvious to readers: Fréron's *Année littéraire* approvingly noted the essay's relevance to "our coun-tryside," as well as to the lands of Eastern Europe.[140] Other entrants took the opportunity to debate the legitimacy and utility both of wage labor and exist-ing distributions of property. The result was a critique of social inequality that anticipates some of the currents of radical thought that emerged during the French Revolution.

Beardé de l'Abbaye deployed the language of patriotic agricultural improve-ment to make a case for *petite culture.* His dissertation enjoyed at least four edi-tions, and it was praised fulsomely in both the *Année littéraire,* which lauded the author's "healthy and patriotic views," and in the *Journal encyclopédique,* which noted that Beardé de l'Abbaye's essay "contains the most useful views, dictated by humanity, by reason and by patriotism."[141] His thesis was that a

[135] Allison, *Lamoignon de Malesherbes,* 87.

[136] Quoted in Bourde, *Agronomie et agronomes,* 1042.

[137] *Gazette d'agriculture, commerce, arts et finances,* December 8, 1778. Quoted by Bourde, *Agronomie et agronomes,* 1045.

[138] Bourde, *Agronomie et agronomes,* 1045.

[139] Franco Venturi, *The End of the Old Regime in Europe, 1768–1776: The First Crisis,* trans. R. Burr Litchfield (Princeton, 1989), 3–19; "Avertissement," in *Dissertation qui a remporté le prix sur la question proposée en 1766 par la Société d'oeconomie & d'agriculture à St. Pétersbourg; à laquelle on a joint les pièces qui ont eües l'accessit* (n.p., 1768).

[140] *Année littéraire* 3 (1770): 241–52. In its review of the essay, the conservative Italian *Notizie letterarie* felt it necessary to insist that the distribution of lands to peasants was only suitable for largely uncultivated places like Russia. Cited in Venturi, *End of the Old Regime,* 20.

[141] *Année littéraire* 3 (1770): 241–52; *Journal encyclopédique* 1 (1770): 201–12.

prospering agriculture is the foundation of powerful and stable states, and that cultivation can flourish only on the basis of peasant proprietorship. He warned that existing prosperity, based on luxury, was an illusory wealth that left the state in a precarious position. "Do not let yourself be seduced by a dazzling illusion," he cautioned. "The plaster that covers the surface of a building, and that embellishes it, perhaps hides ruins ready to crumble at the slightest shock: in a word, the luxury of the cities is rather an abuse of wealth than a proof of opulence."[142] It was only on the land that one could see "the real physical wealth of a state." Beardé de l'Abbaye ascribed British power to its improved agriculture, contrasting Britain favorably with luxurious Spain. To produce children for the state, a key source of power, peasants must have the economic security that only landowning could bring. He also affirmed the benefits of granting distinctions to farmers, citing the example of the emperor of China.[143]

In celebrating the benefits of peasant cultivation, Beardé de l'Abbaye's dissertation had a distinct anti-Physiocratic edge.[144] This emphasis was more marked, however, in the discourse of J.-J.-L. Graslin, which received an honorable mention from the St. Petersburg Society.[145] Graslin was a financier, an entrepreneur, and an urban developer. He acquired the office of *receveur des fermes du roi* in Nantes, used some of his profits to open a manufactory for printed calicoes, and developed a whole new city quarter in Nantes in the 1780s. He also undertook major drainage projects in the 1770s and corresponded with the agricultural societies of Tours and Limoges.[146] Graslin resolutely opposed the "sect."[147] In his contribution to the St. Petersburg competition, he argued that the free proprietor is a more productive cultivator than the serf or the "mercenary." In regions with peasant proprietorship, Graslin argued, owners wrung abundance from the least fertile soils and the land was cov-

---

[142] Beardé de l'Abbaye, *Dissertation qui a remporté le prix*, 5–6.

[143] Ibid., 6, 16–22.

[144] In 1770, Beardé de l'Abbaye launched an attack on the Physiocratic proposal for a single tax falling uniquely on land, accusing the *économistes* of indifference to the poor. Instead of taxing land exclusively, he proposed to tax luxuries, celibacy, and mobile wealth in general. Beardé de l'Abbaye, *Recherches sur les moyens de supprimer les impôts, précédées de l'examen de la nouvelle science* (Amsterdam, 1770), 158–63, 171, 189–90.

[145] Jean-Joseph-Louis Graslin, "Dissertation sur la question proposée par la Société économique de St. Pétersbourg. Est-il plus avantageux et plus utile au bien public, que le paysan possède des terres en propre, ou seulement des biens mobiliers, & jusqu'où doit s'étendre cette propriété?" in *Dissertation qui a remporté le prix sur la question proposée en 1766 par la Société d'oeconomie & d'agriculture à St. Pétersbourg; à laquelle on a joint les pièces qui ont eües l'accessit* (n.p., 1768).

[146] See R.-Marie Luminais, *Recherches sur la vie, les doctrines économiques et les travaux de J.-J.-Louis Graslin* (Nantes, 1862); Jean-Claude Perrot, "Urbanisme et commerce au XVIIIe siècle dans les ports de Nantes et Bordeaux," *Actes du colloque villes et campagnes, XV–XXe siècles* (Lyons, 1977).

[147] See "Avant-Propos," in *Correspondance entre M. Graslin, de l'Académie économique de S. Pétersbourg, auteur de l'Essai analytique sur la richesse et sur l'impôt, et de M. l'abbé Baudeau, auteur des Éphémérides du citoyen, sur un des principes fondamentaux de la doctrine des soi-disants philosophes économistes*, ed. Gino Longhitano (Catania, 1988).

ered with vigorous families which assured the state a numerous population. It was in the interest of society and the sovereign, he insisted, that peasants own as much land as they could cultivate with their own hands. He was pointedly critical of large landowners, "a few powerful men" accustomed to basing their happiness on the "subjugation" of a useful and respectable class. In nearly all nations, he claimed, the natural order, which ordained that the fruits of labor ought to belong to the laborer, had been inverted.[148]

Graslin's comments were not the most radical of those expressed by entrants to the St. Petersburg contest. This distinction belongs to Giambattista Vasco, a Piedmontese political economist, whose essay was published in French translation in 1770. As Franco Venturi points out, Vasco's answer to the question went further than Beardé de l'Abbaye's, asking not only whether it was advantageous to the state that peasants own land, but whether it was useful that anyone but peasants should do so.[149] Using a version of the same political economic language as Beardé de l'Abbaye, Vasco assailed agricultural wage labor and existing property arrangements. The wealth of an exclusively commercial nation was "precarious," he argued, and must always depend on "the hazards of commerce." The strength of a state depended on agriculture, and lands worked by their owner were always better farmed.[150] Vasco called for relative equality in land holding, though he regarded absolute equality as neither feasible nor desirable. He suggested that great landowners be prohibited from adding further to their estates, but he opposed forcible land redistribution as a remedy worse than the disease. Rather, laws "which hide the secret goal of the Legislator," especially legislation to divide inheritances equally, ought to be employed to redistribute land.[151]

Vasco criticized agricultural wage labor, mixing Lockean natural rights claims with a quasi republican vocabulary. To have to work on the land of others, which placed one "in a too vile dependence" on the proprietor, he argued, was not much better than slavery. Drawing on Locke's labor theory of property, he argued that all human beings originally had the same right to gather the fruits of the earth, and that private property was justified only because it increased production. The inventors of property, however, never envisioned that a small number of "idle" and "useless" men would seize all the land and permit those who worked it only a modest wage. Not only was wage labor contrary to natural right, he argued, it destroyed the moral advantages of country life. The *moeurs* attributed by so many ancient philosophers to those who lived on the land were vitiated for the man who had to work as the hireling of another.[152]

---

[148] Graslin, "Dissertation sur la question," 111, 142–48.

[149] Venturi, *End of the Old Regime*, 19–20. According to Venturi, it was "one of the works of greatest importance in Italy in the eighteenth century."

[150] Giambattista Vasco, *La félicité publique considerée dans les paysans cultivateurs de leurs propres terres, traduit de l'italien par M. Vignoli* (Lausanne, 1770), 16–20, 23, 29.

[151] Vasco, *Félicité publique*, 49, 62, 80, 84–86.

[152] Ibid., 10–23, 50.

Vasco combined his attack on estate agriculture with a critique of nobility. He rejected the idea that idleness ought to be the distinguishing mark of gentle status, and called for the participation of gentlemen in commerce; if nobles did not want to trade, they must perform some useful activity in the public service. He questioned the social utility of an hereditary nobility, describing the institution as "an extravagance of the opinion of men," and observed that "a long succession of persons who descend from the purchaser of a fief, and who have always lived in idleness, constitute a very brilliant nobility without virtue or glory having had any part in it." Yet, "Any virtuous father can inspire these sentiments in his sons without being titled."[153]

If a political economy exalting agriculture as the well-spring of national regeneration was pioneered by writers who saw in it a means to regenerate the nobility, clearly it could also be used to advance very different social agendas. In critiques such as Vasco's, and even, to a lesser degree, in those of Graslin and Beardé de l'Abbaye, one sees elements of the same language being mobilized to exalt ordinary peasant farmers, to disparage estate agriculture, and even to censure the nobility itself. What this suggests, in the first place, is the modular character of the anti-plutocratic language deployed by middling elites in the 1750s and early 1760s. The nobility, or nonnoble landowning elites, were not immune to criticisms that they themselves constituted strata that owed their power to money rather than honor or virtue. Indeed, when one took the standpoint of the ordinary men and women who actually worked the land in France it was manifestly obvious that the entire middling elite constituted such a privileged class. Similar criticisms would make their appearance in the 1770s as the critique of luxury was slowly reconfigured. But it was only in the radically changed circumstances of the 1790s that such perspectives would prove politically potent.

---

[153] Ibid., 72–77. Misgivings about property, and a call for greater equality, were articulated in France by Mably. See Gabriel Bonnot de Mably, *Doutes proposées aux philosophes économistes, sur l'ordre naturel et essentiel des sociétés politiques* (The Hague, 1768).

CHAPTER 4

Patriotic Commerce and Aristocratic Luxury

[Luxury] remains subordinated to [civic spirit] unless the system of government has freed it from this subordination, unless, in a nation possessing wealth, industry, and luxury, the administration has extinguished civic spirit.

—Saint-Lambert, "Luxe," *Encyclopédie* (1765)

The 1770s was a decade of defeat, decline, and retrenchment for those who sought to regenerate France by reinvigorating agriculture. Partisans of an agriculture-centered program of reform moved into a weaker position in the 1770s because they lost the cooperative links with the royal government that had developed in the previous decade. In December 1770 the king dismissed the duc de Choiseul. The measures that followed Choiseul's disgrace were thoroughly reactionary from the point of view of those who saw agriculture as the well-spring of national renewal. The abbé Terray, controller general since December 1769, reestablished the regulation of the grain trade and stifled debate on economic reform.[1] He ordered the suppression of the Physiocratic *Éphémérides du citoyen* in 1772.[2] The enthusiasm of most of the agricultural societies had long since cooled, and a majority ceased to meet in the chilly climate of the early 1770s.

The death of Louis XV in 1774, and the accession of his grandson to the throne, heralded new possibilities for reform, but hope was quickly followed by disillusionment. Louis XVI disgraced the ministerial triumvirate of Terray, Maupeou, and d'Aiguillon and brought Jacques Turgot into the government, at first as minister of the navy, and a month later as controller general. The new minister was a former acolyte of Vincent de Gournay, and after the latter's death in 1759 he gravitated toward the Physiocrats. In his brief ministry, Turgot set out

---

[1] He encouraged the dissemination of the abbé Galiani's *Dialogues sur le commerce des blés,* a tract attacking free trade in grain, and had the police seize the abbé Morellet's counterattack, the *Réfutation de l'ouvrage qui a pour titre, Dialogues sur le commerce des blés.* See Goodman, *Republic of Letters,* 213.

[2] Schelle, *Du Pont de Nemours,* 145.

to remodel the kingdom's economic structures: he reestablished freedom of trade in grain, abolished the craft guilds, and transformed the corvée into a money tax. He had more ambitious changes planned, including a comprehensive reform of the fiscal system and the introduction of a system of local assemblies intended to foster the civic spirit which he believed France sorely lacked. However, after only two years in office, Turgot was forced out. His fall was a blow to the advocates of fundamental economic reform. Turgot's replacement at the *contrôle générale*—the Genevan banker, Jacques Necker—advocated the creative use of public credit to regenerate the finances of the state. He was, in some respects, a reformer, but his ascendancy represented an abandonment by the royal government of an agriculture-led strategy of national regeneration.

New themes began to resound in public discussion of political economic issues. The 1770s was a critical period for the emergence and dissemination of representations validating commerce as a patriotic and honorable social activity. Developing the arguments adumbrated by Gournay's circle in the 1750s, commentators increasingly differentiated the negative effects of mobile wealth under the institutional conditions of the old regime from the likely beneficial effects of commerce in a different institutional framework. As commerce was detached from luxury, blame for the moral corruption and economic precariousness associated with *luxe* was tied more and more closely to political and social institutions. This was a momentous shift in emphasis: first, because it made luxury a political problem rather than an unavoidable adjunct to modern life; and second, because it removed a central obstacle to the emergence of representations of a virtuous commercial society. At the same time, champions of commerce sought to represent merchants in positive terms: as patriots and, perhaps most significantly, as emulators rather than profit-seekers. To some extent, the forces behind this shift lay in the world of commerce itself. Merchants, commercial journalists, and men of letters linked to the world of trade recognized the challenge that agriculture-centered discourses of patriotic regeneration posed to their social and self-legitimation, and they countered the agrarians with their own claims for the patriotic importance of commerce.

By the 1770s it had become obvious to many defenders of trade that the attempt to redefine luxury as a mere form of consumption, or sign of prosperity, tainted their principal message. The ascendancy of a new royal mistress, Madame du Barry, fired anxieties about luxury in the same fashion as the rise of Madame de Pompadour had in the 1740s. The public was inundated with information about the machinations of du Barry and her supposed protégés— Maupeou, d'Aiguillon, and Terray. Much of this material was collected together and published in the *Anecdotes sur Mme la comtesse du Barry,* which Robert Darnton lists as the second most popular clandestine work sold in eighteenth-century France.[3] The presumed author of the *Anecdotes,* Mathieu-François Pi-

---

[3] Robert Darnton, *The Forbidden Best-Sellers of Pre-Revolutionary France* (New York, 1995), 63.

dansat de Mairobert, had been arrested in 1749 for disseminating verses that slandered Madame de Pompadour, and he had been producing *libelles* ever since.[4] In relating the career of du Barry, he drew on many of the same tropes used to attack Pompadour. Du Barry's social origins made those of the marquise seem positively exalted. Of humble birth, she had worked for a time as a shop girl until she was recruited as a prostitute. The *Anecdotes* stressed du Barry's prodigality and love of luxury; indeed, it was her desire for fine clothing and jewelry, according to Pidansat de Mairobert, that drew her to prostitution. By the end of 1773, he claimed, du Barry had cost the treasury the fantastic sum of 18 million livres. Though she did not have the obvious connections to financiers that her predecessor had, du Barry's biographer claimed that she was the daughter of a minor official in the tax farms and that a financier found guilty of misconduct in the early 1770s, one Billard Dumonceau, was her godfather.[5] He also emphasized that du Barry had been the kept woman of the financier Maximilien Radix de Sainte-Foy.[6]

Attacks on du Barry together with claims that commerce and luxury were conceptually separate tended to push the blame for luxury more firmly onto financiers and courtiers. During the 1770s, the attack on luxury took on an increasingly anti-aristocratic slant. I stress anti-*aristocratic*, as opposed to anti-noble, to emphasize that it was the wealthy nobility of the capital and Versailles, in particular, that was singled out as a luxurious class.[7] There was, perhaps, a certain inevitability about this development. The critique of luxury articulated a rejection of plutocracy, a resistance to the process whereby wealth seemed to be replacing honor as a foundation for social status. As the moneyed class par excellence, the aristocracy of the court and capital was vulnerable to such a critique. Its connection with financiers, both personal and pecuniary, and its engagement with court capitalism, was damaging to the upper nobility's claim to be a class founded on honor rather than money. As early as the 1750s, the marquis de Mirabeau had savaged the luxury of courtiers, and there is evidence that anti-aristocratic sentiment was rife among provincial nobles in the 1770s. But there is also reason to believe that middling nobles had lost control of the anti-luxury critique, for they, too, with growing frequency, were represented as vectors of *luxe*.

---

[4] Durand Echeverria, *The Maupeou Revolution: A Study in the History of Libertarianism: France, 1770–1774* (Baton Rouge, LA, 1985), 23.

[5] On Billard Dumonceau, see Bosher, *French Finances*, 108–9.

[6] Mathieu-François Pidansat de Mairobert, *Anecdotes sur Mme la comtesse du Barry* (London, 1775).

[7] I am not suggesting that people used the term *aristocrat* in the 1770s exclusively to refer to wealthy and powerful nobles; rather I am seeking a convenient means to underline a central division within the Second Estate between the upper nobility and their less exalted provincial peers. C. B. A. Behrens, however, argues that the very term *aristocrat* was new in the eighteenth century, and that it referred not to the nobility as a whole but to *les grands*. *The Ancien Régime* (New York, 1989) [1967], 74.

Fixing the Boundaries between Commerce and Luxury

After the Seven Years' War, writers in an Enlightenment tradition developed the insights of Forbonnais and Dangeul to produce a properly *political* critique of luxury. Conceding that France was indeed corrupted and disordered in many of the ways that the critics of luxury had suggested, they separated luxury conceptually from commerce and, while continuing to validate trade, placed the blame for a dangerous luxury on political economic institutions, and finally on the monarchy. One way commentators separated commerce from luxury was to claim that while privileged, monopoly commerce might give rise to luxury, free trade would not. Some represented privileged commerce as an adjunct of finance—an argument highlighted in the struggle over the fate of the French Indies Company. Writers with links to the world of trade, and periodicals articulating a mercantile perspective, produced sympathetic accounts of commerce, and lauded the merchant's patriotism. Defenders of commerce emphasized that trade was animated as much by emulation, or a desire for honor, as it was by pecuniary interest. The merchant prompted by the stirrings of honor rather than by baser desires could more readily be viewed as public spirited.

A text that bridges the gap between an older Enlightenment perspective on luxury and the view increasingly adopted in the 1760s and 1770s is the marquis de Saint-Lambert's essay, "Luxe," published in the *Encyclopédie* in 1765. A one-time protégé of Voltaire, and lover of the *salonnière* Mme d'Houdetot, Saint-Lambert mounted an apology, of sorts, for luxury. However, the difference between the marquis's position and that of the earlier philosophic apologists was stark. Saint-Lambert accepted virtually every claim of the critics who attacked luxury in the 1750s and 1760s: that consumption was disordered; that social rank was confused; that honor was being lavished on mere wealth with destructive social and moral effects; that patriotism was being undermined and agriculture neglected. He only rejected the notion that luxury was the ultimate source of these maladies.[8]

In European nations suffering such ailments, he insisted, it was a political economic order characterized by fiscalism, monopoly, and public borrowing that was at the root of the problem. In France, Saint-Lambert remarked, luxury had exceeded "acceptable limits" only since the wars of Louis XIV brought disorder to the finances, creating a class of financiers and monopolists. It was for these that he reserved his censure. "The fortunes of the holders of a monopoly, of the administrators and collectors of public funds are the most despicable," he stated. The administration had also failed in its duty to balance wealth and virtue. "A government must foster civic spirit and patriotism in its citizens while at the same time keeping alive and even stimulating their love of property, their desire to increase their possessions and to enjoy them," he ar-

---

[8] Jean-François, marquis de Saint-Lambert, "Luxe," in *Encyclopédie, ou Dictionnaire raisonné des sciences, des arts et des métiers*, vol. 9 (Neufchâtel, 1765).

gued. Luxury, "kept within its proper limits by civic spirit," would reinforce rather than undermine the social order.[9]

Many writers of the late 1760s and 1770s distinguished between a benign luxury which they associated with conveniences and comforts and a vicious luxury that was the fruit of economic privilege and the system of public finance. According to Diderot, a positive luxury characterized by high consumption of necessaries and conveniences was the product of the wealth diffused by a thriving agriculture, while a luxury characterized by "ostentation and misery" was produced by a defective system of public finance and commercial privileges.[10] Such critics saw the solution to the problem of luxury in fiscal reform and the eradication of commercial privileges, but also in economic development. The sign of moderate, beneficial luxury, according to Jean-François Butini, was a prosperous and well-dressed peasantry such as one might find in the English countryside or in the France of Henri IV. Butini celebrated the activity of England's burgeoning industrial centers—Manchester, Yarmouth, and Sheffield— which employed thousands in districts that would otherwise be sterile. A state could enjoy the advantages of luxury without suffering its inconveniences, he insisted, if it fostered the useful arts, founded manufactures, and developed roads and canals. But the law must impose barriers to excessive inequality by abolishing exclusive privileges, tax farming, and primogeniture.[11]

In the late 1760s and 1770s, many critics claimed that privileged commerce sowed luxury by producing artificial income inequalities. Such criticisms uncoupled luxury from trade per se; indeed, free commerce was represented as an antidote to luxury. Saint-Lambert argued that the great inequalities on which a destructive luxury were founded flowed from economic privileges which distorted the natural distribution of commercial wealth.[12] Condillac echoed this claim, arguing that free trade limited inequality, and with it the possibilities for a harmful luxury.[13] This argument owed much to the Physiocratic critique of privilege. In Physiocratic theory, the profits of merchants were composed of a modest salary the trader paid himself, together with the interest on his initial investment. If merchants and manufacturers were making huge gains, as the Physiocrats conceded they were, then this could only be because exclusive privileges allowed them to overcharge the consumer. The abbé Baudeau claimed that the cure for luxury lay in freedom of trade—an end to all monopolies, privileges, and prohibitions. "The liberty of commerce would be the first enemy of luxury," Baudeau affirmed.[14]

[9] Saint-Lambert, "Luxe," 766–67.

[10] Denis Diderot, Diderot on Art, trans. John Goodman (New Haven, 1995), 2:75–78.

[11] Butini, Traité du luxe, 13, 45–47, 182–89, 221.

[12] Saint-Lambert, "Luxe," 766–67.

[13] Étienne Bonnot de Condillac, Le commerce et le gouvernement considérés relativement l'un à l'autre (Amsterdam, 1776), 245, 257–58.

[14] Nicolas Baudeau, Principes de la science morale et politique sur le luxe et les loix somptuaires (Paris, 1767), 22. Twenty years later, the remaining Physiocrats were still making the same argu-

The difference between free commerce and privileged commerce was underlined in the controversy over the fate of the French Indies Company in the summer and fall of 1769. The critics of the company, who sought the abrogation of its exclusive privilege, represented privileged commerce as an adjunct of finance rather than of trade, and linked privilege to speculation. The Indies Company was founded in 1664 and endowed by Louis XIV with the exclusive right to trade with all territories east of the Cape of Good Hope. The War of Austrian Succession proved disastrous for the company, and it limped along through the 1750s, sustained by royal subventions and heavy borrowing. Vincent de Gournay proposed that the monarchy withdraw the company's privilege and open the Asian traffic to all comers.[15] But the Crown held off from any decisive action; the Indies Company was a powerful lobby, with shares in the hands of many courtiers, financiers, and other rich individuals.[16] In the 1760s, according to Louis Cullen, three main factions struggled to determine the destiny of the company: a circle of financiers around the court banker Jean-Joseph de Laborde, and his associate Jean-Baptiste Magon de la Balue; another dominated by the Jacobite commercial nobility of the western ports; and a third led by Jacques Necker. The first two groups formed an alliance aimed at liquidating the company on favorable terms. Both had strong ties to Choiseul, both represented powerful port interests, and both expected to profit from a relaxation of the company's privilege. Necker's group, which represented certain court factions along with Paris commercial banking interests, wished to preserve the company intact and to reopen trade with the Indies.[17]

Matters came to a head in 1769 when, with Choiseul's backing, the controller general Maynon d'Invau sought to revoke the privilege of the company.[18] He turned over its accounts to the abbé Morellet, one of Gournay's former acolytes, and commissioned him to write a critique, the *Mémoire sur la situation actuelle de la Compagnie des Indes*. As represented by Morellet, privileged commercial companies had little to do with trade. Rather, the Compagnie des Indes was a financial shell game borrowing enormous sums to pay dividends to its shareholders, and channeling monies out of public coffers into the hands of its powerful administrators. Unlike real merchants who would be-

---

ment. See J.-N.-M. Guérineau de Saint-Péravi, *Principes du commerce opposé au trafic, développés par un homme d'état* (n.p., 1787), 18.

[15] Édouard Moisson, *Dupont de Nemours et la question de la Compagnie des Indes* (New York, 1968) [1918], 61–63.

[16] Marraud, *Noblesse de Paris*, 320–21.

[17] Louis M. Cullen, "History, Economic Crises, and Revolution: Understanding Eighteenth-Century France," *Economic History Review* 46, no. 4 (1993): 635–57; idem, "Lüthy's La Banque Protestante: A Reassessment," *Bulletin du centre d'histoire des espaces atlantiques* 5 (1990): 229–63. See also Robert D. Harris, *Necker: Reform Statesman of the Ancien Régime* (Berkeley, 1979), 26.

[18] Lüthy, *Banque protestante*, 2:391–95; Chaussinand-Nogaret, *Choiseul*, 206.

come insolvent if their outlay long exceeded their revenues, the enormous size and complexity of the company had allowed it to hide its losses for decades. Morellet argued that its capital had been eroding since the 1720s, that the directors and syndics had paid themselves commissions equivalent to a profit of over 33 million livres during a period when the enterprise was almost always running at a loss. Through creative accounting and over 400 million livres in public subventions, the company had sustained enough confidence to allow it to continue to borrow and thus stave off dissolution. Morellet highlighted the costs to society such a policy entailed. The monies lavished on the company might better have been spent on infrastructure, on tax cuts, or a reduction of the state's debts. He proposed that the privilege of the company be rescinded and free trade opened to the Indies.[19] The memorandum was released to the public on the eve of the government's announcement that it intended to suspend the monopoly. Here, again, we see the strategy of appealing to the public to endorse a major reform initiative. Many of the shareholders were furious. Necker composed a rejoinder to Morellet that the company published at its own expense, and the Physiocrat Pierre-Samuel Dupont weighed in with a lengthy brochure supporting the abbé.[20]

Dupont represented the company as a vehicle for speculation, or *agiotage,* emphasizing the role it played in John Law's infamous "System." Under the Regency, the Scottish financier had tried to use paper money to stimulate the economy and at the same time to pay off the enormous debts left by Louis XIV.[21] Law's scheme quickly produced an explosion of speculation on the notes issued by his Mississippi Company, and when the bubble burst, many investors were ruined. Despite this disastrous experience, projects for a paper money to stimulate economic activity were elaborated intermittently in the 1730s and 1740s.[22] Indeed, one of the factions seeking to reform the Indies Company proposed to transform it into a *caisse d'escompte,* or discount bank, which would issue paper money as a means to promote commercial exchanges.[23] Under Law's superintendancy of the royal finances, the company had been, in Dupont's words, a "servile tool" in the hands of the Scotsman. Its purpose was to borrow from the creditors of the state sums sufficient for the Crown to re-

[19] André Morellet, *Mémoire sur la situation actuelle de la Compagnie des Indes* (n.p., 1769), 26–32, 35–36, 75–79, 130–31, 153–57.

[20] Jacques Necker, "Réponse au mémoire de M. l'abbé Morellet sur la Compagnie des Indes," in *Oeuvres complètes de M. Necker, publiées par M. le baron de Staël* (Paris, 1821), 15:127–202; Pierre-Samuel Dupont de Nemours, *Du commerce et de la Compagnie des Indes, seconde édition . . . augmentée de l'histoire du système de Law* (Paris, 1769). Morellet published a reply to Necker, *Examen de la Réponse au mémoire de M. N . . .* (Paris, 1769).

[21] On Law, see Antoin E. Murphy, *John Law: Economic Theorist and Policy Maker* (Oxford, 1997).

[22] Simone Meyssonnier traces the debate on this subject in the 1730s and 1740s. Meyssonnier, *Balance et l'horloge.* See also Spengler, *French Predecessors of Malthus,* 51–52; Paul Harsin, *Les doctrines monétaires et financières en France du XVIe au XVIIIe siècle* (Paris, 1928).

[23] Lüthy, *Banque protestante,* 2:389–90.

imburse those same creditors. It was part of Law's intention, according to Dupont, to encourage speculation. For the Physiocrat, as for many of his contemporaries, *agiotage* represented the worst excesses to which a commercial society could succumb, a state of affairs in which the avarice, illusion, and irrationality that always threatened commercial society came fully, triumphantly, to the fore. During the time of Law, according to Dupont, "the national spirit was debased for a time;" citizens clamored to pay in gold for paper whose value was "almost entirely imaginary;" good land was sold in exchange for paper, "and that paper for other paper."[24]

Dupont did not limit himself to criticizing the Indies Company; the Asian trade itself, he claimed, was disadvantageous to the nation. This commerce had been a source of endless wars against rival European powers. If France gave up the Indies trade, he argued, wars would be more rare and less costly.[25] The 1770s was a period of considerable skepticism about the commercial humanist claim that trade created pacific relations between peoples. The harshest critics of foreign trade also reversed the claim that commerce is a civilizing force to insist that trade had produced a new barbarism in the form of slavery and colonial oppression. "Oh peoples who claim to be civilized, how barbaric you are!" Paul Boesnier de l'Orme lamented in his *L'esprit du gouvernement économique* (1775). He censured the European desire for conquest and excoriated the policies of commercial monopoly and colonization.[26] Such anti-colonial sentiment became more common after the publication of the abbé Raynal's *Histoire philosophique et politique des deux Indes* (1770), a work that underlined the frightful toll in human life exacted by Europeans in their pursuit of colonial wealth.[27] Others insisted, however, that it was only privileged commerce that sowed injustice. According to André-Daniel Laffon de Ladébat, privileged commerce engendered slavery and the misery of other peoples. By pushing the commerce of a nation beyond its natural limits, it engendered conflicts between peoples. Free trade, however, extended the commerce of a nation "to the limits prescribed by nature and the competition of other nations."[28]

As in the 1750s, when Gournay's circle led the way, the defenses of commerce that proliferated in the 1770s were often elaborated by individuals with roots in the world of trade. Laffon was part of a great Bordeaux merchant

---

[24] Dupont, *Du commerce et de la Compagnie des Indes,* 100–101, 116, 142. Dupont may be attacking the idea that the Indies Company be converted into a discount bank, an institution that would have issued notes functioning as a form of paper money in a manner analogous to Law's Mississippi Company of the 1720s.

[25] Ibid., 54–55, 60.

[26] Paul Boesnier de l'Orme, *De l'esprit du gouvernement économique* (Paris, 1775), 107–8.

[27] Guillaume-Thomas-François Raynal, *Histoire philosophique et politique, des établissemens & du commerce des Européens dans les deux Indes* (Amsterdam, 1770), 271.

[28] André-Daniel Laffon de Ladébat, *Réponse au maire d'Orient, ou Défense d'un mémoire adressé au gouvernement . . . sur les avantages d'une liberté absolue pour le commerce de l'Inde* (n.p., 1776), 9–10, 26–27, 43–45.

family involved in the Asian trade after the suspension of the Indies Company's privilege.[29] His seemingly high-minded critique of commercial privileges was framed within a broader attack on the favored status of the port of Lorient, which, even after the suppression of the Indies Company's monopoly, remained the only port where ships returning from Asia could be off-loaded.[30] Interventions such as Laffon's became more common in the 1770s and 1780s, as merchants engaged more fully in the public sphere. In the seventeenth century, the merchant had been a being on the margins of public discourse. The education of merchants tended to exclude them from literary culture. "In Saint-Malo," according to Daniel Roche, "it was common to say that 'going to school is neither useful nor convenient.'" Instead of being schooled at the *collèges,* sons of merchants were sent to sea or to a merchant house in another country, excluding them from the elite culture of the humanities. Merchants read little and possessed few books. By the middle of the eighteenth century, however, all this was changing. According to Roche, the desire for social advancement brought more merchant children into elite education. Merchants acquired larger libraries and became "adepts of new, more public forms of reading such as lending libraries." Indeed, Roche argues, "the traders of western France led the way in reading works about politics and economics as well as newspapers."[31]

In the 1770s and 1780s, traders became increasingly adept at using publicity to forward their objectives. Fashion merchants and the fashion press sought to separate *la mode* from an association with corruption and luxury by redefining it as a peculiarly feminine concern, and representing it as an expression of tasteful self-expression, rather than courtly display. The fashion press also made the argument that fashion stimulated the national economy and was therefore beneficial to the public.[32] Individuals who bridged the gulf between the world of trade and the world of letters played an especially important role in disseminating positive representations of commerce. Nicolas Bergasse, the son of an important merchant house with branches in Lyons and Marseilles, who trained in the law, articulated an eloquent defense of commerce in 1774, arguing that sympathy was the foundation of trade. Among simple peoples, "pity . . . perhaps gave them the first idea of commerce, and it was without doubt the exchange of the products of their feeble agriculture which, in bringing them closer to each other, rendered them more industrious and less savage." Like so many other defenders of commerce in the 1770s, Bergasse acknowl-

[29] Lüthy, *Banque protestante,* 2:439.
[30] Georges Gaigneux, *Lorient et la Compagnie des Indes* (Lorient, 1957), 15.
[31] Roche, *France in the Enlightenment,* 160–72.
[32] Jennifer M. Jones, "Repackaging Rousseau: Femininity and Fashion in Old Regime France," *French Historical Studies* 18, no. 4 (1994): 939–67. See also Dena Goodman, "Furnishing Discourses: Readings of a Writing Desk in Eighteenth-Century France," in *Luxury in the Eighteenth Century: Debates, Desires, and Delectable Goods,* ed. Maxine Berg and Elizabeth Eger (New York, 2003).

edged the ills of luxury, conceding that it led to the destruction of liberty and precipitated the fall of empires. But he insisted that luxury was not the fruit of commerce.[33]

Another significant agency for the diffusion of positive representations of commerce in the 1770s and 1780s was the advertising press, or *affiches*, analyzed recently by Colin Jones. Published in dozens of provincial cities, and in Paris, these newssheets, targeted at traders and entrepreneurs, carried advertisements along with commercial information: shipping news, prices in local markets, and announcements of sales and auctions. As promoters of consumption, the affiches were anxious to avoid charges of endorsing luxury. Most editors followed the new Enlightenment position that distinguished between a vicious luxury associated with ostentation and a luxury of comfort and convenience characteristic of the virtuous middling ranks.[34] The editor of the *Affiches, annonces, et avis divers*, commonly known as the *Affiches de province*, harshly condemned Georges-Marie Butel-Dumont's *Théorie du luxe*, a work published in 1771, which took a highly favorable view of luxury. He reproached the author for "justifying luxury in the unfortunate circumstances where it is the scandal of mediocre fortunes and the despair of the indigent," and argued forcefully that "luxury, rather than rendering states more flourishing, in fact . . . must necessarily undermine them . . . . It is luxury, uniquely luxury, that general corrupter of manners . . . which prepared, necessitated, consummated the fall of all the great empires."[35] While rejecting luxury, the affiches disseminated positive representations of commerce. According to Jones, "They overlooked their profit-oriented organization to conceive of themselves playing an altruistic role in the diffusion of Enlightened ideas" and diffused belief in "the enlightening and civilizing powers of trade." The self-appointed mission of these newssheets was "the making of happiness, the fostering of national spirit, and the nurturing of citizenship."[36]

Alongside the conceptual separation that was occurring in the 1770s between commerce and luxury, important shifts emerged in the representation of merchants and entrepreneurs. Traditionally the merchant was viewed as a being driven by interest, and therefore incapable of subordinating the profit motive to the general good. Such prejudices were still common in the eighteenth century. In 1757, the Parlement of Grenoble wrote that "No respectable man could embrace the profession of commerce. The honor and sentiments which he would

[33] Nicolas Bergasse, *Discours prononcé à l'hôtel de ville de Lyon, le 21 décembre 1774* (Lyons, 1775) 14, 32–33, 39–41.

[34] Colin Jones, "The Great Chain of Buying: Medical Advertisement, the Bourgeois Public Sphere, and the Origins of the French Revolution," *American Historical Review* 101, no. 1 (1996): 13–40.

[35] "Livres nouveaux," in *Affiches, annonces, et avis divers (Affiches de province)* 50 (December 18, 1771): 201–2.

[36] Jones, "Great Chain of Buying," 24–25.

possess are incompatible with the knowledge of petty details, the grime of mer-
chandise and the dust of bales."[37] Merchants themselves, in many instances,
subscribed to a social ethos that represented commerce as potentially corrupting. As Amalia Kessler has shown in her analysis of eighteenth-century merchant
courts, "the fact that litigants argued without the assistance of lawyers and mer-
chant-court judges received no emolument was crucial to contemporary merchants because it ensured that justice would not be for sale—that it would be
kept outside the realm of commerce and thus shielded from the base commercialization to which the 'normal' courts were deemed so susceptible."[38]

Albert Hirschman claims that pecuniary interest was reimagined in eighteenth-century France as a socially beneficial impulse. According to Hirschman,
moralists who believed that human passions might be kept in check by using
one passion to restrain another came to the conclusion that the role of "bal-
ancing passion" could best be played by *interest*—the passion for wealth. Interest was suitable for this role, according to Hirschman, because it was
regarded as a calm and regular passion, one that, if not exactly laudable, was
at least rational and predictable. Construed as a check on humankind's more
destructive urges, he suggests, interest began a slow transition that transformed
it from a vice into a quasi-virtuous disposition.[39] There is certainly some evidence of writers attempting to present interest in a positive light. The Physiocrats, as Hirschman rightly points out, made interest the cornerstone of their
system. The writers descended intellectually from Gournay were also quite well
disposed toward interest. In his attack on the Indies Company, the abbé Morellet depicted free commerce in very positive terms, representing the mercantile
pursuit of interest as a kind of heroism.[40] I suggest, however, that Morellet and
the Physiocrats were exceptional in this respect.[41] Interest largely retained its
negative associations.

Without contesting the potentially corrupting character of the interest motive, merchants found ways to represent their activities as virtuous and public
spirited. The most important means they found to do so was to represent the
trader as a being driven by emulation. For many commentators who defined
themselves as patriots, emulation offered the only means to induce men to subordinate private interest to the public good in a world corrupted by money. To
reverse the ravages of luxury in a state, Mably's Phocion counsels, "Try to revive in hearts some spark of the love of glory, it is the only one of all the virtues
which, with the assistance of vanity, can show itself in the midst of an extreme

[37] Henri Lévy-Bruhl, "La noblesse de France et le commerce à la fin de l'ancien régime," *Revue
d'histoire moderne* 8 (1933): 226.

[38] Amalia D. Kessler, "Enforcing Virtue: Social Norms and Self-Interest in an Eighteenth-Century Merchant Court," *Law and History Review* 22, no. 1 (2004).

[39] Hirschman, *Passions and the Interests*, passim.

[40] Morellet, *Mémoire sur la situation actuelle*, 154–56.

[41] John Shovlin, "Emulation in Eighteenth-Century French Economic Thought," *Eighteenth-Century Studies* 36, no. 2 (2003): 224–30.

corruption."[42] I am not suggesting that attributing emulative impulses to the merchant was a deliberate strategy to remake him as a patriot—not initially, at least. Rather, the widespread discourse on the need to use honor to animate economic activity, including commerce, disseminated a way of thinking about the merchant as a being responsive to honor at least as much as to profit. Moreover, merchants *were* powerfully attracted by the honorific distinctions that still played such an important role in creating and marking status. The inexorable drain of capital out of commerce and into land, offices, and *rentes*—forms of property less profitable, but more honorable—was proof of this fact.[43]

The view popularized by writers such as Coyer and Dangeul that commerce could be animated by making it honorable enjoyed a hugely successful career in the final decades of the eighteenth century. Instead of arguing that nobles ought to become involved in commerce so that the stigma attached to trade would be lifted, most commentators suggested that merchants who were particularly successful should be honored by the state. Jean Auffray rejected the idea that nobles should enter trade, but he was equally adamant that the monopoly of honors enjoyed by the First and Second Estates be broken; Auffray demanded that merchants be honored.[44] The anonymous author of *Le négociant citoyen* (1764) argued that while merchants and nobles should remain in their respective estates, the administration should "take notice" of the merchants who distinguished themselves through zeal for the *patrie*.[45] Similarly, in *L'apologie du commerce* (1777), Louis-Hippolyte Dudevant pointed out that while among nobles the love of glory drew a man from a quiet country life, or a life of city pleasures, and threw him into wars and battles, among merchants this same love of glory attracted men out of occupations where, for the good of the country, they ought to remain. As a remedy, Dudevant proposed that wholesale merchant families be ennobled who maintained an honorable commerce through three generations, so long as the ennobled generation agreed to remain in trade.[46]

Cumulatively, such arguments helped to recast the meaning of commerce and the status of the traders who pursued it. In the 1760s and 1770s, farming, trade, and industry were widely represented as fields for the pursuit of honor as much as arenas for the accumulation of profit. Economic agency was imagined as a kind of emulation. Through the avenue of emulation, merchants and entrepre-

---

[42] Mably, *Entretiens de Phocion*, 2:144. For similar comments, see also D'Arcq, *Noblesse militaire*, 65–66; Mirabeau, *Ami des hommes*, 2:78.

[43] Doyle, *Venality*, 168–69.

[44] Jean Auffray, *Le luxe considéré relativement à la population et à l'économie* (Lyons, 1762), 26–28.

[45] Anon., *Le négociant citoyen, ou Essai sur la recherche des moyens d'augmenter les lumières de la nation sur le commerce et l'agriculture* (Amsterdam, 1764), 10.

[46] Louis-Hippolyte Dudevant de Bordeaux, *L'apologie du commerce, essai philosophique et politique . . . suivi de diverses réflexions sur le commerce en général, sur celui de la France en particulier, & sur les moyens propres à l'accroître & le perfectionner* (Geneva, 1777), 47–49.

neurs, previously supposed to lack the aptitude for public spirit, might be redeemed as potential patriots. If farmers and merchants were sensitive to considerations of honor, it followed that they were not locked into an interest-based personality structure. Dudevant argued that if merchants were given a chance to win honor in their profession, if the state accorded titles to particularly successful traders, "Commerce will no longer be guided by the sordid spirit of interest . . . it will be jealous to acquire a true glory." He claimed that ennoblement would also deliver merchants from the tendency to console themselves for their low status by an immoderate luxury.[47]

One of the most thoroughgoing attempts to redeem the merchant as a patriot was a book called *Le négociant patriote* originally published in 1779, with a second edition issued in 1784. The author, a merchant named Bedos, did not attempt to remake the trader by claiming that the free play of interest had positive social effects. Rather, he argued that merchants were actuated by patriotism, generosity, and honor. Characterizing interest as "that being which corrupts men," Bedos suggested that a small number of "sublime souls" had managed to hold themselves above this corrupting impulse. He identified great international merchants as a particularly patriotic group. "Patriotism shines more in them than in the others," he claimed, "it activates them; it consumes them." Bedos made it clear that merchants were animated by emulation. Speaking for himself, as a merchant, he stated that "I prefer my honor to the loss of my life." He represented finance as the mutual enemy of agriculture and commerce. In his dedicatory preface to the Chambers of Commerce of France, he claimed to have "sighed" with those leaders of the mercantile community "to see all the goods of this world passing to *traitans* (financial contractors), to the bearers of privilege."[48]

The flourishing of an emulation-centered vision of commerce challenged those conceptions of emulation that had envisioned a privileged role for the nobility. Commentators, such as Mirabeau and the chevalier d'Arcq, argued that honor ought to be confined to nobles. According to their view, the nobility was the only social class capable of consistently placing the public good before private interest, a proclivity that followed from nobles' acute sensitivity to honor. Commoners were incapable of such accomplishments, according to d'Arcq, because they were habituated to placing profit before considerations of honor. If honor were lavished on nonnobles, not only would it be wasted, it would lose its value for the nobility and there would be no stimulus left to spur them to public-spirited action. The kind of thinking that called for the use of honor to encourage commerce and agriculture eroded the view that nonnobles were purely calculators, and thus incapable of the kind of patriotism and heroism

---

[47] Ibid., 52.

[48] Bedos, *Le négociant patriote, contenant un tableau qui réunit les avantages du commerce, la connaissance des spéculations de chaque nation . . . par un négociant qui a voyagé* (Amsterdam, 1784), 106, 67, 224, x.

that nobles alone displayed. It implied that the passion for honor could most successfully be exploited for society's benefit if the competition for honor was extended to as many areas of life and as many social actors as possible, rather than confining that competition to nobles.

The claim that nonnobles were not sensitive enough to honor to be capable of generous emulative impulses was met by a wave of texts arguing that even the meanest members of society were sensitive to honor and could be induced to behave in a socially useful fashion by the prospect of honorific rewards. The sense that a preference for honor over profit was a part of the French national character was widespread in the 1770s. Bounties might be the best means to revivify agriculture in nations where self-interest predominated, argued a member of the agricultural society of Tours in 1778, but "in ours distinctions are necessary: the Frenchman gets more satisfaction from the consideration attached to his profession . . . than from the lucre that follows that profession."[49] The same faith that emulation might inspire socially useful action was also extended to urban craftsmen. The Société libre d'émulation, founded in 1776 by the abbé Baudeau to promote mechanical discoveries and inventions, stated that its objective was "to excite emulation among artists and artisans."[50] The democratization of honor that the discourse on emulation entailed was extended even to beggars by the 1770s. One of the most important works of that decade dealing with the problem of poverty argued that the vagrant's taste for work could be reanimated through the use of emulation. "Let us accord marks of distinction to those who lead a laborious life," the author argued, "let us cover idleness and begging with disdain and ignominy: we are sure to extirpate these vices." It might be objected, the author noted, that beggars are "hardly susceptible to the sentiments of honor," but this, he affirmed, was an error: "the Frenchman forgets himself; but his character is never effaced."[51]

Beginning in the 1760s, a few proponents of this egalitarian conception of emulation developed a critique of hereditary nobility emphasizing that the noble monopoly on honor stifled emulation among nonnobles. Only by making nobility personal and using it to reward virtuous or useful actions, they argued, could the institution be reconciled with the common good. One of the earliest tracts that drew upon and developed the anti-noble potential implicit in the argument that agriculture and commerce should be honored was the abbé Pierre Jaubert's Éloge de la roture (1766). Jaubert, the curé of a parish near Bordeaux, and editor of the Dictionnaire raisonné universel des arts et métiers (1773) was not satisfied with pointing out that commoners ought to be honored, he denied

[49] Fresnais de Beaumont, Noblesse cultivatrice, 5.

[50] Règlements de la Société libre d'émulation, établie à Paris en 1776 pour l'encouragement des inventions qui tendent à perfectionner la pratique des arts et métiers utiles (n.p., 1780), 9.

[51] Abbé Malvaux, Les moyens de détruire la mendicité en France, en rendant les mendians utiles à l'État sans les rendre malheureux; tirés des mémoires qui ont concouru pour le prix accordé en l'année 1777, par l'Académie des sciences, arts & belles-lettres de Châlons-sur-Marne (Paris, 1780), 323–28.

that the nobility deserved the honor that it monopolized. He suggested that personal nobility ought to be substituted for hereditary nobility, because the former encouraged emulation while the latter stifled it. He contended that nobility was a privilege originally granted by commoners to the bravest and wisest of their number in order to encourage emulation. These rewards for virtue were not passed on to descendants except "when . . . they rendered themselves worthy of them through great actions." Being a reward for virtue, nobility must be personal only.[52] Jaubert's argument was echoed by Augustin Rouillé d'Orfeuil, who suggested in 1773 that agriculture should be encouraged by rewarding particularly active and enterprising farmers with honor. He combined this warm endorsement of emulation with a frontal attack on the "hereditary principle," denouncing the latter as an absurdity, on the grounds that nobility must be a purely personal reward for public service if "emulation" was to be encouraged.[53]

What Henry Clark has noted of seventeenth-century France was also true of the eighteenth century: commerce was legitimated principally by attributing to the merchant the kinds of qualities traditionally associated with nobles—love of honor, patriotism, and a sentiment of duty.[54] Rather than embracing some version of "market culture" as a mode of self-legitimation, merchants, and most of those who spoke on their behalf, embraced a strategy of rendering trade "national" by remaking its agents as patriots, driven by the same emulation that inspired noble deeds on the battlefield. What seems to have happened in the process, albeit on the margins of this discourse, was a questioning of the virtues of the nobility, and a reversal of the traditional images of the noble and the merchant. That such a reversal was plausible was due in part, as we shall see, to the increasingly negative representations attaching to nobility in the 1770s, and particularly to symbolic efforts to link nobility and luxury.

A Critique of Aristocracy

In the 1770s, critics of the nobility represented the Second Estate as an adjunct of a social system founded on the power of money. The aristocratic practice of using dazzling displays of consumption to mark and assert an exalted social position could readily be construed as a plutocratic mode of power. With numerous links tying the court nobility to capitalist ventures and tax farming, one could plausibly view the aristocracy as a money-hungry class whose interests were contrary to those of the nation. Much of the hostility to nobility derived from criticisms of court and Parisian nobles, and *grands seigneurs*, rather

[52] Abbé Pierre Jaubert, *Éloge de la roture dédié aux roturiers* (London, 1766), 23–24.
[53] Augustin Rouillé d'Orfeuil, *L'alambic moral, ou Analyse raisonnée de tout ce qui a rapport à l'homme* (Morocco, 1773), 317, 425–27, 526.
[54] Clark, "Commerce, the Virtues, and the Public Sphere," 438.

than the nobility *tout court*. To some extent, indeed, this critique articulated the frustration and anger of provincial nobles. As Rafe Blaufarb has shown, middling nobles, and especially military nobles, spoke "a language of social resentment" in the final decades of the old regime.[55] This resentment was directed not just against the ennobled sons of financiers whose wealth facilitated rapid promotion in the military, but against courtier officers whose rise seemed to be as effortless as it was unmerited. But middling nobles were not immune to criticism themselves. The sheer scale on which venal office had transformed nonnobles into nobles since the seventeenth century left the whole order vulnerable to the charge that nobility had become a mere expression of wealth, indeed, a commodity in its own right. Also, as a disproportionately wealthy class whose local influence was tied as much to money as to honor, the nobility could be fitted without much difficulty into the mold of plutocracy. In the difficult economic conditions of the early 1770s, some critics were ready to blame pauperization on the affluence of the gilded minority.

The contrast between an innocent luxury of comforts and conveniences and a malevolent luxury of ostentation, which emerged as a central contrast in writing on consumption in the 1770s, served to condemn the traditional aristocratic practice of using spectacular appearances to mark and assert social rank. One of the traditional meanings of luxury was the usurpation by the low-born of clothing or other commodities appropriate only to their betters. While spectacular appearances were legitimate for the well-born, they were illicit for those of low origins. In the 1760s and 1770s, this sense of luxury was turned on its head. Critics began to employ the term to refer to *all* uses of spectacular consumption for the purpose of social distinction, regardless of the social position of the user, and the focus of criticism shifted from the low-born to *les grands*. Moralists attacked the use of pomp for purposes of social distinction arguing not that magnificence should be the sole prerogative of the king and the nobility, but that conspicuous consumption should no longer be used to constitute social order or political authority. In the words of one writer, "the crime of luxury is that it makes us judge a man not according to what he is, but according to what surrounds him. We confuse the man with his horses, his liveries, his equipages, his appearance."[56] The aristocracy was sensitive to this critique and started to change its modes of dress, adopting less ornate clothing, often in imitation of English "country" styles.[57] Marie-Antoinette led the way, making fashionable a simple white chemise for elite women.[58]

Criticisms of the nobility as a luxurious class could also flow from the compulsive emphasis on the honorable character of agriculture and the peasants who practiced it. As Amy Wyngaard shows, sentimental drama depicting vir-

[55] Rafe Blaufarb, "Nobles, Aristocrats, and the Origins of the French Revolution," in *Tocqueville and Beyond*, ed. R. M. Schwartz and R. A. Schneider (Newark, DE, 2003).

[56] Jean-François André, *Le Tartare à Paris* (Paris, 1788), 83.

[57] Aileen Ribeiro, *Fashion in the French Revolution* (London, 1988), 39.

[58] Jones, *Sexing La Mode*, 183.

tuous peasants as protagonists in the late 1760s and 1770s carried sharply anti-noble messages.[59] Charles-Simon Favart's *Les moissonneurs* was overtly anti-aristocratic and, though it affirmed the goodness of virtuous country nobles, it contained a more radical subtext. The play turns on a series of events that oc-cur when Candor, a country gentleman, receives a visit at harvest time from his villainous aristocratic nephew Dolival. Candor is the ideal seigneur: he throws himself into agricultural work, treats his peasants as equals, and keeps a pa-ternalistic eye out for their welfare. Dolival sneers at the local manners and tries to seduce the virtuous peasant girl Rosine, the heroine of the play. The good noble and the bad are clearly demarcated by their attitudes toward luxury. To his nephew's horror, Candor dresses in a simple farmer's smock. "Decency de-mands dress in conformity to one's birth," Dolival cautions, "one would take you for a farmer." "I have the honor to be one," replies Candor, "I make my farm valuable and I give myself over entirely to the infinite details which this involves. I take pride in the clothing of the profession." Candor directly op-poses the interests of country people to those of the court nobility: "That species you despise," Candor admonishes Dolival, "is the victim of people who are good for nothing. When you have lost all your goods in gambling, you pressure them to pay for your foolishness."[60]

Such theater was open to two different readings, either as an overt affirma-tion of the virtue and utility of an uncorrupted, provincial noble class in con-trast to a corrupt aristocracy, or as an implicit rejection of nobility in favor of social egalitarianism. As Wyngaard points out, there are deeply egalitarian mes-sages embedded in the text. Humble people are represented as honorable and disinterested. Rosine, who finds a purse of gold, turns it over to Candor, ob-serving that "poor people have honor." Candor constantly acknowledges his equality with ordinary people. The play is ambiguous on the nobility's claim to hereditary virtue. The fact that the corrupt Dolival is the nephew of the virtu-ous Candor implicitly undercuts any claim to the hereditary character of virtue, yet it turns out at the end that Rosine, the paragon of commoner virtue, was well-born all along. Perhaps the most significant message of the drama is that the good noble must cut himself off from virtually every aspect of noble status as traditionally defined: elegant dress, the seigneurial château, a life of leisure. Candor's nobility resides in none of these things, but entirely in his virtue; how-ever, if virtue constitutes true nobility, then any virtuous man or woman is the equal of a noble.[61]

In the salons of the philosophes, there was disagreement about whether no-bility was part of the problem of luxury or part of the solution. Saint-Lambert's argument in the *Encyclopédie* was underpinned by a corporatist vision of soci-ety in which distinctions of estate were still worth preserving. He argued that

---

[59] Wyngaard, *From Savage to Citizen*, 73–74.
[60] Charles-Simon Favart, *Les moissonneurs, comédie en trois actes* (Paris, 1768), 17–18.
[61] Ibid., 60, 79.

luxury was undermining the hierarchical social order, thereby threatening the whole system of authority on which society rested. "If the use of wealth endows the . . . ordinary citizen with the retinue of high station, then the common people will necessarily lose their awe of the men who are destined to lead them. As the proper attributes of each estate disappear, there vanishes even the slightest trace of the general social order." In a reformed polity where government more successfully balanced wealth and virtue, according to Saint-Lambert, consumption would reinforce rather than dissolve the boundaries of society. "The different kinds of luxury goods will then be distributed according to the differences between estates: the military men will have fine weapons and prize horses . . . the luxury of a magistrate will express the importance of his station, it will be dignified and restrained; the businessman and the financier will seek elegance in comfort." As part of this reformed social order, Saint-Lambert envisioned a regenerated nobility, custodian of national honor and the spirit of patriotism. "The nobles will inspire men with love of country and all the feelings of virtuous and uncompromising honor." Such views are unsurprising for a man of Saint-Lambert's background and status. A titled noble, descended from an old Lorraine family, Saint-Lambert served in the royal army at the rank of colonel before turning to a career as a man of letters.[62]

Others in the philosophic party took a different view, placing the blame for a vicious luxury squarely on the nobility. According to Alexandre Deleyre, a collaborator of Raynal on his *Histoire philosophique et politique des deux Indes,* and later a regicide deputy to the revolutionary Convention, it was not the economically active who were corrupted by commercial wealth but the idle classes. Deleyre set out to show that the effects of commerce were almost entirely positive. The source of corruption when a nation grew rich through trade, he suggested, was the ability of the powerful to engross much of the wealth, giving themselves over to "luxury," "intrigue," and a "baseness that is called grandeur." In a thinly veiled attack on the court aristocracy, Deleyre charged that "Nobility is nothing but an odious distinction, when it is not founded on real services, truly useful to the state, such as defending the nation against invasions and conquest, and against the undertakings of despotism. It is only a precarious and often ruinous assistance when, after leading a soft and licentious life in the cities, it goes to lend a feeble defense to the country in the fleet or in the army, and returns to the court to beg for recompenses for its cowardliness, places and honors outrageous and onerous for the People." This was not a critique of noble mores intended to inspire reform; Deleyre posited no simple, industrious country nobility who might serve as a model for aristocrats to emulate. Indeed, he made sneering remarks about provincial nobles in the same vein as Coyer's *Noblesse commerçante.*[63]

[62] Saint-Lambert, "Luxe," 767, 769.

[63] Alexandre Deleyre, *Tableau de l'Europe, pour servir de supplément à l'Histoire philosophique & politique des établissements & du commerce des Européens dans les deux Indes* (Maastricht, 1774).

A few writers argued that the Second Estate had been so corrupted by the influence of money that nobility itself had become an emblem of luxury—a reasonable position, given the massive influx of wealthy nonnobles into the Second Estate over the course of the century. In an extended poem published in 1774, the chevalier du Coudray lashed out at ennoblement, at financiers, at the fact that "merit" and "blood" were no longer esteemed in Paris, and that only money distinguished. Du Coudray claimed that he would esteem the nobility if it were generous, sublime, or great—that is, if nobles were really noble—but nobility, in his view, was nothing more than "an ill introduced by luxury." Du Coudray celebrated a fraternal order of useful and industrious citizens, contrasting them to the idle, aristocratic rich, "those scoundrels" who appropriated the wealth created by their hard-working fellows. What distinguished the parasitic group, above all, from the true citizens was luxury. But for all these swipes at the titled, du Coudray's text is not so much anti-noble as anti-aristocratic. He claims to hail from a provincial noble family, noting with pride that his father is the "Chevalier Seigneur du Coudray," and a former captain of cavalry. It is those nobles whose nobility is a sign of wealth rather than a token of virtue that he condemns; he rejects the commodification of titles rather than the idea of hereditary privilege.[64]

The attack on the aristocracy as a luxurious class was also articulated in the 1770s through critiques of despotism. The charge that Louis XV's monarchy had become despotic was widespread in that decade. The abbé Terray initiated a partial state bankruptcy in 1770—the ultimate in arbitrary political actions.[65] Terray created new taxes on starch and printed matter, made the first *vingtième* permanent, extended the second to 1781, and revised the tax rolls to increase assessments on the privileged, sparking a revolt among Norman nobles.[66] His efforts to stockpile cereals to meet the subsistence needs of the capital seemed to confirm the rumor that the government was speculating in grain.[67] In 1771, royal chancellor Maupeou rudely reasserted the principle that the monarch was the sole legislative authority by stripping the parlements of all but their judicial functions.[68] The Maupeou coup elicited a violent backlash from self-styled patriot defenders of the sovereign courts against what they represented as royal despotism. There was an explosion of patriot propaganda, much of it

[64] Alexandre-Jacques, chevalier du Coudray, *Le luxe, poëme en six chants; orné de gravures, avec des notes historiques et critiques, suivi de poésies diverses* (Paris, 1773), 30, 132.

[65] Terray suspended payments on the *billets* of the Farmers General and on the *rescriptions* of the Receivers General, promissory notes issued by the financiers that functioned as a form of paper money. He converted ruinously expensive *tontine* loans by fiat into simple annuity loans on single lives, thereby slashing the returns on these securities. He cut arrears payable to holders of various kinds of *rentes* by half; and he postponed the repayment of loan principal due for repayment. Echeverria, *Maupeou Revolution*, 20.

[66] Kwass, *Privilege and the Politics of Taxation*, 199–201.

[67] Steven L. Kaplan, *The Famine Plot Persuasion in Eighteenth-Century France* (Philadelphia, 1982).

[68] For a description of Maupeou's reforms see Echeverria, *Maupeou Revolution*, 14–19.

in the form of *libelles* that harped on the despotism and moral corruption of the king, his ministers, and the court.

Some critics, playing on an age-old theme, linked the despotism of the regime with its luxury. In a thinly veiled censure of the king, J.-F. Butini suggested that the despot, sunken in luxury, cared only about maintaining a magnificent court, stocking his seraglio, investing authority in favorites, and multiplying taxes.[69] In his *Essai sur le despotisme*, the comte de Mirabeau (son of the Physiocratic marquis de Mirabeau) claimed that of all the ways a despot could reach his goal, the cultivation of luxury was the most effective.[70] Deleyre suggested that an excessive love of gain that supplanted patriotic virtue was a feature of regimes organized to serve the interest of a single individual, or of a privileged few.[71] Others made the same connection. In a work inspired by English politics, but with obvious French resonances, the future *montagnard* Jean-Paul Marat identified despotism with a social order governed by an opulent class of financiers, speculators, capitalists, and *rentiers*, a society in which "nobility . . . great employments, dignities and magistracies are venal." Marat claimed that the aspiring despot deliberately fostered such luxury in order to destroy the love of glory. The tyrant, he argued, knows that citizens animated by the passion for honor have too much devotion to the public good to permit the destruction of their liberty. "The first effect of luxury is to stifle [this] love of glory; because once one can attract looks with superb equipages, sumptuous clothing, a crowd of valets, one no longer seeks to distinguish oneself by pure *moeurs*, noble sentiments, great actions, heroic virtues." Once the love of glory was eradicated, Marat argued, nothing was left to excite patriotism and public virtue.[72]

These attacks linking a venal aristocracy to despotism represent the rejection of an opposition in French political culture of the seventeenth and eighteenth century that had distinguished despotism and aristocracy. Apologists for the absolute monarchy represented the Crown as the enemy of aristocracy, as the ally of the people, and as its protector from feudal oppression.[73] Critics of absolutism, such as Montesquieu, to the contrary, regarded the vestiges of aristocratic institutions in France—the parlements, seigneurial justice, and indeed the nobility as a whole—as a critical bulwark against tyranny. This common sense broke down in the closing decades of the old regime. Luxury bound the high aristocracy ever more firmly to the Crown. It was only through the massive transfers of wealth brokered by the king that aristocrats were able to produce

---

[69] Butini, *Traité du luxe*, 111–12.

[70] Honoré-Gabriel Riqueti, comte de Mirabeau, *Essai sur le despotisme* (Paris, 1821) [1775], 188.

[71] Deleyre, *Tableau de l'Europe*, 156–57. For Deleyre, with the Maupeou coup, France had "fallen into corruption under the yoke of despotism." See Venturi, *End of the Old Regime*, 353–54.

[72] Jean-Paul Marat, *Les chaînes de l'esclavage* (Paris, Year I) [1774], 77–78.

[73] Nannerl O. Keohane, *Philosophy and the State in France: The Renaissance to the Enlightenment* (Princeton, 1980), 5–7.

the spectacular displays of consumption that were so vital to the maintenance of their power and influence. As Gabriel Sénac de Meilhan observed, the great French aristocratic families had long since become tributaries of the court.[74] The monarchy was no longer the enemy of the high nobility, but its principal source of income. This dependency made the aristocracy a feeble bulwark against despotism.

The high nobility were also seen as enemies of the fundamental economic reforms that many patriots regarded as necessary for national regeneration. In October 1775, the Italian *Gazetta universale* reported that Turgot had presented the king with a plan to abolish all the tax farms, a plan which would not be easy to implement, because "the greatest lords have interests in the finances."[75] The increasing fusion of the court nobility with *la finance* was made dramatically clear in 1776 when a list of the *croupes* and pensions attached to the lease of the General Farm was published by a renegade clerk from the *contrôle général*, Jean-Baptiste-Louis Coquereau.[76] A considerable portion of the revenues of tax farming passed into a complex network of aristocratic creditors and courtly *pensionnaires*. Most Farmers General owed a share of their profits to *croupiers*, sleeping partners who put up a portion of the purchase capital of a share. In 1774, nearly two thirds of the places in the Company were so divided. In many instances, these *croupiers* were associated with the court: among them were Mme du Barry who derived 200,000 livres from the profits of one Farmer General, and Louis XV himself, who was a *croupier* for two quarter shares and one half share. In addition, the profits of most Farmers General were encumbered with an obligation to pay pensions to persons designated by the king. The pensioners in 1776 were a motley assortment of actors and opera girls patronized by members of the court, former lovers of the king, members of the royal family, members of the administration, and relatives of the abbé Terray and of Madame de Pompadour.[77]

Many commentators in the 1770s were critical of the luxury of the rich and their apparent indifference to the fate of the poor.[78] In the *Anecdotes sur Mme la comtesse du Barry*, Pidansat de Mairobert referred regularly to the hard lot of the people.[79] He complained that "the provinces are despoiled to provide tribute to the luxury and ostentation of a few families, as contemptible in their origins as in their behavior, who cannot see anything superfluous in their opu-

[74] Gabriel Sénac de Meilhan, *Considérations sur les richesses et le luxe* (Amsterdam, 1787), 102.

[75] *Gazetta universale*, no. 82 (October 14, 1775): 650. Quoted in Venturi, *End of the Old Regime*, 371.

[76] Jean-Baptiste-Louis Coquereau, *Mémoires concernant l'administration des finances sous le ministère de M. l'abbé Terrai, contrôleur général* (London, 1776); another edition also published in 1776 carries the title *Mémoires de l'abbé Terrai, contrôleur général, concernant sa vie, son administration, ses intrigues & sa chute; avec une relation de l'émeute arrivée à Paris en 1775* (London, 1776).

[77] Matthews, *Royal General Farms*, 235–37.

[78] Echeverria, *Maupeou Revolution*, 51.

[79] Darnton, *Forbidden Best-Sellers*, 212.

lence; while in the other class millions of families, earning scarcely enough from their miserable toil to stay alive, seem a living reproach to providence for this humiliating inequality."[80] Delisle de Sales suggested that without luxury there would be no poverty. He concluded that "Luxury makes for the pomp of a state for a time: but it is a fire that burns only at the expense of the subsistence which it destroys."[81] In *L'an deux mille quatre cent quarante*, the most popular illegal best seller of the century, Louis-Sébastien Mercier was even more disparaging, remarking that "I do not believe the sewers [of Paris carry] anything more foul than the souls of the rich."[82] Lanjuinais's *Le monarque accompli* (1774), cited by Darnton in his index of illicit best sellers, excoriated the luxury of the rich and advocated popular rebellion against vested court interests.[83]

The background to these attacks on the rich was the economic crisis that swept France in 1769 and 1770. The root of the crisis lay in a series of bad harvests that had driven up prices for basic necessities, eroding the purchasing power of ordinary people, with disastrous consequences for French manufactures. Unemployment surged and a rash of bankruptcies unnerved the business world. In 1770, according to Kaplan, reports of "terrible maladies," and "extreme misery" circulated throughout the kingdom. Some contemporaries could not help connecting the poverty they saw all around them with the luxury of the rich. A subdelegate in the Auvergne reported that "We are on the eve of witnessing one of the most horrible famines; there will be risings against the rich .... While so many of the miserable perish in the countryside, luxury and self-indulgence go on just the same in the big cities."[84]

Beyond the crisis conditions of 1770, poverty was becoming a more pressing social problem in the last decades of the old regime. Travelers often commented on the disparity between the poverty of rural France and the wealth of the cities.[85] According to Alan Forrest, the social mechanisms for dealing with mass poverty were breaking down in the second half of the century as charitable institutions tried to deal with a decrease in charitable bequests and a burgeoning population of paupers. Between 1777 and 1779, the academies of Châlons-sur-Marne, Orléans, Lyons, and Soissons held essay competitions dealing with the problem of beggary.[86] This was probably a response to an initiative Turgot had begun in the months preceding his fall to close most of the *dépôts de mendicité,* which had served to repress begging, and to extend outdoor

---

[80] *Journal historique de la révolution opérée dans la constitution de la monarchie françoise par M. de Maupeou, chancelier de France,* 6:207–8.

[81] Jean-Baptiste-Claude Izouard de Delisle de Sales, *Lettre de Brutus sur les chars anciens et modernes* (London, 1771), 114–15.

[82] Cited in Echeverria, *Maupeou Revolution,* 288.

[83] Joseph Lanjuinais, *Le monarque accompli* (Lausanne, 1774).

[84] Kaplan, *Bread, Politics, and Political Economy,* 489, 502–3.

[85] See, for instance, Arthur Young, *Travels in France* (Cambridge, 1929), 117.

[86] Antoine-François Delandine, *Couronnes académiques, ou Recueil des prix proposés par les sociétés savantes* (Paris, 1787).

relief to the aged and infirm, while creating employment for the able-bodied poor. The Châlons academy attracted 118 entries, five or six times the average for academic essay competitions.[87] Beggars and vagabonds were increasingly represented as dangerous, violent, and menacing, leading to forceful calls for repression.[88] However, there was a countervailing tendency among many publicists to blame the destitution of the rural poor on the luxury of the rich and to construe poverty as a function of deeper problems of the political economic order.

A useful bellwether of the debate on the problem of poverty and inequality is *Les moyens de détruire la mendicité en France,* a work commissioned by the Châlons Academy to synthesize the recommendations of the large number of entries it received in response to its essay competition. The volume's editor, the abbé Malvaux, borrowed many of the themes popularized by the agricultural societies in the 1760s to frame the problems of poverty and begging. All the riches of the provinces are concentrated in the capital, he complained, and luxury is carried there to the last excess; peasants quit the land for Paris and "that Babylon vomits them back as vagabonds to terrorize the countryside." He compared the illusory wealth of contemporary France to "a tumbledown hovel, covered with plaster, which must be propped up with all the precautions of wisdom and prudence rather than allowed to crumble under the vain ornaments with which it has been overloaded." It was only when agriculture, commerce, and navigation had been made to flourish that one ought to think of embellishments, he argued, but the Frenchman who "doesn't have a shirt . . . gives himself cuffs!"[89]

One of the striking features of the *Moyens de détruire la mendicité* is the open hostility it manifests toward the rich and especially the court. According to Malvaux, the inequality on which luxury and poverty are founded flowed from the inequity of the fiscal system and from the parasitic extortions of courtiers. In particular, he blamed the heavy weight of taxes falling on the countryside, the arbitrariness of the *taille,* privileges which shifted the tax burden from the rich to the poor, an apparatus of collection that absorbed a large part of what it gathered, and crushed industry "to maintain pride and splendor." Malvaux described the rich as false, faithless, hard, unjust, and corrupting. Indeed, he ascribed to courtiers and the rich the same vices he attributed to vagabonds. In his view, a man who enjoyed a revenue without working differed little from a brigand. To destroy beggary, and to prevent it from returning, a reform of the *moeurs* both of the people and of *les grands* would be necessary, he argued—the mass of the "political blood" would have to be renewed. Ad-

---

[87] Daniel Roche, "La diffusion des lumières," *Annales* 19, no. 5 (1964): 887–922.

[88] Alan Forrest, *The French Revolution and the Poor* (New York, 1981), 17–20. In his *Mémoire sur les vagabonds et sur les mendiants* (1764), the Physiocrat Guillaume-François Le Trosne called for the death penalty for incorrigible vagrants.

[89] Malvaux, *Moyens de détruire la mendicité,* 409–10, 322, 386.

dressing his advice to the "grandees of the court," the abbé admonished all to live within their means, to give up those immense revenues received from the state which were neither the reward of work nor of virtues. Indeed he accused *les grands* themselves of being beggars: they did "not blush to have their hands out!" Nor was Malvaux alone in using this metaphor. Jean-Baptiste Cotton de Houssayes, the petty noble whom we met in an earlier chapter as a founder of the Rouen Agricultural Society, condemned "aristocrats" as beggars.[90]

Echoing the critique of Physiocracy articulated at the end of the 1760s, Malvaux also attacked the concentration of land in great estates. Certainly, states needed wealthy individuals, he argued, but when riches passed certain bounds and were concentrated in the hands of a few, they became dangerous. Circulation and commerce suffered, and begging sprang up. If the fortunes of a few very affluent houses were suddenly divided among a thousand families, he argued, a few lackeys would be laid off, and the jeweler, the gilder, the perfumer, and the pastry cook would suffer, but every other kind of useful manufacture would benefit. Malvaux expressed admiration for the egalitarian societies of the ancient world but did not believe they offered a model for contemporary France. A better means to create equality than a Spartan-style agrarian law, he argued, would be to encourage economic development. Manufactories and workshops ought to be established to give employment; land should be sold in small parcels, and wasteland given gratis to the poor. If the two million *arpents* of common land were divided among half a million beggars, the problem of rural poverty would be solved at a stroke. Malvaux also highlighted the tax system as an engine of social inequality, and hinted at the need for progressive taxation.[91]

The whole of the *Moyens de détruire la mendicité* is tinged with solicitude about the fate of Turgot. The abbé Malvaux was a partisan of the reforming minister: "All eyes appear to turn towards the council of finance," he wrote. "It is from it that public felicity must come. Tyrants of the people tremble: and you unhappy People wipe away your tears, the soul of Henri IV breathes on the throne, France has her Sully, and already Colbert's panegyrist is his rival."[92] The last reference, to Colbert's panegyrist, is an allusion to Jacques Necker, who had received the prize of the Académie française in 1773 for his eulogy of Colbert, Louis XIV's great finance minister.[93] The *Éloge de Colbert* was Necker's first move in a campaign for the controller generalship, a campaign crowned with success in 1777 when he effectively took control of the royal finances.

---

[90] Ibid., 2, 10, 14, 406–8. On Cotton, see Dewald, *Pont-St-Pierre*, 121–22.

[91] Malvaux, *Moyens de détruire la mendicité*, 421–22.

[92] Ibid., 322.

[93] Jacques Necker, *Éloge de Jean-Baptiste Colbert, discours qui a remporté le prix de l'Académie françoise, en 1773* (Paris, 1773).

Turgot versus Necker

The *Entretiens de Périclès et de Sully aux Champs Élisées, sur leur admin-istration* (1776) is a fanciful account of some conversations between the ancient Athenian statesman Pericles, the emblem of commercial and luxurious Athens, and that icon of austerity, love of agriculture, and hatred of financiers, the duc de Sully. Pericles and Sully stand in, respectively, for Necker and Turgot. "Pericles" notes that great luxury is not necessarily a political defect: it stimulates circulation, puts men to work, prompts useful discoveries, and animates the arts and letters. According to "Sully," by contrast, luxury destroys cultivation, causes men to disdain the simplicity of rural life, diverts land to unproductive uses, and concentrates wealth excessively in the hands of a few.[94] To ordinary members of the reading public, the conflict between Necker and Turgot could be viewed as part of the continuing struggle between the apologists of luxury and those who saw in agriculture a means to regenerate the *patrie*. More so-phisticated observers understood that the opposition was between two differ-ent visions of public finance: one focused on reducing borrowing and raising the long-term tax yield by fostering economic development, especially in agri-culture; the other embracing borrowing, committed to holding down taxes, and depending on the intelligent manipulation of public credit to achieve the bal-ancing act.[95]

In his career, and his person, Turgot embodied something of the trajectory of the patriot movement for national regeneration. As a young man, he had been arrested for spreading anti-Pompadour propaganda, but his youth and family connections had saved him from disgrace.[96] Closely associated with Vin-cent de Gournay in his twenties, and gravitating toward Physiocracy after Gournay's death in 1759, he had worked to disseminate reforming views from his intendancy in Limoges, and one of his first actions in office was to reestab-lish free trade in grain. Many believed that Turgot was going to replace the Farmers General with a *régie* (an administrative arrangement more akin to a public bureaucracy than a tax farm), and that he planned to replace the *vingtième* and the *taille* with a universal land tax on Physiocratic lines.[97] In fact, Turgot's fiscal reforms never got further than suppressing a few minor fiscal of-fices and exactions. He condemned economic privileges and moved to abolish the Paris guilds, an action that aroused the wrath of the Parlement of Paris. The magistrate who led the attack on the reforms, Jean-Jacques Duval d'Eprémes-nil, was a shareholder in the Indies Company who had clashed with Morellet

[94] Lalande, *Entretiens de Périclès et de Sully aux Champs Élisées, sur leur administration: ou Ba-lance entre les avantages du luxe, et ceux de l'économie* (London, 1776), 22–25. The work is also attributed to Jean Auffray. For another comparison of Turgot to Sully, this one in the Italian news-paper *Notizie del mondo*, in June 1776, see Venturi, *End of the Old Regime*, 376.
[95] Whatmore, *Republicanism and the French Revolution*, 21–22.
[96] Dakin, *Turgot and the Ancien Régime*, 8.
[97] Ibid., 166–68.

and Dupont in 1769. He condemned the Physiocrats as "an absurd, fanatical, dangerous sect, the more dangerous as they now had one of the King's ministers at their head," and implied that Necker would make a worthy successor to Turgot.[98]

One of the reasons Turgot is most celebrated today is for a project he did not have time to initiate: the establishment of a network of local and provincial consultative assemblies that would have replaced the Receivers General and Particular as the main tax-gathering apparatus. The project is described in detail in the *Mémoire sur les municipalités* that Turgot instructed his secretary, Pierre-Samuel Dupont, to draw up for him in 1774. In addition to replacing the financiers, Turgot projected the assemblies to address the dismal lack of public spirit in France. "Each individual is solely concerned with his own private interests," the *Mémoire* complained, "and almost no one bothers to fulfill his duties or recognize his relationships to other citizens."[99] The assemblies, by educating men in the practice of public affairs, would instill in them a civic outlook.[100] In Turgot's conception, citizenship was ineluctably tied to land holding. The *Mémoire* proposed a system of representation based exclusively on landed property. Those owning enough land to support a family were to be considered full citizens, those owning less, fractional citizens. Men owning land enough to support more than one family would have as many votes as they had shares. No property other than property in land was to be used for purposes of determining representation; in all of Paris there would have been no more than a few hundred citizens. Turgot noted that "Mobile wealth is as fugitive as talent; and unfortunately those who possess no land have a country only through their hearts, through their opinions, through the happy prejudices of childhood. Necessity gives them none."[101] His assemblies would have empowered landholders at the expense of those who owned urban and mobile property, but would have extended no special privileges to nobles. Like the later Mirabeau, Turgot was determined to efface traditional distinctions of status, and to privilege only landowning.

Turgot's rival, Necker, rejected a vision of national regeneration centered on agriculture in favor of neo-Colbertism and the manipulation of public credit. In the words of Cullen, he stood for "Paris as opposed to the provinces: the management of debt rather than radical fiscal reform. . . . He appeared as a rising figurehead of all the forces opposed to reform in the real economy, and which sought a reassertion of controls rather than liberalization."[102] Necker's

[98] Ibid., 243.

[99] Anne-Robert-Jacques Turgot, baron de l'Aulne, *Oeuvres de Turgot et documents le concernant, avec biographie et notes*, ed. Gustave Schelle (Paris, 1913–23), 4:576.

[100] Cavanaugh, "Turgot."

[101] Turgot, *Oeuvres*, 4:584. On Turgot's conception of property, see William H. Sewell, Jr., *Work and Revolution in France: The Language of Labor from the Old Regime to 1848* (Cambridge, 1980), 131–32.

[102] Cullen, "History, Economic Crises, and Revolution," 646.

entire political career before the controller generalship was premised on defending exclusive privileges and criticizing free trade in grain. He made his reputation as a leading shareholder in the Indies Company, where he lobbied to renew the company's trade after the Seven Years' War. He always insisted on the need to maintain the company's exclusive privilege, and he led the fight against its suppression in 1769. In his *Éloge de Colbert,* he defended privileged companies, and extolled the virtues of the Indies Company.[103] In 1775, he published an attack on free trade in grain at the height of the "Flour War"—a rash of popular riots and protests unleashed by Turgot's policy of liberalization.[104] Necker was no doctrinaire opponent of freedom of trade, but he was unwilling to risk popular disturbances in order to maintain a liberal policy.[105] Mobilizing some of the anti-Physiocratic themes and suspicion of the rich articulated in the early 1770s, he argued that there was a structural conflict of interest between proprietors and the working poor, and he implied that freedom of the grain trade was a rich man's conspiracy against the underprivileged.[106]

Necker's central strategy for regenerating the finances of the state, as revealed in the *Éloge de Colbert,* involved the manipulation of public credit. He argued that borrowing rather than taxes ought to be used to meet the obligations of the state. If the state needed 100 million livres, he suggested, this sum could be obtained by raising a tax of 100 million, or by borrowing 100 million and raising a tax to pay the interest. Necker championed the second option as the better solution for "moral" reasons—a great tax increase, he observed, could lead to "convulsions."[107] Necker placed significant emphasis on management of the money supply. He argued that low interest rates are one of the primary motors of useful enterprises, and claimed that by increasing the sum of money in circulation, the government could lower interest rates—a theory that Hume had decisively condemned twenty years before.[108] In a country such as England where the circulation of money was rapid, Necker argued, it was easier for the government to borrow money. It was his confidence that he could revivify the royal finances by short-term manipulation of public credit that won Necker his ministry in 1777. The king and some of his closest advisers saw the revolt of the American colonies against British control as an opportunity to recover the prestige France had lost in the Seven Years' War. Turgot argued that pouring money into a new war would require either bankruptcy or higher taxes. Necker, however, promised to service war costs by borrowing, supplemented by domestic economies.[109]

[103] Necker, *Éloge de Colbert,* 39–40.
[104] Jacques Necker, *Sur la législation et le commerce des grains* (Paris, 1775). See also Harris, *Necker,* 46.
[105] Harris, *Necker,* 62–64; Necker, *Éloge de Colbert,* 27–30.
[106] See also *Éloge de Colbert,* 32–33.
[107] Ibid., 121–22.
[108] Hume, "Of Interest," *Essays.*
[109] John Hardman, *Louis XVI: The Silent King* (London, 2000), 42–49.

One of the central themes of the *Éloge de Colbert* was a defense of luxury, but Necker adhered to a moderate and cautious line in this respect. Luxury, Necker insisted, was an inevitable consequence of wealth, and did not undermine the power of states.[110] Money, not virtue, was the basis of power in the modern world. In *De l'administration des finances*, his three-volume *magnum opus* on financial administration, published in 1784, the Genevan suggested that the growth of luxury was a consequence of fixed "social laws." The wages of the laboring poor would always remain at a level proportional to the simple necessities of life. The wealth of the class of proprietors, however, is ever increasing as a consequence of improvements in the cultivation of the land, combined with technical advances that increased the productivity of industry.[111] Thus a growing income gap was inevitable, and luxury must be its fruit. He conceded that luxury could be excessive and that poor government could exacerbate its spread. The chief problem was the diversion of wealth into the hands of a small number of individuals through unwarranted gifts or emoluments, the excessive profits of finance, and heavy interest payments paid to *rentiers*. A sound administration, he argued, would introduce economies in government, diminish taxes, reduce the rate of interest, and restrain favoritism and prodigality.[112] A chapter on the fortunes of financiers followed directly on Necker's consideration of luxury. "This subject," he remarked, "naturally presents itself following considerations on luxury." Necker noted that in his own ministry he made great efforts to reduce the number of financiers and to diminish their profits, but the American War made it impossible to deal decisively with the problem.[113]

This was true. Necker was a reformer to the extent that he sought to diminish the dependence of the monarchy on financiers, and to move the system of public finance toward something more like a centralized bureaucracy with a single treasury. To this end, as controller general, he abolished a large number of financial offices. He hived off from the General Farm the collection of certain excise taxes and the management of dues from the royal domain, placing each under the control of a *régie*, an institution that still employed venal office holders, but that operated more like a true public bureaucracy. He also drastically cut the number of Receivers General, the venal office holders responsible for the collection of direct taxes, and reorganized the remaining ones into a *régie* known as the *recette générale*.[114] The other way in which Necker reduced direct dependence on financiers was by increasing government borrowing on international money markets. Turgot had already initiated such a policy, but Necker

[110] Other defenders of the Indies Company justified luxury on similar grounds. See Claude-François-Joseph d'Auxiron, *Examen des de'cisions de M. l'abbé Morelet, sur les trois questions importantes qui sont le sujet de son mémoire* (n.p., 1769).

[111] Jacques Necker, *De l'administration des finances de la France* (n.p., 1784), 3:57–60.

[112] Ibid., 3:64–66.

[113] Ibid., 3:76, 78–80.

[114] Bosher, *French Finances*, 149–50, 160–62.

greatly expanded it as he strained to meet the enormous needs of the state during the American War.[115]

Whatever Necker's virtues as a reformer, among the partisans of Turgot there was little doubt that the Genevan's accession to power was a disaster. For those individuals, like the abbé Malvaux, who had pinned their hopes on Turgot, Necker's ministry was a bitter pill. Friends of Turgot resented the role that the Genevan had played in the downfall of their champion. Aside from his strategically timed interventions in the grain trade debate, Necker provided ammunition to Turgot's enemies by writing an evaluation of his budget in 1776 that disputed the minister's figures. Morellet believed that Necker's intervention had led to Turgot's fall and he refused to visit Necker's house for several years thereafter.[116] Giambattista Vasco criticized Necker's writings on the grain trade, arguing that the kind of limited and regulated liberty that Necker favored would lead to "ill-gotten gains for a few," while complete freedom would "multiply the products of agriculture, keeping them at a more moderate price," thereby increasing the wealth of the nation.[117] Baudeau attacked his *Administration des finances,* claiming that Necker's system entailed sacrificing the interests of landowners and farmers to "idle *rentiers,* speculative bankers, international merchants, [and] manufacturers of the most trifling and extravagant objects." Necker falsely represented the nobility and the landed bourgeoisie as the enemies of the state and as the vectors of luxury, Baudeau complained. He criticized the Genevan for thinking that credit and borrowing were the bases of power. According to Baudeau, the real economy was being starved of capital by the high interest rates engendered by excessive state borrowing. If *rentiers* were making profits of between 6 and 12 percent on government loans, how could agriculture, which returned 3 percent on average, get the investment capital it needed? Baudeau compared the societies of modern Europe, "desolated for two centuries by the new principles of finance" to "a sick man, whom the fever has not yet completely quit after a long and perilous attack."[118]

Criticisms akin to Baudeau's, in some respects, had already been disseminated in a barrage of pamphlets, starting in the spring of 1780, which criticized Necker's administration and questioned his integrity.[119] The attacks were orchestrated principally by a group of disgruntled financiers. The full collection of pamphlets, *Collection complette de tous les ouvrages pour et contre M. Necker* (which is far more "contre" than "pour"), is listed ninth in Darnton's

[115] Matthews, *Royal General Farms,* 229; Lüthy, *Banque protestante,* vol. 2, passim.

[116] Dakin, *Turgot and the Ancien Régime,* 255.

[117] *Gazzetta letteraria,* no. 25 (June 21, 1775), 197ff. Quoted in Venturi, *End of the Old Regime,* 340.

[118] Abbé Nicolas Baudeau, *Principes économiques de Louis XII et du cardinal d'Amboise, de Henri IV et du duc de Sully sur l'administration des finances, opposés aux systêmes des docteurs modernes* (n.p., 1785), 7, 22–23, 25, 96, 51–52.

[119] Harris, *Necker,* 192–207. See also Jeremy Popkin, "Pamphlet Journalism at the End of the Old Regime," *Eighteenth-Century Studies* 22, no. 3 (1989): 351–67.

inventory of best-selling clandestine literature.[120] The critics questioned Necker's much-vaunted disinterestedness. The author of the *Lettre à M. Necker, directeur général des finances* (better known as the *Liégeoise*) questioned the purity of Necker's motives. How, the author asks, could a banker with a quarter share in a second-tier firm who made a fortune of six million livres for himself since 1760 claim to be disinterested? According to the *Liégeoise*, Necker first gained an immense and dishonest fortune at the expense of the Indies Company.[121] It was there that he "became the pupil and finally the emulator of the virtuous abbé Terray."[122] Other writers claimed that Necker continued to make a fortune in the royal administration by funneling lucrative business to the bank in which his brother was a partner.[123] These aspersions cast on Necker's integrity were linked to a second charge that was almost ubiquitous in the pamphlets: his lack of patriotism. All the publicists harped on Necker's foreignness, and did so primarily to suggest that he could not serve France as his *patrie*. One cannot imagine that Necker sought the administration of the king's finances simply with the desire to increase his fortune, Jacques-Mathieu Augéard observed in his *Sur l'administration de M. Necker, par un citoyen françois*. Perhaps, the pamphleteer speculated, it was the desire to immortalize himself that was the spur, "because it is difficult to attribute to him the sentiments and the zeal of love of country; he was not born French; he has not acquired any real assets in France."[124] A constant theme of the critics is that financiers are better stewards of the royal finances than bankers, because the latter, in the words of Augeard, all have two fatherlands: the first where they borrow money cheaply, and the second where they sell it dear.[125]

Perhaps the most persistent charge against Necker was that he was reviving the infamous "System" of the Scottish financier John Law—a charge Dupont had leveled at the Indies Company ten years earlier, when Necker was a leading shareholder. The allegation was almost ubiquitous in the pamphlets, and was easy to make because Necker, like Law, was a foreigner, a banker, and a Protestant. A broadsheet, reproduced in the *Collection complette,* drew up a detailed comparison of Law's initiatives with measures Necker had undertaken since 1776, tracing a close parallel between the two (see figure 7).[126] Augéard

---

[120] *Collection complette de tous les ouvrages pour et contre M. Necker avec des notes critiques, politiques et secrètes* (Utrecht, 1782). Darnton, *Forbidden Best-Sellers,* 138.

[121] "Lettre à M. Necker, directeur général des finances," *Collection complette,* 1:18–19. (The pagination starts over following the "Tableau comparatif.") The charge is repeated in "Lettre de M. le marquis de Caraccioli à M. d'Alembert," *Collection complette,* 3:43.

[122] J.-M. Augéard also linked Necker with Terray: "the administration of the abbé Terray appears to have been the epoch of the development of the talents of M. N. for high speculations." "Sur l'administration de M. Necker, par un citoyen françois," *Collection complette,* 1:31.

[123] "Lettre de M. Turgot à M. Necker," and "Sur l'administration de M. Necker," *Collection complette,* 1:5–6, 32. The "Lettre" is also attributed to Augéard. Harris, *Necker,* 198.

[124] "Sur l'administration de M. Necker," 1:32.

[125] "Lettre de M. Turgot à M. Necker," 1:10.

[126] "Tableau comparatif de ce qui se passa dans les années 1716, 1717, 1718, 1719 & 1720,

claimed that the *caisse d'escompte* under Necker had become a vehicle for un-
secured paper money in the fashion of Law's Mississippi Company. "The disaster for France when the finances were confided to that foreign banker has not
been forgotten," he warned.[127] In multiplying the notes of the *caisse d'escompte* to an enormous extent, "M. N. has literally followed in the footsteps
of Law."[128] The critics linked Necker with Law by arguing that the excessive
borrowing in which he engaged was giving rise to speculation, just as Law's System had initiated an orgy of *agiotage* during the Regency. Augeard suggested
that Necker pursued a policy of borrowing to meet the costs of the American
War in order to engender this *agiotage* from which he and his banker friends
would reap enormous profits. Necker had nothing to gain personally from the
extension of taxation, Augeard pointed out, but it was quite otherwise with
loans: "speculation in these is enormous and very profitable."[129] The *Liégeoise*
also accused Necker of excessive borrowing and of engendering speculation.
Necker claimed credit for economies, the author complained, while dissipating
the treasures of the state by "the most onerous borrowings, and even more ruinous speculation." Under Necker's system, Augéard warned, French power
had become ungrounded, its whole force in time of war resting on "paper, opinion, and your word."[130]

The argument that Necker neglected to promote real prosperity, choosing to
manipulate public credit and the money supply instead, was not a major theme
of the critics, but it did appear in a few of the brochures. The very title of the
"Lettre de M. Turgot à M. Necker," with the conceit that the work was written by Necker's rival, implied an opposition between the policies of one and the
policies of the other. The *Liégeoise* accused the banker of neglecting the prosperity of agriculture, manufactures, and the arts: what canals had Necker cut,
what roads had he constructed, what rivers had he rendered navigable, what
had he done for the prosperity of France? Augéard claimed that the comments
Necker had made in his work on the grain trade were dangerous and suggested
that, as a banker and a foreigner, he did not understand that "properties are the
base and the essential wealth" of the kingdom.[131]

It is difficult to imagine a more cynical and opportunistic manipulation of
the themes popularized in the political economy of the 1760s than that orchestrated in the campaign against Necker. Financiers had arrogated to themselves the mantle of patriotism and mobilized against Necker, a reformer who

---

d'une part; & de ce qui s'est passé en 1776, 1777, 1778, 1779 & 1780, d'autre part: vérifié d'après
les pièces originales imprimées à la suite de l'Histoire du Système," *Collection complette,* 1: un-
numbered, follows page 112.

[127] "Lettre de M. Turgot à M. Necke," 1:6.

[128] "Sur l'administration de M. Necker," 1:46.

[129] Ibid, 65. The charge that Necker was engaging in borrowing without "limit or measure" was
made in the "Lettre de M. le marquis de Caraccioli à M. d'Alembert."

[130] "Lettre a M. Necker," 1:43. "Lettre de M. Turgot à M. Necker," 1:7.

[131] "Sur l'administration de M. Necker," 1:33.

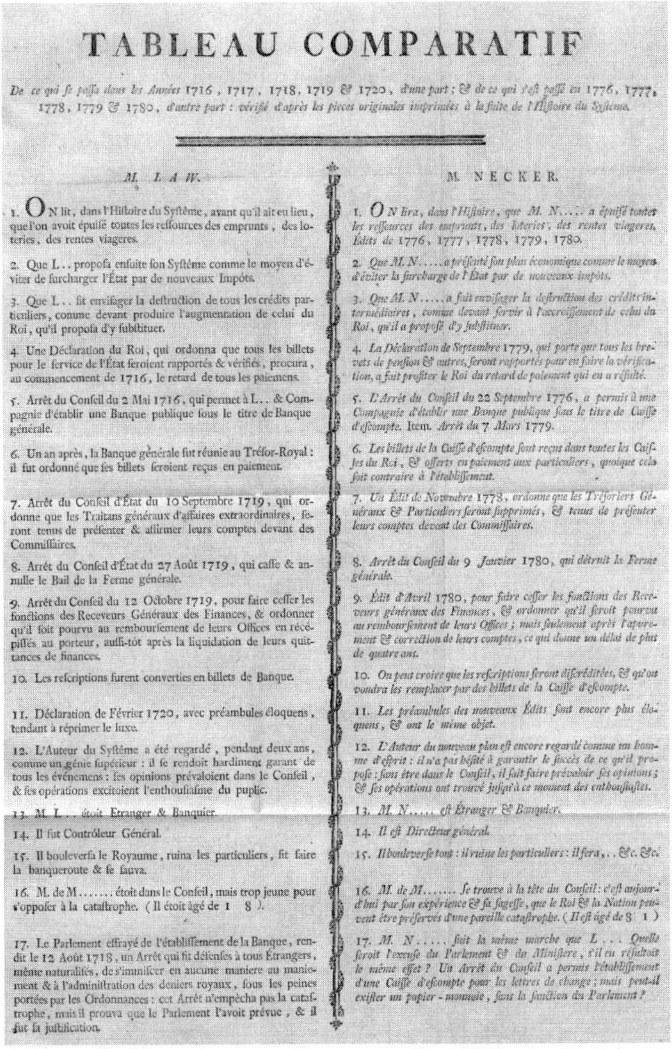

TABLEAU COMPARATIF

De ce qui se passa dans les Années 1716, 1717, 1718, 1719 *&* 1720, *d'une part ; & de ce qui s'est passé en* 1776, 1777, 1778, 1779 *&* 1780, *d'autre part : vérifié d'après les pieces originales imprimées à la suite de l'Histoire du Système.*

M. LAW.	M. NECKER.
1. ON lit, dans l'Histoire du Système, avant qu'il ait eu lieu, que l'on avoit épuisé toutes les ressources des emprunts, des loteries, des rentes viageres.	1. *ON lira, dans l'Histoire, que M. N..... a épuisé toutes les ressources des emprunts, des loteries, des rentes viageres, Édits de* 1776, 1777, 1778, 1779, 1780.
2. Que L.. proposa ensuite son Système comme le moyen d'éviter de surcharger l'État par de nouveaux Impôts.	2. *Que M. N..... a présenté son plan économique comme le moyen d'éviter la surcharge de l'État par de nouveaux impôts.*
3. Que L.. fit envisager la destruction de tous les crédits particuliers, comme devant produire l'augmentation de celui du Roi, qu'il proposa d'y substituer.	3. *Que M. N..... a fait envisager la destruction des crédits intermédiaires, comme devant servir à l'accroissement de celui du Roi, qu'il a proposé d'y substituer.*
4. Une Déclaration du Roi, qui ordonna que tous les billets pour le service de l'État seroient rapportés & vérifiés, procura, au commencement de 1716, le retard de tous les paiemens.	4. *La Déclaration de Septembre* 1779, *qui porte que tous les brevets de pension & autres, seront rapportés pour en faire la vérification, a fait profiter le Roi du retard de paiement qui en a résulté.*
5. Arrêt du Conseil du 2 Mai 1716, qui permet à L.. & Compagnie d'établir une Banque publique sous le titre de Banque générale.	5. *L'Arrêt du Conseil du* 22 *Septembre* 1776, *a permis à une Compagnie d'établir une Banque publique sous le titre de Caisse d'escompte.* Item. *Arrêt du* 7 *Mars* 1779.
6. Un an après, la Banque générale fut réunie au Trésor-Royal : il fut ordonné que ses billets seroient reçus en paiement.	6. *Les billets de la Caisse d'escompte sont reçus dans toutes les Caisses du Roi, & offerts en paiement aux particuliers, quoique cela soit contraire à l'établissement.*
7. Arrêt du Conseil d'État du 10 Septembre 1719, qui ordonne que les Traitans généraux d'affaires extraordinaires, seront tenus de présenter & affirmer leurs comptes devant des Commissaires.	7. *Un Édit de Novembre* 1778, *ordonne que les Trésoriers Généraux & Particuliers seront supprimés, & tenus de présenter leurs comptes devant des Commissaires.*
8. Arrêt du Conseil d'État du 27 Août 1719, qui casse & annulle le Bail de la Ferme générale.	8. *Arrêt du Conseil du* 9 *Janvier* 1780, *qui détruit la Ferme générale.*
9. Arrêt du Conseil du 12 Octobre 1719, pour faire cesser les fonctions des Receveurs Généraux des Finances, & ordonner qu'il soit pourvu au remboursement de leurs Offices en récépissés au porteur, aussi-tôt après la liquidation de leurs quittances de finances.	9. *Édit d'Avril* 1780, *pour faire cesser les fonctions des Receveurs généraux des Finances, & ordonner qu'il seroit pourvu au remboursement de leurs Offices ; mais seulement après l'apurement & correction de leurs comptes, ce qui donne un délai de plus de quatre ans.*
10. Les rescriptions furent converties en billets de Banque.	10. *On peut croire que les rescriptions seront discréditées, & qu'on voudra les remplacer par des billets de la Caisse d'escompte.*
11. Déclaration de Février 1720, avec préambules éloquens, tendant à réprimer le luxe.	11. *Les préambules des nouveaux Édits sont encore plus éloquens, & ont le même objet.*
12. L'Auteur du Système a été regardé, pendant deux ans, comme un génie supérieur : il se rendoit hardiment garant de tous les événemens : ses opinions prévaloient dans le Conseil, & ses opérations excitoient l'enthousiasme du puplic.	12. *L'Auteur du nouveau plan est encore regardé comme un homme d'esprit : il n'a pas hésité à garantir le succès de ce qu'il propose : sans être dans le Conseil, il sait faire prévaloir ses opinions ; & ses opérations ont trouvé jusqu'à ce moment des enthousiastes.*
13. M. L.. étoit Etranger & Banquier.	13. *M. N..... est Étranger & Banquier.*
14. Il fut Contrôleur Général.	14. *Il est Directeur général.*
15. Il bouleversa le Royaume, ruina les particuliers, fit faire la banqueroute & se sauva.	15. *Il bouleverse tout : il ruine les particuliers : il fera,.. &c. &c.*
16. M. de M....... étoit dans le Conseil, mais trop jeune pour s'opposer à la catastrophe. (Il étoit âgé de 1 8).	16. *M. de M....... se trouve à la tête du Conseil : c'est aujourd'hui par son expérience & sa sagesse, que le Roi & la Nation peuvent être préservés d'une pareille catastrophe. (Il est âgé de* 8 1)
17. Le Parlement effrayé de l'établissement de la Banque, rendit le 12 Août 1718, un Arrêt qui fit défenses à tous Étrangers, même naturalisés, de s'immiscer en aucune maniere au maniement & à l'administration des deniers royaux, sous les peines portées par les Ordonnances : cet Arrêt n'empêcha pas la catastrophe, mais il prouva que le Parlement l'avoit prévue, & il fut sa justification.	17. *M. N..... suit la même marche que L... Quelle seroit l'excuse du Parlement & du Ministere, s'il en résultoit le même effet ? Un Arrêt du Conseil a permis l'établissement d'une Caisse d'escompte pour les lettres de change ; mais peut-il exister un papier-monnoie, sans la sanction du Parlement ?*

Fig. 7. Broadside comparing Jacques Necker to John Law from *Collection complette de tous les ouvrages pour et contre M. Necker,* 1782.

This broadside, originally published in 1781 as part of a campaign by disgruntled financiers to unseat the controller general Jacques Necker, compared Necker to the notorious John Law, the Scottish banker who directed royal finances during the Regency and whose name was a byword for the ills of speculation. The broadside is organized into a year-by-year comparison of the tenures of the two ministers—the first line reads: "Comparative Table of what happened in the years 1716, 1717, 1718, 1719 & 1720, on the one hand; and of what happened in 1776, 1777, 1778, 1779 & 1780, on the other"—implying that Necker's administration will lead France to the same kind of disaster that Law's had. Necker and Law were both foreigners, both Protestants, and both fascinated by the possibility of using paper money to solve the financial problems of the monarchy. Courtesy of Kroch Library (Rare and Manuscript Collections), Cornell University, Ithaca.

threatened their interests, rhetorical strategies forged in the 1760s to attack financiers themselves. The campaign, moreover, was successful: Necker resigned his ministry in May 1781. The successful symbolic assault on the minister's position suggests that a political economic idiom emphasizing patriot themes had definitively ceased to be the property of any one social group and had become a common currency of public debate on political economic issues—a weapon available to be used by any interest. In this sense, the critics of Necker were the heirs to those court interests of the 1760s who patronized agronomy and Physiocracy. But in deploying such rhetorical strategies against Necker, his enemies also helped to reenergize the demand for a renewal of the "real" economy, and showed the *parti* Turgot how effectively the John Law card might be played. In the following years, the champions of national regeneration via agricultural renewal would learn to use popular suspicion of financial speculation to dramatic effect.

The partisans of deep economic reform needed all the help they could get by the end of the 1770s; it had been a difficult decade. From the loss of Choiseul's protection in 1770, to the reactionary policies of the abbé Terray, to the dashed hopes of Turgot's ministry, disaster succeeded disaster. Necker's legacy was an especially troubling one. His success in raising money to fight the American War—a resounding victory for France—might be taken to prove that it was not necessary to free the grain trade, foster agriculture, or effect deep political economic reform to regenerate France. The nation had triumphed over Britain, and Necker's manipulations had made it possible. Nevertheless, the Genevan's vulnerability to the charge that he was a new Law, that his system was a conjuror's trick, inimical to the real interests of the nation, suggests that the friends of economic reform still had a deep reservoir of credibility on which to draw.

Beyond the relative stagnation of the body of thought focused on agriculture, the 1770s saw significant changes in the way commerce and luxury were represented in public discourse. Defenders of commerce did important cultural work to produce legitimations of trade, casting merchants as patriots, and distinguishing commerce from luxury. At the same time an anti-aristocratic thread in the critique of luxury became much more prominent. The court nobility, and to a lesser extent, the nobility as a whole, was increasingly blamed for luxury in the 1770s. This anti-aristocratic animus was to prove important in the following years, when the language pioneered by critics of aristocratic luxury would be mobilized in the anti-noble campaign that launched the French Revolution.

CHAPTER *5*

Political Economy and the Prerevolutionary Crisis

[Paris] is the abyss where all riches come to be swallowed up forever, along with honesty, along with *moeurs*. It is the seat of luxury, which corrupts everything: it is the seat of speculation, which finishes by sacrificing all useful industry to the most harmful of all industries.

—J.-B. Secondat de Montesquieu, *Pensées d'un amateur de la vérité,*
sur les affaires présentes (1789)

One of the objectives of this book is to shed new light on the origins of the French Revolution by considering the ways in which widely held political economic perspectives and ideas shaped elite attitudes toward aristocracy and absolutism. The point is not to offer a comprehensive new interpretation of why a revolution occurred in France, but rather to elucidate and clarify the relationship between two influential approaches to understanding revolutionary origins that have developed on largely separate lines. One of these approaches traces the origins of the Revolution to the development of a new political culture in the final decades of the old regime.[1] By focusing on shifts in the language and practices of politics, historians seek to explain the erosion of the authority of the absolute monarchy, and the emergence of rival models for the organization of political power. In so doing, scholars hope to make comprehensible the assault on the absolute monarchy in the late 1780s and the seizure of sovereignty by the revolutionary National Assembly in 1789. The second approach explores the institutional reasons why the old regime's system of public finance collapsed in the late 1780s, bringing the monarchy down with it.[2] Rather than

[1] Among the foundational texts of this literature are Keith Michael Baker, ed., *The Political Culture of the Old Regime*, vol. 1, *The French Revolution and the Creation of Modern Political Culture* (Oxford, 1987); idem, *Inventing the French Revolution: Essays on French Political Culture in the Eighteenth Century* (Cambridge, 1990); and Roger Chartier, *The Cultural Origins of the French Revolution*, trans. Lydia G. Cochrane (Durham, 1991).

[2] The literature on the monarchy's financial tribulations is extensive. For an overview, see Richard Bonney, "What's New about the New French Fiscal History?" *Journal of Modern History* 70, no. 3 (1998): 639–67.

focusing on the strength of opposition to absolutism, practitioners of this "new fiscal history" concentrate on exploring the weaknesses of the French state and the pressures placed on its institutions by fiscal-military competition with rival states.

As a number of scholars have recognized, neither approach alone can adequately explain why the revolution occurred. A new political culture could mediate decisive political transformations only when a power vacuum had been opened by the paralysis of the monarchy. It is difficult to explain this paralysis without falling back on the insights of the institutional approach. On the other hand, it is impossible to account for the fiscal breakdown of the 1780s without understanding the climate of ideas in which the monarchy and its creditors operated. The collapse of the monarchy was not a purely internal crisis but a breakdown in the credibility of monarchical power and in the capacity of the Crown to engage the loyalty of elites.[3]

The political economy explored in this book was at the confluence of old regime political culture and the institutional structures of the fiscal-military state. Middling sections of the elite used this political economy to criticize what they perceived as the failed and ruinous strategies the French state had pursued in its efforts to finance diplomatic and military competition against opposing powers. From the time of the Seven Years' War, they drew on deep-seated cultural anxieties about luxury to argue that France had degenerated. Through a political economic perspective infused with older ideas about luxury, they claimed that the system of public finance, together with a Colbertist bias in economic policy, had not only undermined the wealth of the nation but eroded its virtue. Part of what made such a diagnosis attractive was that such policies were also perceived as damaging the interests of mid-level elites. The monarchy was held to be guilty of neglecting landowners, and sponsoring a tax system that siphoned money out of agriculture and into the hands of rapacious financiers and selfish courtiers. This set of ideas and reflexes powerfully conditioned the perceptions and understandings of French elites in the 1780s, and played a significant role in turning financial crisis into Revolution.

This chapter is concerned to link the structural to the conjunctural, to explain how broad discontent with aspects of the political economic order helped to produce the political crisis out of which the Revolution emerged. By 1786, interest payments on the state's debt were consuming more than 50 percent of current revenue, options for short-term borrowing were almost exhausted, and loans contracted in the 1770s would soon have to be repaid. The Crown was facing insolvency. Crisis gave way to revolution in part because of the way the monarchy elected to deal with these problems. When the financial resources of the state had last been exhausted in the early 1770s, the abbé Terray had opted for a policy of partial repudiation combined with forced renegotiation of the

---

[3] As Kathryn Norberg and Michael Kwass, in particular, have emphasized: see Norberg, "The French Fiscal Crisis of 1788"; Kwass, "A Kingdom of Taxpayers."

monarchy's most onerous obligations; this was the time-honored mode of dealing with fiscal crisis. In 1787, by contrast, the Crown elaborated a program of political economic reforms in the mold of Turgot—a move difficult to understand unless one views it as a strategy to restore the credibility of the monarchy in the eyes of disgruntled elites.[4] But if this was the intention, it failed. When it was announced to the public through the Assembly of Notables in 1787, the reform program created the expectation of an imminent, fundamental transformation that would regenerate France, but it did not restore public confidence in the Crown. Even the replacement of controller general, Charles-Alexandre de Calonne, by a member of the *parti* Turgot, Étienne-Charles Loménie de Brienne, failed to win the support of the Notables. They demanded that the king convene the Estates General, a representative assembly that had not met since 1614.

In part, the skepticism of elites was a function of the two earlier, failed efforts at political economic reform under Choiseul and Turgot; in part it reflected the deep discredit brought on the monarchy in the 1780s by Calonne. The Paris Bourse in the 1780s played host to a frenzy of speculative activity, and in the face of this new threat, the old political economic reflex to decry luxury was reanimated. Critics of speculation argued that it undermined the real sources of national wealth by driving up interest rates, and weakened the moral foundations of public spirit by igniting an excessive and unquenchable desire for wealth. They blamed this speculative fury on the massive borrowing undertaken by the administration, and they also attacked the host of privileged joint-stock companies established in the 1780s whose shares were a stimulus to *agiotage*. Against such a background, Calonne could not credibly put himself forward as a new Turgot, as the Sully who would rescue France by revivifying agriculture and animating patriotism. The odium aroused by the controller general also attached itself, at least temporarily, to the monarchy.

Calonne's successor, Brienne, attempted to execute the royal program of reforms, but it became more and more difficult to sustain credit in the face of elite noncooperation and a growing economic crisis. Hailstorms destroyed crops over much of northern France in the summer of 1788. The consequence was a sharp rise in the price of bread, which forced ordinary people to curtail their consumption of other goods, and led in turn to a recession in the manufacturing sector. There is debate among economic historians about the underlying health of the French economy in the 1780s, but none about the severity of the economic crisis in 1788–89: it was the worst of the century. Employment in the textile industries fell drastically, perhaps by as much as half in 1788.[5] Nothing could have more powerfully validated the claim that many political economists

---

[4] There is no definitive account of why the monarchy did not choose bankruptcy in 1786, a fact underlined by François R. Velde and David R. Weir, "The Financial Market and Government Debt Policy in France, 1746–1793," *Journal of Economic History* 52, no. 1 (1992): 1–39.

[5] William Doyle, *Origins of the French Revolution*, 3rd ed. (Oxford, 1999), 151.

had been making for years—that the existing economic order was ungrounded, subject to "revolutions" that might beggar the nation overnight. The coincidence of economic crisis with the speculation of the 1780s was purely fortuitous. In fact, the recession had been worsened by a trade treaty signed with Britain in 1786, intended to open markets for French agricultural commodities. But the facts did not matter so much as the perception the economic collapse created. Moreover, the crisis tightened credit conditions further and made it more difficult for the government to remain solvent. In August 1788, the treasury ran out of money and Brienne resigned. The Crown had placed sweeping political economic renovation on the agenda but could not secure a mandate to be the agency of that reform.

With Brienne's fall, royal power effectively collapsed, leaving to the Estates General the responsibility for regenerating the nation. The temporary paralysis of the administration, and uncertainty over the form the new representative institutions would take, set off a scramble for power among competing lobbies, some of whom claimed to represent the Third Estate and others the nobility. In the context of this political struggle, publicists resisting what they represented as a noble effort to monopolize power found that political economy yielded a veritable arsenal of rhetorical weapons.[6] Mobilizing criticisms articulated in the 1770s, spokespersons for the Third Estate accused nobles of being part of a corrupt plutocracy inimical both to the prosperity and the virtue of the nation. This charge was largely opportunistic in so far as the provincial nobility was its target. Attacks on noble luxury in the preceding decades made it plausible to tar middling nobles with the same brush as *grands seigneurs;* the motivation for doing so came from the fierce competition between noble and nonnoble elites that was a product of the political crisis. But antipathy to aristocracy, more narrowly construed, was neither opportunistic, nor merely a function of the political crisis. Mid-level elites had long represented absolutism, aristocracy, and plutocracy as different aspects of the same complex of power. They had come to regard special interests in finance and the court as the chief obstacles to reform. That middling elites should attack the court nobility in the context of a fundamental effort to regenerate the nation was entirely predictable.

Calonne and the Apotheosis of Court Capitalism

In November 1783 Calonne was appointed controller general. By the time his administration collapsed in April 1787, the minister's name had become a byword for the disastrous effects of the league between the absolute monarchy and vested interests in finance and the court. Calonne was an important pro-

---

[6] William Sewell offers important insights into the use of political economy as an anti-noble rhetoric by the abbé Sieyès. See William H. Sewell, Jr., *A Rhetoric of Bourgeois Revolution: The Abbé Sieyes and What is the Third Estate?* (Durham, 1994).

moter of court capitalism, subsidizing many of the great industrial enterprises of the late eighteenth century in which aristocrats had an interest. It was under his watch that stock speculation emerged as a major object of public concern; indeed, the minister was intimately involved in the machinations of the stock market himself. Calonne was, perhaps, most notorious for presiding over a massive expansion of the royal debt, though in this he was merely continuing the policies of his three predecessors. When the financial crisis of the monarchy was unveiled to the public in 1787, the public viewed it as the fruit of the malign league between the court, finance, and the monarchy that the minister emblematized.

Calonne was a creature of the financial milieu. His uncle was Jacques Marquet de Bourgade, one of the inner circle of major financiers who participated in the creation of government fiscal policy. His brother-in-law was another of these great financiers, Joseph Micault d'Harvelay, and his cousin was the former court banker Jean-Joseph de Laborde.[7] Calonne was appointed to the ministry after the Farmers General had forced the ouster of his predecessor, Lefèvre d'Ormesson. The latter, in an abortive effort at fiscal reform, had suspended the lease of the General Farm as a preliminary to transforming it from a tax farm into an entity more akin to a state bureaucracy.[8] The tax farmers, with Micault d'Harvelay at their head, warned the king that public credit would collapse if the lease were not immediately reinstated. Thoroughly alarmed, Louis XVI sacked d'Ormesson. Calonne's first undertaking in office was to reinstate the tax farmers' lease.[9] Nor was this merely an act of political expediency. As Bosher has noted, Calonne believed in the system of private enterprise in public finance. Unlike Necker, who sought to make the public finance system more like a government department, Calonne expanded the system of venal financial offices.[10]

If Calonne was a candidate for the ministry welcome to financiers, he was also the choice of that most venal group of courtiers, the *société de la reine*. Munro Price describes the *société* as a group of friends and hangers-on of the queen, interested in her chiefly as a source of patronage. Among these courtiers were the princesse de Lamballe, the duc and duchesse de Polignac, Mme d'Andlau, Mme de Châlons, the ducs de Guines, de Guiche, and de Coigny, the baron

---

[7] Munro Price, *Preserving the Monarchy: The Comte de Vergennes, 1774–1787* (Cambridge, 1995), 64, 88–89. Calonne's wife was a granddaughter of Pâris-Duverney. Chaussinand-Nogaret, *Financiers de Languedoc*, 252.

[8] The plan was to establish a *régie intéressée*, in which the current tax farmers would become administrators who would have to pay over all revenues to the state, but who would continue to enjoy a 10 percent return on the capitals invested in their offices and profit-sharing whenever taxes went above a certain level. Price, *Preserving the Monarchy*, 105–6.

[9] Robert Lacour-Gayet, *Calonne: Financier, réformateur, contre-révolutionnaire, 1734–1802* (Paris, 1963), 75.

[10] Bosher, *French Finances*, 182. See also David D. Bien, "Property in Office under the Old Regime: The Case of the Stockbrokers," in *Early Modern Conceptions of Property*, ed. John Brewer and Susan Staves (London, 1995).

de Besenval, the comte d'Artois, and the comte de Vaudreuil. It was the association with this group of courtiers, more than any other factor, Price suggests, that harmed the reputation of the queen in the eyes of public opinion.[11] Calonne, who was particularly close to Vaudreuil, had been put forward by the *société* in October 1783 as an alternative to d'Ormesson.[12] The new controller general, in turn, proved a generous patron of the queen's friends. Nearly half the money paid out in pensions between 1774 and 1789 was disbursed during the three and a half years of Calonne's term in office. He was particularly generous to the duc and duchesse de Polignac.[13] So closely were the fortunes of the *société* linked to Calonne, Price argues, that after the controller general broke with the queen at the end of 1784 and joined Vergennes's opposing ministerial clique, the courtiers began to transfer their allegiance also.

Calonne has been credited with attempting to promote the modernization of the French economy, especially in the manufacturing sector, but it is truer to say that he was the chief sponsor of court capitalism in the 1780s.[14] Calonne financed significant improvements to infrastructure.[15] He increased the fund for the building of roads and bridges, made grants to individual entrepreneurs to aid in the construction of roads and canals, directed money to improve the harbors of Cherbourg, Dieppe, Dunkirk, La Rochelle, and Le Havre, improved markets and bridges in Paris, and financed the construction of new quays in Marseilles. He also directed government subsidies to assist in the establishment of manufactures using modern machinery and developing new industrial processes.[16] However, these subsidies must also be seen as subventions to the aristocratic and financier shareholders of the companies in question. The Neuville cotton manufactory, which Calonne subsidized, was financed in part by the duc d'Orléans, the comte de Vergennes, and the comte d'Angiviller. The Le Creusot works, which received 600,000 livres from the royal treasury in 1785, had among its major shareholders the financiers Baudard de Sainte-James and Mégret de Sérilly; Sérilly's chief clerk, Nicolas Bettinger; and the commissioner of the postal service, Palteau de Veymeranges. Later, the king took a one-twelfth share in the company.[17] Calonne cemented his association with court capitalism in 1785 when he presided over the reestablishment of the Indies Company whose monopoly had been suspended in 1769.[18]

[11] Price, *Preserving the Monarchy*, 28.

[12] Ibid., 107.

[13] Lacour-Gayet, *Calonne*, 96–100.

[14] Wilma J. Pugh, "Calonne's 'New Deal,'" *Journal of Modern History* 11, no. 3 (1939): 289–312; Lacour-Gayet, *Calonne*, 154–56.

[15] In his own career as an intendant, Calonne had noted the importance of infrastructural improvements. See Charles-Alexandre de Calonne, *Mémoire sur la navigation des rivières de la province de Metz* (Metz, 1773).

[16] Frederick L. Nussbaum, "The Deputies Extraordinary of Commerce and the French Monarchy," *Political Science Quarterly* 48, no. 4 (1933): 534–55.

[17] Lacour-Gayet, *Calonne*, 154–56.

[18] Frederick L. Nussbaum, "The Formation of the New East India Company of Calonne," *American Historical Review* 38, no. 3 (1933): 475–97.

Calonne continued the policy of his immediate predecessors of borrowing vast sums to cover the gap between government revenue and expenditure. Between 1777 and 1788 the administration offered over a billion livres in loans for public subscription, much of it at ruinous rates of interest. A standard form of loan the French government floated in the 1770s and 1780s was the life annuity, or *rente viagère*, constituted on from one to four "heads." Between 1777 and 1788, the Crown obtained 776 million livres on loans of this sort. Because the French government calculated annuities crudely, making no allowances for the age or health of the head on which the annuity was constituted, these *rentes viagères* proved a ruinous form of borrowing. In the 1770s, Genevan investors figured out that by carefully selecting as their heads children of well-off parents who had already survived smallpox, they could prolong payments on French life annuities for decades. An investor like Étienne Clavière, a refugee in Paris from the Genevan Revolution of 1782, could borrow money at 5 percent from bankers in Amsterdam or London, repay the loan from income on a life annuity in fifteen years, and for the rest of the life, or lives, specified on the annuity enjoy an 8 to 10 percent income on capital that was never actually his.

The massive government borrowing of the 1780s fueled the greatest episode of speculation seen in Paris since the days of John Law.[19] Syndicates of speculators sought profit in short-term price fluctuations, buying and selling financial instruments in large volume, usually on credit. They struggled to create and take advantage of price variations by coordinating their activities and publishing brochures intended either to buoy up or to undermine public confidence in targeted securities. They drew heavily on political support to secure advantageous investment opportunities and to undercut the maneuvers of rival cabals. The speculative boom of the 1780s resulted from an explosion in the quantity and variety of financial instruments sold on the Paris Bourse. This expansion was initially a consequence of the massive increase in the number and type of government *rentes* sold to the public. Nor was the link between government borrowing and speculation inadvertent. Speculators were a conduit connecting the French monarchy to the hundreds of millions of livres of capital available on the money markets of Amsterdam, London, and Geneva. The administration built features into loans to make them attractive to speculators, developing a symbiotic relationship with the rue Vivienne. During his term as controller general, Calonne borrowed over 420 million livres, nearly 195 million of it in high-interest life annuity bonds calculated to appeal to speculators.[20]

There were further lucrative opportunities for speculative gain in buying and selling the shares of joint-stock companies. Among the new companies established in Paris in the 1780s were the Paris Water Company, the reconstituted Indies Company, two rival fire insurance companies, a life insurance company,

[19] See George V. Taylor, "The Paris Bourse on the Eve of the French Revolution, 1781–1789," *American Historical Review* 67, no. 4 (1962): 951–77. Other essential sources are Lüthy, *Banque protestante*, and Jean Bouchary, *Les manieurs d'argent à Paris à la fin du XVIIIe siècle* (Paris, 1939).
[20] J. C. Riley, "Dutch Investment in France, 1781–1787," *Journal of Economic History* 33, no. 4 (1973): 732–60.

the West African Trading Company, and the Northern Trading Company. Some of these ventures were actually engaged in productive economic activity, but many were simply vehicles for speculation established by syndicates of investors seeking new opportunities for profit. The enterprises Clavière started in the 1780s, notably a venture to rival the Paris Water Company, and a life insurance company, seem to have been purely speculative projects. Other cases were more ambiguous. The royal cotton-spinning manufactory established at Neuville in 1782, for instance, was one of the most modern, mechanized textile concerns in the world, but it may have doubled as a speculation for some of its investors. Three quarters of the original shares were marketed through the Parisian notary C.-O.-J. Baroud, one of the most infamous speculators of the 1780s.[21] By the end of 1788, promoters of the various joint-stock companies had created shares worth 76 million livres at par, and in the summer of 1786, many of these companies were trading on the Bourse for double their nominal value.

Speculation had traditionally been a facet of court capitalism. The need for access to large sums on credit, combined with the importance of inside information, made it a natural domain for financiers and the court nobility. Commercial or manufacturing ventures often doubled as an opportunity for speculation, at least for some of the shareholders. In 1768, for example, Thomas Sutton, comte de Clonard, a member of the Jacobite trading aristocracy and a syndic of the Indies Company, secured a silver mining concession from the king of Spain at Guadalcanal in the Sierre Morena mountains. Among the shareholders of the new company, capitalized at three million livres, were the duc d'Harcourt, the duc de Châtelet, the duc de Liancourt, and the marquise de Marboeuf. When the company broke up a few years later, Sutton, who speculated on his shares, seems to have been the only shareholder to turn a profit.[22] The court nobility and the upper tiers of finance were very much involved in the stock speculation of the 1780s, though they shared the field with a wide variety of outsiders, many of them foreign bankers. Among the most notable aristocratic speculators of that decade were the duc de Lauzun, illegitimate son of the duc de Choiseul, the abbé de Périgord, better known to history as Talleyrand, the abbé Marc-René d'Espagnac, the comte de Narbonne, and the marquis de Lafayette.

Although there is no evidence that Calonne engaged in stock speculation on his own account, his administration had compromising links to speculators. He exchanged lands from the royal domain worth 200,000 livres a year for a property supposedly worth only 90,000 a year owned by the baron d'Espagnac, the brother of a leading speculator.[23] The controller general lived in constant fear of a stock market crash, and the collapse of public credit that must ensue. To

[21] On the ownership of the Neuville company, see Chaussinand-Nogaret, *French Nobility,* 103. On Baroud's career as a speculator, see Bouchary, *Manieurs d'argent.*

[22] Chaussinand-Nogaret, *French Nobility,* 108. On Sutton's speculation, see Chaussinand-Nogaret, *Gens de finance,* 77.

[23] Lacour-Gayet, *Calonne,* 139–41.

prevent this from happening, he intervened in capital markets on several occasions with treasury funds. Late in 1786, the stock of the new Indies Company had just been doubled, and investors who already owned shares were offered the opportunity to buy more at par, guaranteeing them an instant profit. However, in order to create the liquidity necessary to take advantage of this tempting offer, many investors would have to sell some of the shares they already owned which, together with the huge increase in the total number of shares, would have depressed the price, perhaps leading to a sell-off and a crash. Calonne intervened to prevent this from happening. He gave 11.5 million livres in treasury funds to a syndicate of speculators to be used to shore up the value of falling Indies stock.[24] In December 1786 and January 1787, this cartel used the funds Calonne had supplied, together with their own credit, to establish a corner on the market for Indies shares. In essence, they placed those investors selling short in Indies stock in the ruinous situation of having to buy shares from the syndicate, at monopoly prices, in order to fulfill their contracts. In this manner, quite contrary to his original intention, Calonne had gotten himself embroiled in machinations of dubious legality. To make matters worse, the investors caught in the trap, led by Clavière, exposed this maneuver to the public in the comte de Mirabeau's *Dénonciation de l'agiotage au roi et à l'Assemblée des notables* (1787).

The Revival of the Agricultural Societies

The speculative boom of the 1780s, and Calonne's compromised administration, prompted a resurgence of patriotic calls for the regeneration of agriculture. Critics of speculation represented it as the newest and most disturbing avatar of luxury. They charged that the rapid and easy fortunes made by speculators disseminated an excessive greed and love of money to other social groups, and that speculative wealth was illusory and unstable. They held that speculation dried up the sources of real wealth in agriculture and commerce by sucking all money toward Paris, and raising interest rates to exorbitant levels, making it impossible for farmers and merchants to get the credit they needed. Critics contrasted the virtuous provinces to Paris, which they represented as a corrupt Babylon, shimmering in the gaudy brilliance of its false wealth.

The agricultural societies and the agronomic press reemerged as centers for the dissemination of this revivified anti-luxury language. According to André Bourde, the 1780s saw the apogee of the agronomic movement in France.[25] The specialized agronomic press expanded in the 1780s. The *Journal et la gazette*

---

[24] This was not the first of his interventions to shore up credit, nor would it be the last. On his intervention in the affairs of the *caisse d'escompte* in 1785, see J. Bénétruy, *L'atelier de Mirabeau: Quatre proscrits genevois dans la tourmente révolutionnaire* (Geneva, 1962), 97. For his handling of the Indies Company scandal in 1787, see Taylor, "Paris Bourse."

[25] Bourde, *Agronomie et agronomes*, 1311.

de l'agriculture began publishing in January 1782.[26] That same year, the *Bibliothèque physico-économique,* a collaboration involving the agronomists A.-A. Parmentier, J.-M. Roland de la Platière, and the abbé Carlier, also got off the ground. In 1787, the *Journal général de France* began to publish a twice-monthly agricultural supplement which became a weekly feature early in 1788. In 1790 this supplement was to branch off as the *Feuille d'agriculture et d'économie rurale,* changing its name once again in September of that year to the *Feuille du cultivateur.*[27] Initially published by the agronomist Sarcey de Sutières, the editorship passed in May 1790 to J.-B. Dubois de Jacingny, an active associate of the Paris agricultural society. In the 1780s, prizes for essays dealing with rural improvement were offered by academies and learned societies in Amiens, Angers, Arras, Bordeaux, Nancy, and Châlons-sur-Marne.[28] Following a lull in activity, provincial agricultural societies started to revive in the mid 1780s. In 1784, a Society of Agriculture, Sciences, and Arts was established at Agen. Other new societies followed at Moulins (1786), in the Médoc (1787), and at Poitiers (1789).[29] Not having met with any regularity since 1769, the Caen society sputtered back to life in 1785.[30]

The provincial agricultural societies were bastions of a patriotic political economy, often of a kind little changed since the 1760s. In 1783, the vice-secretary of the Orléans agricultural society, the abbé Genty, published a *Discours sur le luxe* which reiterated the old theme that agriculture is the foundation of the prosperity of states.[31] It is all very well for small republics like Holland and Genoa to concentrate on commerce, Genty argued, their soils are sterile and inadequate. But great states, while they can benefit from a limited trade, should concentrate on cultivation. In his account of the sources of an immoderate and harmful luxury, the abbé blamed the excessive profits of finance and the prodigality of sovereigns in lavishing gifts and pensions on favorites. He attacked exclusive privileges because they generated greater inequality and denied men the use of their talents, condemning them to poverty. He charged that privileges stifled economic activity and that in their absence "free competition would open a vast field to emulation and would distribute the precious fruits of industry."

---

[26] According to Musset, *Bibliographie agronomique.* The work is not listed in *Dictionnaire des journaux,* ed. Sgard.

[27] Sgard, ed., *Dictionnaire des journaux.*

[28] Antoine-François Delandine, *Couronnes académiques, ou Recueil des prix proposés par les sociétés savantes* (Paris, 1787); Charles-Sigisbert Sonnini de Manoncourt, *Mémoire sur la culture et les avantages du chou-navet de Laponie; lu à l'assemblée publique de l'Académie royale des sciences, arts & belles-lettres de Nancy, le 25 août 1787* (Paris, 1788); Daniel Roche, "La diffusion des lumières. Un exemple: l'Académie de Châlons-sur-Marne," *Annales: E.S.C.* 19 (1964): 887–922.

[29] Eugène Lefèvre-Pontalis, *Bibliographie des sociétés savantes de la France* (Paris, 1887); Justin, *Sociétés royales d'agriculture,* 112.

[30] André Rostand, "La Société d'agriculture de la généralité de Caen (1762–1790)," *Bulletin de la Société des antiquaires de Normandie* 37 (1926–27): 334–35.

[31] The Orléans agricultural society had never ceased to meet; it held its 592nd meeting on May 12, 1789. Justin, *Sociétés royales d'agriculture,* 257.

He criticized royal borrowing, charging that it raised both interest rates and taxes. Genty noted that luxury made it more difficult for men to devote themselves to the public good. When a disordered imagination keeps creating new needs, interest must become mankind's foremost passion, he warned, and as a consequence "the heart closes itself to philanthropy and pity."[32]

Similar ideas were mooted in the Lyons agricultural society, which enjoyed a renaissance in the late 1780s.[33] One member of the society who would later play a prominent role in the Revolution as Girondin Minister of the Interior, J.-M. Roland de la Platière, deployed a familiar anti-luxury discourse, castigating proprietors for failing to live on their estates and exalting the *moeurs* of individuals who occupied themselves with agriculture. "Peace, gentle affections, all the sentiments dear to the heart of man, essential to his existence, are allied with the country life," Roland argued; "Virtue seems to be strengthened there through the spectacle of nature that one has always before one's eyes."[34] Another active member of the Lyons society, C.-J. Mathon de la Cour, published a discourse in 1787, claiming that *moeurs* could be regenerated, and with them the patriotism of the nation, through the revivification of commerce and agriculture.[35] The constant enemies of *moeurs* and patriotism, he argued, is luxury. Everywhere, men are corrupted by interest; merchants leave useful commerce for speculation; a "spirit of inconstancy and ambition" induces people to leave their estate. Mathon's primary argument is that agriculture, commerce and the arts must be reanimated if *moeurs* and patriotism are to be regenerated.

The most significant institutional development for champions of agricultural improvement was the capture and reinvigoration of the Paris agricultural society by the partisans of Turgot. In 1783, the duc de Liancourt,[36] the duc de La Rochefoucauld, the duc de Béthune-Charost, and the comte d'Angiviller all became members of the society. They were followed in 1784 by P.-S. Dupont, and in 1785 by C.-G. Lamoignon de Malesherbes. Béthune-Charost and Liancourt were prominent agricultural improvers, while the others were former friends

[32] Louis Genty, *Discours sur le luxe, qui a remporté le prix d'éloquence à l'Académie des sciences, belles-lettres & arts de Besançon, en 1783* (n.p., 1783).

[33] In 1786, the society moved into new premises. By 1788 the intendant was reporting that the society had redoubled its efforts, that its assemblies were numerous and its memoirs interesting. Justin, *Sociétés royales d'agriculture*, 257. For evidence of the thriving character of the Lyons society, see *Séance publique de la Société royale d'agriculture de la généralité de Lyon, tenue le 5 janvier 1787* (Geneva, 1788).

[34] Jean-Marie Roland de la Platière, "Mémoire sur la culture de France, comparée à celle d'Angleterre," in *Séance publique de la Société royale d'agriculture de la généralité de Lyon.* Most of the memorandum was devoted to practical suggestions for the improvement of agriculture.

[35] Charles-Joseph Mathon de la Cour, *Discours sur les meilleurs moyens de faire naître et d'encourager le patriotisme dans une monarchie, sans gêner ou affoiblir en rien l'étendue de pouvoir d'exécution qui est propre à ce genre de gouvernement* (Paris, 1787).

[36] François-Alexandre-Frédéric de La Rochefoucauld, duc de Liancourt (1747–1827), became the duc de La Rochefoucauld-Liancourt in 1792, following the death of his first cousin Louis-Alexandre, duc de la Rochefoucauld (1743–1792). As the duc de Liancourt lived much of his life as the duc de La Rochefoucauld-Liancourt, he is often referred to retroactively by this title.

and collaborators of Turgot.[37] The society also recruited a host of luminaries from the Academy of Sciences, among them L.-J.-M. Daubenton, curator of the royal cabinet of natural history; André Thouin, chief gardener at the Jardin du roi; A.-L. Lavoisier, France's leading chemist, and an enthusiastic experimental agronomist; the abbé Tessier, director of the king's experimental farm at Rambouillet; and Fougeroux de Bondaroy, the nephew and collaborator of H.-L. Duhamel du Monceau, founder of the French agronomic movement in the 1750s.[38] The social caché of the society was increased by celebrity associates such as George Washington (a serious agronomist, and often represented in France as a Cincinnatus figure), and the heir to the Spanish throne, Don Ferdinand, duke of Parma.[39] By 1787, the society was thriving. It published regular compendia of its proceedings, offered prizes to encourage agricultural improvements, and held public sessions in Paris. The revival of the society culminated in 1788 when it was reconstituted as the Royal Society of Agriculture with the king as its protector.[40]

Like the provincial societies, members of the Paris agricultural society made frequent patriotic calls for economic regeneration. At the first public session of the revivified society on March 30, 1786, the duc de Béthune-Charost gave an address encouraging great proprietors to spend money on agricultural improvements instead of lavishing it on "a superfluous luxury." He also sounded the familiar theme of the power of emulation to stimulate agricultural improvement: "A look from the Sovereign, a mark of satisfaction, are powerful means of encouragement in the hands of the Government."[41] That agricultural wealth is the only solid foundation for the power of states was the central theme of a discourse given in the society on July 10, 1788 by the *prévôt des marchands* of the city of Paris, an ex officio member of the society. He observed that "agriculture, protected and encouraged, can alone raise empires to true splendor, to effective power, which is never the result of anything but real wealth. The success and the decadence of nations attest to this truth, such that it ought always to influence in a direct and invariable manner the principles of good governments, and all the operations they adopt."[42]

[37] R. Mantel, *La Rochefoucauld-Liancourt, un novateur français dans la pratique agricole du XVIIIe siècle* (Paris, 1965); Dakin, *Turgot and the Ancien Régime*, 17, 153, 212.

[38] Among the other scientific luminaries recruited by the society were Antoine-François Fourcroy, Jean-Antoine-Claude Chaptal, Jean-Henri Hassenfratz, and Antoine-Auguste Parmentier.

[39] In announcing Washington's recruitment, the secretary invoked the Cincinnatus trope. The general who had bestowed liberty on his country had now given himself over to the peaceful occupations of agriculture. *Discours prononcé à la séance publique tenue par la Société royale d'agriculture, dans la grande salle de l'archévêché le 28 décembre 1789* (Paris, 1790).

[40] "Règlement fait par le roi, du 30 mai 1788," in *Mémoires d'agriculture, d'économie rurale et domestique, publiés par la Société royale d'agriculture de Paris, année 1788, trimestre d'été* (Paris, 1788).

[41] Armand-Joseph, duc de Béthune-Charost, *Copie d'un mémoire lu à la première séance publique de la Société royale d'agriculture de Paris, du 30 mars 1786* (n.p., n.d.), 10.

[42] "Règlement fait par le roi, du 30 mai 1788," xvi.

Fig. 8. *Oath of the Horatii* by Jacques-Louis David, 1786.

Fig. 9. *Oath of the Horatii* by Jacques-Louis David, detail, 1786.

In this reduced version of Jacques-Louis David's celebrated *Oath of the Horatii* (Paris, Musée du Louvre), the original painting's narrative of patriotism and virtue is reinforced by the addition of a simple wooden plow in the background of the picture, partially obscured by one of the pillars (see detail), and a distaff lying at the feet of the women on the right side of the image. The inclusion of the plow ties the painting to discourses linking agriculture, regeneration, and civic virtue, a tradition that was being renewed in the 1780s in opposition to the court capitalism and speculation that Calonne's administration had come to symbolize. Courtesy of the Toledo Museum of Art. Purchased with funds from the Libbey Endowment, Gift of Edmund Drummond Libbey.

The same themes were sounded by a new generation of patriot agricultural improvers who assumed prominent roles in the agricultural society during the late 1780s. An exemplary voice among these new men was J.-B. Rougier de la Bergerie, a young landowner from Poitou who enjoyed a meteoric rise in the agricultural society: he was named a correspondent in 1787, became a full member in 1788, and was one of the intellectual leaders of the body by the autumn of 1789.[43] For de la Bergerie agricultural regeneration would be the foundation of political regeneration. He drew on the intellectual legacy of the 1760s and modified it to meet the new challenges of the late 1780s, particularly speculation. In his *Recherches sur les principaux abus qui s'opposent aux progrès de l'agriculture* (1788), he argued that agriculture is the basis for good *moeurs*, and is the foundation of patriotism. In contrast to the man who only pursues money, he argues, the cultivator is "attached to his *patrie*."[44] De la Bergerie favorably contrasted cultivators "whose hearts are as pure as their works are useful" to city dwellers with their "spirit of calculation." His book is framed by concerns about the dangers of *agiotage*. "A false speculation, a dangerous system, [a] mania for representative riches, which the opinion of the age has unfortunately endorsed, can in a moment cause an immense fortune to disappear," he noted. Society and the state must be refounded on more stable and surer bases than "that fictive and fantastic wealth, which luxury, idleness, and systems have imagined." Citing the example of the Roman republic, he observed that states are stable so long as they are based on agriculture.[45]

To encourage agriculture and to refound society on surer bases, de la Bergerie argued, it would be necessary to assign the farmer "a distinguished rank" in society. There should be equal consideration for the zealous cultivator as for the true gentleman. The proper economy of honor had been deranged, he suggested, because honor was lavished on "men depraved on the inside, since gold is everything in their eyes, and a fatal prejudice brings you to welcome and consider them, solely because they are superbly attired and have plenty of money." The fact that agriculture was honored in ancient Rome while it was now despised could be attributed, he suggested, to "the false opinion that gold is the most solid, the most real wealth of society."[46] De la Bergerie was a strong advocate of the use of honors and prizes to animate agricultural improvement and to keep peasants on the land. Indeed, he personally organized a country festival for his neighbors with a distribution of prizes to worthy cultivators.[47]

[43] He is one of six signatories of the *Mémoire présenté par la Société royale d'agriculture à l'Assemblée nationale, le 24 octobre 1789, sur les abus qui s'opposent aux progrès de l'agriculture,* the principal policy brief produced by the society during the Revolution. Indeed large parts of the brief were closely based on Rougier de la Bergerie's *Recherches sur les principaux abus qui s'opposent aux progrès de l'agriculture* (Paris, 1788).

[44] Rougier de la Bergerie, *Recherches sur les principaux abus,* 111.

[45] Ibid., 12, 200, 3.

[46] Ibid., 10, 12.

[47] See the account given in Broussonet, *Discours prononcé à la séance publique tenue par la Société royale d'agriculture,* 15–16. Rougier de la Bergerie praises the intendant of Paris, Louis-

The idea that moral regeneration could be effected through a return to agriculture was premised on the notion that by altering the physical environment in which men lived—for example, by transferring them from the city to the countryside—their *moeurs* could be transformed. By the late 1770s, the notion that a return to agriculture would have regenerative effects, especially with respect to luxury, had become something of a cliché. The essay "Of Commerce and of Luxury," that J.-B. Robinet selected for publication in his *Dictionnaire universel des sciences morales, économique, politique et diplomatique* in 1780, for example, notes that "agriculture is besides in itself proper to repressing luxury; and it is not without reason that a great philosopher regards it as the school of wisdom and good *moeurs*. It accustoms [one] to a simple and laborious life: these gentle and innocent occupations draw one away from fantasies."[48] "Natural history and agriculture," Emma Spary argues "appeared to many to offer solutions to the problems of moral and physical degeneration of the nation."[49] The experts on natural history brought over to the Paris agricultural society from the Academy of Sciences and the Jardin du roi in the 1780s were technicians in this science of regeneration.

One of the most important sites for French discussions of the morally regenerative possibilities of agricultural work and landowning in the 1780s was in discourse about America. If France could be made more like America—by decreasing social inequalities, by limiting luxury, by simplifying *moeurs,* but most of all by increasing the number of land owners and the centrality of agriculture in national life—then perhaps French *moeurs* might become more like those of their American counterparts. Nowhere was the argument that agriculture has the capacity to regenerate *moeurs* more clearly expressed than in the paradigmatic French work on America, *Letters from an American Farmer,* published in 1784 by the returned French expatriate M.-G. St-Jean de Crèvecoeur.[50] In the *Letters,* he represents America as a land uncorrupted by luxury,

---

Bénigne-François Berthier de Sauvigny, for paying special attention to farmers and peasants and for distributing medals to encourage them on his twice yearly rounds of his generality. *Recherches sur les principaux abus,* 14.

[48] "Du commerce et du luxe," in *Dictionnaire universel des sciences morales, économique, politique et diplomatique; ou Bibliothèque de l'homme-d'état et du citoyen* (1780), 12:557.

[49] Emma C. Spary, *Utopia's Garden: French Natural History from Old Regime to Revolution* (Chicago, 2000), 125.

[50] Michel-Guillaume Saint-Jean de Crèvecoeur, *Letters from an American Farmer: Describing Certain Provincial Situations, Manners, and Customs, Not Generally Known; and Conveying Some Idea of the Late and Present Circumstances of the British Colonies in North America* (London, 1783). First published in English in 1782; translated by the author and published in France in 1784. Crèvecoeur had emigrated to America in 1754 where, in 1769, he bought and cleared a 120 acre farm in Orange County, New York. He refused to support the rebellion in the 13 colonies, was ostracized by his neighbors, and returned to France in 1781. Keeping his Tory past a secret, Crèvecoeur became the darling of Paris salon society for a time in the early 1780s. In May 1782 he was invited to take up residence in the hôtel of Mme d'Houdetot, where he was introduced to the ducs de La Rochefoucauld, and de Liancourt, and to Marmontel, Delille, d'Alembert, Suard, La Harpe, Grimm, Necker, and Target. Julia Post Mitchell, *St. Jean de Crèvecoeur* (New York, 1916).

a society of small farmers unmarked by the brutal contrasts of wealth and poverty that characterized the Old World. Crèvecoeur emphasizes the power of the American environment to regenerate the corrupted *moeurs* of European immigrants. In America, he argues, "every thing has tended to regenerate them;" after acquiring land, the new American "begins to feel the effects of a sort of resurrection." For Crèvecoeur, rule of law and relative social equality are important regenerative features of the American environment, but the decisive transformation is effected by the acquisition of land. The new landholder quickly "forgets that mechanism of subordination, that servility of disposition, which poverty had taught him." That agriculture is the decisive source of regeneration, rather than liberty, or the American environment, is attested to by Crèvecoeur's discussion of the immigrants who settle in the American backwoods and become hunters rather than farmers. These backwoodsmen, unlike their agricultural brethren, "degenerate a little," becoming "ferocious, gloomy, and unsocial."[51]

Here Crèvecoeur is drawing on ideas commonplace in the latter half of the eighteenth century. As an essay on the moral effects of the arts had observed in 1762, "in a wild and sterile place the mind is quite differently modified than in the bosom of a smiling and fertile countryside."[52] The mechanism whereby *moeurs* are differently affected by an untamed environment than by an agricultural setting was analyzed in 1776 by Georges-Louis Schmidt: "The hideous and tedious aspect of a savage country fills the imagination with sad ideas, and these ideas continually reproduced, turn into a habit, and form a sad, hard and ferocious character. . . . A well-cultivated land excites on the contrary soft and cheerful ideas, which contribute to the softening of *moeurs*."[53]

Crèvecoeur evokes the pure *moeurs* of the farming life in a sentimentalized account of his own domestic felicity: "When I contemplate my wife, by my fireside, while she either spins, knits, darns, or suckles our child, I cannot describe the various emotions of love, of gratitude, of conscious pride, which thrill in my heart, and often overflow in involuntary tears." Crèvecoeur links this domestic bliss to his life as a farmer: "My wife would often come with her knitting in her hand, and sit under the shady tree, praising the straightness of my furrows and the docility of my horses." On such occasions, he would place his son on a seat attached to the plough, symbolically uniting domestic affections with agricultural labors. "The father, thus ploughing with his child" he remarks, "is inferior only to the emperor of China ploughing as an example to his kingdom."[54]

These images of virtue and regeneration, as the reference to the Chinese emperor underlines, are in fact direct borrowings from the French political econ-

---

[51] Crèvecoeur, *Letters from an American Farmer*, 53–54, 73–75, 63–65.

[52] "Réflexions sur la partie morale & politique des arts," *Journal étranger* (August 1762), 27.

[53] Georges-Louis Schmidt, *Principes de la législation universelle* (Amsterdam, 1776), 1:54.

[54] Crèvecoeur, *Letters from an American Farmer*, 23–27.

omy of the 1760s, transplanted to a setting where political economic conditions made it possible to imagine such virtue and regeneration as a possibility for everyone. Crèvecoeur was steeped in the agronomic literature of the late eighteenth century. His father had been a member of the agricultural society of Caen in the 1760s,[55] and Crèvecoeur the younger, on returning to France in the 1780s, established links with the resurgent Paris society.[56]

So authoritative had idioms of patriotic political economic regeneration become by the mid 1780s, that speculators began to draw on them tactically in the course of struggles against competing speculative interests. The world of financial speculation was wracked by bitter conflicts between groups of speculators attempting to push up the value of stock, and others who had sold short and who needed to depress the price of the same shares. In 1785 Étienne Clavière led a cabal of bearish speculators who had sold short in Paris Water Company shares and sought to push down the value of the stock in order to cover their commitments at a profit. They were opposed by a powerful syndicate of financiers, among them Joseph Micault d'Harvelay, Claude Baudard de Sainte-James, Mégret de Sérilly, and Magon de la Balue. The syndicate was led by Isaac Panchaud, a former associate of Clavière's, and now a financial adviser to Calonne. Clavière employed the comte de Mirabeau to be the front man for an attack on the practicality of the Water Company scheme—an inspired choice, because the comte was the son of the founding father of Physiocracy, the marquis de Mirabeau. In a pamphlet ostensibly written by the younger Mirabeau, Clavière savaged the Paris Water Company as a vehicle for speculation, causing the shares of the company to fall in value by 500 livres apiece.[57] The following year, Clavière attempted to further sink the value of the stock by establishing a competing venture. This time, the Panchaud syndicate managed to have the claims of Clavière's company quashed in the royal council where Calonne backed Panchaud's faction while the baron de Breteuil backed Clavière's.[58]

The struggle continued when Clavière sought to torpedo a fire insurance

[55] Rostand, "La Société d'agriculture de la généralité de Caen," 301.

[56] This contact was facilitated by the fact that Turgot's brother, the marquis de Turgot, who was a founding member of the Paris society, was related to Crèvecoeur by marriage and allowed the "American" to stay with him for a time when he first arrived in Paris. Crèvecoeur published a brochure on potato cultivation, the *Traité de la culture de la pomme de terre* (1786) and followed it with a treatise on the acacia, *Mémoire sur la culture et l'usage du faux acacia dans les États-Unis* (1786). After the French Revolution, he became an associate of the Institut national, and a member of the agricultural society of Meaux, outside Paris, where he had bought land in 1801. Mitchell, *St. Jean de Crèvecoeur*, 171.

[57] Honoré-Gabriel Riqueti, comte de Mirabeau, *Sur les actions de la Compagnie des eaux de Paris* (Paris, 1785). See Bénétruy, *Atelier de Mirabeau*, 109–112.

[58] On the role of the government in adjudicating these competing claims, see Taylor, "Paris Bourse," 972–73. Early in 1788, the royal council again had to rule between the claims of two competing life insurance companies both seeking an exclusive privilege. This time, with Loménie de Brienne at the helm, and both Baudard de Sainte-James and Mégret de Sérilly in bankruptcy proceedings, Clavière's group triumphed.

company established by Panchaud by having J.-P. Brissot write a brochure exposing it as a vehicle for speculation.[59] Claiming to speak as a patriot, Brissot proceeded to unmask the fire insurance company as a snare to capture the money of the credulous. The directors of the new fire insurance company, he claims, have no thought that it will succeed in its avowed business. Indeed, that is not their ambition. Rather, "speculation, one of the most cruel scourges of civilized nations, is the sole aim of these companies and of their shareholders." With some subtlety, Brissot deploys central tropes of political economy to represent the new company as a threat to "real wealth." These insurance companies actually cause financial losses, he argues, because once insured, people no longer try to save their possessions from fires. He claims that the establishment of such a company will cause insurance fraud to take off in Paris, "a city the immensity of which favors new means of corruption, where a great inequality of fortunes reigns, where the desire for splendor is universal, because it alone obtains consideration." Brissot's principal objection to all such companies lies in their destructive effects on *moeurs*. In a metaphor for the difference between a society based on public spirit and a society based on interest, Brissot draws an unfavorable contrast between villagers, who courageously and disinterestedly save the homes and possessions of their neighbors, and the paltry efforts of those "mercenaries" paid to fight fires. Worse still, he argues, such companies orient people excessively toward private interest, toward money, leading to a slackening of the bonds of society. "They banish from society all moral bonds," and transform it into a jungle where people do not scruple to steal from, or even to assassinate, a fellow being if they can do so with impunity. To allow the company to go forward, Brissot laments, "would cause general sensibility to disappear from society, which is one of its bases."[60]

Regenerating the Royal Finances

By the summer of 1786, the royal finances were on the verge of collapse. Calonne informed the king in August that he expected a deficit of 100 million livres for the year on revenues of 475 million. Matters would only become worse in the near future: the third *vingtième* tax would expire in 1787, exacerbating the shortfall of revenues over expenditures, and by the end of the year the state would have spent 280 million livres of its future tax revenues in the form of advances from financiers. The financial situation would reach a criti-

[59] J.-P. Brissot, *Dénonciation au public d'un nouveau projet d'agiotage, ou Lettre à M. le comte de S*** sur un nouveau projet de compagnie d'assurance contre les incendies à Paris, sur ses inconvéniens, & en général sur les inconvéniens des compagnies par actions* (London, 1786).

[60] Ibid., 27–29, 39–40, 33–34, 53. See also *Agio, ou Traité de l'agiotage à l'usage des agents de change, courtiers, marrons et agioteurs, d'après le plan d'éducation de MM. les Lionnois & Genevois. Par un grenadier du régiment d'Anjou* (Paris, 1789); and *Lettre à l'auteur d'un libelle ayant pour titre: Agio, ou Traité de l'agiotage* (n.p., 1789).

cal point in 1790 when the state would begin to repay loans floated during the American War at an additional annual expense of 50 million livres. The controller general revealed the dreadful state of the royal finances to the nation in February 1787 when he convoked an Assembly of Notables which, he hoped, would endorse a series of reforms to save the monarchy from bankruptcy. Calonne's initiative, combined with the Assembly's refusal to sanction it, set in motion the political crisis out of which the French Revolution was born.[61]

Historians often regard the deficit crisis as a trigger, a pretext for French elites to demand a share of political representation, an occasion for the Revolution rather than a cause.[62] But the relationship between the deficit crisis and the Revolution was more direct. The Revolution began, in part, because the public assumed that piecemeal reforms would not constitute an adequate solution to the financial problems of the monarchy and that a sweeping, comprehensive program of national regeneration would be required. Contemporaries arrived at this conclusion because they understood the deficit crisis within a framework that construed it as a symptom of disorders that extended deep into the political economic fabric of the monarchy, disorders amounting to a modernized version of a luxury crisis. Profound institutional changes would be needed to resolve these deeper problems, changes which were expected not only to create national prosperity but to revive public virtue. Calonne introduced his comprehensive reform plan in order to play to public opinion, and thereby turn a bleak situation to some political advantage for the monarchy.

In so doing, the minister implicitly endorsed the perception that a regenerative political economy was the appropriate framework in which to view the deficit crisis. In order "to bring real order into the finances," he told the king, it would be necessary "to revitalize the entire state by reforming all that is defective in its constitution."[63] Calonne's plan to save the royal finances drew heavily on the literature of political economic reform elaborated since the 1750s. Indeed, in drawing up his proposals he called upon the experience and ideas of two prominent political economists—the Physiocrats Dupont de Nemours, and Le Mercier de la Rivière.[64] Calonne proposed to replace the *vingtième* with a universal land tax, payable in kind, to be collected by the taxpayers themselves, organized for this purpose in provincial assemblies. He held that the assemblies would excite "a sort of patriotic effervescence that, if managed wisely, can do much good."[65] He also proposed a range of procedures to

[61] Jean Egret, *The French Prerevolution, 1787–1788*, trans. Wesley D. Camp (Chicago, 1977), 1–2.

[62] Michael Sonenscher is a notable exception. See "The Nation's Debt and the Birth of the Modern Republic: The French Fiscal Deficit and the Politics of the Revolution of 1789," *History of Political Thought* 18, no. 1–2 (1997): 64–103, 267–325.

[63] Egret, *French Prerevolution*, 2.

[64] Lacour-Gayet, *Calonne*, 70.

[65] Quoted in Vivian R. Gruder, "A Mutation in Elite Political Culture: The French Notables and the Defense of Property and Participation, 1787," *Journal of Modern History* 56 (1984): 598.

stimulate economic growth and increase the tax-bearing capacity of the king's subjects. In order to liberate agriculture from "the bondage and afflictions that oppress it even more than do taxes," he proposed to establish free trade in grain, to replace the corvée with a money tax, to reduce the weight of the salt tax, and to suppress internal customs barriers.[66]

However much Calonne's proposals might have owed to patriotic political economy, the Assembly of Notables refused to endorse his reform plan. Not that the notables were against reform; indeed, among the leaders of opposition to the controller general were some of the most progressive figures in the body—the duc de Béthune-Charost, the duc de La Rochefoucauld, and the marquis de Lafayette. The notables were, in fact, strongly in favor of some aspects of the plan, notably the establishment of free trade in grain, the commutation of the corvée into a tax, and reform of the *gabelle*. They criticized Calonne's plan for provincial assemblies not in principle but on the grounds that these bodies would not have enough independence from the monarchy. Their opposition to the proposed land tax, as Vivian Gruder has noted, was not couched as a defense of tradition or privilege; indeed, they favored the principle of fiscal equality.[67] Rather, critics argued that the new tax, in the form Calonne proposed to levy it, would be harmful to agriculture. The tax, which would be levied in kind, ought to fall not on the gross product of the land, they argued, but on its net product, so that the imposition was proportional to the fertility of the soil. If the notables adhered to an orthodox Physiocratic position here, they rejected the Physiocratic doctrine of a single, universal land tax. The notables sought to shift the tax burden off the land and onto paper wealth, calling for taxes to fall equally on "capitalists" and *rentiers*.[68]

Even if the notables had agreed with every detail of Calonne's plan they would almost certainly still have opposed him. The moderate revolutionary Malouet later observed of the controller general that he "appeared to be a combination of all the abuses he wanted to reform. So vast a plan, even though skillfully contrived, was bound to collapse in the hands of a man lacking public confidence and esteem."[69] Whatever shreds of public confidence Calonne re-

[66] Egret, *French Prerevolution*, 3.

[67] Gruder, "Mutation in Elite Political Culture."

[68] They also objected to the unlimited nature of the tax, both in duration and size. Traditionally, taxes had been levied for a fixed period of time, and in a quantity fixed in advance and supposedly in proportion to the needs of the state. The new land tax was a potentially limitless resource for administrative waste. The notables also preferred a tax that was constant so that any increase in agricultural output would be tax-free, creating incentives for improvements. Gruder, "Mutation in Elite Political Culture."

[69] Egret, *French Prerevolution*, 29–30. In Egret's words, "The liberal aristocrats, who shaped opinions, could welcome, with bewildered if profound satisfaction, the unexpected conversion to the Physiocratic doctrine of a minister who had recently reestablished the East India Company. But they were obliged to reject the pretensions of this determined agent of the administrative monarchy who conceived provincial assemblies without real power, demanded a proportional tax that would be indefinite and perpetual, and paid no attention to the privileges of individuals, corporate bodies, and provinces."

tained were undermined by damaging revelations during the Assembly of Notables concerning the involvement of his administration with speculators. That Calonne's administration was fostering and protecting speculation was the central thesis of a pamphlet which Darnton describes as the second most influential tract published during the prerevolutionary crisis: the *Dénonciation de l'agiotage au roi et à l'Assemblée des notables* (1787).[70] The brochure, published under the comte de Mirabeau's name, but probably written by Brissot in collaboration with Clavière, was intended to force Calonne to annul contracts made by speculators who had sold Indies Company shares short and who were now at the mercy of another group of speculators who had established a corner on the market for such shares using treasury funds.

The *Dénonciation de l'agiotage* was a critical political intervention because, more successfully than any other work, it framed the monarchy's financial crisis in terms of a political economy of patriotic regeneration. Because of this framing it was significant that Mirabeau's name was attached to the pamphlet (and for that reason I shall preserve the fiction that he was the author). "Mirabeau" argued that speculation would have to be eradicated if the nation were to be regenerated, and curtailing speculation would require a move against both the court-capitalist joint-stock companies and excessive government borrowing. A principal impetus to speculation, he notes, is the multitude of shares with which privileged companies inundate the marketplace. These companies, he claims, are "enemies of our true industry." The reestablishment of the monopolistic Indies Company, for example, flies in the face of the general consensus that liberty is what animates commerce; why, he asks, was the Indies trade not left to our industrious ship owners? Mirabeau also identified the corrupt administration of the Paris Discount Bank (*caisse d'escompte*) as a stimulus to speculation; he claimed that the bank had been hijacked by its banker administrators who extended cheap credit to their cronies for speculative purposes. Besides the court capitalist sector, the other great spur to speculation, according to Mirabeau, was the excessive borrowing the royal administration had indulged in since the American War. The explosion of government *rentes* had become a fuel for speculation.[71]

One of Mirabeau's central arguments was that speculation creates a false wealth which undermines real sources of riches in agriculture and commerce. He described the paper wealth circulating in Paris as a "Sterile pomposity! A sickly abundance! Ready to vanish at the slightest reverse." "Its final product," he complained, "is an unbridled gaming, where millions [of livres] have no other movement than to pass from one portfolio to another, without creating anything other than a collection of chimeras that the madness of the day parades with pomp, and which that of tomorrow will cause to vanish." Mirabeau charged that speculation had raised interest rates to prodigious levels, and cre-

[70] Robert Darnton, "The Brissot Dossier," *French Historical Studies* 17, no. 1 (1991): 191–208.
[71] Honoré-Gabriel Riqueti, comte de Mirabeau, *Dénonciation de l'agiotage au roi et à l'Assemblée des notables* (n.p., 1787), 25–28, 87–89.

ated a money famine in the provinces, making it impossible for farmers and merchants to get the credit they needed to increase their production. He also suggested that the obscure but mighty gains of the speculators were a disincentive to work. Their overnight fortunes sowed a disenchantment among ordinary laborious people with their own modest profits. "One would wish that the honest merchant, the artisan of simple *moeurs,* the modestly-salaried worker would have the virtue to resist this intoxicating spectacle of enormous gains, of ostentatious luxury, of fortunes born in a day," Mirabeau observed, but such a hope was vain.[72]

Describing speculation as "the most redoubtable enemy" of the kingdom, Mirabeau suggested that unless it was suppressed, the public finances would never be righted. The only way to put the public finances back permanently on a sound footing was to generate economic development. By drying up investment, speculation made it impossible to create prosperity in the real economy. "Is it not necessary to send back to our fields the money that Paris absorbs only to corrupt everything?" Mirabeau pleaded. The other reason why the public finances would not be regenerated so long as speculation persisted was that speculation destroyed the public spirit necessary for any significant reform. According to the comte, "the lack of public spirit is our primary vice." He warned that the nation must choose between catastrophe and a constitution that would "substitute regenerative public spirit for inflammatory struggles." Later, he returned to the same theme, noting the "harsh greed, the culpable indifference to means" that speculation fostered in all classes of society. He bemoaned the lack of social solidarity—everyone was "occupied solely with his particular interest." To destroy speculation, Mirabeau argued, would be to save the state, to reestablish order in the finances, and to prepare the way for a return of public spirit.[73]

Appearing two weeks after the opening of the Assembly of Notables, the *Dénonciation de l'agiotage* was deeply damaging to Calonne's position.[74] The controller general had learned of its contents before it was actually published, and had tried to buy off Mirabeau, but printing was already underway.[75] He issued a warrant for the author's arrest, and Mirabeau had to flee to the Netherlands. It was not just Mirabeau's ad hominem charges that resonated with Calonne's critics; his claim that speculation had raised interest rates in the provinces to exorbitant levels, thus destroying the prosperity of the real economy, was echoed both in the Assembly of Notables and in the nation at large. The notables criticized the credit policies the royal government had pursued,

[72] Mirabeau, *Dénonciation de l'agiotage,* 7–8, 27–30, 44.

[73] Ibid., 12, 15, 32–3, 69–70, 126. Jean-Louis Carra deployed a similar set of arguments against Calonne in his *M. de Calonne tout entier, tel qu'il s'est comporté dans l'administration des finances, dans son commissariat en Bretagne, &c. &c.* (Brussels, 1788).

[74] Bosher, *French Finances,* 190.

[75] The *Dénonciation de l'agiotage* appeared on 6 March, 1787, two weeks after the Assembly of Notables got underway. For details surrounding its publication, see Bénétruy, *Atelier de Mirabeau,* 129–30.

particularly the high interest rates offered on government loans which, they argued, raised interest rates to exorbitant levels and starved agriculture and commerce of investment.[76] The Chamber of Commerce of Lyons drafted a memorandum arguing that speculation was ruining provincial trade and forwarded it to the controller general. The Lyonnais complained that interest rates were as high as 16 percent, forced up by the activities of Paris speculators.[77] The last vestiges of his credibility damaged, and the assembly slipping out of his hands, Calonne tried a desperate gamble, publishing a pamphlet claiming that the notables were resisting necessary reforms in order to protect their own privileged position. The brochure served only to further incense the assembly; Calonne's last chance to reach an accommodation slipped away. Recognizing this, the king demanded his resignation and appointed Étienne-Charles Loménie de Brienne, the archbishop of Toulouse, in his stead.

The appointment of Loménie de Brienne is usually seen as a sop to the notables, because the archbishop had been one of the leaders of opposition to Calonne in the Assembly. But there was a deeper significance to his selection. Loménie de Brienne was regarded as a prospective second Turgot, and in appointing him the king surely meant to link the monarchy to projects for patriotic economic renewal. It is a measure of the distance between 1774 and 1787 that this strategy proved so futile. Turgot is supposed to have remarked once of Brienne that "I shall be consoled for my disgrace if some day the Archbishop of Toulouse can take my place."[78] Brienne had been a school friend of Turgot's, sharing quarters with him and the abbé Morellet when they were students together at the Sorbonne. Turgot's ally, Morellet, remained close to Brienne.[79] Shortly after his accession to power, Brienne brought two other Turgot associates, Malesherbes and the duc de Nivernais, into the government as ministers without portfolio. (Malesherbes had served alongside Turgot as minister of the king's household and shared his disgrace; Nivernais was a long-time protector of the Physiocrats). Loménie de Brienne made the program of the patriot agricultural improvers his own. In July 1787, the archbishop became an associate of the Paris agricultural society and, in May of the following year, he reorganized the body as the Royal Society of Agriculture with the king as its patron. Brienne gave the society a consultative role to the royal government on issues of economic development. He also protected the Physiocratic journal, the *Nouvelles éphémérides économiques*, revived by the abbé Baudeau in January 1788.[80] Brienne moved publicly to control the excesses of speculation by ap-

[76] Gruder, "Mutation in Elite Political Culture."

[77] Taylor, "Paris Bourse."

[78] Quoted in Egret, *French Prerevolution*, 39.

[79] Morellet spent part of each year at the château de Brienne in Champagne. Léonce de Lavergne, *Économistes français*, 333, 356.

[80] Weulersse, *Physiocratie à l'aube de la Révolution*, 19. He dispensed, however, with the services of the Physiocratic P.-S. Dupont de Nemours, who was compromised by his close association with Calonne.

pointing a commission to investigate the new Indies Company, and by dismissing Panchaud who had served Calonne and his two predecessors.[81] In December he appointed another commission to investigate an apparently fraudulent land deal between Calonne and the baron d'Espagnac, brother of a notorious speculator.[82]

Brienne took Calonne's reform plan and modified it to meet the criticisms of the notables, but he had little more success in getting the Assembly to endorse the reforms than had his predecessor.[83] On May 25, Brienne dismissed the Notables and the following month attempted to get the Parlement of Paris to register the main edicts of the reform plan. He had little trouble securing assent for provincial assemblies and free trade in grain, but the court refused to register any new taxes. Béthune-Charost emerged as a leader of opposition to the ministry, joined later by La Rochefoucauld. On July 26, the Court presented a remonstrance to the king demanding the convocation of the Estates General. Loménie de Brienne was suffering the costs of the almost total breakdown in trust of the royal government that Calonne's administration had provoked. Some of the most vocal advocates for the Estates General were personally sympathetic toward Brienne: the duc de Montmorency-Luxembourg was a friend of his, while Lafayette extolled his virtues. The abbé Morellet understood the logic of the situation and explained it to the chief minister: "We need some bar to the repetition of abuses: we need the Estates General or the equivalent. That is what people everywhere are saying."[84] On August 10, at the height of the struggle between Loménie de Brienne and the parlement, the parlementary leader Adrien Duport was still attacking Calonne, while the chief prosecutor of the parlement, Joly de Fleury, charged the former controller general with "maladministration of the finances, whether by exchanges and acquisitions detrimental to the state, or by extension of loans beyond the limits set by the edicts or declarations registered in the court . . . or by secretly using the funds of the Royal Treasury to cover stock speculation detrimental to the state."[85]

Brienne's struggle with the parlement dragged on to May of 1788. On August 14, 1787 the parlement was exiled to Troyes. However, when Prussia invaded the Dutch Republic on September 13, and the French could do nothing to help their Dutch Patriot allies, Brienne decided to reconcile with the parlement. On September 20 he withdrew the tax edicts, presented a new loan edict, together with a five-year plan of financial retrenchment, and a promise to convene the Estates General in 1792. The compromise foundered, however, when in the course of a special session, with the king in attendance, on November 19, Louis grew impatient and ordered the edicts registered. When the duc d'Orléans denounced

---

[81] Nussbaum, "Deputies Extraordinary of Commerce."

[82] Egret, *French Prerevolution*, 54.

[83] Jean Egret suggests that at this point the notables were too concerned about compromising themselves in the eyes of public opinion to endorse any increase in taxation. Egret, *French Prerevolution*, 34.

[84] Ibid., 108.

[85] Ibid., 100.

this as illegal, the king replied: "I don't care . . . it's legal because I wish it." After the king left, the parlement disassociated itself from the registration. Rumors abounded of a royal coup against the parlements like that of chancellor Maupeou in 1771. The blow came in May 1788 when the parlements were reduced to simple appeals courts, and the right to register edicts was vested in a new institution, the Plenary Court. In the following weeks, a wave of protest swept the country akin to that which followed the Maupeou coup.

The attack on the authority of the parlements made Brienne as unpopular as his predecessor chancellor Maupeou, but even at this late stage compromise might have been reached and revolution averted. It was not popular protest but empty coffers that precipitated Brienne's fall. Early in August, the minister was informed that the treasury could not raise the 240 million livres in short-term credit that it needed to meet its obligations for the rest of the year. Brienne suspected a plot by financiers to leave the treasury empty. In a bid to shore up confidence, he announced that the Estates General would be convened in May 1789, and he postponed until that date the establishment of the new Plenary Court: significant concessions to the patriot opposition. According to Jean Egret, patriots such as Lafayette rallied promptly to the administration.[86] But to no avail. On August 16 the treasury ran out of money and began to make payments in interest-bearing treasury bills. One might view this as a form of bankruptcy or, as John Bosher argues, as the creation of a state-backed paper money to replace the short-term credit supplied by financiers.[87] Though the furor created among investors by the treasury bonds quickly died down, it provided a pretext for Brienne's enemies to move against him. Brienne asked Necker to join the government but Necker delayed for five days and during this period the *société de la reine* moved against Brienne. The duchesse de Polignac worked on Marie-Antoinette while the comte d'Artois tried to persuade the king to abandon his unpopular minister.[88] On August 25, seeing that the royal couple were no longer behind him, Brienne resigned. Necker abandoned the initiatives of his predecessors; his policy was to wait for the Estates General to regenerate France rather than have the monarchy do so. It was quite natural for the forces opposed to reform to think that a delaying action of this sort might yield them some advantage—Brienne's policies would have been disastrous for them. But in assuming that the devil they didn't know might be better than the devil they did, they were sorely mistaken.

The Attack on Aristocracy

With the fall of Brienne, the political crisis moved into a new phase. Once it became clear that the monarchy had abdicated responsibility for regenerating

---

[86] Ibid., 183.
[87] Bosher, *French Finances*, 198–99.
[88] Ibid., 199; Egret, *French Prerevolution*, 185–86.

the nation to the Estates General, the composition of that body became a matter of the greatest political importance. The Parlement of Paris declared in September that the Estates General would be structured in the same manner as in 1614, the last time it had convened, an arrangement that would have given the nobility a preponderant voice in the assembly. Catalyzed by this apparent power grab, protest against royal despotism was transformed, between the fall of 1788 and the spring of 1789, into a struggle that pitted spokesmen claiming to speak for the Third Estate against both the monarchy and the so-called privileged orders. In the course of this struggle, critics drew heavily, and to brilliant effect, on themes from the political economy of the preceding decades to depict nobles as corrupted by luxury, and their order as an obstacle to patriotic renewal. Partially a product of the intense political rivalries produced by the dispute over the form the Estates General should take, the attack on aristocracy was also a product of long-standing tensions. Court nobles and their financier cousins had long been viewed both as the beneficiaries of political economic institutions that were the root cause of French degeneration, and as the chief impediments to the reform of those institutions. It was much more difficult to cast the provincial nobility in such a role, but critics could draw on the anti-noble motifs elaborated during the 1770s, and middling nobles made it easier for these critics by seeming to throw in their lot with *grands seigneurs* in the elections to the Estates General.

Middling nobles can only have confirmed the claim that they were no different than aristocrats when, in the spring of 1789, the electoral assemblies of the Second Estate, which were dominated by provincial nobles, elected *grands seigneurs* in large numbers. In its choice of deputies, the nobility expressed a desire to reassert as clearly as could be the dividing line that separated nobles from nonnobles, a dividing line that, in social terms, had been profoundly blurred by financial and commercial wealth. The nobility overwhelmingly elected men of impeccable and long-standing noble status who had served in the military; they shunned the recently ennobled. Eighty percent of the noble deputies had acquired their nobility before 1600 while perhaps two-thirds of all nobles had been ennobled after 1600. Only 6 percent of deputies for the nobility were from families ennobled in the eighteenth century, compared to about one-third of the order as a whole.[89] In selecting its deputies, the nobility produced a representation of itself very different from its true composition, something closer to an authentic, pure, ancient nobility unblemished by the corrupting admixtures of commerce and finance. The irony is that, in so doing, it elected a delegation that was very rich and heavily weighted to Paris. Half of the deputies had addresses in the capital; a majority had incomes above the median for the nobility, and many of them were very wealthy. In such circumstances, it was difficult to sustain the distinction between a virtuous, provincial nobility and a corrupt aristocracy wallowing in luxury.

[89] Timothy Tackett, *Becoming a Revolutionary: The Deputies of the French National Assembly and the Emergence of a Revolutionary Culture (1789–1790)* (Princeton, 1996), 28–29, 32.

In treating all nobles as part of a luxurious class allied with despotism, propagandists for the Third Estate were able to twist political economic categories to their own ends. The anonymous author of *Le dernier mot du Tiers-État à la noblesse de France* identified the Third Estate with the "farmers" and the "merchants" who created all the wealth of the kingdom, and counterposed them to nobles who did no work but nevertheless reaped the treasure of the state.[90] The same contrast was central to the comte de Volney's *Sentinelle du peuple,* a radical newspaper that pioneered anti-noble language in Brittany. Volney used the traditional contrast between nobles who fight and commoners who work to establish an invidious contrast between the two estates. All of the arts useful and necessary for life are concentrated among the Third Estate while the nobles know nothing of them, Volney argued; nobles fight, but to defend their own privileges rather than for the sake of the *patrie*. He blamed the nobility for exclusive economic privileges: is it not the gentlemen, by exclusions of all kinds, who chain our industry, he asked? The provincial nobility was pushed back into the same category as the court nobility—all parts of a group that consumed but did not work.[91]

The language political economists had evolved in the old regime to criticize plutocracy was turned on the nobility as a whole in 1789. Volney attacked the "vicious inequality of wealth," blaming riches for the intolerable pride of the nobility. He also turned his pen against financiers, advising his readers to "attack those rich commoners who aspire only to betray their Order: dismiss those corrupted men, who make of honor a prize of finance." Volney turned traditional pro-noble language on its head, accusing nobles of excessive interest in money and insufficient attachment to honor: "Those French gentlemen, so jealous of honor, so free with their blood, we thought them avid for glory, [but] they were [avid] only for money: and for a little of that vile metal, they have set fire to their *patrie,* and preferred the loss of their Nation to the loss of their tyranny."[92] The claim that the nobility was interested in money rather than honor—that is, that they were corrupted by luxury—was a central feature of the attack on the privileged late in 1788 and early in 1789. Rougier de la Bergerie, the rising star of the Paris agricultural society, reversed the standard traits of the noble and the commoner, attributing to farmers qualities traditionally seen as noble, and attributing to nobles the interest in money long considered a characteristic of the ignoble. The cultivator, he argues, is "always useful, always virtuous, always honest, always beneficent, always attached to his *patrie*, to his king." He is willing to spend his whole fortune and spill his blood for their glory and interest. De la Bergerie implies that the modern nobility has been corrupted by pecuniary interest: if you had proposed to a soldier that he become a Farmer General under the reign of Louis XIV, he would have

[90] Anon., *Le dernier mot du Tiers-État à la noblesse de France* (n.p., 1788).
[91] *La sentinelle du peuple, aux gens de toutes professions, sciences, arts, commerce et métiers, composant le Tiers-État de la province de Bretagne,* no. 1 (10 November 1788), 5; no. 4 (15 December 1788), 8.
[92] *Sentinelle du peuple,* no. 5 (25 December 1788), 15, 18.

been insulted, he claimed, but today chevaliers de Saint-Louis clamor for such positions.[93]

Luxury was the critical failing of the nobility, according to Pierre-Laurent Berenger's *Les quatre états de la France*.[94] Calling for sumptuary legislation to reintroduce order and simplicity among nobles, Berenger argued that the nobility must be made to see that the way to win consideration was through virtue, not through dress.[95] Berenger leveled these charges within the context of a work that attacked exclusive privileges and fiscalism as sources of rapid fortunes and destructive inequality; he warned about the poor state of the countryside, and called for the encouragement of agriculture; and he condemned tax farmers, financiers, and courtly extravagance. Even more damning conclusions were drawn by the abbé Emmanuel-Joseph Sieyès, who emerged briefly in 1789 as a leader of the Revolution. In his *Essai sur les privilèges* (1788) Sieyès suggested that, as a consequence of their luxury, nobles were more interested in money than nonnobles. According to Sieyès, "they are even more prone to give themselves over to that ardent passion, because the prejudice of their superiority inflames them ceaselessly to overdo their expenditure." While prejudice pushed nobles to spend, it cut them off from almost all honest ways to replenish their fortunes. Considerations of honor restrained nobles less than commoners, Sieyès argued, because, being born with honor, it was difficult for them to lose it. As a consequence, "intrigue" and "beggary" had become the "industry" of the nobility.[96]

The argument that hereditary nobility was an impediment to emulation—an argument first adumbrated in the 1760s and 1770s—emerged in the late 1780s as a decisive feature of the revolutionary critique of nobility. The thesis of the *Essai sur les privilèges* is that the existence of honorific distinctions, such as titles of nobility, along with a social class which monopolizes such honors, made it difficult or impossible to harness the passion for honor for the public good. According to Sieyès, the desire for honor leads people naturally to perform actions which advantage society because, in return for such actions, they receive the approbation and esteem of others. The desire for money, by contrast, is an anti-social force which the passion for honor might be used to tame. "The desire to merit the public esteem," Sieyès argued, "is a necessary brake on the passion for riches." Because titles could be inherited, there existed a class of people—the privileged—who enjoyed honor as a birthright. They had little to gain from acts of public virtue, and nothing to lose from the anti-social pursuit of gain. As honor was theirs by right, they could not be deprived of it by the public. Sieyès demanded the abolition of the whole institution of honorific "distinctions," along with the class that monopolized them, to open a "free competition of all" for public esteem.[97]

[93] Rougier de la Bergerie, *Recherches sur les principaux abus*, 111, 8.

[94] Pierre-Laurent Berenger, *Les quatre états de la France* (n.p., 1789).

[95] See also Pierre-Toussaint Durand de Maillane's *La noblimanie*, published on February 25, 1789, which laid the blame for luxury squarely on nobles.

[96] Emmanuel-Joseph Sieyès, *Essai sur les privilèges* (Paris, 1788), 32–3.

[97] Sieyès, *Essai sur les privilèges*, 13.

Nicolas Bergasse, a leading apologist for commerce in the 1770s, and a leader of the moderate *monarchien* faction in the National Assembly in 1789, concurred with Sieyès arguing that nobility destroys "emulation" and "encouragement." Bergasse asked the reader to imagine the progress society would make "if the hope of success encouraged work and talent in all orders of Society; if finally, the field of honor and glory was open equally to all kinds of merit." Bergasse suggested that the French nation accord its homage "only to justly merited glory," and held out the prospect of this people—"so sensitive to honor"—"delivered finally to the energy of the most free emulation."[98] Other revolutionaries advocated the abolition of hereditary nobility but welcomed honorific distinctions for the life of the bearer. The anonymous author of the *Abolition de la noblesse héréditaire en France* proposed that nobles of old stock be permitted to keep their titles for life, but not to pass them on to their heirs. He also advocated that three chivalric orders be maintained: "one of *Saint-Esprit* for persons who fill the highest offices in the state, and for all those who signal themselves by a brilliant patriotism in whatever class of society they should be; the other of *Saint-Michel* for all those who excel in the sciences, the arts, commerce and navigation; and the third finally of *Saint-Louis,* destined solely for the military estate."[99] But the *chevaliers* of the various orders were to be ennobled for life only. "Respect . . . ought to be free," he contended, "it is against the nature of things to . . . accord this respect independent of the sentiment of those who give it and the merit of those who are its object."[100]

A version of this emulation-based critique of nobility provided language to justify the abolition of nobility and titles in 1790. During the debate on the suppression of nobility on the night of June 19, 1790, the deputy Joseph-Marie Lambel proposed a motion to eliminate titles.[101] Charles de Lameth seconded Lambel's motion and demanded the abolition of nobility outright. Echoing Sieyès's *Essai,* he suggested that distinctions which confer honor on people, regardless of how they behave, are a disincentive to virtuous action. "There is no emulation of virtue where citizens have another dignity than those attached to the functions confided in them, another glory than that which they owe to their actions." Opposing Lameth's proposition, the marquis de Foucault demanded to know how a man ennobled for saving the state could be recompensed for the

---

[98] *Observations sur le préjugé de la noblesse héréditaire* (London, 1789), 28, 42. On Bergasse's parliamentary career, see Jean-Denis Bergasse, *D'un rêve de réformation à une considération européenne: MM. les députés Bergasse (XVIIIe–XIXe siècles)* (Cessenon, 1990).

[99] *Abolition de la noblesse héréditaire en France, proposée à l'Assemblée nationale; par un philanthrope, citoyen de Belan* (n.p., n.d), 42–43.

[100] Ibid., 26. Similarly, an anonymous pamphlet entitled *L'anéantissement total de la noblesse héréditaire, ou Requête urgente à l'Assemblée nationale* (Paris, 1789) noted that "the French nation ought not to recognize any distinction but that acquired through talent or merit, that is to say, that it ought not admit into its bosom any other nobility than personal nobility, because that is the only one which may support the analysis of reason" (6). The author complained that, "a ridiculous prejudice seems to exclude [the commoner] from everything having to do with the honorific, which ought to belong only to talent, to merit and to capacity . . ." (5).

[101] *Réimpression de l'ancien Moniteur* (Paris, 1847) 4:676.

loss of his title. The marquis de Lafayette countered that the real distinction lay not in the title but in the patriotic action of the hypothetical noble; instead of saying that such a man was ennobled, one ought simply to say, "this man has saved the state." Sieyès made the same point in his *Essai* when he noted that "the true distinction is in the service which you have rendered to the *patrie,* to humanity . . . public regard and consideration cannot fail to go where this kind of merit calls them."[102]

Under the more radical of the emulation-based critiques of aristocracy, even a well-regulated and individually virtuous nobility was represented as antithetical to the public welfare. This view is perhaps most clearly articulated in an article which appeared in the aftermath of the abolition of the Second Estate. In response to a query raised by two provincial readers, the revolutionary newspaper, *La feuille villageoise,* published a scathing attack on hereditary distinctions. The readers in question wrote to the editors of the paper to praise a local noble whom they described as a friend of the people. So popular was this ex-noble locally that he had just been elected a justice of the peace. The two correspondents noted, however, that their new magistrate was bitterly opposed to the suppression of nobility, titles, and other symbolic distinctions. They asked the editors of the *Feuille* to explain for their benefit, and for that of their *seigneur,* the advantage to be gained from abolishing nobility and titles. The editors replied with an article couched in language similar to Sieyès's *Essai.* Addressing their remarks to the ex-noble mentioned by the two correspondents, the editors suggested that, in a nation of philosophers, "your claim to be born with the right to public consideration would excite only a contemptuous laugh." They went on to compare nobility, titles, and distinctions to a counterfeit money which the privileged had used to buy the respect and consideration of the common people, asking whether the government should tolerate the circulation of such a "false money." Then, implying that honor ought to be at the disposal of the public to reward meritorious action, and that the existence of nobility destroys the incentive for virtuous behavior, they suggested that "esteem, consideration, the homage of citizens . . . forms a part of the public wealth: because it is the fund for recompensing those who have served the *patrie.* How will it be then if this treasure of honors is dissipated to the profit of the false merit of birth, if a sterile nobility extorts with impunity the share of genius and virtue?"[103]

Nobles had, perhaps, always been courting trouble in claiming that the public interest was being subordinated to the advantage of a wealthy and luxuri-

---

[102] Sieyès, *Essai sur les privilèges,* 9–10.

[103] *Feuille villageoise* 18 (January 26, 1792), 420–21. The piece was probably written by Philippe-Antoine Grouvelle, one of the collaborators on the *Feuille villageoise.* He had used a similar argument, comparing titles to a "false money," in the journal of the Society of 1789 in July 1790, immediately after the suppression of nobility. Grouvelle, "Considérations sur le décret du 18 juin, et sur l'opinion de M. Necker à ce sujet," *Journal de la Société de 1789,* no. 6 (July 10, 1790), 36.

ous few. They saw themselves as the victims of this pernicious plutocracy—in the army where they found it hard to compete with court nobles and the sons of *anoblis,* and facing a system of taxation and public finance that transferred wealth out of their pockets and into those of tax farmers, "capitalists," and aristocrats. From the perspective of their countrymen, however, nobles could readily be seen as part of an elite defined largely by money and enjoying a preferential position within the larger political economic order. Most nobles had acquired their nobility through purchase, many within living memory. If the consumption patterns of lesser nobles were frugal and austere by comparison with financiers and grandees, they were often lavish by the standards of small-town France. The way middling nobles championed a critique of the old regime's luxury is analogous in many ways to their claim that merit should serve as the basis for promotion in the army. They seem to have been quite blind to the possibility that this demand could be turned against them. But those nonnoble elites who wielded the charge of luxury against the nobility were not invulnerable to such a critique themselves. Within a few years they were being attacked as a "bourgeois aristocracy" by the radical sans culottes; their relative wealth had become a pretext to question their patriotism.

CHAPTER 6

The Agrarian Law and the Republican Farmer

The regime of liberty and equality cannot be sustained except in tending always, in so far as possible, to the leveling of fortunes: to divide the soil, to multiply land holders and small properties, ought thus to be the goal of the new government.

—J.-M. Lequinio, *Richesse de la république* (1792)

It is easy to declaim against luxury; its pernicious effects are easily recognized; but it is not so easy to discover the means to disengage from its influence the population and the power of an empire, without falling into ills infinitely greater.

—Germain Garnier, *Abrégé élémentaire des principes de l'économie politique* (1796)

The preoccupation with luxury that animated debates in political economy during the forty years before the Revolution declined sharply during the 1790s. In part, this development was a consequence of revolutionary reforms that destroyed the political and institutional order which old regime critics had identified as the principal source of luxury. Revolutionary legislatures abolished tax farming, monopoly companies, courtly pensions, the whole institutional complex linking polity and economy that critics had identified as a source of luxury in the ancien régime. The power of the court aristocracy and the financiers was broken. Early in 1791, most of the indirect taxes of the old regime were abolished and the General Farm was liquidated. By the end of 1791, the exclusive privileges and monopolies enjoyed by court capitalist enterprises had been abrogated. In the logic of patriot political economy, such reforms would eliminate luxury and permit the emergence of a virtuous commercial society. However, lessening concern about luxury was not simply a consequence of the reform of economic structures.

It was not luxury, but its inverse, that seemed the more pressing problem in the 1790s. An issue that overshadowed political economic analysis in that decade was the concern that political transformation might precipitate a collapse of wealth-creating capacity and the ruin of the civil society it sustained.

A significant guise in which this anxiety was expressed was as fear of an "agrarian law." Many commentators voiced concern that a modern-day Lycurgus would operate a scheme of forcible property redistribution modeled on the anti-luxury reforms of ancient legislators, and reduce France to economic primitivism. When revolutionaries worried that reforms intended to curtail luxury might precipitate economic collapse, they were still struggling with a version of the old political economic predicament of constructing a durable compromise between wealth and virtue. In the circumstances of the 1790s, with a revolutionary state in place dedicated to the regeneration of patriotic virtue, the sense developed that it was now wealth rather than virtue that was under threat. Fears of complete economic breakdown were the more credible in the 1790s in view of the sharp decline of the most dynamic sectors of the economy and the stark visibility of poverty. Of the Faubourg Saint-Germain, one of the most fashionable neighborhoods of Paris before the Revolution, one foreign observer wrote in 1796 that the district was "quite depopulated; its hotels almost all seized by the Government, and the streets near the Boulevard are choked with weeds."[1]

Unease about revolutionary economic reforms was, in part, a consequence of the radical mutation in the nature of politics that the Revolution had brought about. The revolution transformed politics from a realm governed, at least prescriptively, by custom and tradition into an instrument for the recasting of society by the sovereign will of the people. After the abolition of the monarchy, in particular, politics seemed to have become a pure instrument of sovereign will.[2] If the life of a nation could be remade through political action, in disregard for precedent and history, what were the limits of such a reconstruction? It was in the nature of the revolutionary conjuncture that the ground rules of civil life were *all* potentially open to alteration. In this context, it seemed possible that property, and the wealth-producing resources of the nation, might also be open to radical reconfiguration. Such fears were powerfully aggravated by sans-culotte critiques of existing inequalities of wealth and property, which became increasingly forceful and strident in 1793. This was the climate in which apprehensions about the agrarian law erupted.

Some revolutionaries responded to the threat of the agrarian law, and to the general sense that the post-revolutionary world was foundationless by seizing upon the economy as an entity that would limit the exercise of political will. From 1792, revolutionaries who sought to resist the regulation of the grain trade or the imposition of price controls argued that further interference with property would precipitate economic collapse. They painted such a breakdown in the darkest terms—as the inauguration of a new barbarism. The economic

---

[1] William Doyle, *Oxford History of the French Revolution* (Oxford, 1989), 402.

[2] See, in particular, Lynn Hunt, *Politics, Culture, and Class in the French Revolution* (Berkeley, 1984); idem, *The Family Romance of the French Revolution* (Berkeley, 1992); idem, "The World We Have Gained: The Future of the French Revolution," *American Historical Review* 108, no. 1 (2003): 1–19.

realm, they suggested, was refractory to the exercise of sovereign will; legislative action would have effects entirely contrary to those anticipated. After the fall of Robespierre in 1794, surviving revolutionaries claimed that the Jacobin Republic over which he had presided was bent on initiating such a decivilizing process. To symbolize the path away from Jacobinism that the Revolution was now taking, they adopted a rhetoric that cast the Republic as a protector of agriculture, trade, and manufactures. By 1795, republicans were representing economic activities as foundations of the civic order. The new vision promised to produce citizens who were patriotically engaged, but who expressed their civic spirit in a privatized fashion as farmers, merchants, or entrepreneurs. It calmed fears for property and soothed apprehensions that the republic would undermine civilization. This virtual "invention" of the economy turned out to be a useful way to stabilize the post-revolutionary order. Revolutionaries adopted and disseminated such conceptions in order to stabilize a world haunted by the dread that everything is political.

Political Economy and the New Civic Order

In the fall of 1789, with the struggle between the Third Estate and the nobility resolved in favor of the former, and with the dramatic events of July 14 and August 4 behind them, the deputies to the Constituent Assembly (as the Estates General was now known) turned once again to the question of the political economic regeneration of France. Some measures for regeneration had already been taken. In August, the deputies had lifted regulations on the grain trade. During the night of August 4, 1789, when much of the fabric of privilege was destroyed, they abrogated most of the exclusive privileges and monopolies enjoyed by court capitalist enterprises; the Saint-Gobain Company, for example, lost its privilege.[3] The Indies Company escaped this first onslaught, but its privilege was revoked in April 1790.[4] The Constituent Assembly set about regulating French policy on external trade with a view to regenerating France as an economic power capable of rivaling England.[5] It opted to do away with all internal customs and duties in favor of a single duty imposed at the national frontiers, a policy that effectively did away with much of the business of the Farmers General.[6] In March 1791, the General Farm was suppressed, completing the abrogation of the old regime of indirect taxes. The former direct taxes had already been suppressed. In November 1790, the offices of the tax re-

[3] René Sédillot, *Le coût de la Révolution française* (Paris, 1987), 195.
[4] *Réimpression de l'ancien Moniteur* (Paris, 1859–63), 3:649, 4:5, 7–8, 23–24, 30–32, 38–40.
[5] Jeremy J. Whiteman, "Trade and the Regeneration of France, 1789–91: Liberalism, Protectionism, and the Commercial Policy of the National Constituent Assembly," *European History Quarterly* 31, no. 2 (2001): 171–204.
[6] J. F. Bosher, *The Single Duty Project: A Study of the Movement for a French Customs Union in the Eighteenth Century* (London, 1964), 163, 171.

ceivers were abolished and public employees were hired to collect the new taxes that replaced the *taille*, the *capitation*, and the *vingtième*.

The centerpiece of the Constituent Assembly's effort to regenerate the nation economically was its assault on the whole system of private enterprise in public finance, an agenda that also entailed the creation of the revolutionary paper currency, the *assignats*. The process whereby the *assignats* emerged as the agency that would liberate France from the financiers was a complex, even a tortuous one. It began with Étienne Clavière, who argued in June 1789 that the route to regeneration of the finances lay in the creation of a paper money which, he argued, would revivify the national economy.[7] The shortage of money, he claimed, was a major obstacle to prosperity, leading to high interest rates that starved agriculture of investment. The best means to stimulate "general industry" would be to increase the money supply promptly by using a "fictive currency." Criticism of Clavière's proposal emerged quickly. No one should be taken in by the "illusions" of paper money, wrote the anonymous author of an *Essai sur la dette nationale et sur la régénération de la France*, published in October of 1789. Instead, the state should sell the lands of the church, a measure that would expand the number of proprietors and help to stimulate agriculture.[8] Agricultural improvers rallied around this proposal for resolving the financial difficulties of the state. In October 1789, the Royal Agricultural Society called for the nationalization of church lands. A policy brief adopted at an extraordinary general meeting held on September 26, and forwarded to the National Assembly, held that "the regeneration of the kingdom . . . has as its principal basis the regeneration of cultivation," and a vehicle of that regeneration might be the nationalization of ecclesiastical properties.[9] In selling the lands of the church to resolve the financial problems of the state, moreover, the Assembly would supply a powerful antidote to the ravages of speculation. "Soon, even our capitalists, who have exercised their industry, their genius, only to augment riches that are often imaginary, no longer finding means to make their funds serve for speculation . . . will employ them in commerce or in buying estates."[10] The deputies concurred, and on November 2 the Constituent Assembly appropriated the lands of the church.

---

[7] Étienne Clavière, *Opinions d'un créancier de l'État, sur quelques matières de finance importantes dans le moment actuel* (London, 1789), 64–89.

[8] *Essai sur la dette nationale et sur la régénération de la France* (n.p., n.d.).

[9] *Mémoire présenté par la Société royale d'agriculture* (Paris, 1789). The memorandum was signed by the four officers of the society—the marquis de Buillion, Parmentier, the abbé Lefebvre, and Broussonet, and also by the duc de Béthune-Charost and Rougier de la Bergerie, suggesting that these last two played some role in drafting it. Indeed, parts of the brief were taken word for word from Rougier de la Bergerie's *Recherches sur les principaux abus qui s'opposent aux progrès de l'agriculture* published the previous year. The meeting at which this program was adopted was held two weeks before Talleyrand proposed the nationalization of Church lands in the National Assembly, and the *mémoire* was presented to the Assembly on October 24, at the height of debate on the motion.

[10] *Mémoire présenté par la Société royale d'agriculture*, 55–56.

Ultimately, however, the nationalization of clerical properties to pay off the public debt facilitated the paper money scheme Clavière championed. The transition from Clavière's original paper money project to the *assignats* was mediated by proposals to create a land bank which would issue paper money backed by the estates of proprietors who would borrow these paper funds for agricultural investment. The establishment of such a bank was another recommendation of the Royal Agricultural Society. The society reminded the deputies that there was still a money famine in the provinces, a state of affairs it attributed partially to luxury. To meet the extreme shortage of money, the society recommended the establishment of a rural bank at which proprietors could borrow up to half the value of their lands at generous terms in paper money. This paper, which would function as legal tender, could then be used to finance the rural investment that would revivify agriculture, while the interest that proprietors would pay on their loans would be a source of revenue for the state. The agricultural society complained that interest was being charged at 10 percent on money loaned to cultivators, a consequence of "the effects of speculation." The diminution of interest rates that would follow the establishment of the rural bank with its paper money would force the capitalists to lend money at lower rates of interest.

The society was anxious to block any invidious comparisons between this proposed scheme and that of John Law. They assured the Assembly that "the notes or bank papers could never occasion the dangers of Law's fatal system, the memory of which still terrifies, in that they would have a truly real, truly sure, representation, independent of all events and of all public revolutions." Indeed the memorandum suggested that because of the direct connection of this paper currency to the land, it would, in a sense, be more real than metallic money. "These notes would have, perhaps, a credit more real than minted pieces of gold and silver, which are in themselves only conventional signs." Similar land bank schemes were proposed by numerous agricultural improvers unaffiliated with the Paris society.[11] This proved to be the formula that resolved the psychological and political obstacles to the creation of paper money. By tying the value of any new currency to land, the claim could be made that paper money was as real, indeed more real, than metallic money.

A second factor that mediated the creation of the *assignats* was the short-term funding crisis of the state in the autumn of 1789, and Necker's proposal

---

[11] Ibid., 57n, 142–46. For other land bank proposals, see Jacques-Annibal Ferrières, *Plan d'un nouveau genre de banque nationale et territoriale, présenté à l'Assemblée nationale* (Paris, 1789); François Ébaudy de Fresne, *Plan de restauration et de libération. Analyse d'un nouveau plan de culture, de finance & d'économie . . . principes sur lesquels on doit établir la répartition des impôts . . . & la création d'un nouveau signe, pour encourager la culture & le commerce, pour assurer la dette & pour détruire l'usure & l'agiotage* (n.p., n.d.); Leblanc de l'Arbreaupré, *Plan sur l'agriculture et le commerce, suivi de l'établissement d'une banque rurale, & d'un autre pour la formation des galères de terre* (Paris, 1789). From his exile in London, Calonne proposed a similar scheme: *Observations sur les finances à l'Assemblée* (London, 1790).

that this crisis should be met by allowing the *caisse d'escompte* to print paper money. On November 14, 1789, Necker told the Assembly he would need a subvention of 90 million livres to make all payments due in 1789, and he projected a deficit of 294 million for 1790. He proposed to meet the funding crisis by turning the *caisse d'escompte* into a National Bank, increasing its capital by 50 percent, and having it issue 240 million livres in paper money to lend to the government. The *caisse d'escompte* had originally been founded under Turgot to facilitate trade by discounting bills of exchange and other commercial papers. Under Necker, and his successors, its capital was raised to 100 million livres, and it became, principally, a bank to bankers. It played a role in the speculative boom of the 1780s by extending cheap credit for speculative purposes and, under Calonne, it made substantial loans to the Crown. Mirabeau had fiercely criticized the *caisse d'escompte* as a vehicle for speculation in a series of addresses during the preceding months.[12]

The Constituent Assembly rejected Necker's proposal. The marquis de Montesquiou, speaking for the Committee on Finance on November 18, asked the assembly to consider its short-term financial problems within a larger framework. Implicitly attacking Necker's scheme for raising money, Montesquiou stated that "it is not a question of combining the petty resources of fiscality and speculation to fiddle with the taxes and to solicit cupidity. Those talents so commended, and regarded for so long as commendable, will no longer prosper among us. . . . What we need is a general plan, a plan for regeneration."[13] Montesquiou was reflecting the thinking of a majority of the deputies, especially the provincial deputies, whose aversion to relying on the services of bankers and financiers was palpable in the debate that followed.[14] He argued that the principal obstacle to national regeneration was the money owed to financiers in the form of anticipations "which render the administration tributary to capitalists," together with the surety bonds advanced by "companies of finance" that placed the administration in perpetual dependence on these companies. The total of these obligations amounted to well over half a billion livres, but without paying off this debt, and breaking the dependence on financiers, Montesquiou argued, a deeper regeneration of the state would be impossible. He proposed the issue of 400 million livres worth of interest-bearing *assignats*, exchangeable for national lands, to be used to meet the state's most pressing financial obligations. On December 19, the assembly adopted this proposal.

It is worth stopping for a moment to consider what the Finance Committee was proposing here and what the assembly agreed to. The deputies had inherited an enormous public debt from the old regime; it was the crushing size of this debt that precipitated the crisis out of which the Revolution developed. Montesquiou proposed to add considerably to the burden of those inherited

---

[12] *Archives parlementaires*, 9:17–23, 705–11.

[13] *Réimpression de l'ancien Moniteur* (Paris, 1859–63), 2:197–98.

[14] Bosher, *French Finances*, 261–62.

obligations in order to liberate the nation from its dependency on financiers. Despite the enormous size of the public debt, the Assembly did not hesitate to increase the nation's financial obligations in order to bring about a deep reform of the political economic order. Indeed, to these costs of winding up the old regime's system of public finance were ultimately added the more than half a billion livres owed to the owners of venal offices, the 150 million livres of debt taken over from the clergy with the nationalization of clerical property, 100 million livres in compensation payments to former owners of feudal dues, as well as miscellaneous other sums that brought the total debt created by the Revolution itself to about two billion livres. It was this debt—the so-called *dette exigible,* or floating debt—not the obligations inherited from the old regime, that the first truly large emission of *assignats* was created to pay in the autumn of 1790.

Those who wished to use *assignats* to pay off the two billion livres in new debt were able to marshal a series of arguments, developed first by the Royal Agricultural Society, that paper money grounded on land was more real than metallic money and that it would stamp out speculation. Opponents of the proposal drew on the same set of arguments to argue that the debt be paid with interest-bearing *quittances de finance,* which would not function as money, and which would be exclusively exchangeable for national lands. The debate over the rival schemes was dominated by concerns about speculation and the regeneration of the "real" economy. Numerous commentators argued that the *assignats* would revivify a flagging commerce and agriculture. Jérôme Pétion claimed that the emission of *assignats* would give a new life to the "social body." The more that money is abundant, he argued, the more interest rates fall, the more agriculture and commerce flourish, the more the proprietor and the merchant are enriched, the more employment there is for the poor.[15] Mirabeau agreed, arguing that it was necessary to revivify the economy, which was depressed by a shortage of money caused by a "vampire" government.[16]

Critics of the *assignats,* by contrast, claimed that the new paper money would undermine agriculture and commerce. J.-N. Démeunier argued that the issue of two billion livres worth of *assignats* would cause a disastrous inflation.[17] While it was true that wages would eventually rise to equilibrium with prices, this process would take years, and in the meantime those living on a wage or on small *rentes* would become destitute. Twenty-four million people would suffer to enrich the few. A.-F. Delandine claimed that the creditors of the state receiving *assignats* would expect and fear their devaluation. Thus the *assignats* would not be used to acquire land but to repay debts. Ultimately, they would end up in the hands of proprietors, and because the latter would also

---

[15] *Archives parlementaires,* 18:516ff.

[16] *Archives parlementaires,* 19:267.

[17] Jean-Nicolas Démeunier, *Opinion sur le projet de rembourser, en assignats-monnaie, les dix-neuf cent millions de la dette qu'on appelle exigible* (Paris, 1790).

fear depreciation, they would invest this paper in buying more land, increasing the size of their estates without giving themselves the wherewithal to make them fertile. The state would suffer from the lack of general prosperity, the concentration of property, and the weakness of agriculture that must follow. *Quittances de finances,* by contrast, would force the creditors of the state to buy land, attaching to the state "men of the court, men of the bank, men of the law." These would be forced to behave like citizens. "It is not the people, it is not the proprietor who must be taught to love the *patrie,*" Delandine pointed out, "it is for the men who have concentrated all their vices, all their happiness in a portfolio that you must create a *patrie.*" With the "capitalists" investing in land, one would see "civic mindedness reawakening suddenly in certain classes, after a profound lethargy."[18]

The promoters of the *assignats* made exactly the same claim for their scheme. In a speech given at the Paris Jacobin Club on August 13, 1790, before debate had even begun in the Assembly, a member of the club, Gouget-Deslandes, argued that the *assignats* would spell the death knell of speculation, which he represented as the root of the nation's financial problems.[19] Through their maneuvers, he argued, speculators had "dried up industry, ruined agriculture, and increased their fortune at the expense of others." Interest rates had been raised to absurd levels by government borrowing, to the sole benefit of speculators who borrowed money and then lent it at usurious profit to the state. If interest rates were lower, land would become a more profitable investment than such *agiotage.* Similarly, in the National Assembly J.-L. Gouttes supported the proposal to pay the debt in *assignats* claiming that "in creating *assignats* you destroy papers abandoned to speculators, papers which corrupt morals, and you replace them by a fictive money which will protect them; you will favor agriculture and commerce by forcing the creditor to turn his speculations towards commerce and agriculture."[20]

Far from ending speculation, the critics argued, *assignats* in such large issues would return France to the days of John Law. In a memorandum sent to the Finance Committee, the marquis de Condorcet implied that the *assignats* scheme was the brainchild of speculators and would unleash speculation on a national scale.[21] *Assignats,* made legal tender by fiat, would be the ideal fuel for *agiotage,* he argued, because their value was exposed to circumstances and artificial variations, which were forever the speculator's source of profit. In launching this huge issue of *assignats,* the National Assembly would be inviting the nation to the gaming table. The duc de La Rochefoucauld agreed. He anticipated speculation on the basis of fluctuations in the value of the paper currency rela-

[18] *Archives parlementaires,* 18:520–24.

[19] Gouget-Deslandes, "Discours sur les finances prononcé à la séance du 13 août 1790, de la Société des amis de la Constitution," in *Archives parlementaires,* 18:538ff.

[20] *Archives parlementaires,* 18:387.

[21] Marie-Jean-Antoine-Nicolas, marquis de Condorcet, "Mémoire sur la proposition d'acquitter la dette exigible en assignats," *Archives parlementaires,* 18:530ff.

tive to metallic money.[22] J.-N. Démeunier denounced the proposal to pay the debt in *assignats* as a revival of Law's System.[23] "The two billions in *assignats*-currency," he insisted, "will be a rain of gold for a few speculators; but other than that they will spread sterility and poverty."[24]

Defenders of the *assignats* rejected such invidious comparisons. The abbé J.-M. Brousse asserted that the dangers associated with paper money did not attach to the *assignats*, whose "value is as sure . . . as the land they represent." They were the "sign" of a "thing productive by nature" and "in this way are better than money."[25] J.-B.-C. Chabroud agreed, arguing that *assignats*, "the essential analog of land, which is the source of all value," could prove more "solid" even than existing money. One could not make the land itself circulate, "but the paper becomes the representation of this value."[26] Mirabeau claimed that *assignats* are not what is commonly known as paper money.[27] Founded on national lands, the "sacred base of all our projects of regeneration," the value of the *assignats* is more "real" than that of money itself. "I ask all the philosophers, all the economists, all the nations of the Earth," Mirabeau declaimed, "if there is not more reality, more real wealth, in the thing of which the *assignats* are the type, than in the thing denominated under the name of money?" Acres of land could not by their nature be made to circulate, Mirabeau observed, but "their sign" could circulate and "it ought to be taken for the thing itself." Two days after Mirabeau's final speech, which was interrupted a dozen times by tumultuous applause, the National Assembly decreed that the floating debt be paid in *assignats*, though no more than 1.2 billion livres in *assignats* should be allowed to circulate at any one time.

Both sides in the debate had accused one another of wishing to foster speculation. Was there any truth in these accusations? Was the scheme to use *assignats* to pay the debt a grand speculative project of Clavière and Mirabeau? Clavière was, after all, very much involved in speculation still, running a life insurance company that never actually sold any policies but still managed to turn

[22] "Opinion de M. de la Rochefoucauld, député de Paris, sur la proposition d'une émission nouvelle d'assignats-monnaie," *Archives parlementaires*, 19:280–83.

[23] Démeunier, *Opinion sur le projet*. Démeunier conceded that the first paper money issue of four hundred million had been successful, and that three to four hundred million more would probably be beneficial. He proposed that the total sum of *assignats* in circulation not exceed eight hundred million, and that this money not be used to pay the floating debt.

[24] Mirabeau condemned the *quittances de finance* scheme on similar grounds, warning that it would give rise to a new speculation that would ruin all the branches of "useful" commerce and every kind of industry. *Archives parlementaires*, 19:271.

[25] *Archives parlementaires*, 18:390–92.

[26] Ibid., 397. Pétion assured his colleagues that the *assignats* had nothing in common with Law's banknotes: "Law's notes were mortgaged on chimeras . . . while the *assignats* are based on solid, unchanging properties . . . which is to say that the system of Law had no base, while the system of the *assignats* has the surest base, the only true, the only invariable one . . . the land." Ibid., 516ff.

[27] *Archives parlementaires*, 19:263ff.

a healthy profit.[28] A letter of Étienne Dumont, one of Clavière's circle of exiled Genevans, written in January 1791, noted that since the issue of the *assignats* his friends, and Clavière in particular, were "like convalescents in improving health." "Clav[ière] has not gained as people have claimed," Dumont wrote, "but he has felt the beneficial effects of the *assignats* like all those who had payments to make . . . . Speculation has become considerable."[29]

What of the claim, also made by both sides, that the methods they championed to pay the debt would transform speculators into landowners? As much speculation as the *assignats* gave rise to, in the long run they drove a lot of investors to purchase land. Originally intended for debt payment only, the revolutionary paper currency was later used to meet the state's short-term obligations. In October 1792, with the revolutionary war underway, the ceiling on the quantity of *assignats* in circulation was raised to 2.4 billion; it was to be the first of many such increases. On October 19, 1795, the floor of the building that housed the *assignat* printing shop collapsed due to the tremendous activity of the presses. By February 1796, when those presses finally ceased turning, 45 billion livres worth of *assignats* had been issued.[30] Naturally, such massive issues, combined with the effects of war, led to steep inflation. By 1795, *assignats* were worth only a tiny fraction of their nominal value. The only safe haven for assets in conditions of spiraling inflation was in land, and enormous quantities of land could be had at bargain prices. A significantly larger portion of all private French capital was invested in land in 1800 than in 1789.

The Agrarian Law and the Revolutionary Crisis

Anxiety about the security of property was a thread that ran through the Revolution from 1789 until 1799. One curious, but revealing, form in which fears for property were expressed was in worries about the prospect of an "agrarian law," a massive, forcible redistribution of land on an egalitarian basis. Peter Jones has described apprehensions about the agrarian law as a "bourgeois Great Fear."[31] The National Convention was so exercised about the prospect of the agrarian law that, on March 18, 1793, it decreed the death penalty for anyone proposing such a measure.[32] Describing the *loi agraire* as "a law subversive of all social order," the spokesman for the Committee of Public Safety, Bertrand Barère, asserted that, if he did not regard them as mad, he would propose the death penalty for those who called for such a measure. At

---

[28] Taylor, "Paris Bourse."

[29] Bénétruy, *Atelier de Mirabeau*, 304.

[30] Doyle, *Oxford History of the French Revolution*, 322, 403.

[31] P. M. Jones, "The 'Agrarian Law': Schemes for Land Redistribution during the French Revolution," *Past and Present* 133 (1991): 99.

[32] *Archives parlementaires*, 60: 292–93.

once, several deputies demanded that the death penalty be mandated for this crime, and the measure was adopted by acclamation "amid scenes," as Barrie Rose puts it, "of general and almost hysterical enthusiasm."[33] The remainder of this section will explore the revolutionary anxiety about the agrarian law. Analysis of this fixation offers a singularly effective means to grasp the problem the Revolution posed for men and women whose thinking was framed by the political economic debates of the old regime.

During the 1790s, worry about the agrarian law expressed, to some extent, the actual insecurity of property. In 1789, rural France was swept by the "Great Fear," when rumors spread like wild fire that nobles were plotting to starve the common people by employing brigands to destroy the crops. Peasants armed themselves and launched preemptive and punitive strikes against noble châteaux and against the symbols of seigneurial power: gibbets, dovecotes, and lordly battlements. The French countryside remained the scene of an extended, episodic rebellion against seigneurial rights until the summer of 1793. John Markoff enumerates over 4700 violent incidents involving crowd actions in the French countryside between June 1788 and June 1793, a large proportion of them attacks on property.[34] Georges Lefebvre gathered hundreds of petitions from rural France between 1792 and 1794 that called for limitations to be placed on the extent or use of property. A small number were extremely radical. One from the municipal officers of the town of Nantua in the Côte d'Or, drafted in September 1792, called for the abolition of private property and the cancellation of debts. The drafters represented this reform as a means to revitalize agriculture and to eradicate luxury. "Thus you will encourage agriculture, the first of the arts; thus you will force to work those idle Sybarites, corrupted and corrupting, useless to the land which nourishes them . . . to the *patrie* of which they are the denatured children. Thus you will destroy that afflicting spectacle of poor and unhappy virtue beside a triumphant and honored vice."[35] However, as Lefebvre notes, such expressions were unusual; calls for redistribution rarely went farther than the demand that the size of lease-hold farms be limited.

An attention to the term "agrarian law" itself reveals something about the sources of revolutionary apprehensions concerning the security of property. The expression was a borrowing from Roman republican history where it referred to efforts championed by reformers, such as the Gracchi, to distribute public lands to the poor. In practice, as Rose has noted, revolutionaries also used the term to refer to the far more radical redistributive scheme of Lycurgus, who is supposed to have expropriated all private land in Sparta and apportioned it

[33] R. B. Rose, "The 'Red Scare' of the 1790s: The French Revolution and the Agrarian Law," *Past and Present* 103 (1984): 113–30.

[34] John Markoff, "Violence, Emancipation, and Democracy: The Countryside and the French Revolution," *American Historical Review* 100, no. 2 (1995): 360–86.

[35] Georges Lefebvre, *Questions agraires au temps de la Terreur* (Paris, 1989) [1932], 176–77.

equally among the citizens.[36] In using the expression agrarian law, the implication was that this measure would come from above rather than below—it is the Legislator not the landless who ordain an agrarian law. The agrarian law, especially in its Lycurgan variant, was an anti-luxury measure, an effort to reestablish virtue by recreating the conditions of equality and simplicity in which such virtue was supposed to flourish. In manifesting their apprehensions about the agrarian law, revolutionaries were expressing an anxiety that their *own* anti-luxury measures might go too far, that in trying to regenerate virtue, they might destroy the mainsprings of national wealth.

Some anxiety about the prospect of such excessive anti-luxury measures was generated by the small number of revolutionaries who insisted on the need to establish caps on how much property a person could own, or who called for a distribution of land to all citizens. A debate on land redistribution was initiated in the autumn of 1790 by Claude Fauchet, the chief ideologist of the Confédération des amis de la vérité, or Cercle social, a Paris political club whose meetings attracted crowds of several thousand individuals.[37] At the November 19 meeting of the Confédération, Fauchet claimed that "every man has a right to the earth and must possess enough land for his existence." He argued that no individual ought to own more than 50,000 livres worth of land (still a fairly substantial holding). He did not propose to expropriate those who owned more than this, but held that they should not be allowed to acquire more. Fauchet also proposed to make the equal division of inheritances compulsory, a measure that would break up great estates, level fortunes, and create a nation of small farmers. In December, he went on to say that "it is impossible to create a viable social constitution without assuring real property to all members of society."[38]

Others continued the discussion of property redistribution in the revolutionary press over the following months, but they did so gingerly. In January 1791, James Rutledge, a leader of the popular Cordelier Club, suggested that to consolidate the revolutionary abolition of aristocracy, some redistribution of property might be necessary. He dismissed forcible property redistribution as both impractical and destructive and rejected the agrarian law outright. But he suggested that some limits on property might be advisable.[39] More radical proposals were made by Sylvain Maréchal in the *Révolutions de Paris*, one of the most successful and widely-read revolutionary journals.[40] Maréchal, who was later associated with the 1796 Conspiracy of Equals, orchestrated by the com-

[36] On this point, see Rose, "'Red Scare' of the 1790s." The classic accounts of both the Gracchi and Lycurgus were to be found in Plutarch's *Lives*.

[37] Gary Kates, *The Cercle Social, the Girondins, and the French Revolution* (Princeton, 1985).

[38] *Bouche de fer*, no. 22 (November 1790): 346. Quoted in Kates, *Cercle Social*, 112–13.

[39] *Le creuset*, no. 1 (January 3, 1791), 1–24.

[40] "Des pauvres et des riches," *Révolutions de Paris*, no. 82 (January 29–February 5, 1791): 169–75.

munistic "Gracchus" Babeuf, noted that, in time, the new revolutionary institutions would produce equality. In the meantime, however, he counseled the
rich to make proprietors of poor men by relinquishing a portion of their possessions. He also advised the poor to demand that uncleared land be divided
among them. These tentative calls for a more equitable distribution of property
may have encouraged Antoine de Cournand to publish *De la propriété, ou La
cause du pauvre,* perhaps the most radical call for a redistribution of property.
Cournand proposed that all private land be expropriated by the state, that one
third of it be leased out, with the rents to replace taxation, and that the remaining two-thirds be divided equally among every man, woman, and child.[41]

In many respects, such calls were merely extreme versions of ideas made
commonplace in the political economic debates of the 1770s and 1780s. Those
who called for a measure of redistribution did so from within the terms of a political economy focused on patriotic regeneration; the purpose of redistribution
was to foster social virtue. The greatest boon of egalitarian property arrangements, Cournand argued, would be the regeneration of *moeurs,* "that nerve of
empires." "Every man being obliged to work for his subsistence," he claimed,
"*moeurs* will little by little be regenerated." Though at points in his argument
Cournand seems to incline toward a social order almost entirely agricultural,
subsistence oriented, and autarkic, ultimately he was committed to reconciling
virtue with commercial wealth. He claimed that his scheme would perfect commerce rather than destroy it. Many individuals would choose to remain in cities,
he argued, but those who continued to desire luxuries, not being able to acquire
them with landed revenues, would be forced to work for them. Under such circumstances, far from disappearing, manufactures, commerce, and the useful
arts might be exalted to new heights.[42]

Those who condemned the agrarian law were, in many cases, as committed
to making property available to the poor as was the radical fringe that called
for the division of common lands, or landholding maxima. From the beginning
of the Revolution, moderate revolutionaries argued that a better distribution of
landed property would regenerate virtue, improve the prosperity of agriculture,
and ameliorate poverty. In a policy brief exploring the means to animate rural
development sent by the Royal Agricultural Society to the National Assembly
in October 1789, for instance, the agricultural society called for the diffusion
of property to wider social strata through the enclosure of common lands. The
society represented enclosure as a critical impetus to English agricultural development since the Glorious Revolution. However, in its recommendations for
enclosure, the brief stressed the importance of increasing the *number* of holdings, not their size. The brief complained that entail, a legal institution governing the inheritance of property, tended to maintain "immense fortunes" in

---

[41] Antoine de Cournand, *De la propriété, ou La cause du pauvre, plaidée au tribunal de la raison,
de la justice et de la vérité* (Paris, 1791).
[42] Cournand, *De la propriété,* 39–40.

families and to diminish the number of proprietors. "A wise government," the society cautioned, "tends to divide great properties, because experience instructs it that they are worse cultivated and impolitic; it tends moreover to . . . give the People the chance to own properties . . . . The status of Citizen is strengthened by the title of Proprietor."[43]

The debate on property redistribution—initiated by Fauchet in November 1790 and continued by Rutledge, Maréchal, and Cournand in 1791—was marginal to mainstream revolutionary politics, yet it aroused consternation among contemporaries. When he made his initial statement in favor of redistribution at the Confédération des amis de la vérité, Fauchet's audience hissed him for a full half hour.[44] This, despite the fact that the Confédération was a forum where radical democratic ideas, among them, women's rights, could expect at least a polite hearing. The reaction of more conventional revolutionaries was harshly critical. Choderlos de Laclos, editing the Jacobin-sponsored *Journal des amis de la Constitution,* criticized Fauchet for promoting "the absurd notion of equality of property."[45] Rutledge was shouted down in the Jacobin Club when he repeated the comments he had made earlier. In April 1791, J.-F. de La Harpe accused Rutledge and Maréchal of trying to foist a disastrous "agrarian law" on France.[46] He agreed that great inequality was pernicious, that there could be "monstrous" excesses in the inequality of fortunes—as there were in the old regime. But the natural result of the new legal order would be to diminish such inequality.

Scare-mongering about the agrarian law could function as a weapon in factional struggles. The accusation that an opponent was proposing radical property redistribution was a useful way to cast him as an irresponsible and dangerous man. There was undoubtedly much of this in the Jacobin attacks on Rutledge and Fauchet, figures who represented political competition to the left of the Jacobin Club, or, again, in La Harpe's criticism of Maréchal, the editor of the rival *Révolutions de Paris.* A clear case of the political manipulation of the charge may be found in a letter of June 1790 to the Minister of the Interior written by M.-G.-A. Vadier; it described Vadier's bitter local rivals, the Darmaing clan, as "new Gracchi." Vadier, who was later to become a notorious agent of the Terror, was attempting to prevent the division of a piece of common land among local active citizens and to capitalize on the antagonism this move generated among the local poor. If anyone was playing the role of Gracchus in this situation, it was Vadier himself. Later, by one of those ironies in which the Revolution abounds, Vadier too was charged with promoting the agrarian law and narrowly avoided conviction with Babeuf in 1797.[47] How-

[43] *Mémoire présenté par la Société royale d'agriculture,* 73.

[44] Rose, "'Red Scare' of the 1790s," 121.

[45] Kates, *Cercle Social,* 95.

[46] "De la chimère absurde d'une loi agraire," *Mercure de France,* no. 17 (April 23, 1791): 142–52.

[47] Martyn Lyons, "M.-G.-A. Vadier (1736–1828): The Formation of the Jacobin Mentality," *French Historical Studies* 10, no. 1 (1977): 81.

ever, if politics tells us much about why the accusation of promoting the agrarian law was thrown about in the 1790s, it does not explain the symbolic charge of that allegation. What was it about this bogey that gave it such power to provoke and disturb?

The agrarian law was a raw nerve for many revolutionaries because of their own unease about the basis of property in the new civic order: their disquiet that property had no firmer foundation than political will. Official revolutionary attitudes were predicated on the Lockean axiom that property exists prior to political institutions, which merely function to secure this pre-existing right. This conception of property was enshrined in the Declaration of the Rights of Man and Citizen and, subsequently, in all the revolutionary constitutions. Yet the revolutionaries' own actions manifestly conflicted with this view of property. In the autumn of 1789, the National Assembly had presided over one of the greatest expropriations in European history with the nationalization of the lands of the Catholic Church. The seizure was enacted with the justification that the land belonged to the nation and that the church was merely its steward, but opponents were not fooled. The abbé Maury described nationalization of clerical lands as an "agrarian law."[48] Earlier, in August 1789, the deputies had initiated another radical redefinition of property rights with the so-called abolition of feudalism. The privileges that the revolutionaries abolished on the celebrated Night of August 4, 1789, were forms of property, and recognized as such in French law. If the state could intervene to confiscate property, or to change the rules under which it was held, was this not a tacit acknowledgment that property itself was a political convention, and therefore liable to radical reconfiguration? One might conclude that property rights are positive, political creations subject to redefinition or even extinction with changes in the political order, but this was a conception of property to which most revolutionaries were deeply resistant.

The possibility that wealth and property had no underpinning more stable than the sovereign will was symbolized for the revolutionaries by Lycurgus, the legislator who instituted an agrarian law in ancient Sparta, persuading citizens "to pool all the land and then redistribute it afresh." Lycurgus was a familiar figure for the legislators, because his reforms in ancient Sparta were related in Plutarch's *Lives,* a text widely used in the *collèges* where most deputies had been educated. He was also a stock figure in the political economy of the eighteenth century where he represented the extreme anti-luxury position that virtually all commentators rejected. To economic writers in the old regime, the Lycurgan reforms in Sparta represented a failure to balance the imperatives of creating wealth and virtue by a too great solicitude for the latter.[49] The story of Lycur-

---

[48] Quoted in André Lichtenberger, *Le socialisme et la Révolution française: Études sur les idées socialistes en France de 1789 à 1796* (Paris, 1899), 64.

[49] Mirabeau, *Ami des hommes,* 2:113; Couanier Deslandes, *Éloge de Maximilien de Béthune, marquis de Rosny, duc de Sully* (Paris, 1763), n. 38; Saint-Lambert, "Luxe," 771; *Éphémérides du citoyen* 1 (1767), 116; D. Browne Dignan, *Essai sur les principes politiques de l'économie publique*

gus can also be read as a myth about the purely political origins of both property and wealth; Lycurgus not only redistributed property, he declared by fiat that gold and silver had no value, he replaced them as a medium of exchange with iron, and he arbitrarily set the value of this iron money.[50] The implication of the story is that the ultimate grounding of property and value is political will. The worry about the agrarian law expressed so often and so vehemently by the revolutionaries was, ultimately, an expression of uneasiness that the foundations of property and wealth were political. It is striking that in March 1793 the Convention did not decree the death penalty for actual attacks on property, but rather for anyone who *proposed* the agrarian law—that is, symbolically, anyone who claimed that property could be redistributed by political fiat.

Significantly, one individual who clearly recognized property as a political convention to be made and unmade by human will—Maximilien Robespierre—was among the few revolutionaries untroubled by the specter of the agrarian law. Robespierre dismissed fears of forcible property redistribution, remarking that the "agrarian law of which you have spoken so much is nothing but a phantom created by scoundrels to terrify imbeciles." Robespierre saw property not as a natural right but as a positive right, created and regulated by law; for the slave trader of the old regime, the men shackled in the hold of his ship were property. Noting that the Constitution of 1793 recognized that liberty was limited by the rights of others to liberty, he charged that property right ought to be similarly constrained; it should not prejudice the security, the liberty, the existence, or indeed the property of others. Such limitations ought to be recognized all the more because, unlike liberty, which was a natural right, property was a "social institution," one of the "conventions of man."[51]

Toward a New Sparta?

The Revolution in France took a more radical turn in the summer of 1792. On August 10, following an insurrection of the Paris sections, the Legislative Assembly suspended the monarchy, abandoned the constitution laboriously created between 1789 and 1791, disbanded itself, and called a constitutional Convention to design a new political order. The first act of this body was to declare a republic. A few months later, the Convention tried and executed the king. The foundation of the republic exacerbated anxieties about the security of property and wealth. How much more likely was the emergence of a Lycur-

(London, 1776), 27–28; Chrétien Le Roy, *Le commerce vengé, ou Réfutation du discours couronné par l'Académie de Marseille en 1777, sur cette question: Quelle a été l'influence du commerce sur l'esprit & les moeurs des peuples,* nouvelle édition (Brussels, 1779), 23–24.

[50] *Plutarch on Sparta,* trans. Richard J. A. Talbert (Harmondsworth, 1988), 17.

[51] Maximilien Robespierre, "Sur la propriété," in *Robespierre. Écrits,* ed. Claude Mazauric (Paris, 1989).

gus in a republican order, which—as Montesquieu had taught—must be predicated on the principles of virtue and equality? With the death of Louis XVI,
the final linchpin of the old order had vanished, and possibilities for transformation could appear unbounded. This state of affairs gave rise to feelings of
euphoria, but it also provoked deep apprehension.[52] Some revolutionaries suffered a kind of ontological insecurity, a disquiet that they might be living in a
world without foundations or boundaries. If France could abandon monarchy,
what other institution might it discard or transform? What limit might it trans-
gress? What restriction might it throw off?[53]

Claims that an agrarian law was in the offing escalated also for more tangible reasons: the revolution of August 1792 had been made by the sans culottes,
and these Paris radicals exercised enormous power over the following year and
a half. According to Richard Mowery Andrews, the sans culottes articulated a
distinct political economic vision that was linked to their social position in the
Paris sections. Rejecting Albert Soboul's characterization of the sans culottes as
a motley coalition of journeymen, master artisans, and the popular masses, Andrews argues that a few thousand sectional officials, overwhelmingly drawn
from a stratum of bourgeois Paris, "formed almost a numerical majority of the
entire 'sans-culotterie.'" He suggests that many of the sans culottes were substantial employers. Men who had worked with their own hands, they built busi-
nesses that, in many cases, were more like manufactories than simple artisanal
workshops. According to Andrews, their bourgeois social location was expressed in a distinctive political economic vision: they valued labor and deplored "usury," idleness, and parasitism. It was not wealth, but unearned
income and inherited riches that they disliked. "By this language," Andrews
claims, "revolutionary bourgeois of work allied with a citizenry of labor vio-
lently repudiated Old Regime plutocracy and an emerging class of speculators
in national properties, currency, and the grain trade. The repudiation was tem-
pered: by renouncing usury and luxury, by sacrifice and service, these persons
could join the Republic."

Andrews attributes an aspiration for structural political economic transformation to the sans culottes: "the divestiture of speculative landed, mercantile
and finance capital, and a statist transformation of the French economy centered on expanded production and just distribution of vital commodities."[54]
This political economy was manifestly a version of the critique of plutocracy
and luxury pioneered by wealthier social strata in the eighteenth century, but it
was a version that construed much of the new revolutionary elite as the pluto-

[52] Hunt, *Politics, Culture, and Class*, 32.

[53] Hunt has suggested that this sense of revolutionary vertigo manifested itself in fears that the
distinction between the sexes might be eroded, or that regenerated man might be exposed to incest.
Hunt, *Family Romance*, 89–123.

[54] Richard Mowery Andrews, "Social Structures, Political Elites and Ideology in Revolutionary
Paris, 1792–94: A Critical Evaluation of Albert Soboul's *Les sans-culottes parisiens en l'an II*,"
Journal of Social History 19, no. 1 (1985): 71–112.

cratic enemy. Mistrust of luxury was central to sans-culotte politics. The very term "sans culottes" denoted a rejection of the sartorial insignia of ease and leisure—the knee breeches of elite men. Hostility to wealth, and to the wealthy classes of the old regime, was also a defining feature of the sans-culotte perspective. A petition sent to the Convention in 1793 denounced wealth as "a form of gangrene which corrupts everything it touches" while another called for the exclusion from government posts of sons of *secrétaires du roi*, commercial brokers, and all persons with an income in excess of 3,000 livres.[55] As I have noted, this anti-plutocratic perspective was modular. Just as nonnoble elites used it against its original progenitors, the provincial nobility, so it could be used in turn against those same nonnoble elites by less exalted social strata.

Some of these revolutionary elites struck back against the sans culottes claiming that their demands represented an agrarian law which would have potentially disastrous consequences. The sans culotte certainly left themselves open to such a charge. One sans-culotte militant stated in May 1793 that "it was necessary to apply an agrarian law to all incomes between 4,000 and 5,000 lives."[56] The agrarian law also became a stake in the conflict that divided two factions in the Convention, the Girondins and the Montagnards. The Montagnards, who were closer to the sans culottes, were tarred by their opponents as proponents of a radical and dangerous redistribution of property. The Girondins made increasingly hyperbolic claims that any interference with property would move French society back into a savage or barbaric state. Such wild claims could serve as a means to impose limits on political economic transformation. If interference with property would precipitate economic collapse, then legislators must eschew such meddling. The Girondins claimed that the economic order was resistant to exertions of political will, an argument used for strategic purposes in eighteenth-century political economy, and especially in Physiocracy. In the debates over the regulation of the grain trade in the 1760s and 1770s, the Physiocrats never tired of arguing that regulatory measures intended to assure abundance had the perverse effect of destroying it.[57]

For elite revolutionaries, disquiet about the possibility that the Revolution might threaten a new barbarism could not be separated from uneasiness about the role of the populace in politics. From the beginning, counterrevolutionaries had leveled the charge that the Revolution might engender a crisis of civilization that would precipitate France into an age of iron. The Paris crowd that stormed the Bastille in July 1789 was, for the royalist journalist Antoine Rivarol, the "barbarian town." After the events of October 5–6, 1789, when a crowd led by market women marched on Versailles and forced the royal family to return to Paris, he wrote that "there is no century of Enlightenment for

[55] Albert Soboul, *The Sans-Culottes: The Popular Movement and Revolutionary Government 1793-1794*, trans. Rémy Inglis Hall (Princeton, NJ, 1980) [1968], 10, 12.

[56] Ibid., 10. For other examples, see ibid., 56–58, 61.

[57] Other arguments of this sort are explored in Hirschman, *Passions and the Interests*, 70–81.

the populace . . . . The populace is always and in every country the same: always cannibal, always man-eating."[58] Though those committed to the sovereignty of the people rejected such attitudes, on occasion they too harbored misgivings that a sort of barbarism might be intrinsic to the Revolution. This anxiety was particularly acute following explosions of popular violence such as the mob killings of the intendant of Paris, L.-B.-F. Berthier de Sauvigny, and his father-in-law, Joseph Foulon, or the prison massacres of September 1792, when sans culottes entered the jails of Paris and butchered hundreds of prisoners.[59]

One of the primary forces that brought the people into politics were problems of provisioning—the march on Versailles began as a protest against high bread prices, while Berthier de Sauvigny and Foulon had been accused of hoarding and speculating on grain. It was the provisioning question again in the fall and winter of 1792 that catalyzed concerns about the menace of the agrarian law. Some controls on the grain trade had been reinstituted as an emergency measure in September. There were widespread calls from municipalities for the reimposition of more comprehensive regulation in October and November in the face of a rash of popular protests. From September, the grain trade was a central preoccupation of the Convention. The Girondin press insisted that regulation was an attack on property that presaged the agrarian law, as did the minister of the interior, Roland. On November 19, a delegation from the electoral assembly of the Seine-et-Oise brought matters to a head with a petition claiming that "the liberty of commerce in grain is incompatible with the existence of our Republic" because the price of grain relative to wages made survival impossible for the poor. The petitioners demanded price controls. The president of the Convention, Henri Grégoire, read a letter from Roland arguing that the source of high prices had been the reintroduction of regulation in September. The Convention ordered Roland's letter to be printed, while refusing to publish the competing petition. Within days, a protest movement swept the Beauce; at Courville, on November 29, deputies sent by the Convention to impose order were forced by an angry mob to institute price controls.[60]

On December 8, the Convention devoted most of a session to the grain trade. J.-A. Creuzé-Latouche gave the crucial speech around which supporters of freedom of trade rallied.[61] Creuzé-Latouche had been a provincial correspondent of the Royal Agricultural Society in Paris and would later serve as the first president of the reconstituted Agricultural Society of the Seine. He argued that agriculture had been "oppressed and despised" before the Revolution, and that it

[58] Bronislaw Baczko, *Ending the Terror: The French Revolution after Robespierre*, trans. Michel Petheram (Cambridge, 1994), 192–95.

[59] See Colin Lucas, "Revolutionary Violence, the People, and the Terror," in *The Terror*, vol. 4 of *The French Revolution and the Creation of Modern Political Culture*, ed. Keith Michael Baker (Oxford, 1994).

[60] Albert Mathiez, *La vie chère et le mouvement social sous la Terreur* (Paris, 1973), 1:92–102.

[61] Subsequently published as Jacques-Antoine Creuzé-Latouche, *Sur les subsistances* (Paris, 1793). Citations refer to this edition.

was still misunderstood. Those who wanted to impose controls were deceived by the false glitter of the cities. Dazzled by "edifices, elegant furnishings, charming fabrics," they judged the cultivator, who lived completely without luxuries, "on false appearances," and wished to trouble and menace him with "the most revolting laws." Did the deputies wish to cause cultivators to abandon their land and crowd into the cities, he asked? Did they want all capital to be consecrated to speculation instead of being invested in agriculture? Creuzé-Latouche invoked the specter of the Revolution ending in economic collapse, and a return to a kind of primitivism. The choice facing legislators, he argued, was to respect property and enjoy prosperity and progress, or to attack property and descend into barbarism or savagery. He defended large-scale, commercial agriculture and attacked the idea that restrictions should be placed on the amount of land anyone could farm. He criticized the view that large farms were harmful to the subsistence of the people, arguing that such holdings fed the cities by absorbing a smaller percentage of their own production.[62] While disavowing as a "revolting absurdity" the notion that *all* land should be held in large farms, Creuzé-Latouche equated efforts to limit farm size with the Spartan system of equality, and with the practice of savages. "A step further in our reforms," he warned, "will lead us immediately . . . to the savage state."[63]

In the short term Creuzé-Latouche won his argument. Not only did the Convention reject further controls on the grain trade, it abandoned those reinstated in September. But this was not the end of the matter. There were renewed calls for price controls in the spring of 1792, and, on February 25, mobs attacked grocery stores and warehouses in Paris, engaging in spontaneous price fixing. By the end of April, the Montagnards had changed tack and successfully championed price controls for grain and bread in the Convention. The classic interpretation of these developments, first elaborated by Albert Mathiez, was that the Maximum was an opportunistic move on the part of the Montagnards, a means to win the support of the sans culottes in the struggle against the Girondins. The current consensus suggests that the Montagnards were economic liberals who did not believe in price controls, but acceded to them as a tactical exigency.[64] An alternative view advanced by some scholars is that while the Girondins were liberals, the Montagnards participated in a current of anti-liberal economic thinking focused on the right to subsistence. It is my view that the Girondins and the Montagnards were indeed similar in their beliefs, but that liberalism is not a particularly useful way to characterize those commitments.

The basic framework of both Montagnard and Girondin thinking was a political economy focused on balancing the imperatives of wealth and virtue. The

---

[62] Ibid., 95, 101–3.

[63] Ibid., 107–8, 112–41. Creuzé-Latouche's warnings were echoed by several of his colleagues in the course of the same debate. *Archives parlementaires*, 54:695–96, 698.

[64] François Furet, "Maximum," in *Critical Dictionary of the French Revolution*, ed. François Furet and Mona Ozouf (Cambridge, MA, 1989), 504. Soboul's view is similar. Soboul, *The Sans-Culottes*, 60.

Girondins had more confidence in the power of market forces to create abundance, but ultimately, like the Montagnards, they were only instrumental liberals—economic freedom, for them, was a means to achieve republican goals. They were illiberal in their willingness to subordinate economic policy to a republican imperative—the creation of a material foundation for civic virtue. They regarded the concentration of wealth as a major political problem. Many of them were as committed as the Montagnards to the view that all citizens ought to own property. They strongly supported measures to force fathers to divide inheritances equally among all children. Some of them called for schemes of progressive taxation which would lessen inequalities of property. The Girondin minister for taxation, Étienne Clavière, advocated an estate tax to replace all existing taxation—essentially a scheme for the state to expropriate a substantial portion of all inheritances.

In his comments on property maxima, Creuzé-Latouche did not reject the objectives of the levelers, but what he claimed were their means. The relative equality of fortunes they sought to create would, with a little patience, develop of its own accord in the new institutional order. He argued that the excessive inequalities of the old regime sprang from institutional distortions of the natural circulation of fortunes. "Under our former government," he argued, "perfidious institutions ceaselessly thwarted and arrested that natural order which calls citizens turn by turn from poverty to riches and from opulence to mediocrity." All the laws tended to keep people either in poverty or affluence. Government acted to concentrate wealth in privileged "castes." The pomp of noble families was maintained by keeping vast estates in their hands. To repair the dissipations of these families the idea of ennobling financiers was conceived. However, since the beginning of the Revolution these unnatural institutions had been dismantled. Creuzé-Latouche acknowledged that many landed properties were still disproportionate in size, but held that a forcible redistribution would do immeasurable harm, while the new regime of laws would eventually reestablish relative equality. One ought to leave to "time and to these new laws the care of bringing things back to their just proportions," he argued.[65]

The Girondins were certainly being opportunistic and tactical when they charged that the Montagnards were promoting the agrarian law. Such charges, however, also articulated a nervousness about their own position. The Girondins were uneasy, in part, because they could not help but see themselves, too, in the role of Lycurgus. They were guilty of every charge they threw at the Montagnards. In January 1793, J.-P. Rabaut Saint-Étienne, subsequently proscribed and executed as a Girondin, toyed with the idea that property maxima might be necessary in a republic.[66] The arch "liberal" Roland went further. For all his apocalyptic rhetoric about the agrarian law, in January 1793 he advocated the

---

[65] Creuzé-Latouche, *Sur les subsistances*, 84–85, 92–94.
[66] Jean-Paul Rabaut Saint-Étienne, "De l'égalité," *Chronique de Paris*, no. 19 (January 19, 1793), 74–75.

free distribution of émigré lands to soldiers—a measure strikingly similar to the one proposed by the Gracchi of republican Rome.[67]

Defeat at the hands of the Montagnards in the fight to prevent price controls sparked gloomy Girondin reflections about the way the republic as a constitutional form seemed specially to threaten a rash attempt to destroy economic modernity. On May 8, 1793, four days after the Convention instituted the first "Maximum" on cereal prices, the Girondin leader Vergniaud gave a speech warning his colleagues against pursuing the model of the classical republic in the economic sphere. Rousseau, Montesquieu, and all the other philosophers who have written on government, he observed, "tell us that the equality of democracy vanishes where luxury is introduced, that republics cannot sustain themselves except through virtue; and that virtue is corrupted by riches." To apply such maxims rigorously, he argued, one would have to divide the land equally among all citizens; to proscribe money, even the *assignats;* to stifle industry; to abandon all useful professions; to dishonor the arts and agriculture; to introduce foreigners to serve as merchants; and to enslave men to cultivate the earth. But it was not necessary to destroy a modern economy in order to establish the republic on a solid footing, he argued. He compared the abandonment of agriculture, commerce, and manufactures to "chasing after an ideal perfection, a chimerical virtue," rendering yourself in the process "akin to brutes." The Constitution must find the *juste milieu* in preventing "the corruption that infallibly results from the too great inequality of fortunes," but at the same time afford the most total protection to properties.[68]

If one of the ways the Girondins dealt with the fear that the Revolution might be intrinsically barbaric was to project it onto the Montagnards, the latter deployed the same strategy against their opponents on the left who included the radical journalist Hébert and his followers.[69] In a report of January 10, 1794, recommending measures to preserve ancient inscriptions, Henri Grégoire exonerated the sovereign people from accusations of barbaric, or "vandal" behavior by transferring blame for the wanton destruction of art objects onto a faction which, he claimed, was plotting against the Revolution. In encouraging vandalism, Grégoire argued, this faction sought to undermine the *moeurs* of the nation and prepare it for tyranny. The Hébertists were purged and executed in March 1794, but the rhetoric of "vandalism" proved so useful that in July 1794 the Committee of Public Instruction gave Grégoire and A.-F. Fourcroy responsibility for drafting a report on the maneuvers of another vandal faction purportedly attempting to undermine *moeurs*. We do not know who the intended object of this attack was; before the report was finished, Robespierre and his

[67] See Marcel Dorigny, "Les Girondins et le droit de propriété," *Bulletin d'histoire économique et sociale de la Révolution française* (1980–81): 15–31.

[68] *Archives parlementaires*, 64:330–32.

[69] Baczko, *Ending the Terror,* 195.

closest associates were purged by their colleagues in the Convention and Grégoire redeployed the plastic idiom of vandalism against them.[70]

The leaders of the Revolution after Robespierre's fall seized upon the rhetoric
of vandalism because it solved a pressing ideological problem. With powerful
public demands for the punishment of former terrorists, they needed a symbolic
means to distance themselves from the Terror. This was a challenging imperative, because the Convention had sanctioned each of the ever-bloodier measures
introduced by the Committee of Public Safety in 1793 and 1794. The same
deputies continued to govern France after the fall and execution of Robespierre.
Like the Girondins and the Montagnards before them, they projected the barbarism of the Revolution onto a scapegoat, representing vandalism as a Robes-
pierrist attack on the republic intended to paralyze public education, to
persecute men of learning, and to precipitate the nation into barbarism. There
existed "a plan to dry up all the springs of enlightenment," Grégoire argued,
"in a word, to barbarize us." The idiom of vandalism spread with lightening
speed. Just ten days after the execution of Robespierre, the *Décade philosophique* proclaimed: "The arts have done everything for the Republic! and it is
these arts which an impious faction wished to destroy to reestablish the shameful cult of ignorance! O France, thus you would fall back into barbarism."[71]

Refounding the Republic on Agriculture, Commerce, and Industry

The language of vandalism was the dominant political rhetoric of the Year
III (the year in the revolutionary calendar running from late September 1794 to
late September 1795). In order to distance itself from the legacy of the Terror,
the Convention sought to represent itself as an anti-vandal force, a protector of
civilization rather than a threat to it. At both a rhetorical level, and in the institutions they founded and sponsored, republicans in the Year III sought to
transform the republic's image. They endeavored to stabilize the new order they
had created, to resolve the sense of vertigo created by the perception that everything was political. They pursued policies calculated to represent the Republic
as a protector of the arts and sciences culminating in the establishment of the
Institut national to replace the academies abolished in 1793.[72] They breathed
new life into the patriarchal family, recentering this "natural" social unit at the
heart of the civic order.[73]

As part of this politics of stabilization, revolutionary leaders represented the
republic as a guardian of the wealth-producing—and civilization-sustaining—
activities of farmers and traders. One of the central charges against Robespierre
was that he had "terrorized" commerce and agriculture. By 1794 the most dy-

[70] Ibid., 199–200.
[71] *Décade philosophique, littéraire et politique; par une société de républicains*, 2 (1794): 147.
[72] Martin S. Staum, *Minerva's Message: Stabilizing the French Revolution* (Montreal, 1996).
[73] Hunt, *Family Romance*, 151–91.

namic sectors of the French economy had declined visibly and disastrously. As a consequence of the dislocations of war and the slave revolt in Haiti, colonial commerce was almost eliminated.[74] The port of Bordeaux, once the success story of the eighteenth-century commercial economy, was in steep decline. Its population fell sharply in the 1790s.[75] The numerous industries that depended on the traffic of the ports—rope- and sail-making, shipbuilding, sugar-refining, glass-making, and distilling—collapsed in the 1790s.[76] The luxury trades went into deep recession. Between 1789 and 1799, the number of silk workshops in Lyons fell by half, and the population of the city dropped by 30 percent. On September 20, 1794, Robert Lindet highlighted the destruction of the preceding years and called for economic renewal.[77]

The new republic, dedicated to fostering prosperity, would no longer embody the danger that in trying to regenerate virtue the nation might be precipitated into Spartan barbarism. A program of regenerating agriculture and commerce was articulated in the autumn of 1794 in two addresses by Joseph Eschassériaux, a leading figure on the Convention's agricultural committee. In his first speech, Eschassériaux accused Robespierre of "terrorizing" cultivators. He proposed a series of symbolic and practical measures to accord agriculture a privileged status in the new civic order. He asked that the busts of the agricultural improvers Bernard Palissy and Olivier de Serres be placed in the Convention, along with some farming implements. He suggested that communes celebrate a festival in honor of agriculture each year, and he called for a decree stating that "for a free people agriculture is the first of the arts." He also proposed a number of practical measures to stimulate agricultural improvement including a national survey of soil quality and methods of cultivation, the allocation of funds for the distribution of seed for artificial meadows, and the establishment of a national fund from which farmers could borrow investment capital.[78] In a second speech the following month, Eschassériaux warned that a revolution should not look like a "Tartar conquest." He gave a bleak portrait of the economic condition of the country, and he demanded the abrogation of price controls on non-subsistence goods, a law which, he claimed, had "given birth to another speculation more dangerous perhaps than that which you have destroyed in finances and which . . . dried up all the channels of prosperity."[79]

For Eschassériaux, regenerating agriculture and trade would allow the rev-

---

[74] Doyle, *Oxford History of the French Revolution*, 401–7.

[75] Crouzet, "Bordeaux."

[76] François Crouzet, "Wars, Blockade, and Economic Change in Europe, 1792–1815," *Journal of Economic History* 24, no. 4 (1964): 567–88.

[77] Robert Lindet, *Rapport fait à la Convention nationale, dans la séance du 4e des sans-cullotides de l'an 2e, au nom des Comités de salut public, de sûreté générale et de législation, par Lindet* (Paris, Year II).

[78] Joseph Eschassériaux, *Opinion sur la nécessité et les moyens de régénérer promptement l'agriculture, par Eschassériaux aîné* (Paris, Year III).

[79] Joseph Eschassériaux, *Opinion sur les causes de l'état présent du commerce et de l'industrie, et les moyens de les rétablir sur les véritables bases de l'économie politique, par Eschassériaux aîné* (Paris, Year III).

olutionaries to find an equilibrium between the dangers of luxury on the one hand, and the threat of a collapse of civilization on the other. He acknowledged that "In the last century, Colbert sacrificed all to manufactures, threw a part of the population into workshops and, by this preference, caused all capital to flow into the arts of luxury, ruining the primary source of national wealth, agriculture," but, he insisted, the regeneration of commerce would not entail a resurgence of luxury—the commerce of the republic would be based on agriculture. The most flourishing manufactures and commerce, he suggested, always belonged to the nation with the most prosperous agriculture. Eschassériaux downplayed the dangers of luxury. Some, he observed, had seized on the idea that commerce generates luxury to justify the wrongs done to trade during the Terror. However, he reassured his colleagues, "commerce ought not to be accused of the ills of luxury." Rather it was the faulty institutions of peoples, and especially their idleness, that left them prey to luxury. Industrious nations need have no such apprehensions because "corruption and labor never walk together." Besides, he suggested, the inconveniences attached to commerce could not justify abandoning it altogether. Trade played too important a role in stimulating the agricultural economy and in civilizing *moeurs*. A nation foolish enough to neglect commerce in contemporary Europe would soon lose its "political rank" among other nations. Here was a frank acknowledgment of the limitations imposed on a modern polity by the structure of international competition.[80]

The anti-vandalism rhetoric expanded in 1795 and, under the Directory (1795–99), it turned into a comprehensive effort to remodel the republic by casting agriculture, commerce, and manufacturing as its foundations. This was an attempt to exorcise the ghost of the agrarian law, to defend the republic from the charge that it was incompatible with modern forms of economic life.[81] James Livesey sees this campaign as a direct response to those critics of the republic who argued that republican liberty was suitable only to the antique polis and was incompatible with economic modernity—critics such as the former Genevan revolutionary, François d'Ivernois, who wrote a series of tracts to prove that only a constitutional monarchy could foster commerce, manufactures, and the arts.[82] According to Livesey, republicans after the fall of Robespierre were forced to elaborate a concept of citizenship that could mediate between the demands of republican political participation, on the one hand,

[80] Eschassériaux, *Opinion sur les causes,* 10–12.

[81] James Livesey, *Making Democracy in the French Revolution* (Cambridge, MA, 2001); idem, "Agrarian Ideology and Commercial Republicanism in the French Revolution," *Past and Present* 157 (1997): 94–121.

[82] François d'Ivernois, *Des révolutions de France et de Genève* (London, 1795); idem, *État des finances et des ressources de la République française, au 1er janvier 1796* (London, 1796); idem, *Tableau historique et politique des pertes que la Révolution et la guerre ont causées au peuple français dans sa population, son agriculture, ses colonies, ses manufactures et son commerce* (London, 1799).

and modern economic life on the other. To meet this challenge, they elaborated a "commercial republicanism" with the citizen farmer at its core. Agriculture, for republicans, was the foundation not only of civic virtue, but of the *moeurs* necessary to sustain a republic in the modern world.

The view I take of the late 1790s is indebted to Livesey's but my own assessment differs from his in two significant ways. First, I suggest, the notion of a commercial republicanism with the farmer as its archetypal citizen was not an innovation of the 1790s. One of the central thrusts of political economy in the prerevolutionary decades was precisely to produce a language that would reconcile commercial modernity with the need to preserve and regenerate public virtue. Since the 1760s, agriculture had been the ground on which this tension was resolved. The challenge of effecting this reconciliation had become newly pressing in the 1790s, but the solution republicans opted for was not fundamentally new. I am also inclined to disagree with Livesey that this celebration of the farmer was democratic in spirit. It can also be interpreted as an attempt to fashion a model of passive, depoliticized patriotism that would close the Revolution, while consolidating its benefits. Sentiments similar to those of the republic's critics were articulated by the drafters of the Constitution of 1795, which established the Directory regime. F.-A. Boissy d'Anglas, a member of the commission charged with drafting the new constitution, argued that "to make France a country in continual assembly was to deprive agriculture of those men who should attend to it with assiduity, and to deprive the warehouse and the workshop of those who would better serve the country with their work than by useless speeches and superficial discussions."[83] The Constitution of 1795 was intended to deprive the populace of any share in government without stripping away all vestiges of citizenship. Any adult male paying some direct tax could vote, but only the thirty thousand richest men in the country could be elected to the parliamentary assemblies. Livesey's commercial republicanism may certainly have been put to democratic uses in the 1790s, but it lent itself equally well to the purposes of men like Boissy d'Anglas, and subsequently to those of Napoleon Bonaparte.

From late 1794, the Convention, and after it the Directory regime, followed a policy of fostering agriculture, commerce, and manufactures, and supporting the development and dissemination of both political economy and agronomy. In October 1794, at the behest of Grégoire, the Convention created the National Conservatory of Arts and Trades. Its function was to promote manufactures and agriculture by creating a depository for machines and inventions that the public could access.[84] At the suggestion of J.-A. Creuzé-Latouche, the Convention nominated Alexandre Vandermonde to the first chair of political econ-

[83] F.-A. Boissy d'Anglas, *Discours préliminaire au projet de constitution pour la République française* (Paris, 1795), 25.

[84] Alain Mercier, *1794, l'abbé Grégoire et la création du Conservatoire national des arts et métiers* (Paris, 1989).

omy at the newly established École normale in 1795.[85] Political economy also found institutional support in the Institut national. A section of the Institut was devoted to political economy with Creuzé-Latouche, Dupont de Nemours, Sieyès, Roederer, Talleyrand, and Forbonnais among the members and associates.[86] In the same period, the Ministry of the Interior established a Bureau of Political Economy under P.-L. Ginguené, who was already the Director of Public Instruction.[87] The subject was taught at some of the departmental *écoles centrales*, which had replaced the church-controlled *collèges* of the old regime.[88] In September 1797, the Festival of the Foundation of the Republic was celebrated on the Champs de Mars with a five-day exhibit of French manufactured goods. That such a spectacle should have seemed a fitting way to celebrate the founding of the French Republic bears witness to the recasting of the polity in the years after 1794.

The governments that controlled France from 1794 to 1799 promoted agronomy even more vigorously than they championed political economy. As Livesey notes, Nicolas François de Neufchâteau, twice Minister of the Interior under the Directory, was one of the most active of the republican promoters of agriculture. Two months before he became minister for the first time, in a speech before the central administration of the department of the Vosges, he remarked on the "necessity of making a praiseworthy and public luxury, suitable to a free state, succeed the shameful and private luxury which is the devouring ulcer of despotic states." Describing agriculture as "the source of comfort and of power, school of labor, the companion of good *moeurs*, the true mine republicans ought to strive to exploit," he called for a program of rural regeneration. François de Neufchâteau singled out as inspirations for agricultural improvers the work of Duhamel du Monceau and the marquis de Mirabeau.[89]

In the late 1790s, agricultural improvers who had played a prominent role in the agricultural societies of the old regime returned to public life where they assumed consultative roles to the administration. The agronomists J.-B. Dubois, J.-B. Rougier de la Bergerie, and H.-A. Tessier, all prominent members of the old Royal Agricultural Society, found positions in the Ministry of the Inte-

---

[85] Charles R. Sullivan, "The First Chair of Political Economy in France: Alexandre Vandermonde and the *Principles* of Sir James Steuart at the École normale of the Year III," *French Historical Studies* 20, no. 4 (1997): 635–64.

[86] Martin S. Staum, "The Class of Moral and Political Sciences, 1795–1803," *French Historical Studies* 11, no. 3 (1980): 371–97; idem, "The Institute Economists: From Physiocracy to Entrepreneurial Capitalism," *History of Political Economy* 19, no. 4 (1987): 525–50.

[87] Livesey, *Making Democracy,* 67.

[88] See for example, Berriat Saint-Prix, "Discours prononcé par le citoyen Berriat Saint-Prix, professeur de législation à l'école centrale de l'Isère, pour l'ouverture du cours particulier d'économie publique," in *Mémoires d'économie publique, de morale et de politique; publiés par Roederer* (Year V), 383–402.

[89] Nicolas François de Neufchâteau, *Des améliorations dont la paix doit être l'époque. No. 1er. Moyen préliminaire d'encourager l'agriculture dans les départemens où les terres sont morcelées et divisées à l'infini, en les réunissant sur un plan régulier* (Épinal, Year V), 4, 12, 59–60.

rior.[90] The duc de Béthune-Charost, a former president of the society, was invited to testify before the Convention's committees on agriculture and public instruction where he called for an ambitious scheme of agricultural education.[91] The administration's attention to agricultural improvement made the editorial team at *La feuille du cultivateur* feel vindicated. "We have not ceased to repeat to France, for the last six years," they asserted in 1796, "that it should rest its faith in its soil and its labor, and that agriculture is the basis, and the only basis, for the political and moral regeneration of the country."[92] The periodical, which had been appearing since October 1790, was virtually an organ of the Royal Agricultural Society.[93] Under François de Neufchâteau, the Ministry of the Interior subsidized three thousand copies per week of the *Feuille* for distribution to the departments.[94]

Agricultural societies were created to replace those swept away with the academies in 1793. In 1796, Béthune-Charost founded a new association for rural improvement in the department of the Cher.[95] By 1797 the Ministry of the Interior was actively establishing agricultural societies, and forty such bodies had been founded by 1800.[96] An agricultural society was reestablished in Paris in February 1799 with Creuzé-Latouche as its first president.[97] Many of the prominent names from the old Royal Society of Agriculture reappeared on the roster of the new body. Among them were L.-J.-M. Daubenton, J.-B. Dubois, A.-F. Fourcroy, the duc de La Rochefoucauld-Liancourt, J.-L. Lefebvre, A.-A. Parmentier, J.-B. Rougier de la Bergerie, the abbé Tessier, and André Thouin. The associates included the "American Farmer," Saint-Jean de Crèvecoeur, Béthune-Charost, P.-M.-A. Broussonet, and Dupont de Nemours. Other prominent members were Eschassériaux, François de Neufchâteau, and the abbé Grégoire. In addition to the new agricultural societies, a section of the Institut national was devoted to rural economy, and Thouin, Tessier, Parmentier, and Rougier de la Bergerie were appointed to it.[98]

Agricultural improvers represented themselves as the bearers of a patriotism

---

[90] Livesey, *Making Democracy*, 103–4.

[91] Armand-Joseph Béthune-Charost, *Vues générales sur l'organisation de l'instruction rurale en France, présentées aux Comités d'instruction publique et d'agriculture de la Convention nationale et à la Commission d'agriculture et des arts* (Paris, Year III).

[92] *Feuille du cultivateur* (Year VI), 6:1. Quoted in Livesey, "Agrarian Ideology," 104.

[93] It was originally edited by J.-B. Dubois, P.-M.-A. Broussonet, and J.-L. Lefebvre—all prominent members of the society—while A.-A. Parmentier, another member, was brought onto the paper in December 1793. André Martin and Gérard Walter, *Écrits de la période révolutionnaire, journaux et almanachs*, vol. 5 of *Catalogue de l'histoire de la Révolution française* (Paris, 1943).

[94] Livesey, *Making Democracy*, 104.

[95] *Annales, mémoires & observations de la Société d'agriculture et économie rurale de Meillant, Département du Cher* (Bourges, Year V), 75–76, 83.

[96] Livesey, *Making Democracy*, 118–19.

[97] *Mémoires d'agriculture, d'économie rurale et domestique, publiés par la Société d'agriculture du Département de la Seine*, vol. 1 (Paris, Year IX).

[98] Jean-Baptiste Rougier de la Bergerie, *Essai politique et philosophique sur le commerce et la paix* (Paris, 1797); Jean Tulard, *Dictionnaire napoléon* (Paris, 1987), 932.

antithetical to that of the Montagnard Republic, claiming to have embraced liberty in 1789 but to have subsequently fallen victim to the Terror. In a eulogy for Béthune-Charost, who died in 1800, Augustin-François Silvestre, the secretary of the new Agricultural Society of the Seine, noted that "when the terror weighed on all of France, the virtues of citizen Béthune-Charost were no guarantee for his name or his fortune, he was, with so many other innocent victims, dragged into the dungeons."[99] Béthune-Charost himself had made the same claim about other improvers. Zealous proprietors had assembled together in the prisons of the Year II, he maintained, to discuss the attentions required by agriculture and the institutions needed to disseminate agronomic knowledge.[100] In fact, many prominent agricultural improvers *had* fallen victim to revolutionary violence: Berthier de Sauvigny, the intendant of Paris who played a key role in reviving the Paris agricultural society in the 1780s, was one of the earliest victims of mob violence in 1789. Lavoisier, the chemist, agronomist, and tax farmer, was executed in 1794, as was Malesherbes, the original patron of the *Journal oeconomique*. François de Neufchâteau was imprisoned as a suspect in 1793, while Pierre-François Boncerf, an ally of Turgot who had proposed the abolition of seigneurial rights in the 1770s, narrowly escaped with his life before the revolutionary tribunal (in his defense, he cited his numerous works of drainage and land clearance).[101] The marquise de Marboeuf, whose fields Arthur Young had admired, was declared a suspect, and subsequently executed, for planting part of her estates with artificial meadows instead of sowing the whole with cereals.[102]

Agronomists celebrated economic improvement as a manifestation of patriotism above, or outside of, politics. In his opening address to the society he founded in 1796, Béthune-Charost emphasized the patriotic dimension of working to establish national prosperity. He observed that "agriculture and industry are the bases of territorial wealth and of public prosperity . . . it is they that furnish to commerce, which unified peoples, the primary materials and manufactured works . . . thus, none of these objects can be indifferent in the eyes of those who love their *patrie*." The large proportion of the society's members who were municipal officials suggests the extent to which economic improvement had become an official badge of public spirit. The Minister of the Interior, Pierre Bénézech, wrote to Béthune-Charost, praising the establishment of the society. "To occupy oneself with pushing back the limitations of the most

[99] "Notice historique sur le C. Béthune-Charost," in *Mémoires d'agriculture, d'économie rurale et domestique publiés par la Société d'agriculture du Département de la Seine* (Paris, Year X), 3:349–52. See also Rougier de la Bergerie's eulogy of Cretté de Palluel, a member of the old Royal Agricultural Society. "Notice sur Cretté de Palluel, agriculteur," *Mémoires d'agriculture, d'économie rurale et domestique* (Year IX), 1:435–36.

[100] Béthune-Charost, *Vues générales*, 8–9n.

[101] Pierre-François Boncerf, *Extrait de la défense du citoyen Boncerf, au Tribunal révolutionnaire, le 18 ventôse, l'an deuxième de la République françoise, une, indivisible* (Paris, Year II).

[102] Spary, *Utopia's Garden*, 131.

Fig. 10. *The Plowing Lesson* by François-André Vincent, 1798.
   Vincent's painting of a well-dressed boy learning to till the soil under the tutelage of a weathered plowman emphasizes the importance of agriculture in the formation of good citizens. The painting was publicly exhibited in 1798 under the title *Agriculture* with the following caption: "Convinced that agriculture is the foundation of the prosperity of states, the painter has represented a father, accompanied by his wife and his young daughter, who have come to visit a plowman at work. The father renders him homage by attending a lesson he had pressed the farmer to give to his son, whose education he would regard as incomplete without this knowledge." An addendum follows, noting that paintings representing "commerce and other interesting aspects of education" ought to be produced to accompany this work. Réunion des Musées Nationaux/Art Resource, NY.

useful art, that from which ought to flow abundance, the purity of *moeurs* and public prosperity is truly to have earned the recognition of the *patrie*," he stated; "I can only see with the greatest satisfaction a society, free and disengaged from all political connections, elevate itself under the aegis of the Constitution and give itself over without reserve to the most important works."[103] For Bénézech, agricultural improvement was the expression of a depoliticized patriotism, one free of dangerous party spirit.

   A notable example of the foregrounding of economic activity as a form of passive citizenship and patriotism was a tract published in 1800 by a Lyons banker, Vital-Roux, who subsequently became a regent of the Bank of France. *De l'influence du gouvernement sur la prospérité du commerce* built upon the

---

[103] *Annales, mémoires & observations de la Société d'agriculture et économie rurale de Meillant, Département du Cher* (Bourges, Year V), 17–24, 31, 101–2.

foundations of the rhetoric of vandalism. The happiness of the barbarian lies in destruction, he noted, while that of commercial peoples lies in creating prosperity for all. Under the Revolution, he complained, merchants were treated with contempt because commerce was regarded as an obstacle to that "chimerical equality" to which so many victims were sacrificed. The revolutionaries attempted to turn France into a nation of Spartans. Vital-Roux rejected not only vandalism, but politics itself. The Revolution "carried the destructive hammer into our workshops," he complained, "and the parties which it engendered have, in their criminal furies, shattered all the bonds of society." He elaborated a new, economized vision of citizenship that drew on the old stereotype of the merchant as a man without political personality, drawn away from public affairs by his private business. Vital-Roux presented this representation as the ideal for the modern citizen. One does not see the "peaceful merchant" on the public square agitating and whipping up passions, he observed; the merchant is not "ambitious." It is all the same to him if he is governed by a senate or a monarch; he does not discuss the laws, he submits to them. He rejected an active, participatory patriotism in favor of economic activity in the service of national prosperity. "It is not by artificial discourse, by superb phrases, that he proves his patriotism, his virtues," Vital-Roux wrote of his ideal merchant, "it is through useful actions, by an assiduous labor, that he serves his country." The virtues of citizenship were the virtues of the privatized individual acting in the marketplace: "A sound judgment, an upright sense, a frank probity, a severe order, a settled economy, such are the qualities of the merchant, such also are the virtues of a good citizen."[104]

[104] Vital-Roux, *De l'influence du gouvernement sur la prospérité du commerce* (Paris, 1800), 6–9, 14–15, 20–21, 275.

Conclusion: The Political Economy of the Notables

By the beginning of the nineteenth century, economic discourse had become an everyday and indispensable part of the language of public life. Fifty years of vigorous public discussion of the nature of the material order had transformed the cultural status of economic activity, and made the pursuits of profit-seekers appear central to the life of the nation in a way they had not a century earlier. This change occurred not as a direct response to the expansion of the commercial economy, but as French elites considered the structures that imposed tangible limits on the success of the political community with which they identified. The language of political economy evolved in an effort to make sense of those limits, to consider how the disposition of resources within countries, and among them, affected the balance of power. The language that emerged from the confluence of patriotism and political economy was an attempt to reach an accommodation with the economic realities that constrained national success without succumbing to a wholly mercantile ethos. To make this adjustment, French elites had to find ways to moderate their own prejudices against profit-directed activities, to square their rejection of luxury with the imperative for prosperity. Political economy was the cultural space in which economic activity was reconstituted as a patriotic endeavor. Merchants, farmers, and entrepreneurs were remade as patriots. The new status of the economic was assured when the French Republic, anxious to distance itself from the perceived excesses of Jacobinism, embraced a language that cast commerce and agriculture as foundations of the civic order.

The close attention to agriculture, commerce, and manufactures that was such a hallmark of the Directory was continued under the Napoleonic regimes of the Consulate (1799–1804) and the Empire (1804–1815). Indeed, a language promoting economic improvement as a form of patriotism was one of the ideological foundations of the post-revolutionary order. Agricultural improvers claimed that the regeneration of agriculture would close the Revolution and reestablish order. The Prefect of the Calvados reminded the members of the Society of Agriculture and Commerce of Caen of the services rendered to the *patrie* by the agronomist Olivier de Serres who, under Henri IV, "repaired the ravages of the civil war by reanimating the cultivation of devastated lands."[1] The lesson for the agricultural society was obvious. Rougier de la Bergerie made a similar point when he observed that "the means to maintain or to bring back calm in an empire is to inspire the taste for agriculture there."[2] These views were welcome to Napoleon, who appointed de la Bergerie prefect of the Yonne in 1800. Patronized and promoted by local and national authorities under Napoleon, societies for the encouragement of agriculture flourished. Agronomists sat in large numbers in the official cultural and political institutions—the National Institute, the corps of prefects, and the various Napoleonic legislative bodies. Under Napoleon, involvement in agricultural improvement or the promotion of other kinds of economic progress remained important expressions of patriotism. But this was a privatized and depoliticized patriotism, the mere shadow of republican public spirit.

The Georgic, that poetic form so beloved of agricultural improvers in the 1760s, became something of an official art form under the Consulate and the Empire, and continued to be pressed into service in the task of economic regeneration. Explaining the advantages of the Georgic form, the secretary of the Caen agricultural society noted that it was "not only agreeable, but useful, since it inspires in rich men the taste for country life and the desire to enhance the value of their properties."[3] In the autumn of 1801, the prefect of the Deux-Sèvres offered a prize of a gold medal for a poem dealing with dredging the local river, the Seine niortaise, to be awarded at the Festival of the Foundation of the Republic in Year XI.[4] Lest his fellow citizens find internal waterways a strange subject for poetry, he reminded them that the Canal de Languedoc had been the subject of one of the finest passages in Delille's *L'homme des champs,* a "French Georgic" that the poet published to considerable acclaim in the Year VIII (between 1800 and 1808, the work enjoyed eight editions).[5] At least two other contemporary Georgics were published to rival Delille's effort, the anonymous *Les quatres saisons, ou les Géorgiques françaises,* and Rougier de la Bergerie's *Géorgiques françaises,* published in 1805.[6] Yet another translation of Virgil's *Georgics* was published the same year, this one by the same abbé Cournand who had called for the agrarian law in 1791.[7]

---

[1] Pierre-Aimé Lair, *Précis des travaux de la Société royale d'agriculture et de commerce de Caen, depuis son rétablissement en 1801 jusqu'en 1810* (Caen, 1827), 26–27.

[2] Jean-Baptiste Rougier de la Bergerie, *Observations sur l'institution des sociétés d'agriculture, et sur les moyens d'utiliser leurs travaux; imprimées par arrêté de la Société d'agriculture de la Seine* (Paris, Year VIII), 28–29, 52–54.

[3] Lair, *Précis des travaux,* 81. Internal evidence indicates that this passage was written before 1809.

[4] *Journal officiel du Département des Deux-Sèvres,* no. 4, 25.

[5] Jacques Delille, *L'homme des champs, ou les Géorgiques françaises avec des notes* (Strasbourg, Year VIII).

[6] Musset, *Bibliographie agronomique.*

[7] Antoine Cournand, *Géorgiques de Virgile, traduites en vers français avec le texte latin à côté, accompagnées des notes relatives à l'agriculture* (Paris, 1805).

Fig. 11. *The Emperor Plows a Furrow,* by Loeillot, c. 1823.

This print picturing the exiled Napoleon Bonaparte trying his hand at plowing a field picks up on the motif, so dear to agricultural improvers, of the emperor of China, who plowed a field each year in order to honor agriculture. Like the story of the Chinese emperor or Boizot's engraving depicting Louis XVI as dauphin behind the plow (Fig. 5), this nostalgic image of the Emperor links effective good governance of the nation with a personal commitment to the land. One of a large number of prints that helped to create and disseminate the myth of Napoleon after his death, the theme of Loeillot's lithograph suggests the ideological continuities linking the post-revolutionary society of notables to the pre-revolutionary patriot movement for agricultural regeneration. Bibliothèque Nationale de France.

Manufactures were fostered under the Consulate and encouraged by bodies analogous to the agricultural societies. The industrial exhibitions, begun by François de Neufchâteau in 1797, continued, and departmental societies of agriculture and commerce used exhibitions to stimulate improvements in local manufacturing. The Caen society, for instance, held regular expositions to encourage the "industrial arts."[8] In 1802, a Society for the Encouragement of National Industry was established in Paris to stimulate the discovery and adoption of technical improvements in manufactures and the arts. Though based in Paris, the society was truly national, with nearly a quarter of its original membership resident in Lyons. Like the societies of agriculture and commerce, it offered prizes to stimulate inventors, and its competitions were advertised in the official gazettes of the departments.[9] The society was heavily patronized by the Napoleonic administrative elite. By 1803, twenty-one prefects and fourteen sub-prefects had become members, along with a sprinkling of senators and tribunes from the legislative bodies.[10]

The promoters of industrial innovation under the Consulate represented the drive to improve French manufactures as a part of the patriotic contest against England. A journal called the *Annales des arts et manufactures,* which ran from 1800 to 1815, focused on disseminating new technical inventions and discoveries, and aimed to spread knowledge of those innovations that had afforded Britain "that astonishing influence that she has acquired in Europe." The editors, one of whom was also a member of the Society for the Encouragement of National Industry, claimed that because of 1789 France now had every chance to catch up with England. Individuals that prejudice would formerly have dissuaded from engaging in trade and manufacturing were becoming sensitive to the "delights inseparable from industrial occupations," while "parasitic members" were becoming useful to the *patrie* through employment in workshops. Proprietors had begun to live in the country and improve their lands. As a consequence, the *Annales* foresaw "manufacturing and agricultural France rivaling a jealous neighbor, and her soil, so fertile in productions, being covered with workshops and manufactories."[11]

The theory that economic activities required honor if they were to thrive continued to flourish under the Consulate. According to Vital-Roux, if France had not realized her commercial potential under the monarchy, it was because "the monarchy had relegated the useful professions to a harmful contempt, and because honor and consideration were the prize of birth and fortune." There can be "no emulation where there is no glory," he pointed out. If commerce was given

[8] Lair, *Précis des travaux,* 181–82, 262–66.

[9] See, for example, *Journal officiel du Département des Deux-Sèvres,* no. 31, 242–44 (Year X).

[10] *Bulletin de la Société d'encouragement de l'industrie nationale. Première année* (Paris, Year XI).

[11] "Prospectus," *Annales des arts et manufactures, ou Mémoires technologiques sur les découvertes modernes concernant les arts, les manufactures, l'agriculture et le commerce* (Paris, Year VIII), 1–2. The editor, one M. O'Reilly, is listed as a member of the society since 8 Thermidor Year X. See full list in *Bulletin de la Société d'encouragement,* 236–42.

the consideration that excites industry and nourishes emulation, he argued, it would quickly make France more prosperous than other nations.[12] The desire to "excite that noble emulation which develops talents" prompted the Society of Agriculture and Commerce of Caen to organize an exhibition of local manufactures in April 1803. "Considering that it is particularly by honoring the manufacturers that one can succeed in improving the manufactories," the report of the society read, "on April 26 the society will hold a public session at which nine silver medals will be distributed to manufacturers who will be judged the most worthy." The mayor of Caen, who presided at the prize giving ceremony, opened the meeting with a discourse in which he "made sensible the power of emulation over men." The citation delivered with one of the medals suggests how completely the representation of the businessman had changed since the 1750s. The winners, a group of investors who had established a porcelain factory in the town in 1797, were described as "several individuals, directed less by personal interest than by love of their country." Under the auspices of emulation, the profit motive had disappeared and the entrepreneur had been remade as a patriot.[13]

The Napoleonic regime took seriously the idea that social competition for honor could induce people to pursue the public welfare. In the army, there was careful attention to the use of honorific incentives to encourage soldiers.[14] This was also the basic impetus behind the foundation of the Legion of Honor in 1802. The legion was a replacement for the nobility of the old regime, and indeed it was later transformed by Napoleon into a service nobility. In a report on the projected Legion of Honor delivered to the Corps législatif in May 1802, Pierre-Louis Roederer represented a social order based on the pursuit of honor and distinction, harnessed to patriotic ends, as a viable substitute for competitive economic individualism. Roederer described the establishment of the legion as "the creation of a new money," a money the source of which lay in the French sense of honor.[15] (In 1793, Roederer had suggested that honors might be used to induce the rich to expend their wealth in projects of public assistance.)[16] Honor had been compared sporadically to money in the course of eighteenth-century debates about emulation and in the revolutionary debate on the abolition of nobility.[17] The metaphor is a significant one; it suggests the ex-

---

[12] Vital-Roux, *Influence du gouvernement,* 10, 13–14, 18–19.

[13] Lair, *Précis des travaux de la Société royale d'agriculture et de commerce de Caen,* 183–87. The minister of the interior, Chaptal, showed his faith in public spirit as an animator of national economic life in a letter to the Prefect of the Deux-Sèvres in which he expressed the hope that "the sentiment of national interest and the rebirth of public spirit will finally produce among us what neither coercive laws nor considerations of policy have been able to." *Journal officiel du Département des Deux-Sèvres,* no. 3 (Year X), 17.

[14] John A. Lynn, "Toward an Army of Honor: The Moral Evolution of the French Army, 1789–1815," *French Historical Studies* 16, no. 1 (1989): 152–73.

[15] Jean Daniel, *La Légion d'honneur* (Paris, 1957), 24.

[16] "Roederer à J.-P. Rabaut," *Journal de Paris,* no. 23 (January 23, 1793), 91–92.

[17] See Mirabeau, *Ami des hommes,* 1:128; Helvétius, *De l'esprit,* essay 3, chap. 24; Sieyès, *Essai sur les privilèges,* 10; *La feuille villageoise,* no. 18 (January 26, 1792).

tent to which the socially beneficial competition for honor could be imagined as an alternative to the rational and self-interested pursuit of profit in an exchange economy.[18]

The kind of regime that emerged after the Revolution corresponded in striking ways to the interests and values of those middling elites whose resentment at the political economic order of the old regime, I have argued, was such an important impetus to revolution in 1789.[19] From 1799 to 1814, France was governed by the son of a provincial noble family, a graduate of one of those royal military schools intended to reduce the influence of money in military recruitment and to induct less affluent nobles into the service. The Napoleonic Consulate and Empire saw an expansion of career prospects highly favorable to middling elites in general and nobles in particular. Napoleon designated a stratum of 100,000 men as "notables," and recruited from this pool for his administration. "For most aspiring provincial families," Robert Forster argues, "this was an improvement over the Court favoritism of the Old Regime, a clear recognition that land and local name would carry more weight than liquid wealth and intrigue at Paris."[20] In its recruitment and promotion of military officers the Napoleonic regime favored the sons of provincial noble families. Though large numbers of men were promoted from the ranks, these subaltern officers rarely rose to a grade higher than captain; middling elites, especially those with a tradition of military service, largely monopolized the higher ranks.[21] Military officers constituted a pool from which the regime often drew for civil functionaries: nearly sixty officers served as mayors of major cities and 30 percent of Napoleonic prefects were recruited from the officer corps; 40 percent were old regime nobles.[22]

It was under the auspices of another provincial noble, the comte de Villèle, that the Restoration completed the process of financial reform initiated by Necker and largely accomplished by the Constituent Assembly: the destruction of private enterprise in public finance. Under the pressures of war and financial

[18] On emulation in nineteenth-century bourgeois culture, see Carol E. Harrison *The Bourgeois Citizen in Nineteenth-Century France: Gender, Sociability, and the Uses of Emulation* (Oxford, 1999).

[19] On this theme, see Rafe Blaufarb, "The Ancien Régime Origins of Napoleonic Social Reconstruction," *French History* 14, no. 4 (2000): 408–23.

[20] Robert Forster, "The French Revolution and the 'New' Elite, 1800–1850," *The American and European Revolutions, 1776–1848: Sociopolitical and Ideological Aspects*, ed. Jaroslaw Pelenski (Iowa City, 1980), 188.

[21] Rafe Blaufarb, "The Social Contours of Meritocracy in the Napoleonic Officer Corps," in *Taking Liberties: Problems of a New Order from the French Revolution to Napoleon*, ed. Howard G. Brown and Judith A. Miller (Manchester, 2002).

[22] Louis Bergeron, Guy Chaussinand-Nogaret, and Robert Forster, "Les notables du «Grand Empire» en 1810," *Annales: E.S.C.* 26, no. 5 (1971): 1052–75; Edward A. Whitcomb, "Napoleon's Prefects," *American Historical Review* 79 (1974). Matters were even better under the Restoration, when nobles from provincial families were recruited in large numbers by the administration of Louis XVIII and Charles X. See, Nicholas Richardson, *The French Prefectoral Corps 1814–1830* (Cambridge, 1966), 179–86.

stringency, some of the old abuses had crept back in during the late 1790s and under Napoleon. Villèle finished the process of placing French finances in the hands of a public bureaucracy.[23] In his personal trajectory, Villèle could stand as a kind of emblem for the political economic commitments of middling elites. The son of a provincial noble family in the Toulouse region, he was known for his antipathy to frivolity and luxury, his asceticism, taste for work, and his "domestic virtues."[24] His father had been an important agricultural improver, "a pioneer in the movement towards the suppression of the fallow and the establishment of artificial meadows," and Villèle himself "supervised the family estate with the same minute attention to every detail."[25]

In the long run, it was landowning rather than nobility that constituted the primary basis of status in the new order. Napoleonic France was a society in which the elite was even more firmly rooted in landholding than under the old regime. As a consequence of the destruction of colonial commerce, the collapse of the industrial sector in the western ports, and the fact that land was such a bargain during the 1790s, the social elite was significantly more landed by 1800 than it had been in 1789. To some extent, the dream of the Physiocrats and agricultural improvers such as Rougier de la Bergerie, that landholding rather than noble birth be acknowledged as the basis of status, was achieved. According to the journalist Joseph Fiévée, a leading advocate for this new "society of notables," "Territorial property has always been and always will be aristocratic, even though the proprietors are not nobles by birth."[26] Substantial landowners would continue to dominate French economic, cultural, and political life until well into the nineteenth century.

The debates of the prerevolutionary decades and the 1790s created a distinctive French economic imaginary that would shape perceptions of material life in France through the following century. Fears that the pursuit of private interest could undermine patriotism and sap social cohesiveness persisted among French elites. "By the late 1820s," Victoria Thompson writes, "concerns regarding the effects of market forces and market ideologies were beginning to surface with increasing frequency. These criticisms maintained that rather than promoting the public good, free competition destroyed social bonds. Individualism, defined as the self-interested pursuit of wealth, was said to overwhelm family and national loyalties, creating a society in which each individual was concerned only with the satisfaction of his or her own personal needs and desires." A central goal of social commentators in the middle decades of the century, she argues, was to create a "virtuous marketplace—one in which money making could be seen as an honorable pursuit, one in which self-interest ac-

[23] Bosher, *French Finances*, 314–15, 318.

[24] André Jardin and André-Jean Tudesq, *Restoration and Reaction, 1815–1848*, trans. Elborg Forster (Cambridge, 1983), 55–56.

[25] Forster, *Nobility of Toulouse*, 154.

[26] Quoted in Forster, "French Revolution and the 'New' Elite," 196–7. On Fiévée, see Jeremy D. Popkin, "Conservatism under Napoleon: The Political Writings of Joseph Fiévée," *History of European Ideas* 5, no. 4 (1984): 385–400.

corded with the public good."[27] The problem was never definitively resolved and, in the 1890s, the problem of luxury remained vital. According to Rosalind Williams, who has studied French reactions to mass consumption in the late nineteenth century, "the category most frequently used to criticize the implications of the consumer revolution was that of luxury."[28] The Ministry of Commerce and Industry continued to organize industrial exhibits and to award decorations to encourage entrepreneurs. A central commitment of the state was to support a "balanced economy," an economic order oriented not to maximum economic growth but to preserving an equilibrium between industry, commerce, and agriculture. The land was seen as a critical reservoir of social values, especially patriotism. The official view was that the aggressive pursuit of industrial development would generate turmoil.[29]

Is it too much to suggest that the French were still trying to balance the imperative of prosperity with that of avoiding luxury and materialism well into the twentieth century? One of the features of Vichy's "National Revolution," a program to create a new France free of decadence, was a rhetorical commitment to return to the land. Looking forward from the perspective of the late eighteenth century, it is hard not to see in this an echo of earlier preoccupations with luxury and agriculture. But more than the conservatives, traditionalists, and fascists, it was perhaps those who rejected Vichy's vision and fought for a France that would embrace the economic challenges of the twentieth century who most clearly echoed their eighteenth-century forebears. The historian and resistance fighter Marc Bloch condemned Vichy's back to the soil ideology in 1940, arguing that a failure to modernize would render France permanently vulnerable to its neighbor across the Rhine. Bloch insisted that if France were to survive, "we must adapt ourselves to the claims of a new age." He did not reject the premise that agriculture was the source of critical social virtues and that the land might continue to lend a stability and rootedness to an economically modernizing France. "I am convinced that even to-day a people can gain much from having its life rooted in the soil," he wrote, "for only thus will it give to its economic development a solidity which is rare in the modern world." Most strikingly, Bloch's call for postwar economic development was framed within a broader argument that it was a failure of civic virtue that had led to the "strange defeat" of 1940. He ended his account with a quotation from Montesquieu insisting that a republic requires republican patriotism: "A state founded on the people needs a mainspring: and that mainspring is virtue."[30]

[27] Thompson, *Virtuous Marketplace*, 3, 9.

[28] Rosalind H. Williams, *Dream Worlds: Mass Consumption in Late Nineteenth-Century France* (Berkeley, 1982), 213.

[29] Richard F. Kuisel, *Capitalism and the State in Modern France: Renovation and Economic Management in the Twentieth Century* (Cambridge, 1981), 1–20.

[30] Marc Bloch, *Strange Defeat: A Statement of Evidence Written in 1940*, trans. Gerard Hopkins (New York, 1999) [1948], 148–49, 176.

Bibliography

Primary Sources

Eighteenth- and Nineteenth-Century Journals

L'ami du gouvernement, Journal de littérature et d'économie politique. 1800.
Annales des arts et manufactures, ou Mémoires technologiques sur les découvertes modernes concernant les arts, les manufactures, l'agriculture et le commerce. Year VIII–1815.
Annales de statistique, ou Journal général d'économie politique. 1802–3.
Année littéraire. 1754–90.
Bibliothèque physico-économique instructive et amusante. 1782–97, 1802–16.
Bibliothèque des propriétaires ruraux, ou Journal d'économie rurale et domestique. 1803–13.
Chronique de Paris. 1791–93.
Décade philosophique, littéraire et politique; par une société de républicains. 1794–1804.
Éphémérides du citoyen, ou Chronique de l'esprit national. 1765–66; becomes the *Éphémérides du citoyen, ou Bibliothèque raisonnée des sciences morales et politiques.* 1767–72.
Éphémérides de l'humanité, ou Bibliothèque raisonnée des sciences morales. 1789.
Feuille d'agriculture et d'économie rurale. 1790; becomes the *Feuille du cultivateur.* 1790–1800.
Feuille villageoise. 1791–96.
Gazette de commerce. 1765; becomes the *Gazette du commerce, de l'agriculture et des finances.* 1765–1768; becomes the *Gazette d'agriculture, commerce, arts et finances.* 1769–81; becomes the *Gazette d'agriculture, commerce, finances et arts.* 1782–83.
Journal d'agriculture et des arts et feuille d'avis. 1808–14.
Journal de l'agriculture, du commerce et des finances. 1765–69; becomes the *Journal de l'agriculture, du commerce, des arts et des finances.* 1769–81; becomes the *Journal d'agriculture, commerce, finances et arts.* 1782–83.
Journal d'agriculture et d'économie rurale. 1794–95.
Journal d'agriculture et de prospérité publique, publié en l'an II par les membres du Comité central du Ministère de l'intérieur. 1793–94.
Journal d'agriculture à l'usage des habitans de la campagne. 1791–92.
Journal des arts et manufactures. 1795–97.
Journal de commerce. 1759–62.

Journal d'économie publique, de morale, et de politique. 1796–97.
Journal encyclopédique. 1756–93.
Journal étranger. 1754–62.
Journal et la gazette de l'agriculture. 1782–?
Journal d'instruction sociale; par les citoyens Condorcet, Sieyès et Duhamel. 1793.
Journal du laboureur. 1791–92.
Journal oeconomique, ou Mémoires, notes et avis sur les arts, l'agriculture, le commerce et tout ce qui peut y avoir rapport. 1751–72.
Journal officiel du Département des Deux-Sèvres. 1801–2.
Journal de Paris. 1777–91.
Journal de la Société de 1789. 1790.
Lettres campagnardes. 1789.
Nouvelles éphémérides économiques. 1774–76, 1788.
Nouvelliste oeconomique et littéraire. 1754–61.
Révolutions de Paris. 1789–94.
Sentinelle du peuple, aux gens de toutes professions, sciences, arts, commerce et métiers, composant le Tiers-État de la province de Bretagne. 1788.

SERIAL WORKS

Annales, mémoires et observations de la Société d'agriculture et économie rurale de Meillant. Bourges, Year V.
Archives parlementaires de 1787 à 1860: Recueil complet des débats législatifs et politiques des chambres françaises, 1789–1794. 82 vols. Paris, 1862–1914.
Bulletin de la Société d'encouragement de l'industrie nationale. Première année. Year XI.
Dictionnaire universel des sciences morales, économique, politique et diplomatique; ou Bibliothèque de l'homme-d'état et du citoyen. 30 vols. London, 1777–83.
Encyclopédie, ou Dictionnaire raisonné des sciences, des arts et des métiers, par une société de gens de lettres. Paris, 1751–65.
Encyclopédie méthodique. Économie politique et diplomatique, Paris, 1784–87.
Mémoires d'agriculture, d'économie rurale et domestique publiés par la Société d'agriculture du Département de la Seine. Paris, Year IX.
Mémoires d'agriculture, d'économie rurale et domestique, publiés par la Société royale d'agriculture de Paris. 14 vols. Paris, 1785–91.
Réimpression de l'ancien Moniteur. 30 vols. Paris, 1859–1863.

PRINTED PRIMARY SOURCES

Abeille, Louis-Paul, and Jean-Gabriel Montaudouin de la Touche. *Corps d'observations de la Société d'agriculture, de commerce et des arts, établie par les États de Bretagne, années 1757 & 1758.* Rennes, 1760.
Abolition de la noblesse héréditaire en France, proposée à l'Assemblée nationale; par un philanthrope, citoyen de Belan. N.p., n.d.
Agio, ou Traité de l'agiotage à l'usage des agents de change, courtiers, marrons et agioteurs, d'après le plan d'éducation de MM. les Lionnois & Genevois. Par un grenadier du régiment d'Anjou. Paris, 1789.
André, abbé Jean-François. *Le Tartare à Paris.* Paris, 1788.
L'anéantissement total de la noblesse héréditaire, ou Requête urgente à l'Assemblée nationale. Paris, 1789.
Antraigues, Emmanuel-Henri-Louis Alexandre de Launay, comte d'. *Mémoire sur les États généraux, leurs droits, et la manière de les convoquer.* N.p., 1789.
Arcère, Louis-Étienne. *De l'état de l'agriculture chez les Romains, depuis le commencement de la république jusqu'au siècle de Jules-César, relativement au gouvernement, aux moeurs & au commerce. Dissertation qui a obtenu l'accessit du prix de l'Académie royale des inscriptions & belles-lettres, en 1776.* Paris, 1777.

Arcq, Philippe-Auguste de Sainte-Foix, chevalier d'. *De la convocation des États-généraux, et de la nécessité de former un quatrième ordre de l'État.* N.p., 1789.

——. *Mes loisirs.* Paris, 1755.

——. *La noblesse militaire, ou Le patriote françois.* N.p., 1756.

Argenson, René-Louis le Voyer, marquis d'. *Considérations sur le gouvernement ancien et présent de la France, comparé avec celui des autres états; suivies d'un nouveau plan d'administration.* Amsterdam, 1784.

Auffray, Jean. *Idées patriotiques sur la nécessité de rendre la liberté au commerce.* Lyons, 1762.

——. *Le luxe considéré relativement à la population et à l'économie.* Lyons, 1762.

Autroche. *Mémoire sur l'amélioration de la Sologne, par M. d'Autroche, membre de la Société royale d'agriculture d'Orléans.* Orléans, 1787.

Auxiron, Claude-François-Joseph d'. *Examen des de'cisions de M. l'abbé Morelet, sur les trois questions importantes qui sont le subject de son mémoire.* N.p., 1769.

Avis à la noblesse. N.p., 1788.

Babeuf, Gracchus. *Écrits.* Edited by Claude Mazauric. Paris, 1988.

Bade, Charles-Frederick, grand duke of. *Abrégé des principes de l'économie politique.* Basel, 1773.

Baert-Duholant, Charles-Alexandre. *Le consommateur, dialogue entre un homme d'état et un consommateur, sur divers objets d'économie politique.* Paris, Year X.

Bailleul, Jacques-Charles. *Théorie des institutions sociales.* Paris, 1801.

La balance égale, ou La juste imposition des droits du roi: Ouvrage digne d'un grand ministre, & d'un contrôleur citoyen. N.p., n.d.

Bancal, Jean-Henri. *Du nouvel ordre social fondé sur la religion.* Paris, Year V.

Bar. *Discours sur les inconvéniens du luxe. Pièce présentée à l'Académie françoise en 1770.* N.p., 1770.

Barbier, Edmond-Jean-François. *Chronique de la Régence et du règne de Louis XV (1718–1763), ou Journal de Barbier.* 4 vols. Paris, 1885.

Barère, Bertrand. *Éloge de Louis XII.* N.p., 1782.

——. *Premier rapport fait au nom du Comité de salut public, sur les moyens d'extirper la mendicité dans les campagnes, et sur les secours que la République doit accorder aux citoyens indigens.* Paris, Year III.

Barnave, Antoine. *Introduction à la Révolution française.* Paris, 1971 [1792].

Barrot. *Observations sur quelques moyens à prendre pour faire prospérer la République.* Paris, Year III.

Barruel, abbé Augustin. *Le patriote véridique, ou Discours sur les vraies causes de la révolution actuelle.* Paris, 1789.

Barthoul, abbé. *Lettre à l'auteur de La noblesse commerçante.* Bordeaux, 1756.

Basset de la Marelle, Louis. *La différence du patriotisme national chez les François et chez les Anglois.* Paris, 1766.

Batbedat, François. *Mémoire badin sur un sujet sérieux, dédié aux campagnards & aux curés du Département des Landes. Par un citoyen.* London, n.d.

Baudeau, Nicolas, ed. *Économies royales de Sully. Nouvelle édition, par M. l'abbé Baudeau; contenant le texte original, avec des discours préliminaire à chaque tome . . . des observations critiques, historiques, & politiques.* Amsterdam, 1775.

——. *Idées d'un citoyen sur l'administration des finances du roi.* Amsterdam, 1763.

——. *Idée d'une souscription patriotique, en faveur de l'agriculture, du commerce, et des arts.* Amsterdam, 1765.

——. *Principes économiques de Louis XII et du cardinal d'Amboise, de Henri IV et du duc de Sully sur l'administration des finances, opposés aux systèmes des docteurs modernes.* N.p., 1785.

——. *Principes de la science morale et politique sur le luxe et les loix somptuaires.* Paris, 1767.

Beardé de l'Abbaye. *Dissertation qui a remporté le prix à la Société libre et économique de St. Pétersbourg, en l'année MDCCLXVIII. Sur cette question proposée par la même société: Est-il plus avantageux à un état, que les paysans possèdent en propre du terrain, ou qu'ils n'aient que des biens meubles? Et jusqu'où doit s'étendre cette propriété?* Amsterdam, 1768.

——. *Recherches sur les moyens de supprimer les impôts, précédées de l'examen de la nouvelle science.* Amsterdam, 1770.

Beccaria, Cesare Bonesana, marquis de. *Discours de Mr. le marquis Cesar Beccaria Bonesana . . . prononcé à son installation dans les écoles palatines.* Lausanne, 1769.

——. *Principes d'économie politique appliqués à l'agriculture.* Paris, 1852.

Bedos. *Le négociant patriote, contenant un tableau qui réunit les avantages du commerce, la connaissance des spéculations de chaque nation . . . Par un négociant qui a voyagé.* Amsterdam, 1784.

Béliard. *Lettres critiques sur le luxe et les moeurs de ce siècle, à Madame D***.* Amsterdam, 1771.

Bellepierre de Neuve-Église, Louis-Joseph. *Le patriote artésien.* Paris, 1761.

Belot, Octavie Guichard, dame. *Observations sur la noblesse et le Tiers-État.* Amsterdam, 1758.

Berenger, Pierre-Laurent. *Les quatre états de la France.* N.p., 1789.

Bergasse, Nicolas. *Considérations sur la liberté du commerce; ouvrage où l'on examine, s'il est avantageux ou nuisible au commerce de réduire en privilège exclusif le transport des denrées & des marchandises.* The Hague, 1780.

——. *Discours prononcé à l'hôtel de ville de Lyon, le 21 décembre 1774.* Lyons, 1775.

——. *Observations sur le préjugé de la noblesse héréditaire.* London, 1789.

Berthelé, Joseph, ed. *Montpellier en 1768, d'après le manuscrit anonyme, intitulé: État et description de la ville de Montpellier, fait en 1768.* Montpellier, 1909.

Béthune-Charost, Armand-Joseph, duc de. *Copie d'un mémoire lu à la première séance publique de la Société royale d'agriculture de Paris, du 30 mars 1786, par M. le duc de Charost.* N.p., n.d.

——. *Vues générales sur l'organisation de l'instruction rurale en France, présentées aux Comités d'instruction publique et d'agriculture de la Convention nationale et à la Commission d'agriculture et des arts.* Paris, Year III.

Béthune-Charost, Armand-Joseph, duc de, Pierre-François Boncerf, and de la Noue. *Extrait des registres de la Société d'agriculture. Rapport fait à la société, le 27 mai 1790, par MM. le duc de Charost, de Boncerf & de la Noue.* N.p., n.d.

Bloch, Camille, and Alexandre Tuetey, ed. *Procès-verbaux et rapports du Comité de mendicité de la Constituante, 1790–1791.* Paris, 1911.

Boesnier de l'Orme, Paul. *De l'esprit du gouvernement économique.* Paris, 1775.

——. *Essai sur les principes de la morale naturelle.* Blois, 1792.

Boileau, Nicolas. *Boileau: Oeuvres.* Edited by Jérôme Vercruysse. Paris, 1969.

Bonald, Louis-Gabriel-Ambroise, vicomte de. *De la famille agricole, de la famille industrielle, et du droit d'aînesse.* Paris, 1826.

——. *Oeuvres complètes.* Vol. 2. Paris, 1859.

——. *Réflexions sur l'intérêt général de l'Europe, suivies de quelques considérations sur la noblesse.* Paris, 1815.

Boncerf, Pierre-François. *Extrait de la défense du citoyen Boncerf, au Tribunal révolutionnaire, le 18 ventôse, l'an deuxième de la République françoise, une, indivisible.* Paris, Year II.

——. *Les inconvéniens des droits féodaux.* London, 1776.

——. *Notice des principaux travaux à faire en faveur de l'agriculture et du commerce dans les différens départemens.* N.p., n.d.

Bonnet, abbé J.-Esprit. *Essai sur l'art de rendre les révolutions utiles.* 2 vols. Paris, 1801.

Borde, Charles. *Discours sur les avantages des sciences et des arts, prononcé dans l'as-*

semblée publique de l'Académie des sciences & belles-lettres de Lyon, le 22 juin 1751. Geneva, 1752.

Boudier de Villemaire, Pierre-Joseph. *L'ami des femmes, ou La philosophe du beau sexe.* N.p., 1774.

——. *L'andrométrie, ou Examen philosophique de l'homme.* Paris, 1753.

Boullainvilliers, Henri, comte de. *Essais sur la noblesse de la France, contenant une dissertation sur son origine et abaissement.* Amsterdam, 1732.

Bourdon, Louis-Gabriel. *Le patriote, ou Préservatif contre l'anglomanie.* London, 1789.

Boureau-Deslandes, François-André. *Lettre sur le luxe.* Frankfurt, 1745.

Brissot de Warville, Jacques-Pierre. *Correspondance et papiers.* Edited by Claude Perroud. Paris, 1912.

——. *Dénonciation au public d'un nouveau projet d'agiotage, ou Lettre à M. le comte de S*** sur un nouveau projet de compagnie d'assurance contre les incendies à Paris, sur ses inconvéniens, & en général sur les inconvéniens des compagnies par actions.* London, 1786.

——. *Mémoires (1754–1793).* Edited by Claude Perroud. 2 vols. Paris, 1911.

Brissot de Warville, Jacques-Pierre, and Étienne Clavière. *De la France et des États-Unis, ou L'importance de la Révolution de l'Amérique pour le bonheur de la France.* Edited by Marcel Dorigny. Paris, 1996 [1787].

——. *Point de banqueroute, ou Lettre à un créancier de l'État, sur l'impossibilité de la banqueroute nationale, et sur les moyens de ramener le crédit & la paix.* London, 1787.

Broussonet, Pierre-Marie-Auguste. *Discours prononcé à la séance publique tenue par la Société royale d'agriculture, dans la grande salle de l'archevêché le 28 décembre 1789.* Paris, 1790.

——. *Exposé des travaux de la Société royale d'agriculture dans le courant de l'année 1786.* N.p., 1788.

Broussonet, Pierre-Marie-Auguste, and abbé Jean-Louis Lefebvre. *Projet d'association pour l'encouragement de l'agriculture et des arts agricoles.* Paris, 1791.

Brown, John. *An Estimate of the Manners and Principles of the Times,* 7th ed. 2 vols. London, 1758.

Browne Dignan, D. *Essai sur les principes politiques de l'économie publique.* London, 1776.

Bury, Richard de. *Éloge de Maximilien de Béthune, duc de Sully, principal ministre de Henri IV.* Paris, 1763.

Butel-Dumont, Georges-Marie. *Recherches historiques et critiques sur l'administration publique et privée des terres chez les Romains depuis le commencement de la république jusqu'au siècle de Jules-César.* Paris, 1779.

——. *Théorie du luxe, ou Traité dans lequel on entreprend d'établir que le luxe est un ressort non seulement utile, mais même indispensablement nécessaire à la prospérité des états.* N.p., 1771.

Butini, Jean-François. *Traité du luxe.* Geneva, 1774.

Calonne, Charles-Alexandre de. *Observations sur les finances à l'Assemblée.* London, 1790.

Cantillon, Richard. *Essai sur la nature du commerce en général.* Edited by Henry Higgs. London, 1964 [1755].

Carpentier. *Ébauche des principes sûr pour estimer exactement le revenu net au propriétaire des biens-fonds, & fixer ce que le cultivateur peut & doit en donner de ferme.* Amsterdam, 1774.

Carra, Jean-Louis. *M. de Calonne tout entier, tel qu'il s'est comporté dans l'administration des finances, dans son commissariat en Bretagne.* Brussels, 1788.

Casaux, Charles, marquis de. *Considérations sur quelques parties du méchanisme des sociétés.* 5 vols. London, 1785–88.

Catalogue général des collections du Conservatoire royal des arts et métiers. Paris, 1818.

Challan. *Rapport sur les moyens de concourir au projet de la Société d'agriculture de la Seine, relatif au perfectionnement des charrues*. Versailles, Year X.

Chastellux, François-Jean, marquis de. *Discours sur les avantages ou les désavantages qui résultent, pour Europe, de la découverte de l'Amérique*. London, 1787.

——. *De la félicité publique, ou Considérations sur le sort des hommes dans les différentes époques de l'histoire*. 2 vols. Amsterdam, 1772.

Chaussard, Pierre-Jean-Baptiste [Publicola]. *Coup d'oeil sur l'intérieur de la République française, ou Esquisse des principes d'une révolution morale*. Paris, 1799.

Le citoyen philosophe, ou Examen critique de la noblesse militaire. N.p., 1756.

Clavière, Étienne. *De la foi publique envers les créanciers de l'État. Lettres à Linguet sur le no. CXVI de ses Annales par M***. Ouvrage dans lequel . . . on prouve que la banqueroute n'est ni nécessaire, ni utile, ni politique; et que la confiance doit ranimer l'esprit public*. London, 1788.

——. *Opinions d'un créancier de l'État, sur quelques matières de finance importantes dans le moment actuel*. London, 1789.

Clicquot de Blervache, Simon. *Dissertation sur les effets que produit le taux de l'intérest de l'argent sur le commerce et l'agriculture, qui a remporté le prix, au jugement de l'Académie des sciences, belles-lettres & arts d'Amiens, en l'année 1755*. Amiens, 1755.

Clicquot de Blervache, Simon, and Jacques-Claude-Marie Vincent de Gournay. *Considérations sur le commerce, et en particulier sur les compagnies, sociétés et maîtrises*. Amsterdam, 1758.

Collection complette de tous les ouvrages pour et contre M. Necker avec des notes critiques, politiques et secrètes. 3 vols. Utrecht, 1782.

Condillac, Étienne Bonnot de. *Le commerce et le gouvernement considérés relativement l'un à l'autre*. Amsterdam, 1776.

Condorcet, Jean-Antoine-Nicolas Caritat, marquis de. *Esquisse d'un tableau historique des progrès de l'esprit humain*. Paris, 1988 [1793].

Constant, Benjamin. *De la liberté chez les modernes: Écrits politiques*. Paris, 1980.

Cotte, Louis. *Leçons élémentaires d'agriculture, par demandes et par réponses, à l'usage des enfants, avec une suite de questions sur l'agriculture, la topographie & la minéralogie*. Paris, 1790.

Couanier Deslandes, abbé Claude-Henri. *Éloge de Maximilien de Béthune, marquis de Rosny, duc de Sully, principal ministre sous Henri le Grand, avec des notes historiques tirées du chaos des Mémoires de Sully*. Paris, 1763.

Coupé, Jacques-Michel. *De l'amélioration générale du sol français dans les parties négligées ou dégradées*. Paris, Year III.

——. *De la multiplication des légumes et plantes potagères*. Paris, Year III.

Cournand, Antoine de. *De la propriété, ou La cause du pauvre, plaidée au tribunal de la raison, de la justice et de la vérité*. Paris, 1791.

Coyer, abbé Gabriel-François. *L'année merveilleuse*. N.p., 1748.

——. *Bagatelles morales*. London, 1754.

——. *Chinki, histoire cochinchinoise qui peut servir à d'autres pays*. London, 1768.

——. *Développement, et défense du système de la noblesse commerçante*. London, 1768 [1757].

——. "Dissertation sur le vieux mot de Patrie." In *Gabriel-François Coyer, Jacob-Nicolas Moreau: Écrits sur le patriotisme l'esprit publique et la propagande au milieu du XVIIIe siècle*, edited by Edmond Dziembowski. La Rochelle, 1997 [1755].

——. *La noblesse commerçante*. London, 1756.

Cressy, Louis-Claude de. *Essais sur les moeurs, ou Point de constitution durable sans moeurs; ouvrage adressé à l'Assemblée nationale*. Paris, 1790.

Creuzé-Latouche, Jacques-Antoine. *Sur les subsistances*. Paris, 1793.

Crèvecoeur, Michel-Guillaume Saint-Jean de. *Letters from an American Farmer: Describing Certain Provincial Situations, Manners, and Customs, Not Generally Known; and Conveying Some Idea of the Late and Present Circumstances of the British Colonies in North America.* London, 1783.

Daire, Eugène, ed. *Économistes-financiers du XVIIIe siècle.* Paris, 1843.

Daire, Eugène, and G. de Molinari, eds. *Mélanges d'économie politique.* Geneva, 1984.

Dangeul, Louis-Joseph Plumard de. *Remarques sur les avantages et les désavantages de la France et de la Grande Bretagne, par rapport au commerce, & aux autres sources de la puissance des États. Traduction de l'anglois du Chevalier John Nickolls,* 2nd ed. Leiden, 1754.

Darigrand, Edmé-François. *L'anti-financier, ou Relevé de quelques-unes des malversations dont se rendent journellement coupable les fermiers généraux, & les vexations qu'ils commettent dans les provinces.* Amsterdam, 1763.

Delandine, Antoine-François. *Couronnes académiques, ou Recueil des prix proposés par les sociétés savantes.* Paris, 1787.

Delaure, Jacques-Antoine. *Histoire critique de la noblesse.* Paris, 1790.

Delegorgue. *Mémoire sur cette question, est-il utile en Artois de diviser les fermes & exploitations des terres; & dans le cas de l'affirmative, quelles bornes doit-on garder dans cette division? Ouvrage qui a remporté le prix à l'Académie d'Arras le 26 avril 1786.* N.p., 1786.

Deleyre, Alexandre. *Tableau de l'Europe, pour servir de supplément à l'Histoire philosophique & politique des établissements & du commerce des Européens dans les deux Indes.* Maastricht, 1774.

Delille, Jacques. *Les Géorgiques de Virgile, traduction nouvelle en vers françois avec des notes.* Paris, 1770.

——. *L'homme des champs, ou les Géorgiques françaises avec des notes.* Strasbourg, Year VIII.

Delisle de Sales, Jean-Baptiste-Claude Izouard de. *Lettre de Brutus sur les chars anciens et modernes.* London, 1771.

Démeunier, Jean-Nicolas. *Essai sur les États-Unis.* Paris, 1786.

——. *Opinion sur le projet de rembourser, en assignats-monnaie, les dix-neuf cent millions de la dette qu'on appelle exigible. Prononcée à la séance du 18 septembre 1790.* Paris, 1790.

Denesle. *Les préjugés du public sur l'honneur.* Paris, 1766 [1746].

Depère, Mathieu. *Manuel d'agriculture pratique. Ma vie agricole, ou Essais sur l'amélioration d'agriculture dans le canton de Mézin, Département de Lot-et-Garonne, pour préparer l'abolition des jachères.* N.p., n.d.

——. *Manuel d'agriculture pratique, ou Instructions sur la manière de cultiver nos domaines, et particulièrement la ferme expérimentale de Reffy.* N.p., 1806.

Le dernier mot du Tiers-État à la noblesse de France. N.p., 1788.

Desplaces, Laurent-Benoît. *Préservatif contre l'agromanie, ou L'agriculture réduite à ses vrais principes.* Paris, 1762.

Destutt de Tracy, Antoine-Louis-Claude. *Traité de l'économie politique.* Paris, 1823.

Diderot, Denis. *Diderot on Art.* 2 vols. Translated by John Goodman. New Haven, 1995.

Discours prononcé à l'Assemblée de notables du vendredi 25 mai 1787. Versailles, 1787.

Dissertation qui a remporté le prix sur la question proposée en 1766 par la Société d'oeconomie & d'agriculture à St. Pétersbourg; à laquelle on a joint les pièces qui ont eües l'accessit. N.p., 1768.

Du Coudray, Alexandre-Jacques, chevalier. *Le luxe, poëme en six chants.* Paris, 1773.

Dubignon, abbé, *Qu'est-ce que la noblesse?* Paris, 1789.

Dubuisson, Hubert-Dominique-Joseph. *Restauration de l'agriculture en France, et moyen de prévenir toute disette. Par un cultivateur, député à l'Assemblée nationale.* Paris, 1790.

Duchesne de Voiron, Louis-Henri. *Mémoire remis à MM. les députés de l'Assemblée nationale le 6 juin 1790.* N.p., n.d.

———. *Observations sur le mémoire de M. Necker, lu à l'Assemblée nationale le 14 novembre 1789.* N.p., 1789.

———. *Premiers principes d'une bonne administration, et causes de la décadence d'un royaume.* N.p., n.d.

———. *Projet pour libérer l'État sans emprunt, sans innovations, et en soulageant les peuples.* N.p., 1789.

Duclos, Charles Pinot. *Considérations sur les moeurs de ce siècle.* Edited by F. C. Green. Cambridge, 1939 [1750].

Dudevant de Bordeaux, Louis-Hippolyte. *L'apologie du commerce, essai philosophique et politique . . . suivi de diverses réflexions sur le commerce en général, sur celui de la France en particulier, & sur les moyens propres à l'accroître & le perfectionner.* Geneva, 1777.

Dufour, Jules-Michel. *Diogène à Paris.* Athens, 1787.

Duhamel du Monceau, Henri-Louis. *École d'agriculture.* Paris, 1759.

———. *Traité de la culture des terres, suivant les principes de M. Tull, Anglois.* Paris, 1750–61.

Dupont de Nemours, Pierre-Samuel. *Du commerce et de la Compagnie des Indes, seconde édition . . . augmentée de l'histoire du système de Law.* Paris, 1769.

———. *L'enfance et la jeunesse de Du Pont de Nemours racontées par lui-même.* Edited by H. A. Du Pont de Nemours. Paris, 1906.

———. *De la manière la plus favorable d'effectuer les emprunts.* Paris, 1789.

———. *Physiocratie, ou Constitution naturelle du gouvernement le plus avantageux au genre humain.* Leiden, 1768.

———. *Réponse demandée par M. le marquis de * * * à celle qu'il a fait aux Réflexions sur l'écrit intitulé: Richesse de l'État.* N.p., n.d.

Dupré de Saint-Maur, Nicolas-François. *Essai sur les monnoies, ou Réflexions sur le rapport entre l'argent et les denrées.* Paris, 1746.

Dupuy Demportes, Jean-Baptiste. *Le gentilhomme cultivateur, ou Corps complet d'agriculture, traduit de l'anglois de M. Hale.* Paris, 1761.

Durand de Maillane, Pierre-Toussaint. *La noblimanie.* N.p., 1789.

Ébaudy de Fresne, François. *Plan de restauration et de libération. Analyse d'un nouveau plan de culture, de finance & d'économie. . . . Principes sur lesquels on doit établir la répartition des impôts . . . & la création d'un nouveau signe, pour encourager la culture & le commerce, pour assurer la dette & pour détruire l'usure & l'agiotage.* N.p., n.d.

———. *Traité d'agriculture et d'économie de la culture et des arts, considérés tant en eux-mêmes, que dans leurs rapports d'économie politique. Avec les preuves, tirées de la comparaison de l'agriculture, du commerce et de la navigation de la France et de l'Angleterre.* Paris, 1788.

Éloge de Maximilien de Béthune, duc de Sully, surintendant des finances sous Henri IV. Paris, 1763.

Eschassériaux, Joseph. *Opinion sur les causes de l'état présent du commerce et de l'industrie, et les moyens de les rétablir sur les véritables bases de l'économie politique.* Paris, Year III.

———. *Opinion sur la nécessité et les moyens de régénérer promptement l'agriculture.* Paris, Year III.

Essai sur l'administration des terres. Paris, 1759.

Essai sur la dette nationale et sur la régénération de la France. N.p., n.d.

Établissement d'une société d'agriculture, de commerce, et des arts dans la province de Bretagne, délibérations des États. Rennes, 1757.

Faiguet de Villeneuve, Joachim. *L'ami des pauvres, ou L'économie politique.* Paris, 1766.

———. *L'économie politique, projet pour enrichir et pour perfectionner l'espèce humaine.* London, 1763.

Fauchet, Claude. *Discours sur les moeurs rurales, prononcé dans l'église de Surenne, le 10 d'août 1788, pour la fête de la rosière.* Paris, 1788.

Favart, Charles-Simon. *Les moissonneurs, comédie en trois actes.* Paris, 1768.

Fénelon, François de Salignac de La Mothe-. *Aventures de Télémaque.* Edited by Jacques Le Brun. Paris, 1995 [1699].

———. *Oeuvres.* Edited by Jacques le Brun. Paris, 1997.

Ferrières, Jacques-Annibal. *Plan d'un nouveau genre de banque nationale et territoriale, présenté à l'Assemblée nationale.* Paris, 1789.

Flamen d'Assigny. *De l'agriculture considérée dans ses rapports avec l'économie politique, d'ou l'on déduit la nécessité d'établir des fermes expérimentales pour fonder l'art agricole.* Paris, Year XII.

Forbonnais, François Véron de. *Considérations sur les finances d'Espagne.* Dresden, 1753.

———. *Élémens du commerce.* 2 vols. Leiden, 1754.

———. "Du gouvernement d'Angleterre, comparé par l'auteur de l'Esprit des loix au gouvernement de France." *Opuscules de M. F***.* Vol. 3. Amsterdam, 1753.

Fougeret de Montbron, Louis-Charles. *Préservatif contre l'anglomanie.* Minorca, 1757.

François de Neufchâteau, Nicolas. *Des améliorations dont la paix doit être l'époque. No. 1er. Moyen préliminaire d'encourager l'agriculture dans les départemens où les terres sont morcelées et divisées à l'infini, en les réunissant sur un plan régulier.* Épinal, 1797.

———. *Recueil des lettres circulaires, instructions, programmes, discours, et autres actes publics, émanés du C. François (de Neufchâteau) pendant ses deux exercices du Ministère de l'intérieur.* Paris, Year VII.

Fresnais de Beaumont. *La noblesse cultivatrice, ou Moyens d'élever en France la culture de toutes les denrées que son sol comporte, au plus haut degré de production.* Paris, 1778.

Froger. *Instructions de morale, d'agriculture, et d'économie pour les habitans de la campagne, ou Avis d'un homme de campagne à son fils.* Paris, 1769.

Garnier, Germain. *Abrégé élémentaire des principes de l'économie politique.* Paris, 1796.

Garnier, J.-J. *Le commerce remis à sa place; réponse d'un pédant de collège aux novateurs politiques.* n.p, 1756.

Gauthier, abbé François-Louis. *Traité contre l'amour des parures, et le luxe des habits.* Paris, 1779.

Gautier, Jean-Jacques. *Essai sur les moeurs champêtres.* London, 1787.

Genty, Louis. *Discours sur le luxe, qui a remporté le prix d'éloquence à l'Académie des sciences, belles-lettres & arts de Besançon, en 1783.* N.p., 1783.

Gerdolle. *L'abeille, ou Recueil de philosophie de littérature et d'histoire.* The Hague, 1755.

Goudar, Ange. *Les intérêts de la France mal entendus, dans les branches de l'agriculture, de la population, des finances, du commerce, de la marine et de l'industrie, par un citoyen.* Amsterdam, 1756.

Gournay, Jacques-Claude-Marie Vincent de. *Mémoires et lettres de Vincent de Gournay.* Edited by Takumi Tsuda. Tokyo, 1993.

Goyon de la Plombanie, Henri. *La France agricole et marchande.* Avignon, 1762.

Graslin, Jean-Joseph-Louis. *Correspondance entre M. Graslin, de l'Académie écono-*

mique de St. Pétersbourg, auteur de l'Essai analytique sur la richesse et sur l'impôt, et de M. l'abbé Baudeau, auteur des Éphémérides du citoyen, sur un des principes fondamentaux de la doctrine des soi-disants philosophes économistes. Edited by Gino Longhitano. Catania, 1988 [1767].

———. "Dissertation sur la question proposée par la Société économique de St. Pétersbourg. Est-il plus avantageux et plus utile au bien public, que le paysan possède des terres en propre, ou seulement des biens mobiliers, & jusqu'où doit s'étendre cette propriété?" In *Dissertation qui a remporté le prix sur la question proposée en 1766 par la Société d'oeconomie & d'agriculture à St. Pétersbourg; à laquelle on a joint les pièces qui ont eües l'accessit.* N.p., 1768.

Grimm, baron Friedrich-Melchior, Denis Diderot, Guillaume-Thomas Raynal, Henri Meister. *Correspondance littéraire.* Edited by Maurice Tourneux. 16 vols. Paris, 1877–82.

Hausse, *La noblesse telle qu'elle doit être, ou Moyen de l'employer utilement pour elle-même et pour la patrie.* Amsterdam, 1758.

Hell, François-Antoine-Joseph. *Voeu d'un agriculteur rheno-françois.* Paris, 1791.

Helvétius, Claude-Adrien. *De l'esprit.* Paris, 1758.

Herbert, Jacques-Claude. *Essai sur la police générale des grains.* London, 1754.

Hirzel, Jean-Gaspard. *Le Socrate rustique, ou Description de la conduite économique et morale d'un paysan philosophe.* Zurich, 1762.

Histoire de la fondation de la Société d'encouragement pour l'industrie nationale, ou Recueil des procès-verbaux des séances de cette société, depuis l'époque de sa fondation, le 9 brumaire an X (1 nov 1801), jusqu'au 1er vendémiaire an XI (22 sept 1802). Paris, 1850.

Hume, David. *Discours politiques de Monsieur Hume traduits de l'anglois.* 2 vols. Translated by Jean-Bernard Le Blanc. Amsterdam, 1754.

———. *Essays. Moral, Political, and Literary.* Edited by Eugene F. Miller. Indianapolis, 1985.

———. *Philosophical Essays concerning Human Understanding.* 2nd ed. London, 1753.

Isnard, Achille-Nicolas. *Observations sur le principe qui a produit les révolutions de France, de Genève et d'Amérique, dans le dix-huitième siècle.* Évreux, 1789.

———. *Traité des richesses, contenant l'analyse de l'usage des richesses en général & de leurs valeurs; les principes & les loix naturelles de la circulation des richesses, de leur distribution, du commerce, de la circulation des monnoies & de l'impôt, & des recherches historiques sur les révolutions que les droits de propriété publics & particuliers ont éprouvées en France depuis l'origine de la monarchie.* London, 1781.

Jaubert, Pierre. *Éloge de la roture, dédié aux roturiers.* London, 1766.

Jefferson, Thomas. *Notes on the State of Virginia; written in the year 1781.* N.p., 1782.

Johannot. *Rapport et projet de décret présentés au nom des Comités de commerce, de législation et des finances; par Johannot, sur les établissements de commerce ou manufactures dont les entrepreneurs sont tombés sous la glaive de la loi.* Paris, Year III.

Laffon de Ladébat, André-Daniel. *Réponse au maire d'Orient, ou Défense d'un mémoire adressé au gouvernement . . . sur les avantages d'un liberté absolue pour le commerce de l'Inde.* N.p., 1776.

La Font de Saint-Yenne, Étienne de. *Réflexions sur quelques causes de l'état présent de la peinture en France.* The Hague, 1747.

———. *Sentimens sur quelques ouvrages de peinture, sculpture et gravure, écrits à un particulier en province.* N.p., 1754.

Lair, Pierre-Aimé. *Catalogue de la bibliothèque de la Société royale d'agriculture et du commerce de Caen.* Caen, 1829.

———. *Notices historiques lues à la Société d'agriculture et du commerce de Caen.* Caen, 1807.

——. *Précis des travaux de la Société royale d'agriculture et de commerce de Caen, depuis son rétablissement en 1801 jusqu'en 1810*. Caen, 1827.

Lair Duvaucelles. *Mémoire sur l'utilité des encouragemens donnés à l'agriculture, lu dans une séance publique de la Société nationale des neuf soeurs*. Paris, 1791.

Lalande. *Entretiens de Périclès et de Sully aux Champs-Élisées, sur leur administration, ou Balance entre les avantages du luxe, et ceux de l'économie*. London, 1776.

La Maillardière, vicomte de. *Traité d'économie-politique, embrassant toutes ses branches, ou Les intérêts de la population, de l'agriculture, des arts, du commerce, de la navigation, des finances, de la justice, du militaire & de la politique, à concilier pour la richesse & prospérité de l'État & des citoyens*. N.p., 1783.

Lamerville, J.-L.-T. Heurtault, comte de. *Discours prononcé à l'Assemblée de la noblesse de la vicomté de Paris*. N.p., n.d.

——. *De l'impôt territorial, combiné avec les principes de l'administration de Sully et de Colbert, adaptés à la situation actuelle de la France*. Strasbourg, 1788.

La Rochefoucauld-Liancourt, François-Alexandre-Frédéric, duc de. *Rapport fait au nom des Comités des finances, d'agriculture & commerce, des domaines & de mendicité, le 16 juin 1791*. Paris, 1791.

La Salle d'Offemont, marquis de. *Développement d'une ressource immense et légitime pour la régénération de l'État, l'acquittement de sa dette, l'abolition de la gabelle, et autres droits onéreux*. N.p., 1789.

Leblanc de l'Arbreaupré. *Plan sur l'agriculture et le commerce, suivi de l'établissement d'une banque rurale, & d'un autre pour la formation des galères de terre*. Paris, 1789.

Le Carpentier, Charles. *Notice nécrologique sur feu M. Masquelier, graveur à Paris, associé correspondant de la Société d'émulation de Rouen, lue dans la séance du 1 juillet 1811*. Rouen, 1811.

Lefebvre, abbé Jean-Louis. *Compte rendu à la Société d'agriculture de Paris de ses travaux faits, commencés et projetés, depuis le 30 mai 1788, jusques et compris le 30 septembre 1793*. Paris, Year VII.

Legros, abbé, *Analyse et examen du systême des philosophes économistes, par un solitaire*. Geneva, 1787.

Le Mercier de la Rivière, Paul-Pierre. *L'heureuse nation, ou Relations du gouvernement des Féliciens, peuple souverainement libre sous l'empire absolu de ses loix*. Paris, 1792.

——. *Mémoires et textes inédits sur le gouvernement économique des Antilles*. Edited by L. Ph. May. Paris, 1978.

——. *L'ordre naturel et essentiel des sociétés politiques*. Paris, 2001 [1767].

Lequinio de Kerblay, Joseph-Marie. *École des laboureurs . . . ou Lettre familière aux laboureurs de Bretagne*. Rennes, 1790.

——. *Philosophie du peuple, ou Élémens de philosophie politique et morale, mis à la portée des habitans des campagnes*. Paris, 1796.

——. *Richesse de la république*. Paris, 1792.

Le Roy, Chrétien. *Le commerce vengé, ou Réfutation du discours couronné par l'Académie de Marseille, en 1777, sur cette question: Quelle a été l'influence du commerce sur l'esprit & les moeurs des peuples?* Brussels, 1779.

Lindet, Robert. *Projet de décret présenté au nom des Comités de salut public, d'agriculture et de commerce, dans la séance du 14 brumaire, Robert Lindet*. Paris, Year III.

Linguet, Simon-Henri. *De la dette nationale et du crédit publique en France*. Brussels, 1789.

Liquier, André. *Discours qui a remporté le prix de l'Académie de Marseille, en 1777, sur cette question: Quelle a été dans tous les temps l'influence du commerce sur l'esprit et sur les moeurs des peuples?* Amsterdam, 1777.

Locke, John. *Two Treatises of Government*. Cambridge, 1960 [1689].

Lormoy. *Mémoire sur l'agriculture.* N.p., 1789.

Lottin, Antoine-Prosper. *Discours contre le luxe, il corrompt les moeurs, & détruit les empires.* Paris, 1783.

Loyseau, Jean-René. *Réponse aux observations de M. Necker, sur le décret qui supprime la noblesse, qui défend de porter les titres, les noms de fiefs et les armoiries.* Paris, 1790.

Mably, Gabriel Bonnot de. *Doutes proposés aux philosophes économistes, sur l'ordre naturel et essentiel des sociétés politiques.* The Hague, 1768.

——. *Entretiens de Phocion, sur le rapport de la morale avec la politique.* 2 vols. Paris, Year II [1763].

——. *Des principes des négociations, pour servir d'introduction au droit public de l'Europe, fondé sur les traités.* The Hague, 1757.

Le maire de village à Paris, ou Conversation entre M. le vicomte de Mir . . . . et un de ses fermiers. N.p., n.d.

Malesherbes, Chrétien-Guillaume Lamoignon de. *Idées d'un agriculteur patriote, sur le défrichement des terres incultes, sèches & maigres, connus sous les noms de landes, garrigues, gâtines, friches, &c.* N.p., n.d.

Malthus, Thomas Robert. *An Essay on the Principle of Population.* 2 vols. Edited by Patricia James. Cambridge, 1989 [1798].

Malvaux, abbé J. de. *Les moyens de détruire la mendicité en France, en rendant les mendians utiles à l'État sans les rendre malheureux; tirés des mémoires qui ont concouru pour le prix accordé en l'année 1777, par l'Académie des sciences, arts & belles-lettres de Châlons-sur-Marne.* Paris, 1780.

Mandeville, Bernard. *The Fable of the Bees: or Private Vices, Publick Benefits.* Edited by F. B. Kaye. Indianapolis, 1988.

Manoncourt, Charles-Sigisbert Sonnini de. *Mémoire sur la culture et les avantages du chou-navet de Laponie; lu à l'assemblée publique de l'Académie royale des sciences, arts & belles-lettres de Nancy, le 25 août 1787.* Paris, 1788.

——. *Le voeu d'un agriculteur, ou Essai sur quelques moyens de remédier aux ravages de la grêle & à la disette des grains.* Belin, 1788.

Marat, Jean-Paul. *Les chaînes de l'esclavage.* Paris, Year I.

Marchand, J.-H. *La noblesse commerçable ou ubiquiste.* Amsterdam, 1756.

Marragon, J.-B. *Rapport et projet de décret sur la jonction de l'Oise à la Sambre, présenté au nom du Comité des travaux publics.* Paris, Year III.

Mascarany. *Éloge historique de Maximilien de Béthune, duc de Sully, grand-maître de l'artillerie, maréchal de France, et principal ministre de Henri IV.* The Hague, 1763.

Massabiau, François. *Essai sur la valeur intrinsèque des fonds, ou Le moyen de les apprécier, de faire connoître leurs bornes, leurs limites, leurs servitudes, de pénétrer dans leurs charges, & d'en donner le rapport exact & précis en justice.* London, 1764.

Massac, Pierre-Louis-Raimond de, and Sélébran. *Discours et mémoires relatifs à l'agriculture.* Paris, 1763.

Mathon de la Cour, C.-J. *Discours sur les meilleurs moyens de faire naître et d'encourager le patriotisme dans une monarchie, sans gêner ou affoiblir en rien l'étendue de pouvoir d'exécution qui est propre à ce genre de gouvernement.* Paris, 1787.

Melon, Jean-François. *Essai politique sur le commerce.* N.p., 1734.

Mémoire présenté par la Société royale d'agriculture à l'Assemblée nationale, le 24 octobre 1789, sur les abus qui s'opposent aux progrès de l'agriculture, & sur les encouragemens qu'il est nécessaire d'accorder à ce premier des arts. Paris, 1789.

Mémoires pour servir à l'histoire de la marquise de Pompadour. London, 1763.

Mercier, Louis-Sébastien. *Adresse de l'agriculture à messieurs de l'Assemblée nationale, régénératrice de l'empire français.* Paris, 1791.

——. *L'an deux mille quatre cent quarante.* London, 1774.

——. *Tableau de Paris.* Amsterdam, 1782.

Meude-Monpas, J.-J.-O. de. *Réponse à la question proposée par M. l'abbé Raynal, adressée à l'Académie de Lyon: Les richesses toujours ont causé nos malheurs?* Paris, 1788.

Millin, Aubin-Louis. *Réfutation du pamphlet de M. Necker, contre le décret de l'Assemblée nationale, qui supprime les titres, les armoiries et les livrées.* N.p., n.d.

Mirabeau, Honoré-Gabriel Riqueti, comte de. *De la Caisse d'escompte.* N.p., 1785.

———. *Dénonciation de l'agiotage au roi et à l'Assemblée des notables.* N.p., 1787.

———. *Esprit de Mirabeau, ou Manuel de l'homme d'État, des publicistes, des fonctionnaires et des orateurs . . . embrassant les différentes branches de l'économie politique.* Edited by P.-J.-B. Chaussard. 2 vols. Paris, 1797.

———. *Essai sur le despotisme.* Paris, 1821. [1775].

———. *Lettre du comte de Mirabeau à M. Le Couteulx de la Noraye, sur la Banque de Saint-Charles & sur la Caisse d'escompte.* Brussels, 1785.

———. *Opinion du comte de Mirabeau sur la noblesse ancienne et moderne. Considérations sur l'ordre de Cincinnatus.* Paris, 1815 [1784].

Mirabeau, Victor Riqueti, marquis de. *L'ami des hommes, ou Traité de la population.* Avignon, 1756.

———. *Lettres sur la législation, ou L'ordre légal, dépravé, rétabli et perpétué.* Bern, 1775.

———. *Mémoire concernant l'utilité des états provinciaux.* Rome, 1750.

———. *Théorie de l'impôt.* N.p., 1760.

Mirabeau, Victor Riqueti, marquis de, and François Quesnay, *Philosophie rurale, ou Économie générale et politique de l'agriculture.* Amsterdam, 1763.

Montesquieu, Charles de Secondat, baron de. *Les lettres persanes.* Paris, 1973 [1721].

———. *The Spirit of the Laws.* Translated by Anne M. Cohler, Basia Carolyn Miller, and Harold Samuel Stone. Cambridge, 1989.

Montesquieu, J.-B. Secondat de. *Pensées d'un amateur de la vérité, sur les affaires présentes.* N.p., 1789.

Montvert, Pierre-Esprit Sambuc de. *Analyse des principales causes qui, depuis environ un siècle et demi, ont concouru à faire diminuer en France la surabondance des objets de première nécessité; et les moyens que le nouvel ordre de choses peut fournir, pour rétablir cette surabondance, surtout par l'intérêt qu'un plus grand nombre d'hommes auront à diriger leur industrie et leurs ressources vers les objets d'agriculture, de fabrique et de commerce, comme les sources de la prospérité public.* Sens, 1802.

———. *Observations sur les divers degrés de fertilité ou de dégradation du sol du royaume, suivant l'état des propriétaires.* Paris, 1787.

———. *De la restauration des campagnes, à opérer au physique & au moral, par une division mieux entendue des possessions rurales, au plus grand avantage de tout propriétaire.* Avignon, 1789.

———. *Troisième moyen d'acquitter les dettes de l'État, d'amener la prospérité dans les campagnes, & de soulager les villes d'une partie des individus qui leurs sont à charge, par le manque de travail ou d'occupation.* Paris, 1789.

Moreau, Marie-François. *Rapport fait à la Convention nationale sur l'invention du citoyen Barneville, qui a pour objet d'établir en France des manufactures de mousselines superfines.* Paris, Year III.

Morellet, abbé André. *Mémoire sur la situation actuelle de la Compagnie des Indes.* N.p., 1769.

———. *Prospectus d'un nouveau dictionnaire de commerce.* Paris, 1769.

———. *Réflexions sur les avantages de la fabrication et de l'usage des toiles peintes en France.* Geneva, 1758.

Murat-Montferrand, comte de. *Qu'est-ce que la noblesse, et que sont ses privilèges?* Amsterdam, 1789.

Naveau, Jean-Baptiste. *Le financier citoyen.* N.p., 1757.

Necker, Jacques. *De l'administration des finances de la France.* 3 vols. N.p., 1784.

——. *Compte rendu au roi, par M. Necker, directeur général des finances.* Paris, 1781.

——. *Éloge de Jean-Baptiste Colbert, discours qui a remporté le prix de l'Académie française, en 1773.* Paris, 1773.

——. "Réponse au mémoire de M. l'abbé Morellet sur la Compagnie des Indes." In *Oeuvres complètes de M. Necker.* Vol. 15. Paris, 1821.

Le négociant citoyen, ou Essai sur la recherche des moyens d'augmenter les lumières de la nation sur le commerce et l'agriculture. Amsterdam, 1764.

Papion, N. *Adresse sur les moyens de prospérité du commerce, & sur les secours à lui donner.* Paris, 1791.

——. *Considérations sur les établissemens nécessaires à la prospérité de l'agriculture, du commerce, et des manufactures dans l'Empire français.* Tours, 1805.

Pattullo, Henry. *Essai sur l'amélioration des terres.* Paris, 1758.

Pelissard, L.-L. *L'assurance du commerce.* N.p., 1772.

Perreau, Jean-André. *Le roi voyageur, ou Examen des abus de l'administration de la Lydie.* London, 1784.

Pétion, Jérôme. *Opinion sur le commerce du tabac.* Paris, n.d.

Pezerols, abbé de. *Le conciliateur, ou La noblesse militaire et commerçante; en réponse aux objections faites par l'auteur de La noblesse militaire.* Amsterdam, 1756.

Pfliéger. *Motion d'ordre faite par Pfliéger, député du Haut-Rhin, sur les moyens d'une prompte amélioration de l'agriculture dans la République française.* Paris, Year VI.

Pinczon du Sel des Mons. *Considérations sur le commerce de Bretagne.* N.p., 1756.

Pomme. *Rapport et projet de décret présentés au nom des Comités de marine et colonies et des finances, sur la pétition de Ferdinand Berthoud, auteur des horloges marines.* Paris, Year III.

Price, Richard. *Observations sur l'importance de la Révolution de l'Amérique et sur les moyens de le rendre utile au monde.* N.p., n.d.

Priestley, Joseph. *An Essay on the First Principles of Government and the Nature of Political, Civil, and Religious Liberty.* Dublin, 1768.

Prix nationaux d'agriculture, dans le Département de la Seine Inférieure. Arrêté du directoire du Département de la Seine Inférieure, sur les cultivateurs qui . . . ont mérité les prix nationaux d'agriculture. Rouen, 1795.

Programme des prix distribués et proposés et notice des médailles d'encouragement données par la Société d'agriculture du Département de la Seine, dans sa séance publique du 30 fructidor an IX. Paris, n.d.

Programme des prix proposés par la Société d'agriculture du Département de la Seine, dans sa séance publique du 20 messidor an 8 de la République. N.p., n.d.

Programme des prix proposés par la Société libre d'émulation, établie à l'imitation de celle de Londres, pour l'encouragement des inventions qui tendent à perfectionner la pratique des arts et des métiers utiles. N.p., 1776.

Le publicole françois, ou Mémoire sur les moyens d'augmenter la richesse du prince, par l'aisance des peuples. Paris, 1776.

Quesnay, François. *Les manuscrits économiques de François Quesnay et du marquis de Mirabeau aux Archives nationales (M. 778 à M. 785).* Edited by Georges Weulersse. Paris, 1910.

——. *Oeuvres économiques et philosophiques de F. Quesnay fondateur du système physiocratique.* Edited by Auguste Oncken. Frankfurt, 1888.

Questions sur l'agriculture, les sciences, les arts, les fabriques et manufactures, le commerce, etc. adressées par le Comité de salut public aux administrations de département. N.p., Year III.

Raynal, abbé Guillaume-Thomas. *Histoire philosophique et politique des établissemens & du commerce des Européens dans les deux Indes.* Amsterdam, 1770.

Recueil contenant les délibérations de la Société royale d'agriculture de la généralité de Paris, au bureau de Paris, depuis le 12 mars jusqu'au 10 septembre 1761. Paris, 1761.

Réflexions sur la liberté du commerce des grains, extrait du corps d'observations de la Société d'agriculture de Bretagne. N.p., 1763.

Le réformateur. Paris, 1756.

Règlemens de la Société libre d'émulation pour l'encouragement des inventions qui tendent à la perfection de la pratique des arts et métiers utiles . . . traduits de l'anglois. Brussels, 1778.

Règlements de la Société libre d'émulation, établie à Paris en 1776 pour l'encouragement des inventions qui tendent à perfectionner la pratique des arts et métiers utiles. N.p., 1780.

Remi, Charles. *Considérations philosophiques sur les moeurs, les plaisirs et les préjugés de la capitale.* London, 1787.

Remonstrance de la Chambre des comptes. N.p., 1787.

Ressource actuelle pour les besoins de l'État, ou Supplément à la brochure intitulée Richesse de l'État. N.p., n.d.

Ribaucourt. *Mémoire sur les usages de la tourbe, et de ses engrais, lu à la Société royale d'agriculture de Paris.* Paris, 1787.

Richesse de l'État, à laquelle on a ajouté les pièces qui ont paru pour et contre. Amsterdam, 1764.

Rieussec. *Discours sur les causes morales de la dégradation de l'agriculture, et les moyens d'y remédier. Séance publique de la Société royale d'agriculture de la généralité de Lyon, tenue le 5 janvier 1787.* Geneva, 1788.

Rioux de Maillou. *Vues simples et patriotiques d'un citoyen pour la régénération de la France, dans les États généraux de 1789, où il propose un impôt unique sous la dénomination de droit royal réuni.* Paris, 1789.

Robespierre, Maximilien. *Robespierre: Écrits.* Edited by Claude Mazauric. Paris, 1989.

Robinet, Jean-Baptiste. *De la nature.* Amsterdam, 1761.

Rochon de Chabonnes, M.-A. *La noblesse oisive.* N.p., 1756.

Roland de la Platière, Jean-Marie. "Mémoire sur la culture de France, comparée à celle d'Angleterre," in *Séance publique de la Société royale d'agriculture de la généralité de Lyon, tenue le 5 janvier 1787.* Geneva, 1788.

Rougier de la Bergerie, Jean-Baptiste. *Discours prononcé par M. Rougier-la-Bergerie, député du Département de l'Yonne, membre du Comité d'agriculture et de la Société d'agriculture de Paris, sur les encouragemens à accorder aux départements, pour l'agriculture, le 11 septembre 1792.* Paris, 1792.

——. *Essai politique et philosophique sur le commerce et la paix, considérés sous leurs rapports avec l'agriculture.* Paris, 1797.

——. *Histoire de l'agriculture française, considérée dans ses rapports avec les lois, les cultes, les moeurs et le commerce; précédé d'une notice sur l'empire des Gaules et sur l'agriculture des anciens.* Paris, 1815.

——. *Observations sur l'institution des sociétés d'agriculture, et sur les moyens d'utiliser leurs travaux, imprimées par arrêté de la Société d'agriculture de la Seine.* Paris, Year VIII.

——. *Recherches sur les principaux abus qui s'opposent aux progrès de l'agriculture.* Paris, 1788.

Rouillé d'Orfeuil, Augustin. *L'alambic moral, ou Analyse raisonnée de tout ce qui a rapport à l'homme.* Morocco, 1773.

——. *L'ami des François.* Constantinople, 1771.

Rousseau, Jean-Jacques. *Discours sur l'économie politique.* Paris, 2002 [1755].

——. *Discours sur l'origine et les fondements de l'inégalité parmi les hommes.* Paris, 1971 [1755].

——. "Discours sur les richesses." *Revue Suisse* 16 (1853): 177–98.

——. *Discours sur les sciences et les arts.* Edited by François Bouchardy. Paris, 1964 [1750].

——. *J. J. Rousseau citoyen de Genève à Mr. d'Alembert . . . sur son article Genève dans le VIIme volume de l'Encyclopédie, et particulièrement sur le projet d'établir un théâtre de comédie en cette ville.* Amsterdam, 1758.

Roussel de la Tour, Pierre-Philippe. *Réflexions sur les avantages inestimables de l'agriculture, relatives aux circonstances présentes.* N.p., n.d.

Rubigny de Berteval, Jean-Antoine de. *Observations importantes, présentées à la Convention nationale, par le citoyen Rubigny, tanneur, l'une des victimes du despotisme en 1778, par un emprisonnement de sa personne à la Bastille, et l'un des électeurs de Paris, en 1789.* N.p., n.d.

——. *Réflexions patriotiques, présentées à la Convention nationale, sur le maximum, le commerce et les approvisionnements.* N.p., n.d.

Saige, Joseph. *L'ami des trois ordres, ou Réflexions sur les dissensions actuelles: par l'auteur du Catéchisme du citoyen.* N.p., n.d.

Saint-Jean. *Pensées et réflexions morales, par un militaire.* Paris, 1768.

Saint-Just, Antoine-Louis. *Oeuvres complètes.* Edited by Anne Kupiec and Miguel Abensour. Paris, 2004.

Saint-Péravi, J.-N.-M. Guérineau de. *Principes du commerce opposé au trafic, développés par un homme d'état.* N.p., 1787.

Saint-Vast, Thérèse de. *L'esprit de Sully; avec le portrait d'Henri IV, ses lettres à M. de Sully, & ses conversations avec le même.* Cologne, 1766.

Say, Jean-Baptiste. *Catéchisme d'économie politique, ou Instruction familière qui montre de quelle façon les richesses sont produites, distribués et consommées dans la société.* Paris, 1815.

——. *Mélanges et correspondance d'économie politique, ouvrage posthume de J.-B. Say.* Paris, 1833.

——. *Olbie, ou Essai sur les moyens de réformer les moeurs d'une nation.* Nancy, 1985 [1799].

——. *Traité d'économie politique, ou Simple exposition de la manière dont se forment, se distribuent et se consomment les richesses.* 2nd ed. Paris, 1814 [1803].

Schmidt, Georges-Louis. *Principes de la législation universelle.* 2 vols. Amsterdam, 1776.

Seconds, Jean-Louis. *De l'art social, ou Des vrais principes de la société politique.* Paris, 1792.

Sedaine, Michel-Jean. *Le roi et le fermier. Comédie en trois actes.* Paris, 1762.

Sénac de Meilhan, Gabriel. *Considérations sur les richesses et le luxe.* Amsterdam, 1787.

——. *Des principes et des causes de la révolution en France.* London, 1790.

Servan, Joseph-Michel-Antoine. *Discours sur le progrès des connoissances humaines en général, de la morale, et de la législation en particulier; lu dans un assemblée publique de l'Académie de Lyon.* N.p., 1781.

Servan, Joseph. *Idées à répandre parmi les habitans de la campagne et les propriétaires fonciers. Imprimé et envoyé dans les départemens par ordre du Comité de salut public.* Paris, Year III.

Sieyès, abbé Emmanuel-Joseph. *Essai sur les privilèges.* Paris, 1788.

——. *Qu'est-ce que le Tiers-État?* Paris, 1789.

Simon, J.-B. *Le gouvernement admirable, ou La république des abeilles.* The Hague, 1740.

Smith, Adam. *An Inquiry into the Nature and Causes of the Wealth of Nations.* Edited by R. H. Campbell and A. S. Skinner. Indianapolis, 1981 [1776].

——. *Theory of Moral Sentiments.* Edited by D. D. Raphael and A. L. Macfie. Oxford, 1976 [1759].

Solomé, Jean-Pierre. *L'anti-banquier, ou Moyens très simples d'éteindre à l'instant toutes les dettes de la France, sans augmenter les contributions publiques; et même de les diminuer de près de moitié dans vingt ans d'ici.* Deux-Ponts, 1790.

Soulavie, abbé Jean-Louis. *Des moeurs et de leur influence sur la prospérité ou la déca-*

dence des empires. Discours pour la cérémonie de l'ouverture des États-généraux de Languedoc. Paris, 1784.

Theremin, Charles. *De l'incompatibilité du systême démagogique avec le systême d'économie politique des peuples modernes.* Paris, 1799.

Thomas, Antoine-Léonard. *Éloge de Maximilien de Béthune, duc de Sully, surintendant des finances, &c. principal ministre sous Henri IV. Discours qui a remporté le prix de l'Académie française en 1763.* Paris, 1763.

Tucker, Josias. *Questions importantes sur le commerce.* Translated by A.-R.-J. Turgot. London, 1755.

Turbilly, Louis-François-Henri de Menon, marquis de. *Essai sur les labours, lu à la première assemblée de la Société royale d'agriculture de la généralité de Paris, au bureau de Paris, le 12 mars 1761.* Paris, 1761.

——. *Mémoire sur les défrichemens.* Paris, 1760.

——. *Observations sur l'établissement des sociétés royales d'agriculture dans les différentes généralités du royaume, lues à l'assemblée de la Société royale d'agriculture de la généralité de Paris, au bureau de Paris, le 10 septembre 1761.* Paris, 1761.

——. *Réflexions sur les sociétés royales d'agriculture, des différentes généralités du royaume, lues à la première assemblée de la Société royale d'agriculture de la généralité de Paris, au bureau de Paris, le 12 mars 1761.* Paris, 1761.

Turgot, Anne-Robert-Jacques, baron de l'Aulne. *Oeuvres de Turgot et documents le concernant, avec biographie et notes.* Edited by Gustave Schelle. 5 vols. Paris, 1913–23.

Udin, Jean-Baptiste. *Adresse à l'Assemblée nationale législative; par Jean-Baptiste Udin, cultivateur, à Saint-Aubin-d'Aubigné, Département de l'Ille et Vilaine.* Paris, n.d.

Vasco, Giambattista. *La félicité publique considérée dans les paysans cultivateurs de leurs propres terres, traduit de l'italien par M. Vignoli.* Lausanne, 1770.

Vaudrey. *Nouveau mémoire sur l'agriculture, sur les distinctions qu'on peut accorder aux riches laboureurs; avec des moyens d'augmenter l'aisance & la population dans les campagnes. Pièce qui a obtenu un accessit au prix de l'Académie de Caen en 1766.* Paris, 1767.

Veau, Athanase. *Opinion sur la nécessité de perfectionner en France l'agriculture, les arts et les sciences, par des établissemens adaptés aux localités et à l'intérêt général de la république.* Paris, Year III.

Les véritables intérêts de la nation, considérés dans la vente des biens ecclésiastiques, et dans la destruction de la noblesse et des parlemens. Paris, 1790.

Vital-Roux. *De l'influence du gouvernement sur la prospérité du commerce.* Paris, 1800.

Voltaire. "Défense du mondain, ou L'apologie du luxe." In *Oeuvres complètes de Voltaire.* Vol. 10. Paris, 1877 [1737].

——. "Le mondain." In *Oeuvres complètes de Voltaire.* Vol. 10. Paris, 1877 [1736].

——. *Philosophical Letters.* Translated by Ernest Dilworth. Indianapolis, 1961 [1734].

Voyo de Rigny. *Établissement d'un corps national et militaire d'agriculture.* N.p., 1789.

Young, Arthur. *Travels in France during the Years 1787, 1788 and 1789.* Edited by C. Maxwell. Cambridge, 1950.

——. *Voyage en France, pendant les années 1787, 1788, 1789, 1790, par Arthur Young, traduit de l'anglais, par F. S., avec des notes et des observations par M. de Casaux.* 3 vols. Paris, Year II.

Secondary Sources

Adams, Christine. "Defining État in Eighteenth-Century France: The Lamothe Family of Bordeaux." *Journal of Family History* 17, no. 1 (1992): 25–45.

——. *A Taste for Comfort and Status: A Bourgeois Family in Eighteenth-Century France.* University Park, PA, 2000.

Adams, Leonard. *Coyer and the Enlightenment.* Banbury, Oxfordshire, 1974.

Aftalion, Florin. *The French Revolution: An Economic Interpretation.* Translated by Martin Thom. Cambridge, 1990.

Airiau, Jean. *L'opposition aux physiocrates à la fin de l'ancien régime.* Paris, 1965.

Akkerman, Tjitske. *Women's Vices, Public Benefits: Women and Commerce in the French Enlightenment.* Amsterdam, 1992.

Albaum, Martin. "The Moral Defenses of the Physiocrats' Laissez-Faire." *Journal of the History of Ideas* 16, no. 2 (1955): 179–97.

Aldrich, Robert. "Late-Comer or Early-Starter? New Views on French Economic History." *Journal of European Economic History* 16, no. 1 (1987): 89–100.

Alexander, R. S. "Restoration Republicanism Reconsidered." *French History* 8, no. 4 (1994): 442–69.

Allison, John M. S. *Lamoignon de Malesherbes: Defender and Reformer of the French Monarchy, 1721–1794.* New Haven, 1938.

Anderson, Gordon K. "Old Nobles and Noblesse d'Empire, 1814–1830: In Search of a Conservative Interest in Post-Revolutionary France." *French History* 8, no. 2 (1994): 149–66.

Anderson, M. S. *The War of the Austrian Succession, 1740–1748.* London, 1995.

Andrews, Richard Mowery. "Social Structures, Political Elites, and Ideology in Revolutionary Paris, 1792–94: A Critical Evaluation of Albert Soboul's *Les sans-culottes parisiens en l'an II.*" *Journal of Social History* 19, no. 1 (1985): 71–112.

Antoine, Michel. *Le conseil du roi sous le règne de Louis XV.* Geneva, 1970.

Apostolidès, Jean-Marie. *Le roi-machine: Spectacle et politique au temps de Louis XIV.* Paris, 1981.

Appleby, Joyce. *Capitalism and a New Social Order: The Republican Vision of the 1790s.* New York, 1984.

——. *Economic Thought and Ideology in Seventeenth-Century England.* Princeton, 1978.

Azimi, Vida. *Un modèle administratif de l'ancien régime: Les commis de la Ferme générale et de la Régie générale des aides.* Paris, 1987.

Baczko, Bronislaw. *Ending the Terror: The French Revolution after Robespierre.* Translated by Michel Petheram. Cambridge, 1994.

Bailey, Colin B. *Patriotic Taste: Collecting Modern Art in Pre-Revolutionary Paris.* New Haven, 2002.

Baker, Keith Michael. *Condorcet: From Natural Philosophy to Social Mathematics.* Chicago, 1975.

——. *Inventing the French Revolution: Essays on French Political Culture in the Eighteenth Century.* Cambridge, 1990.

——. "Politics and Social Science in Eighteenth-Century France: The Société de 1789." In *French Government and Society, 1500–1850: Essays in Memory of Alfred Cobban,* edited by J. F. Bosher. London, 1973.

——. "Transformations of Classical Republicanism in Eighteenth-Century France." *Journal of Modern History* 73, no. 1 (2001): 32–53.

Baker, Keith Michael, François Furet, Colin Lucas, and Mona Ozouf, eds. *The French Revolution and the Creation of Modern Political Culture.* 4 vols. Oxford, 1987–94.

Balcou, Jean. *Fréron contre les philosophes.* Paris, 1975.

Barber, Elinor. *The Bourgeoisie in Eighteenth-Century France.* Princeton, 1955.

Behrens, C. B. A. *The Ancien Régime.* New York, 1989.

Bell, David A. *The Cult of the Nation in France: Inventing Nationalism, 1680–1800.* Cambridge, MA, 2001.

——. *Lawyers and Citizens: The Making of a Political Elite in Old Regime France.* Oxford, 1994.

——. "The 'Public Sphere,' the State, and the World of Law in Eighteenth-Century France." *French Historical Studies* 17, no. 4 (1992): 912–34.

Bénétruy, J. *L'atelier de Mirabeau: Quatre proscrits genevois dans la tourmente révolutionnaire.* Geneva, 1962.

Benoît, A. *L'économiste Arthur Young. Devaux-Panpan. Le fédéré Lazowski.* Vol. 3 of *Lunéville et ses environs.* Lunéville, 1879.

Berg, Maxine, and Helen Clifford, eds. *Consumers and Luxury: Consumer Culture in Europe 1650–1850.* Manchester, 1999.

Berg, Maxine, and Elizabeth Eger, eds. *Luxury in the Eighteenth Century: Debates, Desires and Delectable Goods.* New York, 2003.

Bergasse, Jean-Denis. *D'un rêve de réformation à une considération européenne: MM. les députés Bergasse (XVIIIe–XIXe siècles).* Cessenon, 1990.

Bergeron, Louis. *France under Napoleon.* Translated by R. R. Palmer. Princeton, 1981.

——, Guy Chaussinand-Nogaret, and Robert Forster. "Les notables du «Grand Empire» en 1810." *Annales: E.S.C.* 26, no. 5 (1971): 1052–75.

Berkvens-Stevelinck, Christiane. *Prosper Marchand, la vie et l'oeuvre (1678–1756).* Leiden, 1987.

Berlanstein, Lenard R. *The Barristers of Toulouse in the Eighteenth Century (1740–1793).* Baltimore, 1975.

Bermingham, Ann, and John Brewer, eds. *The Consumption of Culture, 1600–1800: Image, Object, Text.* New York, 1995.

Berry, Christopher J. *The Idea of Luxury: A Conceptual and Historical Investigation.* Cambridge, 1994.

Bien, David. "The Army in the French Enlightenment: Reform, Reaction and Revolution." *Past and Present* 85 (1979): 68–98.

——. "Manufacturing Nobles: The Chancelleries in France to 1789." *Journal of Modern History* 61, no. 3 (1989): 445–86.

——. "Offices, Corps, and a System of State Credit: The Uses of Privilege under the Ancien Régime." In *The Political Culture of the Old Regime.* Vol. 1 of *The French Revolution and the Creation of Modern Political Culture,* edited by Keith Michael Baker. Oxford, 1987.

——. "Old Regime Origins of Democratic Liberty." In *The French Idea of Freedom: The Old Regime and the Declaration of Rights of 1789,* edited by Dale Van Kley. Stanford, 1994.

——. "Property in Office under the Old Regime: The Case of the Stockbrokers." In *Early Modern Conceptions of Property,* edited by John Brewer and Susan Staves. London, 1995.

Blaufarb, Rafe. "The Ancien Régime Origins of Napoleonic Social Reconstruction." *French History* 14, no. 4 (2000): 408–23.

——. *The French Army, 1750–1820: Careers, Talent, Merit.* Manchester, 2002.

——. "Nobles, Aristocrats, and the Origins of the French Revolution." In *Tocqueville and Beyond: Essays on the Old Regime in Honor of David D. Bien,* edited by Robert M. Schwartz and Robert A. Schneider. Newark, DE, 2003.

——. "The Social Contours of Meritocracy in the Napoleonic Officer Corps." In *Taking Liberties: Problems of a New Order from the French Revolution to Napoleon,* edited by Howard G. Brown and Judith A. Miller. Manchester, 2002.

Bloch, Marc. *Strange Defeat: A Statement of Evidence Written in 1940.* Translated by Gerard Hopkins. New York, 1999 [1948].

Block, Fred. "The Roles of the State in the Economy." In *The Handbook of Economic Sociology,* edited by Neil J. Smelser and Richard Swedberg. Princeton, 1994.

Bluche, François. *Les magistrats du Parlement de Paris au XVIIIe siècle (1715–1771).* Paris, 1960.

——. *La noblesse française au XVIIIe siècle.* Paris, 1995 [1973].

Blum, Carol. *Strength in Numbers: Population, Reproduction, and Power in Eighteenth-Century France.* Baltimore, 2002.

Bock, Gisela, Quentin Skinner, and Maurizio Viroli, eds. *Machiavelli and Republicanism*. Cambridge, 1990.

Bonnel, Roland Guy. *Éthique et esthétique du retour à la campagne au XVIIIe siècle: L'oeuvre littéraire et utopique de Lezay-Marnésia, 1735–1800*. New York, 1995.

Bonney, Richard, ed. *Economic Systems and State Finance*. Oxford, 1995.

———. "What's New about the New French Fiscal History?" *Journal of Modern History* 70, no. 3 (1998): 639–67.

Bosher, J. F. *French Finances, 1770–1795: From Business to Bureaucracy*. Cambridge, 1970.

———. *The Single Duty Project: A Study of the Movement for a French Customs Union in the Eighteenth Century*. London, 1964.

Bossenga, Gail. *The Politics of Privilege: Old Regime and Revolution in Lille*. Cambridge, 1991.

Bouchard, Marcel. *L'Académie de Dijon et le premier discours de Rousseau*. Paris, 1950.

Bouchary, Jean. *Les manieurs d'argent à Paris à la fin du XVIIIe siècle*. 3 vols. Paris, 1939–43.

Boulaine, Jean. *Histoire de l'agronomie en France*. Paris, 1992.

Bourde, André J. *Agronomie et agronomes en France au XVIIIe siècle*. 3 vols. Paris, 1967.

———. *The Influence of England on the French Agronomes, 1750–1789*. Cambridge, 1953.

Brailsford, H. N. *Voltaire*. London, 1963.

Braudel, Fernand, and Ernest Labrousse, eds. *Des dernier temps de l'âge seigneurial aux préludes de l'âge industriel (1660–1789)*. Vol. 2 of *Histoire économique et sociale de la France*. Paris, 1970.

Breton, Yves, and Michel Lutfalla, eds. *L'économie politique en France au XIXe siècle*. Paris, 1991.

Brewer, John. *The Sinews of Power: War, Money, and the English State, 1688–1783*. Cambridge, MA, 1988.

Brezis, Elise S., and François Crouzet. "The Role of Assignats during the French Revolution: An Evil or a Rescuer?" *Journal of European Economic History* 24, no. 1 (1995): 7–40.

Brissenden, R. F. *Virtue in Distress: Studies in the Novel of Sentiment from Richardson to Sade*. London, 1974.

Brocard, Lucien. *Les doctrines économiques et sociales du marquis de Mirabeau*. Paris, 1902.

Burke, Peter. *The Fabrication of Louis XIV*. New Haven, 1992.

Burrows, Simon. "A Literary Low-Life Reassessed: Charles Théveneau de Morande in London, 1769–1791." *Eighteenth-Century Life* 22, no. 1 (1998): 76–94.

Burtt, Shelley. *Virtue Transformed: Political Argument in England, 1688–1740*. Cambridge, 1992.

Butel, Paul. *L'économie française au XVIIIe siècle*. Paris, 1993.

Butler, Geoffrey. *Studies in Statecraft*. London, 1970.

Butler, Rohan. *Father and Son, 1719–1754*. Vol. 1 of *Choiseul*. Oxford, 1980.

Callaghan, William J. *Honor, Commerce, and Industry in Eighteenth-Century Spain*. Boston, 1972.

Cameron, Rondo, and Charles E. Freedeman. "French Economic Growth: A Radical Revision." *Social Science History* 7, no. 1 (1983): 3–30.

Campbell, Colin. *The Romantic Ethic and the Spirit of Modern Consumerism*. Oxford, 1987.

Carcassonne, Élie. *Montesquieu et le problème de la constitution française au XVIIIe siècle*. Paris, 1927.

Carpenter, Kenneth E. *The Economic Bestsellers before 1850: A Catalogue of an Exhi-*

bition Prepared for the History of Economics Society Meeting, May 21–24, 1975, at Baker Library. Cambridge, MA, 1975.

Carré, Henri. *La marquise de Pompadour: Le règne d'une favorite.* Paris, 1937.

——. *La noblesse française et l'opinion publique au XVIIIe siècle.* Geneva, 1977 [1920].

Cars, Jean des. *Malesherbes: Gentilhomme des lumières.* Paris, 1994.

Cavanaugh, Gerald J. "Turgot: The Rejection of Enlightened Despotism." *French Historical Studies* 6, no. 1 (1969): 31–58.

Chapman, Stanley D., and Serge Chassagne. *European Textile Printers in the Eighteenth Century: A Study of Peel and Oberkampf.* London, 1981.

Charles, Loïc. "L'économie politique française et le politique dans la deuxième moitié du XVIIIe siècle." In *Histoire du libéralisme en Europe,* edited by Philippe Nemo and Jean Petitot. Paris, 2002.

——. "French Cultural Politics and the Dissemination of Hume's Political Discourses on the Continent (1750–1770)." In *Essays on David Hume's Political Economy,* edited by Margaret Schabas and Carl Wennerlind. London, 2007.

Chartier, Roger. *The Cultural Origins of the French Revolution.* Translated by Lydia G. Cochrane. Durham, 1991.

Chaussinand-Nogaret, Guy. *Choiseul (1719–1785): Naissance de la gauche.* Perrin, 1998.

——. *Les financiers de Languedoc au XVIIIe siècle.* Paris, 1970.

——. *The French Nobility in the Eighteenth Century: From Feudalism to Enlightenment.* Translated by William Doyle. Cambridge, 1985.

——. *Gens de finance au XVIIIe siècle.* Paris, 1972.

Cheney, Paul B. "Les économistes français et l'image de l'Amérique: L'essor du commerce transatlantique et l'effondrement du gouvernement féodal." *Dix-huitième siècle* 33 (2001): 231–45.

——. "The History and Science of Commerce in the Century of Enlightenment: France 1713–1789." Ph.D. diss., Columbia University, 2002.

Cherel, Albert. *Fénelon au XVIIIe siècle en France (1715–1820).* Geneva, 1970 [1917].

Childs, Nick. "New Light on the 'Entresol,' 1724–1731: The Marquis de Balleroy's 'Histoire Politique de l'Europe.'" *French History* 4, no. 1 (1990): 77–109.

Claeys, Gregory. "The French Revolution Debate and British Political Thought." *History of Political Thought* 11, no. 1 (1990): 59–80.

Clark, Henry C. "Commerce, Sociability, and the Public Sphere: Morellet vs. Pluquet on Luxury." *Eighteenth-Century Life* 22, no. 2 (1998): 83–103.

——. "Commerce, the Virtues, and the Public Sphere in Early Seventeenth-Century France." *French Historical Studies* 21, no. 3 (1998): 415–40.

Clark, John G. *La Rochelle and the Atlantic Economy during the Eighteenth Century.* Baltimore, 1981.

Cobban, Alfred. *The Social Interpretation of the French Revolution.* Cambridge, 1964.

Cole, Charles Woolsey. *Colbert and a Century of French Mercantilism.* 2 vols. Hamden, CT, 1964.

Coleman, D. C., ed. *Revisions in Mercantilism.* London, 1969.

Colley, Linda. *Britons: Forging the Nation, 1707–1837.* London, 1992.

Comité pour l'histoire économique et financière de la France. *État, finances et économie pendant la Révolution française: Colloque tenu à Bercy les 12, 13, 14 octobre 1989.* Paris, 1991.

Conlon, Pierre M. *Le siècle des lumières: Bibliographie chronologique.* 18 vols. Paris, 1983–98.

Coquery, Natacha. *L'hôtel aristocratique: Le marché du luxe à Paris au XVIIIe siècle.* Paris, 1998.

——. "The Language of Success: Marketing and Distributing Semi-Luxury Goods in Eighteenth-Century Paris." *Journal of Design History* 17, no. 1 (2004): 71–89.

Cordey, Jean. *Inventaire des biens de Madame de Pompadour rédigé après son décès.* Paris, 1939.

Cousin, Jean. *L'Académie des sciences, belles-lettres et arts de Besançon.* Besançon, 1954.

Crouzet, François. "Bordeaux: An Eighteenth-Century Wirtschaftswunder?" In *Britain, France, and International Commerce: From Louis XIV to Victoria*, edited by François Crouzet. Aldershot, 1996.

——. "England and France in the Eighteenth Century: A Comparative Analysis of Two Economic Growths." In *The Causes of the Industrial Revolution in England*, edited by R. M. Hartwell. London, 1967.

——. *La grande inflation: La monnaie en France de Louis XVI à Napoléon.* Paris, 1993.

——. "Wars, Blockade, and Economic Change in Europe, 1792–1815." *Journal of Economic History* 24, no. 4 (1964): 567–88.

Crow, Thomas E. *Painters and Public Life in Eighteenth-Century Paris.* New Haven, 1985.

Cuche, François-Xavier. *Une pensée sociale catholique: Fleury, La Bruyère, Fénelon.* Paris, 1991.

Cullen, Louis M. "History, Economic Crises, and Revolution: Understanding Eighteenth-Century France." *Economic History Review* 46, no. 4 (1993): 635–57.

——. "Lüthy's La Banque Protestante: A Reassessment." *Bulletin du Centre d'histoire des espaces atlantiques* 5 (1990): 229–63.

Daire, Eugène. *Physiocrates: Quesnay, Dupont de Nemours, Mercier de la Rivière, l'abbé Baudeau, Le Trosne.* Geneva, 1971 [1846].

Dakin, Douglas. *Turgot and the Ancien Régime in France.* New York, 1965 [1939].

Daniel, Jean. *La Légion d'honneur.* Paris, 1957.

Darnton, Robert. "The Brissot Dossier," *French Historical Studies* 17, no. 1 (1991): 191–208.

——. *The Forbidden Best-Sellers of Pre-Revolutionary France.* New York, 1995.

——. *The Great Cat Massacre and Other Episodes in French Cultural History.* New York, 1984.

——. *The Literary Underground of the Old Regime.* Cambridge, MA, 1982.

Davis, James Herbert, Jr. *Fénelon.* Boston, 1979.

Dejoint, Georges. *La politique économique du Directoire.* Paris, 1951.

Denby, David J. *Sentimental Narrative and the Social Order in France, 1760–1820.* Cambridge, 1994.

Dent, Julian. *Crisis in Finance: Crown, Financiers, and Society in Seventeenth-Century France.* New York, 1973.

Dessert, Daniel. *Argent, pouvoir et société au Grand Siècle.* Paris, 1984.

Dewald, Jonathan. *Pont-St-Pierre, 1398–1789: Lordship, Community, and Capitalism in Early Modern France.* Berkeley, 1987.

Deyon, Pierre, and Philippe Guignet. "The Royal Manufactures and Economic and Technological Progress in France before the Industrial Revolution." *Journal of European Economic History* 9, no. 3 (1980): 611–32.

Dioguardi, Gianfranco. *Ange Goudar contre l'ancien régime. Suivi de Le testament politique de Louis Mandrin.* Translated by Annie Oliver. Castelnau-le-Lez, 1994.

Dorigny, Marcel. "Les causes de la Révolution selon Roederer: Une interprétation 'matérialiste' de la révolution bourgeoise." *Annales historiques de la Révolution française* 51 (1979): 330–32.

——. "Les Girondins et le droit de propriété." *Bulletin d'histoire économique et sociale de la Révolution française* (1980–81): 15–31.

Doyle, William. *Origins of the French Revolution.* 3rd ed. Oxford, 1999.

——. *Oxford History of the French Revolution.* Oxford, 1989.

——. *The Parlement of Bordeaux and the End of the Old Regime, 1771–1790*. New York, 1974.

——. *Venality: The Sale of Offices in Eighteenth-Century France*. Oxford, 1996.

——. "Was There an Aristocratic Reaction in Pre-Revolutionary France?" In *French Society and the Revolution,* edited by Douglas Johnson. Cambridge, 1976.

Dreyfus, Ferdinand. *L'assistance sous la Législative et la Convention (1791–1795).* Paris, 1905.

Drouet d'Aubigny, Pierre. *La doctrine économique de Boësnier de l'Orme d'après son ouvrage "De l'esprit du gouvernement économique."* Paris, 1908.

Du Boff, Richard B. "Economic Thought in Revolutionary France, 1789–1792: The Question of Poverty and Unemployment." *French Historical Studies* 4, no. 4 (1966): 434–51.

Dubois, Laurent. *Avengers of the New World: The Story of the Haitian Revolution.* Cambridge, MA, 2004.

Duma, Jean. *Les Bourbon-Penthièvre (1678–1793): Une nébuleuse aristocratique au XVIIIe siècle.* Paris, 1995.

Dumont, Louis. *From Mandeville to Marx: The Genesis and Triumph of Economic Ideology.* Chicago, 1977.

Dupâquier, Jacques. *De la Renaissance à 1789.* Vol. 2 of *Histoire de la population française.* Paris, 1988.

Durand, Yves. *Les fermiers généraux au XVIIIe siècle.* Paris, 1971.

——. *Finance et mécénat: Les fermiers généraux au XVIIIe siècle.* Paris, 1976.

Duval, Louis. *Un gentilhomme cultivateur au XVIIIe siècle: Samuel de Frotté de La Rimblière, membre de la Société royale d'agriculture d'Alençon, son livre de compte.* Alençon, 1908.

Dziembowski, Edmond. "Les débuts d'un publiciste au service de la monarchie: L'activité littéraire de Jacob-Nicolas Moreau pendant la guerre." *Revue d'histoire diplomatique* 4 (1995): 305–22.

——. *Un nouveau patriotisme français, 1750–1770: La France face à la puissance anglaise à l'époque de la guerre de Sept Ans.* Oxford, 1998.

Echeverria, Durand. *The Maupeou Revolution: A Study in the History of Libertarianism. France, 1770–1774.* Baton Rouge, 1985.

Edelstein, Melvin Allen. *La feuille villageoise: Communication et modernisation dans les régions rurales pendant la Révolution.* Paris, 1977.

Egret, Jean. *The French Prerevolution, 1787–1788.* Translated by Wesley D. Camp. Chicago, 1977.

——. *Louis XV et l'opposition parlementaire, 1715–1774.* Paris, 1970.

Faccarello, Gilbert. *Aux origines de l'économie politique libérale: Pierre de Boisguilbert.* Paris, 1986.

——. *Studies in the History of French Political Economy: From Bodin to Walras.* London, 1998.

Faccarello, Gilbert, and Philippe Steiner eds. *La pensée économique pendant la Révolution française.* Grenoble, 1990.

Fairchilds, Cissie. "Fashion and Freedom in the French Revolution." *Continuity and Change,* 15, no. 3 (2000): 1–15.

——. "The Production and Marketing of Populuxe Goods in Eighteenth-Century Paris." *In Consumption and the World of Goods,* edited by John Brewer and Roy Porter. London, 1993.

Farge, Arlette. *Subversive Words: Public Opinion in Eighteenth-Century France.* University Park, PA, 1995.

Faure, Edgar. *La banqueroute de Law, 17 juillet 1720.* Paris, 1977.

——. *La disgrâce de Turgot.* Paris, 1961.

Félix, Joël. *Finances et politiques au siècle des lumières: Le ministère L'Averdy, 1763–1768*. Paris, 1999.

Fitzsimmons, Michael P. "New Light on the Aristocratic Reaction in France." *French History* 10, no. 4 (1996): 418–31.

Fleury, Gabriel. *François Véron de Fortbonnais: Sa famille, sa vie, ses actes, ses oeuvres, 1722–1800*. Mamers, 1915.

Forestié Neveu, E. *Notice biographique: Le comte de Sainte-Foy, chevalier d'Arcq, fils naturel du comte de Toulouse*. N.p. 1878.

Forrest, Alan. *The French Revolution and the Poor*. New York, 1981.

Forster, Robert. "The French Revolution and the 'New' Elite, 1800–1850." In *The American and European Revolutions, 1776–1848: Sociopolitical and Ideological Aspects*, edited by Jaroslaw Pelenski. Iowa City, 1980.

——. *The House of Saulx-Tavanes: Versailles and Burgundy, 1700–1830*. Baltimore, 1971.

——. *Merchants, Landlords, Magistrates: The Depont Family in Eighteenth-Century France*. Baltimore, 1980.

——. *The Nobility of Toulouse in the Eighteenth Century: A Social and Economic Study*. Baltimore, 1971 [1960].

——. "The Provincial Noble: A Reappraisal." *American Historical Review* 68, no. 3 (1963): 681–91.

Foster, Charles A. "Honoring Commerce and Industry in 18th-Century France: A Case Study of Changes in Traditional Social Functions." Ph.D. diss., Harvard University, 1950.

Fox-Genovese, Elizabeth. *The Origins of Physiocracy: Economic Revolution and Social Order in Eighteenth-Century France*. Ithaca, 1976.

Furet, François. *Interpreting the French Revolution*. Translated by Elborg Forster. Cambridge, 1981.

Furet, François, and Mona Ozouf, eds. *Critical Dictionary of the French Revolution*. Cambridge, MA, 1989.

Gaigneux, Georges. *Lorient et la Compagnie des Indes*. Lorient, 1957.

Galliani, Renato. *Rousseau, le luxe et l'idéologie nobiliaire: Étude socio-historique*. Oxford, 1989.

Garrioch, David. *The Formation of the Parisian Bourgeoisie, 1690–1830*. Cambridge, MA, 1996.

Gauthier, Florence, and Guy-Robert Ikni, eds. *La guerre du blé au XVIIIe siècle: La critique populaire contre le libéralisme économique au XVIIIe siècle*. Paris, 1988.

Gay, Peter. *Voltaire's Politics: The Poet as Realist*. New York, 1965.

Gayot, Gérard, and Jean-Pierre Hirsch, eds. *La Révolution française et le développement du capitalisme: Acte du colloque de Lille, 19–21 novembre 1987*. Lille, 1989.

Geiger, Reed G. *Planning the French Canals: Bureaucracy, Politics, and Enterprise under the Restoration*. Newark, DE, 1994.

Geison, Gerald L. *Professions and the French State, 1700–1900*. Philadelphia, 1984.

Gendron, François. *The Gilded Youth of Thermidor*. Translated by James Cookson. Montreal, 1993.

Gidel, Gilbert. *La politique de Fénelon*. Geneva, 1971 [1906].

Godechot, Jacques. *The Counter-Revolution: Doctrine and Action, 1789–1804*. New York, 1971.

Goodman, Dena. *The Republic of Letters: A Cultural History of the French Enlightenment*. Ithaca, 1994.

Gordon, Daniel. *Citizens without Sovereignty: Equality and Sociability in French Thought, 1670–1789*. Princeton, 1994.

Gottschalk, Louis R. "Communism during the French Revolution, 1789–1793." *Political Science Quarterly* 40, no. 3 (1925): 438–50.

Goubert, Pierre. *The Ancien Régime: French Society, 1600–1750.* Translated by Steve Cox. New York, 1973.

Gouda, Frances. *Poverty and Political Culture: The Rhetoric of Social Welfare in the Netherlands and France, 1815–1854.* Lanham, MD, 1995.

Grantham, George. "The French Cliometric Revolution: A Survey of Cliometric Contributions to French Economic History." *European Review of Economic History* 1 (1997): 353–405.

Green, Frederick Charles. *Eighteenth-Century France: Six Essays.* London, 1929.

Greenfeld, Liah. *Nationalism: Five Roads to Modernity.* Cambridge, MA, 1992.

Gross, Jean-Pierre. *Fair Shares for All: Jacobin Egalitarianism in Practice.* Cambridge, 1997.

——. "L'idée de la pauvreté dans la pensée sociale des Jacobins." *Annales historiques de la Révolution française* 248 (1982): 196–223.

——. "Progressive Taxation and Social Justice in Eighteenth-Century France." *Past and Present* 140 (1993): 79–126.

Gruder, Vivian R. "A Mutation in Elite Political Culture: The French Notables and the Defense of Property and Participation, 1787." *Journal of Modern History* 56, no. 4 (1984): 598–634.

——. *The Royal Provincial Intendants: A Governing Elite in Eighteenth-Century France.* Ithaca, 1968.

Gueslin, André. *L'invention de l'économie sociale: Le XIXe siècle français.* Paris, 1987.

Habermas, Jürgen. *The Structural Transformation of the Public Sphere: An Inquiry into a Category of Bourgeois Society.* Translated by Thomas Burger. Cambridge, MA, 1989.

Hamowy, Ronald. "Cato's Letters, John Locke, and the Republican Paradigm." *History of Political Thought* 11, no. 2 (1990): 273–94.

——. *The Scottish Enlightenment and the Theory of Spontaneous Order.* Carbondale, IL, 1987.

Hardman, John. *Louis XVI: The Silent King.* London, 2000.

Harris, Robert D. "French Finances and the American War, 1777–1783." *Journal of Modern History* 48, no. 2 (1976): 233–58.

——. *Necker: Reform Statesman of the Ancien Régime.* Berkeley, 1979.

Harris, S. E. *The Assignats.* Cambridge, MA, 1930.

Harrison, Carol E. *The Bourgeois Citizen in Nineteenth-Century France: Gender, Sociability, and the Uses of Emulation.* Oxford, 1999.

Harsin, Paul. *Les doctrines monétaires et financières en France du XVIe au XVIIIe siècle.* Paris, 1928.

Haskell, Thomas L., and Richard F. Teichgraeber III, eds. *The Culture of the Market: Historical Essays.* Cambridge, 1993.

Henderson, George D. *Chevalier Ramsay.* London, 1952.

Henry, Gilles. *Mirabeau père: 5 octobre 1715–11 juillet 1789.* Paris, 1989.

Higgs, Henry. *Bibliography of Economics, 1751–1775.* Cambridge, 1935.

Higonnet, Patrice. *Class, Ideology, and the Rights of Nobles during the French Revolution.* Oxford, 1981.

——. *Goodness beyond Virtue: Jacobins during the French Revolution.* Cambridge, MA, 1998.

Hirsch, Jean-Pierre. *Les deux rêves du commerce: Entreprise et institution dans la région lilloise (1780–1860).* Paris, 1991.

——. "Revolutionary France, Cradle of Free Enterprise." *American Historical Review* 94, no. 5 (1989): 1281–9.

Hirschman, Albert O. *The Passions and the Interests: Political Arguments for Capitalism before Its Triumph.* Princeton, 1977.

Hoffman, Philip T. *Growth in a Traditional Society: The French Countryside, 1450–1815*. Princeton, 1996.

Hoffman, Philip T., and Kathryn Norberg, eds. *Fiscal Crises, Liberty, and Representative Government, 1450–1789*. Stanford, 1994.

Hoffman, Philip T., Gilles Postel-Vinay, and Jean-Laurent Rosenthal. "Information and Economic History: How the Credit Market in Old Regime Paris Forces Us to Rethink the Transition to Capitalism." *American Historical Review* 104, no. 1 (1999): 69–94.

Holmes, Stephen. *Benjamin Constant and the Making of Modern Liberalism*. New Haven, 1984.

Hont, Istvan. "The Political Economy of the 'Unnatural and Retrograde' Order: Adam Smith and Natural Liberty." In *Französische Revolution und politische Ökonomie*. Trier, 1989.

Hont, Istvan, and Michael Ignatieff, eds. *Wealth and Virtue: The Shaping of Political Economy in the Scottish Enlightenment*. Cambridge, 1983.

Horne, Thomas A. *The Social Thought of Bernard Mandeville: Virtue and Commerce in Early Eighteenth-Century England*. New York, 1978.

Hudson, David. "The Parlementary Crisis of 1763 in France and Its Consequences." *Canadian Journal of History* 7, no. 2 (1972): 97–117.

Hufton, Olwen H. *The Poor of Eighteenth-Century France, 1750–1789*. Oxford, 1974.

Hulliung, Mark. *The Autocritique of Enlightenment: Rousseau and the Philosophes*. Cambridge, MA, 1994.

Hundert, E. G. *The Enlightenment's Fable: Bernard Mandeville and the Discovery of Society*. Cambridge, 1994.

Hunt, Lynn. *The Family Romance of the French Revolution*. Berkeley, 1992.

——. *Politics, Culture, and Class in the French Revolution*. Berkeley, 1984.

Hutchinson, Terence. *Before Adam Smith: The Emergence of Political Economy, 1662–1776*. Oxford, 1988.

I.N.E.D. *François Quesnay et la physiocratie*. 2 vols. Paris, 1958.

Ives, Robin J. "Political Publicity and Political Economy in Eighteenth-Century France." *French History* 17, no. 1 (2003): 1–18.

Jack, Malcolm. *Corruption and Progress: The Eighteenth-Century Debate*. New York, 1989.

Jacob, Margaret C. *The Radical Enlightenment: Pantheists, Freemasons and Republicans*. London, 1981.

Jardin, André, and André-Jean Tudesq. *Restoration and Reaction, 1815–1848*. Translated by Elborg Forster. Cambridge, 1983.

Jobert, Ambroise. *Magnats polonais et physiocrates français (1767–1774)*. Paris, 1941.

Johnstone, Paul H. "The Rural Socrates." *Journal of the History of Ideas* 5, no. 2 (1944): 151–75.

Jollet, Étienne, ed. *La Font de Saint-Yenne: Oeuvre critique*. Paris, 2001.

Jones, Colin. "Bourgeois Revolution Revivified: 1789 and Social Change." In *Rewriting the French Revolution*, edited by Colin Lucas. Oxford, 1991.

——. "The Great Chain of Buying: Medical Advertisement, the Bourgeois Public Sphere, and the Origins of the French Revolution." *American Historical Review* 101, no. 1 (1996): 13–40.

Jones, Gareth Stedman. *Languages of Class: Studies in English Working Class History, 1832–1982*. Cambridge, 1983.

Jones, Jennifer M. "Repackaging Rousseau: Femininity and Fashion in Old Regime France." *French Historical Studies* 18, no. 4 (1994): 939–67.

——. *Sexing La Mode: Gender, Fashion and Commercial Culture in Old Regime France*. Oxford, 2004.

Jones, Peter M. "The 'Agrarian Law': Schemes for Land Redistribution during the French Revolution." *Past and Present* 133 (1991): 96–133.

Joyce, Patrick, ed. *The Social in Question: New Bearings in History and the Social Sciences*. London, 2002.

Justin, Émile. *Les sociétés royales d'agriculture au XVIIIe siècle (1757–1793)*. Saint-Lô, 1935.

Kafker, Frank A., and Serena L. Kafker. *The Encyclopedists as Individuals: A Biographical Dictionary of the Authors of the Encyclopédie*. Oxford, 1988.

Kaiser, Thomas E. "The Drama of Charles Edward Stuart: Jacobite Propaganda and French Political Protest, 1745–1750." *Eighteenth-Century Studies* 30, no. 4 (1997): 365–81.

——. "Madame de Pompadour and the Theaters of Power." *French Historical Studies* 19, no. 4 (1996): 1025–44.

——. "Money, Despotism, and Public Opinion in Early Eighteenth-Century France: John Law and the Debate on Royal Credit." *Journal of Modern History* 63, no. 1 (1991): 1–28.

——. "Politics and Political Economy in the Thought of the Ideologues." *History of Political Economy* 12, no. 2 (1980): 141–60.

Kaplan, Steven Laurence. *Bread, Politics, and Political Economy in the Reign of Louis XV*. 2 vols. The Hague, 1976.

——. *The Famine Plot Persuasion in Eighteenth-Century France*. Philadelphia, 1982.

——. *La fin des corporations*. Paris, 2001.

Kaplan, Steven Laurence, and Cynthia J. Koepp, eds. *Work in France: Representations, Meaning, Organization, and Practice*. Ithaca, 1986.

Kates, Gary. *The Cercle Social, the Girondins, and the French Revolution*. Princeton, 1985.

Kennedy, Paul. *The Rise and Fall of the Great Powers: Economic Change and Military Conflict from 1500 to 2000*. New York, 1989.

Kennett, Lee. *The French Armies in the Seven Years War: A Study in Military Organization and Administration*. Durham, NC, 1967.

Keohane, Nannerl O. *Philosophy and the State in France: The Renaissance to the Enlightenment*. Princeton, 1980.

Kessler, Amalia D. "Enforcing Virtue: Social Norms and Self-Interest in an Eighteenth-Century Merchant Court." *Law and History Review* 22, no. 1 (2004).

Kuisel, Richard F. *Capitalism and the State in Modern France: Renovation and Economic Management in the Twentieth Century*. Cambridge, 1981.

Kwass, Michael. "Consumption and the World of Ideas: Consumer Revolution and the Moral Economy of the Marquis de Mirabeau." *Eighteenth-Century Studies* 37, no. 2 (2003): 187–213.

——. "A Kingdom of Taxpayers: State Formation, Privilege, and Political Culture in Eighteenth-Century France." *Journal of Modern History* 70, no. 2 (1998): 295–339.

——. "Ordering the World Of Goods: Consumer Revolution and the Classification of Objects in Eighteenth-Century France." *Representations* 82 (2003): 87–116.

——. *Privilege and the Politics of Taxation in Eighteenth-Century France: Liberté, Égalité, Fiscalité*. Cambridge, 2000.

Labatut, Jean-Pierre. "Patriotisme et noblesse sous le regne de Louis XIV." *Revue d'histoire moderne et contemporaine* 29 (1982): 622–34.

Labrosse, Claude. "Réception et communication dans les périodiques littéraires (1750–1760)." In *La diffusion et la lecture des journaux de la langue française sous l'ancien régime: Actes du colloque international, Nimègue, 3–5 juin 1987*. Amsterdam, 1988.

Lacour-Gayet, Robert. *Calonne: Financier, réformateur, contre-révolutionnaire, 1734–1802*. Paris, 1963.

Landes, Joan. *Women and the Public Sphere in the Age of the French Revolution*. Ithaca, 1988.

La Rochefoucauld, J.-D. de, C. Wolikow, and G. Ikni. *Le duc de La Rochefoucauld-*

Liancourt, 1747–1827: De Louis XV à Charles X, un grand seigneur patriote et le mouvement populaire. Paris, 1980.

Larrère, Catherine, ed. *1748, l'année de l'Esprit des lois.* Paris, 1999.

———. *L'invention de l'économie au XVIIIe siècle: Du droit naturel à la physiocratie.* Paris, 1992.

Laugier, Lucien. *Un ministère réformateur sous Louis XV: Le triumvirat (1770–1774).* Paris, 1975.

Lavergne, Léonce de. *Les économistes français du dix-huitième siècle.* Geneva, 1970 [1870].

Lefebvre, Georges. *The Coming of the French Revolution.* Translated by R. R. Palmer. Princeton, 1947.

———. *Questions agraires au temps de la Terreur.* Paris, 1989.

———. "Urban Society in the Orléanais in the Late Eighteenth Century." *Past and Present* 19 (1961): 46–75.

Legohérel, Henri. *Les trésoriers généraux de la Marine, (1517–1788).* Paris, 1965.

Leith, James A. *The Idea of Art as Propaganda in France, 1750–1799: A Study in the History of Ideas.* Toronto, 1965.

Lemay, Edna Hindie. *Dictionnaire des constituants, 1789–1791.* 2 vols. Paris, 1991.

Lepetit, Bernard. "Urbanization in Eighteenth-Century France: A Comment." *Journal of Interdisciplinary History* 23, no. 1 (1992): 73–85.

Le Roy Ladurie, Emmanuel, and Jean-François Fitou. *Saint-Simon, and the Court of Louis XIV.* Translated by Arthur Goldhammer. Chicago, 2001.

Lévy-Bruhl, Henri. "La noblesse de France et le commerce à la fin de l'ancien régime." *Revue d'histoire moderne* 8 (1933): 209–35.

Lewis, Gwynne. *The Advent of Modern Capitalism in France, 1770–1840: The Contribution of Pierre-François Tubeuf.* Oxford, 1993.

———. *The French Revolution: Rethinking the Debate.* London, 1993.

Lichtenberger, André. *Le socialisme et la Révolution française: Études sur les idées socialistes en France de 1789 à 1796.* Paris, 1899.

Linton, Marisa. *The Politics of Virtue in Enlightenment France.* New York, 2001.

Livesey, James. "Agrarian Ideology and Commercial Republicanism in the French Revolution." *Past and Present* 157 (1997): 94–121.

———. *Making Democracy in the French Revolution.* Cambridge, MA, 2001.

Lodge, Eleanor C. *Sully, Colbert, and Turgot: A Chapter in French Economic History.* London, 1970.

Loménie, Louis de. *Les Mirabeau: Nouvelles études sur la société française au XVIIIe siècle.* 3 vols. Paris, 1889.

Longhitano, Gino. "Avant-Propos." *Correspondance entre M. Graslin et M. l'abbé Baudeau sur un des principes fondamentaux de la doctrine des soi-disants philosophes économistes.* Catania, 1988.

———. "Avant-Propos." *François Quesnay, examen de l'examen du livre intitulé Principes sur la liberté du commerce des grains (1768).* Catania, 1988.

———, ed. *Marquis de Mirabeau et François Quesnay, Traité de la monarchie (1757–1759).* Paris, 1999.

Lougee, Carolyn C. *Le Paradis des Femmes: Women, Salons, and Social Stratification in Seventeenth-Century France.* Princeton, 1976.

Lucas, Colin. "Nobles, Bourgeois, and the Origins of the French Revolution." *Past and Present* 60 (1973): 84–126.

———. "Revolutionary Violence, the People, and the Terror." In *The Terror.* Vol. 4 of *The French Revolution and the Creation of Modern Political Culture,* edited by Keith Michael Baker. Oxford, 1994.

Luminais, R.-Marie. *Recherches sur la vie, les doctrines économiques et les travaux de J.-J.-Louis Graslin.* Nantes, 1862.

Lüthy, Herbert. *La banque protestante en France de la révocation de l'Édit de Nantes à la Révolution.* 2 vols. Paris, 1959–61.

Lynn, John A. "Toward an Army of Honor: The Moral Evolution of the French Army, 1789–1815." *French Historical Studies* 16, no. 1 (1989): 152–73.

Lyons, Martyn. "M.-G.-A. Vadier (1736–1828): The Formation of the Jacobin Mentality." *French Historical Studies* 10, no. 1 (1977): 74–100.

Mackrell, J. Q. C. *The Attack on "Feudalism" in Eighteenth-Century France.* Toronto, 1973.

Magnusson, Lars. *Mercantilism: The Shaping of an Economic Language.* London, 1994.

Manning, Catherine. *Fortunes à Faire: The French in Asian Trade, 1718–48.* Aldershot, 1996.

Manuel, Frank E. "The Luddite Movement in France." *Journal of Modern History* 10, no. 2 (1938): 180–211.

Maravall, José Antonio. *Culture of the Baroque: Analysis of a Historical Structure.* Minneapolis, 1986.

Marchand, Jean. *Une amitié internationale au XVIIIe siècle: La Rochefoucauld-Liancourt et ses fils, Maximilien Lazowski et Arthur Young.* Paris, 1947.

Marczewski, Jan. "The Take-Off Hypothesis and French Experience." In *The Economics of Take-Off into Sustained Growth,* edited by W. W. Rostow. London, 1963.

Margairaz, Dominique. "L'économie d'ancien régime comme économie de la circulation." In *La circulation des marchandises dans la France de l'ancien régime,* edited by Denis Woronoff. Paris, 1998.

Marion, Marcel. *Histoire financière de la France depuis 1715.* 6 vols. Paris, 1921.

Markoff, John. *The Abolition of Feudalism: Peasants, Lords, and Legislators in the French Revolution.* University Park, PA, 1996.

Marraud, Mathieu. *La noblesse de Paris au XVIIIe siècle.* Paris, 2000.

Mars, Francis L. "Ange Goudar, cet inconnu (1708–1791): Essai bibliographique sur un aventurier polygraphe du XVIIIe siècle." *Casanova Gleanings* 9 (1966).

Martin, André, and Gérard Walter. *Écrits de la période révolutionnaire, journaux et almanachs.* Vol. 5 of *Catalogue de l'histoire de la Révolution française.* Paris, 1943.

Martin, Angus, Vivienne G. Mylne, and Richard Frautschi. *Bibliographie du genre romanesque français, 1751–1800.* London, 1977.

Mason, H. T., and W. Doyle, eds. *The Impact of the French Revolution on European Consciousness.* Wolfboro, NH, 1989.

Mathias, Peter, and Patrick O'Brien. "Taxation in Britain and France, 1715–1810: A Comparison of the Social and Economic Incidence of Taxes Collected for the Central Governments." *Journal of European Economic History* 5 (1976): 601–50.

Mathiez, Albert. *Un procès de corruption sous la Terreur: L'affaire de la Compagnie des Indes.* New York, 1971.

——. *La vie chère et le mouvement social sous la Terreur.* 2 vols. Paris, 1973.

Matthews, George T. *The Royal General Farms in Eighteenth-Century France.* New York, 1958.

May, Louis-Philippe. *Le Mercier de la Rivière (1719–1801): Aux origines de la science économique.* Paris, 1975.

Maza, Sarah. "Luxury, Morality, and Social Change: Why There Was No Middle-Class Consciousness in Prerevolutionary France." *Journal of Modern History* 69, no. 2 (1997): 199–229.

——. *The Myth of the French Bourgeoisie: An Essay on the Social Imaginary, 1750–1850.* Cambridge, MA, 2003.

——. *Private Lives and Public Affairs: The Causes Célèbres of Prerevolutionary France.* Berkeley, 1993.

——. "The Rose Girl of Salency: Representation of Virtue in Prerevolutionary France." *Eighteenth-Century Studies* 22, no. 3 (1989): 395–412.

McCoy, Drew R. *The Elusive Republic: Political Economy in Jeffersonian America.* Chapel Hill, 1980.

McDonald, Stephen L. "Boisguilbert: A Neglected Precursor of Aggregate Demand Theorists." *Quarterly Journal of Economics,* 68, no. 3 (1954): 401–14.

McKendrick, Neil, John Brewer, and J. H. Plumb. *The Birth of a Consumer Society: The Commercialization of Eighteenth-Century England.* Bloomington, 1985.

McNally, David. *Political Economy and the Rise of Capitalism: A Reinterpretation.* Berkeley, 1988.

McPhee, Peter. "The French Revolution, Peasants, and Capitalism." *American Historical Review* 94, no. 5 (1989): 1265–80.

Medlin, Dorothy. "Thomas Jefferson, André Morellet, and the French Version of *Notes on the State of Virginia.*" *William and Mary Quarterly,* 3rd series, 35, no. 1 (1978): 85–99.

Meek, Ronald L. *The Economics of Physiocracy.* Cambridge, MA, 1963.

———. *Social Science and the Ignoble Savage.* Cambridge, 1976.

Mercier, Alain. *1794, l'abbé Grégoire et la création du Conservatoire national des arts et métiers.* Paris, 1989.

Meyer, Jean. *La noblesse bretonne au XVIIIe siècle.* 2 vols. Paris, 1966.

Meyssonnier, Simone. *La balance et l'horloge: La genèse de la pensée libérale en France au XVIIIe siècle.* Montreuil, 1989.

Miller, Judith A. "Economic Ideologies, 1750–1800: The Creation of Modern Political Economy?" *French Historical Studies* 23, no. 3 (2000): 497–511.

———. *Mastering the Market: The State and the Grain Trade in Northern France, 1700–1860.* Cambridge, 1999.

Minard, Philippe. *La fortune du colbertisme: État et industrie dans la France des lumières.* Paris, 1998.

Mitchell, Julia Post. *St. Jean de Crèvecoeur.* New York, 1916.

Moisson, Édouard. *Dupont de Nemours et la question de la Compagnie des Indes.* New York, 1968 [1918].

Montlaur, Humbert de. *Mirabeau: L'ami des hommes.* Paris, 1992.

Morilhat, Claude. *La prise de conscience du capitalisme: Économie et philosophie chez Turgot.* Paris, 1988.

Morineau, Michel. *Les faux-semblants d'un démarrage économique: Agriculture et démographie en France au XVIIIe siècle.* Paris, 1971.

Morize, André. *L'apologie du luxe au XVIIIe siècle et «Le mondain» de Voltaire: Étude critique sur «Le mondain» et ses sources.* Geneva, 1970 [1909].

Mornet, Daniel. "Les enseignements des bibliothèques privées (1750–1780)." *Revue d'histoire littéraire de la France* 17, no. 3 (1910): 449–96.

———. *Les origines intellectuelles de la Révolution française, 1715–1787.* Lyons, 1989 [1933].

Mousnier, Roland. *La vénalité des offices sous Henri IV et Louis XIII.* Paris, 1971.

Muller, Jerry Z. *The Mind and the Market: Capitalism in Modern European Thought.* New York, 2002.

Murphy, Antoin E. "Le développement des idées économiques en France (1750–1756)." *Revue d'histoire moderne et contemporaine* 33 (1986): 521–541.

———. *John Law: Economic Theorist and Policy Maker.* Oxford, 1997.

———. *Richard Cantillon: Entrepreneur and Economist.* Oxford, 1986.

Murphy, Terence. "Jean Baptiste René Robinet: The Career of a Man of Letters." *Studies on Voltaire and the Eighteenth Century* 150 (1976): 183–250.

Musset, Victor-Donatien de. *Bibliographie agronomique, ou Dictionnaire raisonné des ouvrages sur l'économie rurale et domestique et sur l'art vétérinaire.* Paris, 1991 [1810].

Myers, Milton L. *The Soul of Modern Economic Man: Ideas of Self-Interest, Thomas Hobbes to Adam Smith.* Chicago, 1983.

Neill, Thomas P. "Quesnay and Physiocracy." *Journal of the History of Ideas* 9, no. 2 (1948): 153–73.

Nussbaum, Frederick L. "The Deputies Extraordinary of Commerce and the French Monarchy." *Political Science Quarterly* 48, no. 4 (1933): 534–55.

——. "The Formation of the New East India Company of Calonne." *American Historical Review* 38, no. 3 (1933): 475–97.

——. "The Revolutionary Vergennes and Lafayette versus the Farmers General." *Journal of Modern History* 3, no. 4 (1931): 592–604.

O'Neal, John C. "Rousseau's Theory of Wealth." *History of European Ideas* 7, no. 5 (1986): 453–67.

Ozanam, Denise. *Claude Baudard de Sainte-James: Trésorier général de la marine et brasseur d'affaires (1738–1787)*. Geneva, 1969.

Ozouf, Mona. *L'homme régénéré: Essais sur la Révolution française*. Paris, 1989.

Pagden, Anthony. "The 'Defence of Civilisation' in Eighteenth-Century Social Theory." *History of the Human Sciences* 1, no. 1 (1988): 33–45.

——, ed. *The Languages of Political Theory in Early-Modern Europe*. Cambridge, 1987.

Pardailhé-Galabrun, Annik. *La naissance de l'intime: 3000 foyers parisiens, XVIIe–XVIIIe siècles*. Paris, 1988.

Parker, Geoffrey. *The Military Revolution: Military Innovation and the Rise of the West, 1500–1800*. Cambridge, 1988.

Parker, Harold. *The Cult of Antiquity and the French Revolutionaries: A Study in the Development of the Revolutionary Spirit*. Chicago, 1937.

Perrot, Jean-Claude. *Genèse d'une ville moderne: Caen au XVIIIe siècle*. 2 vols. Paris, 1975.

——. *Une histoire intellectuelle de l'économie politique, XVIIe–XVIIIe siècle*. Paris, 1992.

——. "Nouveautés: L'économie politique et ses livres." In *Le livre triomphant*. Vol. 2 of *Histoire de l'édition française*, edited by Henri-Jean Martin and Roger Chartier. Paris, 1984.

Perrot, Philippe. *Les dessus et les dessous de la bourgeoisie: Une histoire du vêtement au XIX siècle*. Paris, 1981.

Pigeonneau, M. H. *Le Comité d'administration de l'agriculture (1785–1787)*. Orléans, 1881.

Pincus, Steve. "Neither Machiavellian Moment nor Possessive Individualism: Commercial Society and the Defenders of the English Commonwealth." *American Historical Review* 103, no. 3 (1998): 705–36.

Pocock, J. G. A. "Early Modern Capitalism—the Augustan Perception." In *Feudalism, Capitalism and Beyond*, edited by Eugene Kamenka and R. S. Neale. New York, 1975.

——. *The Machiavellian Moment: Florentine Political Thought and the Atlantic Republican Tradition*. Princeton, 1975.

——. "The Political Economy of Burke's Analysis of the French Revolution." *The Historical Journal* 25, no. 2 (1982): 331–49.

——. *Virtue, Commerce, and History: Essays on Political Thought and History, Chiefly in the Eighteenth Century*. Cambridge, 1985.

Polanyi, Karl. *The Great Transformation*. Boston, 1944.

Popkin, Jeremy D. "Conservatism under Napoleon: The Political Writings of Joseph Fiévée." *History of European Ideas* 5, no. 4 (1984): 385–400.

——. "Pamphlet Journalism at the End of the Old Regime." *Eighteenth-Century Studies* 22, no. 3 (1989): 351–67.

Post, John D. "Climatic Variability and the European Mortality Wave of the Early 1740s." *Journal of Interdisciplinary History* 15, no. 1 (1984): 1–30.

Pottinger, David T. *The French Book Trade in the Ancien Régime, 1500–1791*. Cambridge, MA, 1958.

Prévost de Lavaud, Étienne. *Les théories de l'intendant Rouillé d'Orfeuil.* Rochechouart, 1909.

Price, Munro. *Preserving the Monarchy: The comte de Vergennes, 1774–1787.* Cambridge, 1995.

Pris, Claude. *Une grande entreprise française sous l'ancien régime: La manufacture royale des glaces de Saint-Gobain (1665–1830).* 2 vols. New York, 1981.

Procacci, Giovanna. *Gouverner la misère: La question sociale en France (1789–1848).* Paris, 1993.

Pugh, Wilma J. "Calonne's 'New Deal.'" *Journal of Modern History* 11, no. 3 (1939): 289–312.

Rawson, Elizabeth. *The Spartan Tradition in European Thought.* Oxford, 1969.

Reddy, William M. *Money and Liberty in Modern Europe: A Critique of Historical Understanding.* Cambridge, 1987.

——. *The Rise of Market Culture: The Textile Trade and French Society, 1750–1900.* Cambridge, 1984.

Reinhard, Marcel. "Sur l'histoire de la Révolution française. Travaux récents et perspectives." *Annales* 14 (1959): 553–70.

Rétat, Pierre. "Luxe." *Dix-huitième siècle* 26 (1994): 79–88.

Ribeiro, Aileen. *The Art of Dress: Fashion in England and France 1750 to 1820.* New Haven, 1995.

——. *Fashion in the French Revolution.* London, 1988.

Richard, Guy. *Noblesse d'affaires au XVIIIe siècle.* Paris, 1974.

Richardson, Nicholas. *The French Prefectoral Corps, 1814–1830.* Cambridge, 1966.

Riley, James C. "Dutch Investment in France, 1781–1787." *Journal of Economic History* 33, no. 4 (1973): 732–60.

——. *International Government Finance and the Amsterdam Capital Market, 1740–1815.* Cambridge, 1980.

——. *Population Thought in the Age of the Demographic Revolution.* Durham, NC, 1985.

——. *The Seven Years War and the Old Regime in France: The Economic and Financial Toll.* Princeton, 1986.

Ripert, Henri. *Le marquis de Mirabeau (L'ami des hommes): Ses théories politiques et économiques.* Paris, 1901.

Robin, Régine. *La société française en 1789: Semur-en-Auxois.* Paris, 1970.

Roche, Daniel. *The Culture of Clothing: Dress and Fashion in the "Ancien Régime."* Translated by Jean Birrell. Cambridge, 1994.

——. "La Diffusion des lumières. Un exemple: l'Académie de Châlons-sur-Marne." *Annales: E.S.C.* 19 (1964): 887–922.

——. *France in the Enlightenment.* Translated by Arthur Goldhammer. Cambridge, MA, 2000.

——. *A History of Everyday Things: The Birth of Consumption in France, 1600–1800.* Cambridge, 2000.

——. *The People of Paris: An Essay in Popular Culture in the Eighteenth Century.* Berkeley, 1987.

Root, Hilton L. *The Fountain of Privilege: Political Foundations of Markets in Old Regime France and England.* Berkeley, 1996.

Rosanvallon, Pierre. *Le libéralisme économique: Histoire de l'idée de marché.* Paris, 1989.

Rose, R. B. *Gracchus Babeuf: The First Revolutionary Communist.* Stanford, 1978.

——. "The 'Red Scare' of the 1790s: The French Revolution and the Agrarian Law." *Past and Present* 103 (1984): 113–30.

Rosenthal, Jean-Laurent. *The Fruits of Revolution: Property Rights, Litigation, and French Agriculture, 1700–1860.* Cambridge, 1992.

Ross, Ellen. "The Debate on Luxury in Eighteenth-Century France: A Study in the Language of Opposition to Change." Ph.D. diss., University of Chicago, 1975.

Rostand, André. "La Société d'agriculture de la généralité de Caen (1762–1790)." *Bulletin de la Société des antiquaires de Normandie* 37 (1926–27): 293–342.

Rothkrug, Lionel. *The Opposition to Louis XIV: The Political and Social Origins of the French Enlightenment.* Princeton, 1965.

Rothschild, Emma. *Economic Sentiments: Adam Smith, Condorcet, and the Enlightenment.* Cambridge, MA, 2001.

Ruggiu, François-Joseph. *Les élites et les villes moyennes en France et en Angleterre (XVIIe–XVIIIe siècles).* Paris, 1997.

Rupin, Charles. *Les idées économiques de Sully et leurs applications à l'agriculture aux finances et à l'industrie.* New York, 1970 [1907].

Saisselin, Rémy G. *The Enlightenment against the Baroque: Economics and Aesthetics in the Eighteenth Century.* Berkeley, 1992.

Sargentson, Carolyn. *Merchants and Luxury Markets: The Marchands Merciers of Eighteenth-Century Paris.* London, 1996.

Sauvy, Alfred. *Deux techniciens précurseurs de Malthus: Boesnier de l'Orme et Auxiron.* Paris, 1956.

——, ed. *Économie et population: Les doctrines françaises avant 1800.* Paris, 1956.

Schaeper, Thomas J. *The French Council of Commerce, 1700–1715: A Study of Mercantilism after Colbert.* Columbus, 1983.

Schama, Simon. *Citizens: A Chronicle of the French Revolution.* New York, 1989.

Schelle, Gustave. *Du Pont de Nemours et l'école physiocratique.* Geneva, 1971 [1888].

——. *Vincent de Gournay.* Geneva, 1984 [1897].

Scott, Katie. *The Rococo Interior: Decoration and Social Spaces in Early Eighteenth-Century Paris.* New Haven, 1995.

Scoville, Warren C. *Capitalism and French Glassmaking, 1640–1789.* Berkeley, 1950.

Sédillot, René. *Le coût de la Révolution française.* Paris, 1987.

See, Henri. "The Ship-Owners of Saint Malo in the Eighteenth Century." *Bulletin of the Business Historical Society* 2, no. 4 (1928): 3–9.

Sekora, John. *Luxury: The Concept in Western Thought, Eden to Smollett.* Baltimore, 1977.

Servet, Jean-Michel, ed. *Idées économiques sous la Révolution, 1789–1794.* Lyons, 1989.

Sewell, William H. Jr. *A Rhetoric of Bourgeois Revolution: The Abbé Sieyes and What Is the Third Estate?* Durham, 1994.

——. *Work and Revolution in France: The Language of Labor from the Old Regime to 1848.* Cambridge, 1980.

Sgard, Jean, ed. *Dictionnaire des journaux, 1660–1789.* Paris, 1991.

——. "L'échelle des revenus." *Dix-huitième siècle* 14 (1982): 425–33.

Shapiro, Gilbert, and John Markoff. *Revolutionary Demands: A Content Analysis of the Cahiers de Doléances of 1789.* Stanford, 1998.

Shovlin, John. "The Cultural Politics of Luxury in Eighteenth-Century France." *French Historical Studies* 23, no. 4 (2000): 673–701.

——. "Emulation in Eighteenth-Century French Economic Thought." *Eighteenth-Century Studies* 36, no. 2 (2003): 224–30.

——. "Towards a Reinterpretation of Revolutionary Anti-Nobilism: The Political Economy of Honor in the Old Regime." *Journal of Modern History* 72, no. 1 (2000): 35–66.

Sibalis, Michael David. "Corporatism after the Corporations: The Debate on Restoring the Guilds under Napoleon I and the Restoration." *French Historical Studies* 15, no. 4 (1988): 718–30.

Skocpol, Theda. *States and Social Revolutions: A Comparative Analysis of France, Russia, and China.* Cambridge, 1979.

Smith, David Kammerling. "Structuring Politics in Early Eighteenth-Century France: The Political Innovations of the French Council of Commerce." *Journal of Modern History* 74, no. 3 (2002): 490–537.

Smith, Jay M. "Between Discourse and Experience: Agency and Ideas in the French Pre-Revolution." *History and Theory* 40, no. 4 (2001): 116–42.

———. *Culture of Merit: Nobility, Royal Service, and the Making of Absolute Monarchy in France, 1600–1789.* Ann Arbor, 1996.

———. "Social Categories, the Language of Patriotism, and the Origins of the French Revolution: The Debate over *Noblesse Commerçante.*" *Journal of Modern History* 72, no. 2 (2000): 339–74.

Soboul, Albert. *The Sans-Culottes: The Popular Movement and Revolutionary Government, 1793–1794.* Translated by Rémy Inglis Hall. Princeton, NJ, 1980 [1968].

Sonenscher, Michael. "The Nation's Debt and the Birth of the Modern Republic: The French Fiscal Deficit and the Politics of the Revolution of 1789." *History of Political Thought* 18, no. 1–2 (1997): 64–103, 267–325.

———. *Work and Wages: Natural Law, Politics, and the Eighteenth-Century French Trades.* Cambridge, 1989.

Spary, Emma C. *Utopia's Garden: French Natural History from Old Regime to Revolution.* Chicago, 2000.

Spengler, Joseph J. *French Predecessors of Malthus: A Study in Eighteenth-Century Wage and Population Theory.* Durham, NC, 1942.

Staum, Martin S. "The Class of Moral and Political Sciences, 1795–1803." *French Historical Studies* 11, no. 3 (1980): 371–97.

———. "The Institute Economists: From Physiocracy to Entrepreneurial Capitalism." *History of Political Economy* 19, no. 4 (1987): 525–50.

———. *Minerva's Message: Stabilizing the French Revolution.* Montreal, 1996.

Steiner, Philippe. *La "science nouvelle" de l'économie politique.* Paris, 1998.

———. *Sociologie de la connaissance économique: Essai sur les rationalisations de la connaissance économique (1750–1850).* Paris, 1998.

Stone, Bailey. *The Genesis of the French Revolution: A Global-Historical Perspective.* Cambridge, 1994.

Sullivan, Charles R. "The First Chair of Political Economy in France: Alexandre Vandermonde and the *Principles* of Sir James Steuart at the École normale of the Year III." *French Historical Studies* 20, no. 4 (1997): 635–64.

Swann, Julian. *Politics and the Parlement of Paris under Louis XV, 1754–1774.* Cambridge, 1995.

Tackett, Timothy. *Becoming a Revolutionary: The Deputies of the French National Assembly and the Emergence of a Revolutionary Culture (1789–1790).* Princeton, 1996.

———. "Nobles and Third Estate in the Revolutionary Dynamic of the National Assembly, 1789–90." *American Historical Review* 94, no. 2 (1989): 271–301.

———. *Priest and Parish in Eighteenth-Century France: A Social and Political Study of the Curés in a Diocese of Dauphiné, 1750–1791.* Princeton, 1977.

Tarrade, Jean. *Le commerce colonial de la France à la fin de l'ancien régime: L'évolution du régime de «l'Exclusif» de 1763 à 1789.* 2 vols. Paris, 1972.

Taylor, George V. "Noncapitalist Wealth and the Origins of the French Revolution." *American Historical Review* 72, no. 2 (1967): 469–96.

———. "The Paris Bourse on the Eve of the French Revolution, 1781–1789." *American Historical Review* 67, no. 4 (1962): 951–77.

———. "Types of Capitalism in Eighteenth-Century France." *English Historical Review* 79 (1964): 478–97.

Teyssendier de La Serve, Pierre. *Mably et les physiocrates.* Geneva, 1971 [1911].

Thompson, Victoria E. *The Virtuous Marketplace: Women and Men, Money and Politics in Paris, 1830–1870.* Baltimore, 2000.

Tiersten, Lisa. *Marianne in the Market: Envisioning Consumer Society in Fin-de-Siècle France*. Berkeley, 2001.

Tisserand, Roger. *Les concurrents de J.-J. Rousseau à l'Académie de Dijon pour le prix de 1754*. Paris, 1936.

Tribe, Keith. *Genealogies of Capitalism*. Atlantic Highlands, NJ, 1981.

——. *Land, Labour, and Economic Discourse*. London, 1978.

Tully, James, ed. *Meaning and Context: Quentin Skinner and His Critics*. Oxford, 1988.

Tzonev, Stoyan. *Le financier dans la comédie française sous l'ancien régime*. Paris, 1926.

Uzereau, François-Constant. *Fondation de la Société d'agriculture, sciences et arts d'Angers*. Angers, 1918.

——. *La Société d'agriculture d'Angers (1798–1806)*. Angers, 1914.

——. *La Société royale d'agriculture d'Angers (1761–1793)*. Angers, 1915.

Van Kley, Dale K. "New Wine in Old Wineskins: Continuity and Rupture in the Pamphlet Debate of the French Prerevolution, 1787–1789." *French Historical Studies* 17, no. 2 (1991): 447–65.

——, ed. *The French Idea of Freedom: The Old Regime and the Declaration of Rights of 1789*. Stanford, 1994.

Vardi, Liana. "The Abolition of the Guilds during the French Revolution." *French Historical Studies* 15, no. 4 (1988): 704–17.

Velde, François R., and David R. Weir. "The Financial Market and Government Debt Policy in France, 1746–1793." *Journal of Economic History* 52, no. 1 (1992): 1–39.

Velema, Wyger R. E. "Ancient and Modern Virtue Compared: De Beaufort and Van Effen on Republican Citizenship." *Eighteenth-Century Studies* 30, no. 4 (1997): 437–48.

Venturi, Franco. *The End of the Old Regime in Europe, 1768–1776*. 2 vols. Translated by R. Burr Litchfield. Princeton, 1984–89.

——. *Europe des Lumières: Recherches sur le 18e siècle*. Paris, 1971.

——. *Utopia and Reform in the Enlightenment*. Cambridge, 1971.

Viles, Perry. "The Slaving Interest in the Atlantic Ports, 1763–1792." *French Historical Studies* 7, no. 4 (1972): 529–43.

Villers, Louis de. *La Chalotais agriculteur*. Rennes, 1894.

——. *Histoire de la Société d'agriculture de commerce & des arts établie par les États de Bretagne (1757)*. Saint-Brieuc, 1898.

Vovelle, Michel, ed. *Les Mirabeau et leur temps: Actes du colloque d'Aix-en-Provence, 17 et 18 décembre 1966*. Paris, 1968.

Vovelle, Michel, and Daniel Roche. "Bourgeois, *Rentiers*, and Property Owners: Elements for Defining a Social Category at the End of the Eighteenth Century." In *New Perspectives on the French Revolution: Readings in Historical Sociology*, edited by Jeffry Kaplow. New York, 1965.

Vyverberg, Henry. *Historical Pessimism in the French Enlightenment*. Cambridge, MA, 1958.

Wahrman, Dror. *Imagining the Middle Class: The Political Representation of Class in Britain, c. 1780–1840*. Cambridge, 1995.

Weir, David R. "Les crises économiques et les origines de la Révolution française." *Annales: E.S.C.* 46, no. 4 (1991): 917–47.

——. "Tontines, Public Finance, and Revolution in France and England, 1688–1789." *Journal of Economic History* 49, no. 1 (1989): 95–124.

Weulersse, Georges. *Le mouvement physiocratique en France (de 1756 à 1770)*. 2 vols. Paris, 1910.

——. *La physiocratie à l'aube de la Révolution, 1781–1792*. Revised and edited by Corinne Beutler. Paris, 1985.

——. *La physiocratie à la fin du règne de Louis XV (1770–1774)*. Paris, 1959.

——. *La physiocratie sous les ministères de Turgot et de Necker (1774–1781)*. Paris, 1950.

Whatmore, Richard. *Republicanism and the French Revolution: An Intellectual History of Jean-Baptiste Say's Political Economy*. Oxford, 2000.

Whitcomb, Edward A. "Napoleon's Prefects." *American Historical Review* 79, no. 4 (1974): 1089–1118.

White, Eugene Nelson. "The French Revolution and the Politics of Government Finance, 1770–1815." *Journal of Economic History* 55, no. 2 (1995): 227–55.

——. "Was There a Solution to the Ancien Regime's Financial Dilemma?" *Journal of Economic History* 49, no. 3 (1989): 545–68.

Whiteman, Jeremy J. *Reform, Revolution and French Global Policy, 1787–1791*. Aldershot, 2003.

——. "Trade and the Regeneration of France, 1789–91: Liberalism, Protectionism and the Commercial Policy of the National Constituent Assembly." *European History Quarterly* 31, no. 2 (2001): 171–204.

Wick, Daniel L. "A Conspiracy of Well-Intentioned Men: The Society of Thirty and the French Revolution." Ph.D. diss., University of California, Davis, 1977.

——. "The Court Nobility and the French Revolution: The Example of the Society of Thirty." *Eighteenth-Century Studies* 13, no. 2 (1980): 263–84.

Williams, Rosalind H. *Dream Worlds: Mass Consumption in Late Nineteenth-Century France*. Berkeley, 1982.

Wright, Johnson Kent. *A Classical Republican in Eighteenth-Century France: The Political Thought of Mably*. Stanford, 1997.

Wyngaard, Amy S. *From Savage to Citizen: The Invention of the Peasant in the French Enlightenment*. Newark, DE, 2004.

Index

Page numbers in italics refer to figures.